Praise for Shadow Lines

'Kinnane ... is a fine writer who mixes well-researched history with family stories and a deep love for, and understanding of, the landscapes of Western Australia. It is hard to imagine a more balanced, intelligent or insightful book about the modern Aboriginal experience. It is a story powerfully told.'
— *Sydney Morning Herald*

'Kinnane's sympathetic portraits of his grandparents' lives offers an irresistible look into the choices, pressures and belief systems available to two very different people living in the early decades of the twentieth century.'
— *Aboriginal History*

'Beautifully written, *Shadow Lines* is a powerful, deeply personal and inspiring story of love and the ability of the human spirit to triumph despite overwhelming odds.'
— *The Age*

'This is a tale of self-discovery, beautifully told ... *Shadow Lines* is a considerable accomplishment — of history, biography and creative writing.'
— *The West Australian*

'... a touching account of courage and family love.'
— *The Canberra Sunday Times*

'*Shadow Lines* is a rich and moving testimony to a sorry, sorry past.'
— *Australian Bookseller and Publisher*

SHADOW LINES

There are different versions of how Edward and Jessie came together ... What I do know is that when he fell, he fell hard. What I do know is that they used every spare moment to spend time with each other ... Edward, 'Eddie' from Emanuel School in Westminster, London, met up with 'Cully', Jessie Argyle, 'Gypsy', a Miriwoong woman from Argyle Station. He was a wiry suntanned Englishman with a kind face and a cheeky way of turning his head when she took his photograph. She was a good-looking solid woman who didn't waste time, who did as she pleased as long as she could get away with it. She was disarming, quick-witted, and in control, and he was all vaudeville and magic tricks and had seen a bit of the world.

They were crossing boundaries of race without care, going places where they would have been noticed and discussed. They were having the time of their lives in their first six months together. They had both travelled a long way from their homelands. They were not supposed to meet. The society in which they met did not approve of mixed-race couples. They were not allowed to meet as far as the Aborigines Department was concerned, and they were about to learn that the hard way.

Steve Kinnane is a Marda Marda from Mirriwoong country in the East Kimberley. He has been an active writer and researcher for more than twenty-five years as well as lecturing and working on community cultural heritage, curatorial and development projects. He co-wrote and produced *The Coolbaroo Club* (1996), an ABC TV documentary awarded the Human Rights and Equal Opportunity Commission Human Rights Award for the Arts, and collaborated with Lauren Marsh and Alice Nannup on *When the Pelican Laughed* (1992), the story of Mrs Alice Nannup (Fremantle Press). *Shadow Lines* was awarded the Western Australian Premier's Book Award for Non-fiction 2003, the Fellowship of Australian Writers Award for Non-fiction 2003 and the Stanner Award 2004, and was shortlisted for the Queensland Premier's Literary Award and South Australian Premier's Award. Steve has lived and worked periodically between Perth and the Kimberley region of Western Australia.

SHADOW LINES

STEPHEN KINNANE

 FREMANTLE PRESS

First published 2003 by
FREMANTLE PRESS

Fremantle Press Inc. trading as Fremantle Press
25 Quarry Street, Fremantle WA 6160
(PO Box 158, North Fremantle WA 6159)
www.fremantlepress.com.au

Consultant Editors Ray Coffey and Janet Blagg.
Printed by McPherson's Printing, Victoria, Australia.

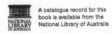 A catalogue record for this
book is available from the
National Library of Australia

ISBN 9781925816709 (paperback)
ISBN 9781925815627 (ebook)

 Department of
Local Government, Sport
and Cultural Industries

Fremantle Press is supported by the State Government through the
Department of Local Government, Sport and Cultural Industries.

  Australia Council for the Arts

Publication of this title was assisted by the Commonwealth Government
through the Australia Council, its arts funding and advisory body.

 MIX
Paper from
responsible sources
FSC® C001695

for Jess

shadow lines

The inflexible boundaries that are laid down by narrow definitions of race, nationalism and religion are shadowed by the boundaries that we ourselves remake as we try to make sense of our world. Our lives are not neatly divided and separated by these demarcations. Our stories are sometimes connected in ways that we can't even fathom, until the diversity of our stories is made clear to us through the inability of rigid boundaries to define, classify and label us.

Shadow lines are wide lines of negotiation that we all use to make sense of our differences, and our interconnections. They shift and change, break and re-form, swell and divide into spaces and patterns within the honesty of those of us who choose to ignore the straight, hard lines and choose to step into a place where our stories have room to move, to dance and exist. These lines of story shadow all of us. They are not always eloquent, or enlightening. Some are brutal and difficult to reconcile.

Contents

I

HOMELANDS

skin

My grandmother's skin was concealed when she was a small child. I am of my grandmother's skin. Her skin leads to my mother's skin, and my mother's skin to mine. My skin is olive and supple. Cuts do not heal quickly but dissolve slowly into raised scars devoid of pigment. The scars last. They show. But this is not the skin I am talking of. I was reunited with my skin when I returned to my grandmother's country, Miriwoong country. *Jalyirri* is my skin. It is how I am placed. It is my skin of reunion. My grandmother was placed by her skin, *Nangarri*, and then taken away to a place where her skin meant nothing more than colour.

A dissecting black border was ruled north–south through the Kimberley, slicing my grandmother's country in two. It cut its way along Empire-red maps dividing the northern frontier into federated Western Australia and the Northern Territory. White people had been in my grandmother's country less than twenty years when she was born. The Europeans saw these countries simply—pastured or rocky, fertile or infertile, inhabited, but from where they stood, under utilised. They saw only two seasons in the East Kimberley, Wet and Dry. The Dry is seen as hot and dusty. The Wet is even hotter, but the heat is broken by the rains. The Miriwoong identify four seasons: Rain, Cold, Windy and Hot. Come the Rain season the country sings into life in rich greens, reds and purples. There is plenty of food and it is Law-time; time to catch up with the mob and rejuvenate the land. The ground is always damp, and can become one vast glass-like flood plain when the afternoon rains thunder down.

Tracks are harder to follow come Rain time. In the Windy season it is cooler and there is no rain. Life swells around the larger water supplies where there's food and business. Tracks last a long time in the dry red earth and the nights are clear and fresh. But the ruling *guddia* saw the world only as wet or dry, black or white. Within a world of 'Empire' they marvelled at their clinical brilliance. They had reduced the world into discrete, simple particles of matter. But it is not so simple. My grandmother's skin had held the story of over two thousand generations of her people's life in their country and then the generations of others. She was born of the crossing of this vertical black line. It cut through her country and into her life.

My grandmother was broken down into 'authentic' parts, half white, half black, but never seen as wholly human. She was the product of the Colonial Frontier to be mapped, traced, labelled and categorised. They called her a 'half-caste'. They thought they had her pegged. But then they didn't know what to do with someone who didn't fit within their neat lines of demarcation so they decided to remove her from their picture. When they took her away they thought they were solving a problem. They thought they were setting the picture straight, clean of their own sins, free of imperfections. They did not see the hole they were tearing. They did not see they were taking someone's daughter, someone's grand-daughter, someone's sister, and someone's future mother. They studied my grandmother, but they did not see her and they did not see the chain of events they were setting in place. They did not think she would remember what had happened to her, or that others would share in this story. They did not think we would one day be leafing through the personal files they created about our grandmother, watching back, as her life was tracked and controlled across those pages for almost half a century. Cuts leave scars. Scars leave tracks. Tracks can be followed.

Lake Argyle stretches the walls of what was once the giant Ord River valley. Tourist brochures boast that it is the largest man-made lake in Australia, containing nine Sydney Harbours nestled neatly within paper-bark-covered hills. It is classified as an inland sea, an unnatural version of the ancient sea that 'explorers' had coveted and mythologised as they searched in vain through an imagined landscape. In reality it is neither a lake nor a sea. A concrete and rock dam wall wedged in a gorge on the Ord River tenuously holds back this enormous body of water.

There is a small tourist village on Lake Argyle. Tourists bring their boats to the lake to fish, ski and sunbathe out on its vast blue surface. You can almost be guaranteed a good catch of freshwater fish on Lake Argyle and, if you're lucky, a rare barramundi that has escaped from the managed fish farm. It is a water playground for southerners escaping cold wet winters, and overseas visitors chasing an illusion of outback Australian life.

But submerged beneath the water's skin, the land remains. This is still my grandmother's country. Hundreds of feet below the surface where the light does not penetrate, the contours of the land, now liquid and dark, hold the story of my grandmother and our ancestors. Not far from an island that was once the tip of a mountain lie the remains of Argyle Station. The old station homestead has been shifted, brick by brick, and rebuilt above the waterline as a heritage site and tourist attraction. It is an instant, transplanted history commemorating the role of the cattlemen in developing the East Kimberley frontier. But this clean, well-tended site is not the house that my grandmother knew.

Before the flooding of the valley, a few bodies were selected for exhumation from the original homestead cemetery, part of the heritage re-creation to celebrate white tenacity in 'overcoming the odds'. But this handful of graves does not speak for the hundreds of blackfellas who died in these lands, whose remains are still held within the now drowned lands of the Miriwoong. Aboriginal accounts of resistance and conflict, of sites of renewal and law, and thousands of years of ancestral story, were left outside the homestead re-creation. These stories had always been left outside, away from sight, and beyond the comfort of the boundary fence in the minds of the whites who came to these lands.

Today, beneath the massive lake's surface the land lies transfixed, cold and silent. Like the hull of a giant sunken ocean liner, my grandmother's country lies trapped in time, holding the memories of thousands of lifetimes, and a moment of disaster when the waters flooded in. If you turn south at the ruins of the old homestead though, and search along the silty floor, you will pick up a trail. These are my grandmother's tracks leading silently out of her country. Although it is dark beneath the silent waters and the tracks are very old, look carefully and you will see them leading all the way back to a place called Wild Dog.

'Ballay Jalyirri, look out for that turn-off now. He be that-a-way a little bit somewhere—turn!' Nangala shouts excitedly. I hit the brakes but the

Valiant just keeps on going, drifting past the Yardungle turn-off, weighed down by a car load of relatives all tooled up with handlines and donkey meat. I reverse back to the turn-off to howls of laughter at my terrible driving. It's hard to get my old station wagon, full of ten people, to stop on the gravel siding. We're going fishing. It is the build-up, coming into Rain time. We are passing down the road that was once the bush track that led my grandmother out of her country.

My partner Lauren is squeezed in the front seat between Nangala and myself, scrabbling with the bag of food to hand around for the journey out of Kununurra. She is listening and nodding good-naturedly as all the women tell her it's time she had some babies now. We have passed, some way back, the re-created Durack homestead where the tourists go. In the back seat Nangala is arguing with Namidge about the best place to stop to catch bait in one of the many side creeks before we head off to the Ord River for some real fishing.

Nangala and Namidge are too old now. They have earned their cataracts well and truly, but Nangala is boasting: 'Even I could drive this mutta-car better than you Jalyirri. I could drive a truck if I put my mind to it, true I could. I'm going to too. I'm going to get a license and drive a big bus and take everyone longa meeting in it, not a small mutta-car like this one. Anyone could drive a little mutta-car like this.'

When we have caught enough bait and piled into the car again, Nangala points me south and we head off to the dam wall. Here the waters of the Ord are stopped dead in their tracks. It is the beginning of the lake that we pass as we round the ridge, drive over the wall and come to the headwaters of what is left of the old river system.

All the way along the country, Nangala is singing, singing, singing. She is singing for the places that we pass, for the big hills and the little trees. She is singing the stories of places and people that overflow through her country, and the other women, Namidge, Nangarri, Nannagoo and Nambijin are singing with her, softly picking up where she leads them. When Nangala stops she will yell out the stories to us because Lauren and I can't speak language. She has to explain to that guddia girl and that 'yella-fella' boy who talks like a guddia what she has been singing about.

At the dam wall freshwater crocs swim against the thrashing waters as they make their way almost imperceptibly against the current, while all the handlines go in and we sit and wait for a bite. Nangala has made her way to her spot, carrying her frail skinny self on her cane, climbing over rocks to find the right position. Crippled from a fall from a tree as a child, Nangala moves awkwardly but swiftly. Her feet, too brittle to be covered by shoe leather, are enclosed in padded layers of bright white socks that stand out against the red soil and granite rock. She will get me to throw her line in for her—but it is never good enough. 'Jalyirri, he even throws like a guddia,' and I'm in for another round of laughs and shaking heads covered in bright scarves.

When I first returned to my grandmother's country, Nangala sat with me in the park in Kununurra and we swapped our stories and talked all afternoon before she decided that my place and my grandmother's place should be settled properly at Yardungle Springs. This is where most of the Elders were then—those who were not at Moongum, or the Reserve, or at Emu Springs, or just beginning the moves to the out-stations.

At Yardungle we sat and listened carefully as Nangala called out my granny's story. All the old men and women talked about it and thought about it, and the boss of Warringarri, who had given me a lift out, translated for me. English, my first language, is only a fourth or fifth language here. My grandmother was placed and it was decided. My skin was placed. Here in Miriwoong country, I am Jalyirri.

Nangala welcomed me back to the country, exhausted but happy. She had stated my case and helped sift through the many stories of children taken away from these lands in order to work out my place. It had been settled. Nangala is my mother, and my own mother, Betty, still thousands of miles south, is also Nangala. Our skins have been reclaimed. My grandmother's skin was Nangarri before she was stolen from her people and placed in a mission thousands of miles south. Our point of reunion is there, back beneath the waters of the lake that was once a river valley, from where my grandmother was taken as a child.

On that same day old Namidge, one of my aunties, sat me down and started teaching me language, making me touch my nose, my ears, my mouth, my hands, my eyes, and calling out the words as if I was just a little kid. Then there were rules to learn. Lauren was given the name of my straight, my rightful, marriage skin, Namirra. With inclusion comes responsibility, and Lauren has to know who she can sit with and who she can't, as do I. We get it all wrong to start off, sit with the wrong people, name people we're not supposed to, but that's okay, because it is a return, and Jalyirri is a southern city fella.

I might be a Nor'wester, but I have grown up in Sou'west country, Noongar country, the country my grandmother was taken to, and so I'm cut some slack.

I call myself a *marda-marda*. It is a Yindjibarndi term that strictly speaking means 'blood-blood'. It is a term that Nor'westers of mixed Aboriginal and non-Aboriginal descent use to describe ourselves. In the south, where northern Aboriginal people such as my grandmother were taken and placed in institutions, terms such as marda-marda were used instead of derogatory words such as 'half-caste' and 'quarter-caste'. Thrown together and forced to learn English, a new language developed, mixing Kimberley Mulba and Yamatji lingo with that of a community of people, mostly women removed from their country, existing in Noongar country.

This place, my skin, has become my starting point, a place from which I am linked and claimed. Being my grandmother's beginning point also, there's an important symmetry, a reconnection to her belonging within country that was disrupted with her removal.

When the fishing was done and we were driving back to Kununurra with our catfish, Nangala pointed south over the lake we were ridging. 'That way Jalyirri, where that road used to slip in that big water there. That's the way, long-way south to that Wild Dog country, true, where they pinched your granny.' It's getting late, and we have to get back to town, and Moongum, and the Reserve, as I drop everyone off black-taxi style. The road is leading us away from Wild Dog, but in the rear-view mirror I can see that lake, that barrier that stands between my present and my grandmother's past. The physical track back to Wild Dog is hidden by the waters of the lake, but there are other ways to go back, guddia ways that I will use to lift my grandmother's story from between the lined pages that were created to document her separation.

Friday 29 June 1906. Wild Dog Police Station. Before they took her away my grandmother's name was Gypsy. She had been taken off a cattle station called Argyle. My grandmother's older half-brother's name was Toby. He had been brought into Wild Dog from the Ord River Cattle Station, which was further south. They waited together. Gypsy was recorded as being five years of age and Toby as being six. They could have been older. They could have been younger. Over the years their ages would fluctuate across the pages of the files that were created about them as figures of authority took wild guesses about their beginnings. For certain, they were too young to be away from their families. They were two small children being held over by the Kimberley police pending their removal. It was all matter-of-factly noted in the Police and Aborigines Department files. The lean sentences, tidy phrases and abbreviated words of bureaucracy were used to begin their story. A simplistic system was in place to decide their future. Although the sentences might be spare, reading these records is like deciphering a code. To be chained and dragged a hundred miles was described as being 'escorted'. To live in a camp with your family was deemed to be 'neglected'. To have fairer coloured skin than your mother meant 'suitable for removal'.

Wild Dog Police Station had a bad reputation. It was as rough and as isolated as it got in the East Kimberley. Smack up against the Northern Territory border; two mounted policemen, four black trackers, young black women, a few old men, a few old women and lots of 'orphaned 'half-caste' children'. Depending on the sort of copper you were, the Wild Dog run was easy money, or a guilty conscience. It was located about forty-three miles south of Argyle Cattle Station near Flying Fox Creek. The police set it up in 1897 as a supposed outpost of white law in the midst of the Killing Times, when open acts of murder and retribution by white authorities against traditional owners of the country were commonplace. In reality, Wild Dog Police Station wasn't there to protect Aboriginal people from being killed by whites, or to protect Aboriginal women from being kidnapped and run as drovers' boys or 'kombos' by itinerant bagmen and stock workers. Wild Dog was set up purely to stop 'the blacks' from killing cattle.

As I leaf through the documents of the archives, I can see the police station in my mind. Rusty corrugated iron flapping loosely in the hot dry wind. Old tins and powdery remains of cold camp fires blow about the station when the morning winds begin. Wild Dog Creek passed nearby; a bed of cracked mud, an invisible promise of water. Way over, up Flying Fox Creek, there was a mob of old people who lived off the scraps of Wild Dog police. Drovers came through here and took young Aboriginal women when they wanted to. Sometimes they brought them back on their way through. Sometimes the women just disappeared.

There was a group of Aboriginal prisoners at Wild Dog waiting with my grandmother and her brother—nine men and two women, chained at the neck. They had been arrested a week earlier at Bow River Station

19

on charges of cattle killing. They were tied to the tree that grew not far from the bough shed, where the trackers lived with a large number of local women. Next to the bough shed was the wreck of a house where the police had their digs. Government-issue blankets shielded the station from the sun. Red, white and blue stripes with the King's crown stamped in the centre. They were supposed to be handed out to old and infirm Aboriginal people on relief at the station depot. But the old folks went without at Wild Dog.

It was the Big Dry of 1906. It had been the driest year in a long time. Water was scarce throughout the Kimberley. There was little traditional game that season due to the drought, so there had been an increase in the number of cattle killed for food by Aboriginal families trying to survive on their county. But the police blamed this increase in cattle killing on the newly arrived Resident Magistrate, James Maloney. Maloney had only been in the district six months and had already got the police and squatters offside. The previous Resident Magistrate, Dodwell Brown, wasn't shy to lock up Aboriginal 'cattle killers' for anything up to two or three years in Wyndham gaol. It didn't matter that the arresting officer was often also the prosecutor. It didn't matter that defendants had no one to defend them, or that the trackers, who were often used as interpreters, might not even speak the same language or, at least, had a vested interest in not crossing the police.

James Maloney made it clear to the police and the squatters that he wasn't going to put cattle killers away without direct proof, which meant cattle station owners coming in to give evidence, something they were loathe to do. The Resident Magistrate called the shots in a place like the East Kimberley. With Maloney on the bench the best the police could hope for was to get prisoners on three- to six-month sentences for the lesser charge of 'possession of beef'. The police didn't need proof for possession, just a few captured Aboriginal women dragged in as coerced witnesses. While in gaol Aboriginal prisoners did hard labour. Effectively, each escort could provide anywhere up to three years' free labour to the guddia.

After serving their time, prisoners would be released back into the country, but with traditional game being driven away by cattle, they would have to again kill cattle to survive. It was a vicious cycle that some police used to their advantage. The police might have complained about the lower sentences, but their arrest rates went through the roof, and along with higher arrest rates came higher ration rates for escorting prisoners to trial in Wyndham. Police received ration money of two and sixpence per day per prisoner. With an average escort of twelve prisoners over ten days, a policeman could earn an extra fifteen pounds each trip. Some policemen lied about the distances they travelled, spent extra days padding out an escort, and made good money out of reimbursement for rations that they rarely provided.

In 1906 the East Kimberley cattle stations carried vast herds, numbering in the thousands. That year the cattle industry shifted over nineteen thousand cows and twenty-two thousand sheep through the port of Wyndham alone. Mostly it was Aboriginal labourers who worked the cows for squatters in return for rations.

Cattle killing was not a threat to this market. Out of fifty-eight reported cases of cattle killing in police files for the East Kimberley in 1906, one hundred and seventy-nine Aboriginal men were brought to trial, of which one hundred and fifty-nine were 'summarily convicted' of the charge. There were a further fifty-eight convictions for the lesser charge of 'possession of beef'. Even allowing for ten times the number of reported cases of cattle killing, that would make maybe five hundred cows being killed out of tens of thousands. Cattle killing was the primary police concern in the district. There were eight police stations, twenty-six policemen and over thirty trackers employed to stop cattle spearing. They were funded by four different government departments, covering wages, rations, horses and equipment. That was expensive law enforcement. The economy of the cow ruled the land.

Wild Dog's police business ended at the Northern Territory border, along with its jurisdiction. The border was the guddia's way of containing themselves in a land they considered without edges. Of course, there were other boundaries that the whites were well aware of but chose to ignore. The guddia were well aware there were tribal boundaries of owned country and the police used this knowledge to their advantage. They preferred Aboriginal trackers from around Wave Hill, across the border in the Northern Territory, country far away from the country they would be employed to patrol. That way, if there was a skirmish, the police hoped these trackers from alien country would not try to protect the local Aboriginal population. It was the old method of divide and conquer.

It was an uneasy relationship of mutual benefit for some. The police made sure to keep their trackers in food, clothes and women, and although the trackers didn't have any real power in the system of policing, when a police party was out in remote country and the finding of water was critical, the coppers knew they couldn't survive without them. The trackers knew it too.

The Wild Dog run was an endless cycle of abuse, use, advantage and imprisonment. Trackers came and went as it suited them. When they had to return to their own homelands, or when they had had enough of the police controlling their lives, they headed across the border where the police would generally not follow. Just before my grandmother was taken, there had been some trouble just west of Wild Dog. While the police were off investigating, the trackers who had been left behind decided it was time to head home, back to Wave Hill country. But new trackers were readily acquired to replace the old ones. The revolving door of the border line crossings swung another turn. The Wild Dog trackers watching over my grandmother were new on the job. These were the men, along with the policeman, who were in charge of the run that would take my grandmother away.

We are sitting by the Ord River near Ivanhoe Crossing. The rains are getting closer. You can feel rain building. From the first light of day the hot air saps your strength, even before the sun has made its way over Kelly's Knob. Even while the town and the valley are still in the shadow of night, the grass in the build-up smells dry and sweet. It is cool under the trees with the river spilling past. Nangala has been telling us of the Killing Times, when bags of flour were poisoned and black men shot on the outskirts of stations. Nangala can remember the Killing Times because they had continued into the early years of her childhood. When Nangala was a little kid there was still trouble that was settled guddia way, by the gun, or by Aboriginal business and Law. As the guddia encroached on Miriwoong country, arresting men for cattle killing, chasing people off their traditional lands or stealing Aboriginal women, the delicate balances between country, culture and Law were damaged. It was a period of outright white domination and control, but also of shifting allegiances, of people forced to track food beyond their own country, causing tensions with other traditional owners, and of conditional brokerage and patronage of station bosses. Nangala tells stories about other people much older than herself, who are long gone now, because it is important to keep those stories alive. When Nangala tells killing stories it is as if they happened just yesterday.

My aunty, Namidge, was only a girl herself when the guddia came looking for her and her father. They had resisted going in with the guddia and had avoided the police, keeping in touch with relatives on stations while remaining out of sight. They hid in the ranges of the valley for months, until her father became sick with leprosy and died. After weeks of trying to care for herself, Namidge was found and brought in. She was young enough to be trained as a house girl for Newry Station, where she spent the rest of her working life.

Government enquiries into the removal of children use dates in their calculations of the numbers of Aboriginal kids taken away from their families. The dates coincide with the passing of legislation when this practice was proclaimed legal. However, these official dates are arbitrary and misleading. From the time the guddia first entered this country Aboriginal children were taken. To really understand what happened, and how it impacted on the lives of Aboriginal communities, you have to listen to stories that have been handed down.

I passed around my grandmother's photograph in the park in Kununurra, the one of her soon after she entered the Mission. In the photo she was a chubby little five-year-old. When she smiled her eyes were all squinty in the sunlight. She was short for her age, fair skinned, big hipped and skinny legged. She had a big birthmark on her left thigh, and a head that was too big for her body. She was a funny-looking little kid, and she was a long way from her home. I wasn't sure if it was permitted to show the photograph so widely, but Nangala said enough time had passed for cheeky spirits not to be a worry. The photo was of great interest and all the women had cooed and sighed, and laughed too, at the sight of my grandmother dressed up in mission clothes.

My grandmother and her brother Toby were some of the first children taken from the East Kimberley by government authorities, but not long after them the yearly toll started to rise. Many of the women sitting in the park had experienced the trauma of having their children taken away. Some of them were younger than my mother and had had their children taken from them as recently as the 1970s and 1980s, when they were sent as babies to Princess Margaret Hospital for treatment, and once there were adopted out without the women's consent. I think this is one of the reasons why they were so welcoming; it was not just about my grandmother, but about every child that was taken away. I could come back and be placed because missing children and their stories are not forgotten. One aunty told me she is still waiting for her son to come back. It is the same in the south, where too many older women waited their entire lives without ever being reunited with their children. This is our community history and an unresolved daily reality for many Aboriginal families.

Later that afternoon the women are off to a ceremony about fifty kilometres out of town. I offer to take them in my station wagon, but Nangala tells me politely, 'No Jalyirri, this is properly business now. You can't come with us longa Yardungle this time. You gotta stop in town. We see you tomorrow, ay? Maybe we go fishing at Ivanhoe Crossing.' And with long arms hauling big bodies into the back of a Toyota, everyone is gone in a cloud of red dust.

I am of here. But I was not born here. There are rules to abide by. There are stories the women are happy to share, and then there are other stories that are not on offer to me. It is all part of the legacy of the policy of removal.

Saturday 30 June 1906. Wild Dog Police Station. The beginning of my grandmother's escort. Mounted Police Constable Joseph Hill was in charge. Hill was a policeman of the ilk to wear his copper's uniform, replete with starched cotton underwear, in the middle of a heatwave. He wasn't good at milking the system for rations, but did his fair share of prisoner round-ups.

My grandmother remembered being taken from her mother by the police. How long she had been at Wild Dog Police Station though is unclear. There were many children kept there at different times, along with the old and infirm who were on rations. She could have been there a month. She could have been there a week. The stories that she told my own mother were not concerned with details and dates. She remembered being taken off Argyle Station and the trek out of her country. She remembered crocodiles and waterholes, rivers and dry red earth. She remembered the sound of her mother crying as her child was taken away. She remembered to have respect for people from the same country.

Constable Hill and the new Wild Dog trackers spent all morning on the day my grandmother's escort began getting the provisions and horses ready for the journey into Wyndham. At two o'clock on a clear blue afternoon, Hill roused up his trackers and they hit the road. It hadn't rained in months and the air was bone dry. It was the hottest part of the day. They moved slowly north out of Wild Dog and into country. Wild Dog Police Station was at the extreme edge of my grandmother's country, bordering Malngin country to the south. The people stuck at Wild Dog Station — an excuse for a border junction — were from all over; from Kidja, Djaru and Malngin country.

It was a typical escort party. There were two black trackers, Paddy and Dickey; nine male prisoners chained at the neck; two women witnesses, Walaumbal and Duiack; my grandmother, Gypsy, and her half-brother, Toby. They started out on the track for the port town of Wyndham, twelve days and one hundred and fifty miles to the north-west. The prisoners, witnesses and the two small children were on foot. The policeman and the trackers rode on horses with five fresh ones trailing spare.

At Sugar Springs the group broke for camp at dusk. The children had been on the road only one day, but the prisoners and witnesses had been on the road and chained at the neck for almost a week. A hunchback moon rose late in the north-west sky over the distant ranges. Later that first night, Constable Hill made a note in his journal: 'Further conveying to Wyndham, two orphans one half-caste girl five years of age and one abo native boy 6 years of age on arrival hand above named orphans to Dr. Maloney for transmission South.'

The details had obviously been worked out months before in telegrams exchanged north and south between the police, the Aborigines Department and the Anglican Church missionaries. The files detailing my grandmother's life were already growing. In neat phrases and minimally constructed sentences, public servants in Perth had begun the process of rewriting a version of my grandmother's story. In the documents they made there is no mention of her mother. No permission was needed because legislation had been passed granting full powers of 'guardianship' to a white man in Perth. There was no discussion, no dialogue, nor any questioning of their actions. The voices of the file makers are self-assured in their powerful ignorance. They do not listen, they only ever instruct.

Sunday 1 July 1906. Octayard. The second day into my grandmother's escort. Constable Hill steered the party further north. Breaking camp early they travelled sixteen miles following small ravines, descending deeper into the huge Ord River valley flood plain. They made camp at five o'clock at the Octayard. The Octayard was primarily a place for breaking horses, and races were held there every year. It was a hub of comings and goings between Argyle Station and Rosewood Station across the border to the east.

When escort parties stopped to camp for the night the prisoners remained chained. Female witnesses were chained by the ankles and fastened to a tree close to the camp. The policeman made his camp slightly away from the group and the trackers were left to guard the prisoners. The women were particularly vulnerable to sexual demands by the trackers, and if the copper knew what was going on, it was in his best interest to turn a blind eye. It was part of the reciprocal arrangement between trackers and their bosses. There are damning instances of such practices recorded in government archives, and it wasn't only the trackers who abused women on the long journey to Wyndham. There is recorded evidence attesting that the police were also often as not abusing Aboriginal women.

I wonder how, in the midst of such a camp, my grandmother and Toby fared. Were they too chained with the women witnesses? Were the children taken by the trackers to sleep near their camp? My grandmother had lived on a station and she was used to a certain way of life. Who made sure the children had sufficient food to eat and water to drink? The rationing of food was solely at the policeman's discretion. If a pecking order existed I'm sure the trackers came first and the women and children were a sorry last.

When PC Hill recorded my grandmother as an orphan he was mistaken. When she later told the story of her removal, my grandmother spoke of growing up on Argyle Station. She said M.P. Durack, who was the main boss, was her father. My grandmother never mentioned whether M.P. Durack was around when the policeman came to take her away; was more concerned about the loss of her mother.

Camped at the Octayard, my grandmother was back in her home country. She would have known this land well. She would have travelled over it when she was a baby. She would have been carried over it, heading out into country for months at a time with family when the wet season came and everyone went into country to rejuvenate the land. She was as close to Argyle Station as she would ever be again in her life, only I doubt she had any understanding of that then. For my grandmother, growing up in the East Kimberley, there was nothing else *but* her own country and it must have been an inconceivable thought, to be taken from your country.

Later that night Constable Hill left the escort party in the hands of his trackers and headed into Argyle Station to catch up with the manager, Ambrose Durack. Ambrose was considered a solid stockman, but also a 'cunning old bugger' by the Aboriginal stockmen working under him. He had their respect, but they liked to call him 'old parrot nose' behind his back.

The East Kimberley police had an uneasy relationship with squatters like the Duracks, which ranged from open hostility to resentful negotiation. The police resented the squatters, who treated them as de facto boundary riders, babysitting cattle in country that they were too busy making money to venture into. The squatters thought they were a cut above the coppers who they wrote off as simple wage earners.

Personal feelings ran high and a few police were shunned and refused food and comfort at stations, although others were welcomed enough to be invited to Christmas dinner. The Duracks had worked out a successful understanding with the Wild Dog police. Of all the runs in the area Argyle Station was the most central, and the most protected. It was dead centre of the richest country of the Ord valley, one million acres of the best-watered prime cattle country in the north. The Wild Dog police run was closest to Argyle Station, and included Lissadell, Carlton, Mentinee and Ivanhoe cattle stations, but these other stations never received the same attention as Argyle.

If you trace it on a map it was Durack country every step of the way into Wyndham. The Durack family leased the biggest and most successful stations in the East Kimberley and they recognised the benefit of controlling other aspects of the industry. Their leases made a quilted pattern over the land for the whole one hundred and fifty miles from the Northern Territory border to the Cambridge Gulf. The smaller station owners complained about the Durack monopoly over shipping and transport, and later their influence in government. If you needed to ship your beef to the south, you had to use Durack-owned transport, and if you wanted to sell a few cows, you had to use a Durack-owned company.

Michael Patrick (M.P.) Durack came from a family of cattlemen. After surveying the East Kimberley in 1885, the Durack boys trekked overland with cattle from their Queensland property to start up Argyle, their first venture in the region. Eventually they ruled over an empire of cattle stations equal to half the total size of their original homeland, Ireland. For a bunch of poor rural white boys originally from County Galway and

Clare, their clan had certainly come up in the world. They were young, rich, self-righteous, and they packed pistols. Nothing was going to stop them making good in the newly opened territory.

The East Kimberley was a good money-making proposition for cattlemen, and by 1906 the Duracks were well established and more than comfortable. Their father, Patsy Durack, had done the same in the west Queensland territories, and it was he who encouraged his sons, nephews and cousins to give it a go in the north-east of Western Australia. This isn't to say they didn't take risks, or put in a hard day's work; they had even buried a good number of their clan in the Kimberley earth by 1906. The Duracks were simply the best at working the system to their profit; they were well connected, and they knew how to court essential government support. With the comfort of political support, and a cheap pool of Aboriginal labour, it was close to a sure proposition. Moreover, the Duracks had worked out how to run the whole show on subsidised rations, without the need to part with their own cash — once again, the 'economy of the cow'.

The labour force that worked Argyle Station was predominantly Aboriginal people. Originally, around the time that my grandmother was born, there was a small nucleus of trusted Aboriginal workers from Queensland, but increasingly workers from the East Kimberley were brought in. The men did the fencing and worked with the cattle, and the women worked up at the house washing, tending the vegetable gardens or feeding the poultry and small livestock. These were the people my grandmother had lived with all her early life.

The Argyle homestead, made of stone and timber, grew out of a high bank on the Behn River. M.P. Durack had personally selected the site. Standing on the shaded front verandah, you could see Mount Misery rising in the distance. At the foot of the mount, a dry grassless plain encircled the perimeter of the station. Heavy Victorian furniture filled the bungalow's rooms, along with a piano for genteel entertainment. But aside from a few trimmings, the homestead was generally quite basic, made for utilitarian living. And it was isolated from distant neighbours.

Around the homestead, chicken-wire fencing attached to rough logs attempted to mark out some form of boundary against the vastness of the surrounding landscape. In windy weather rags and blankets blew from the 'blacks' camp', pinning bedraggled scraps of material to the skeleton wire fencing. A stark windmill pumped hot water into a raised water tank. The stockmen's quarters stood nearby; a smaller, rougher version of the main house. Stone, wood, corrugated iron, red earth, dry grass. The Boss and his family slept up at the homestead. Trusted offsiders sometimes slept on the all-round verandah to protect the white bosses. The main camps were a little way down from the house and occasional camps were further down on the river. Every bit of territory was claimed and marked, from the Boss's bed to the dry earth of the camps. Small borders of rocks marked out red dirt paths from red dirt country, enclosing a manageable space.

When M.P. Durack chose the site for the station he did not know that it stood in the centre of traditional Aboriginal trade routes that ran right through country and into Wyndham. It was an accident in his favour as it guaranteed him labour. Aboriginal people had traded pearl shell, weapons, songs and grinding stones, and shared Law along these routes for centuries, but in the first twenty years of occupation, these practices would be terribly disrupted.

With the aid of trusted black workers the Duracks 'acquired' Aboriginal boys, 'brought in' Aboriginal women and 'coaxed' local Aboriginal people to come 'inside' to serve the new pastoralist order. In return for work and ceasing to kill cattle for food, the Duracks provided rations, clothing and shelter. As more people came 'inside', more 'outside' people were being imprisoned for cattle killing, or were killed in reprisals. In this climate the Duracks' inside world offered more than food and shelter; the Durack's had become brokers of power under the mantle of the gun.

Although coming inside with the Duracks brought its benefits, the bonds of kin and skin were greater than any introduced system. Ceremony and Law continued to be maintained throughout the seasons, especially when the rains came, when insiders and outsiders would gather close to the station for business. There was greater flexibility between groups than the whites liked to admit, and M.P. Durack, hearing the comings and goings at night as he sat in his homestead, was described by his daughter and biographer as disdaining such liaisons.

Living on Argyle Station, my grandmother would have participated in these rhythms of station life, going *pinkeye* each Wet season when everyone headed bush for seasonal hunting and to carry out ceremonies and rituals. As well as participating in the cultural life of her own people, there were occasional entertainments at the homestead. The Duracks were Catholics and they liked to celebrate Christmas in a big way.

The children of the Aboriginal workers were included in some of the festivities and sports organised for the day.

The last Christmas my grandmother spent at Argyle was exceptionally hot: a forewarning of the dry year ahead. It was so hot that the annual races and games held for the Aboriginal kids on the station were postponed and everyone had a lazy day at the homestead. M.P. had gathered together the usual assortment of white workers and managers from his nearby stations, as well as friendly coppers and workers from the Aboriginal camp. The phonograph was dragged out and all the favourite tunes were spun.

In the afternoon M.P. handed out clothes to the station 'boys' (which could mean men as old as fifty). Later that night he sat alone in the hot and still homestead to record the day in his journal. The following day, Boxing Day, they played cricket and, before one of the guests headed back to Wyndham, stopped to take photographs of all the workers and men to mark the passing of another season.

If M.P. Durack acknowledged my grandmother as his daughter, she did not rate any special mention in his records; nor did he appear to oppose her being taken away. Of course, it was common at the time for white fathers to avoid responsibility for their children. Although government archives show a growing population of 'half-caste' children at this time in the East Kimberley, it was rare for white men to come forward and claim responsibility for the care and maintenance of their own children. It was as if they saw the children of their unions with Aboriginal women as not being connected to themselves.

In the short years she lived at Argyle, my grandmother witnessed the coming and going of many travellers and visitors to the station. She saw the Durack brothers as they made the rounds of their empire, and the excitement of anticipated visitors up from Perth. She saw the white drovers passing through on their way to and from Wyndham, and would also have seen the policemen and their trackers leading prisoners on the chain.

On that warm night while my grandmother was camped with Toby and the other prisoners, close to the Argyle Station, M.P. Durack wasn't home. He had left several months after Christmas for a grand world tour. Around the time the group reached Octayard he was on *The Empress of Ireland* sailing from Liverpool to Canada. Writing in his travel diary in his cabin at night, he marvelled at the pure luxury of first-class travel, and recorded his amazement at the sights he had seen.

Monday 2 July 1906. Stoney Bar. Police Constable Hill broke camp from the Octayard early and headed north along the main track into Wyndham. Passing through Stoney Bar, he took his party around the familiar Carr Boyd ranges to the west. The days were long and slow. My grandmother and her brother kept up with the women. Hill made regular notations in his journal each evening. 'Left Camp 7 am and travelled to Stoney Bar and Camped for Night at 6 pm. 15 miles.' He wasn't one to elaborate. Hill had travelled this road dozens of times. He knew the East Kimberley run well, though it wasn't by choice.

Constable Joseph Hill first joined the East Kimberley police in 1899. He was stationed in Wyndham for three years before he managed to win a transfer south to the quiet and relatively safe posting of the Newcastle District, just north-east of the city of Perth. He would have served his time out there if he hadn't gotten greedy for his boss's job. There was an incident where Hill faked a letter defaming his superior officer in an attempt to secure a promotion. The letter was not actually sent, but it was discovered and reported. The District Sergeant took a grim view of Hill's actions. '[Any] Constable who would take this means of injuring a comrade, and degrading the service is not worthy to wear the uniform.'

After an internal investigation Hill was found guilty of writing the letter, but they couldn't prove he was going to send it. Desperate to keep his job he pleaded his case. 'I have always been of good character ever since I have been in the Police Force and I have a wife and child to keep.' The Commissioner considered the charge against Hill a most serious one, 'and instant dismissal would result if the evidence was stronger.' It was only due to lack of evidence that the charges were dismissed. Hill, aware the matter wasn't over, struck a deal. He offered to apply for a transfer and promised that he would 'give no further trouble'. Within three weeks Constable Hill was back on the Wild Dog run; the most remote, isolated and dangerous beat in the East Kimberley.

Wednesday 4 July 1906. Cockatoo Springs. My grandmother had been on the road five days and had covered seventy-four miles barefoot. The moon waxed high above, almost full and steadily drifting west. They had climbed north out of the Ord River valley, through Stoney Bar, over Granite Creek, swung past the Newry Station turn-off to the Northern Territory border, and moved west around the ranges into Cockatoo Springs.

They stopped early, at five o'clock that afternoon, and watered the horses. My grandmother was moving further from home than she'd ever been before. The country was becoming unfamiliar. The children would stay close together. Cockatoo Springs was a common resting point for travellers, stockmen and police escort parties on the Wyndham route. It was an oasis of pandanus palms, shade and fresh water.

Jim Patterson, manager of Ord River Station, also stopped at Cockatoo for the night. He was on his way back to the station from Wyndham. Patterson had once managed Newry Station for the Duracks. Now he was the working partner with the Copley brothers who had purchased Ord River Station from a deceased estate. Patterson did all the sweat work and built the station up. He'd been done out of more than £6,500 in 1903 on a deal that went bad with the Duracks. Hill checked Patterson out. Patterson had no complaints. Having recently been taken off this man's station, young Toby would have known Patterson by sight.

Constable Hill would participate in many more removals of children and Patterson would witness increasing numbers of them being herded along the road into Wyndham for removal to the south.

The removal of my grandmother and her brother, and the removal of hundreds to come after them, came as a direct result of the 1905 Aborigines Act.

Up until the passing of the 1905 Act, the police turned a blind eye to the existence of Aboriginal children by white fathers living in the district. Children were being removed from one district to another, from one station to another, and from stations to ration depots, but the 1905 Act signalled the beginning of decades of carefully planned and institutionalised removals of children to southern missions, thousands of miles from their homelands. My grandmother didn't have any idea of the legislation or why she was being taken to Wyndham, but she would understand the realities of it soon enough.

The new 1905 Act not only gave the Aborigines Department the green light to remove Aboriginal children of mixed descent, but removal was at the core of its intention. Instead of controlling and curtailing the abusers, the Act controlled the abused. Its ratification through state parliament was a defining moment that would set the tone for race relations in Western Australia throughout the rest of the century. Almost one hundred years later the effects of the 1905 Act are still being felt in the

Aboriginal communities of Western Australia, and the intent behind its enactment is still being debated.

The 1905 Aborigines Act legislation resulted in part from the 1904 Roth Royal Commission. Named after Dr W.E. Roth, the former Chief Protector of Aborigines in Queensland who headed it, the Roth Royal Commission was created not only to respond to increasingly alarming reports of abuse of Aboriginal people in the north of Western Australia, but also to address the racist alarm of southern whites who feared the rising population of 'half-caste' Aboriginal people in the south-west of the state. However, the Commission was to focus its investigation on the north, and on the East Kimberley frontier in particular.

The Roth Royal Commission crystallised the already existing differences of opinion between the north and south in regard to the treatment of Aboriginal people. Whites in the south saw the north as being dominated by ruthless squatters whose stations were overrun with 'half-caste' children. Whites in the north saw the south as being peopled by a bunch of urbane city folk who had no idea of the realities of the frontier. In a sense, there were truths in both stereotypes. When Roth's report was released in 1905 these views were inflamed in the resultant controversy. The cries of the pastoralists and pearlers against Roth's scathing assessment of their treatment of Aboriginal people echoed through the press. Official witness evidence given to the Commission was attacked openly in the press and the moral character of witnesses was called into question. Roth himself was attacked by people in the south for not going far enough, and by people in the north for going too far. His methods of collecting evidence, of going into the field and interviewing witnesses, were disputed. He was accused of talking to the wrong people from both sides of the fence.

Witnesses Roth interviewed ranged from clergymen, magistrates and white stockmen to alleged bushrangers, as well as a number of policemen. Few Kimberley pastoralists were included. Everyone giving evidence had an angle. The police painted themselves as white as snow, while expressing grievances against pastoralists. Certain stockmen had a chance to even the score with both the police and the pastoralists, and resident magistrates expressed their dislike for certain police practices. Roth grilled police from the city of Perth, and from all over the North-west. Events in the south of the state hardly rated a mention.

However, of all the allegations of abuse of Aboriginal people levelled at pastoralists, pearlers, missionaries and police, the group most focused upon in Roth's investigation was clearly the Western Australian Police Force. As Roth's evidence mounted he began to smell something particularly bad in the East Kimberley district and decided to close in on it in his questioning. Much of what smelled seemed to come from the direction of Wild Dog Police Station. At the junction of the colonial border separating state and territory, it was a purported gateway to vice and immorality. Immorality was something Roth was particularly keen to uncover and stamp out.

Many records of the paternity of white fathers of Aboriginal children were collected by Roth as he interviewed police and pastoralists eager to inform on each other. In the end though, he decided that it wasn't in the best interests of the state, or of the many well-to-do families involved, to have these details released in the press, and this evidence was expunged from the final report.

The Roth Royal Commission established an integral link between police corruption, frontier abuse of Aboriginal people, the hidden hypocrisy of northern white society, and the increasing population of Aboriginal people of mixed descent. Commissioner Roth repeatedly asked witnesses about the presence of 'half-caste' children like my grandmother, and what they considered would be an appropriate way to deal with them. When asked if sending children to missions for education was a good solution, responses varied from 'Such treatment only ruins them', to 'They should be removed from the black's camps altogether.'

Many white people seemed schizophrenically caught between despising children of mixed race as 'inheriting the worst of both races,' to feeling a responsibility towards the imagined 'white blood' in their veins. There were, of course, examples of successful unions between Aboriginal women and men of other cultures, and there are instances in the archives of men wanting to act in their children's best interests who were undermined by the authorities. However, these cases are in the minority. In the East Kimberley at the turn of the century, Aboriginal women were being traded and abused by a steady stream of men who passed through the district.

If Aboriginal children of white fathers were living in deplorable conditions, and if some, as was reported, were involved in prostitution, it had nothing to do with fanciful notions of inferiority due to the calculated admixture of race. What it had everything to do with was the dominant European attitudes in regard to racial superiority, and a corresponding repugnance to the concept of mixed race.

At the core of the corruption revealed by Roth's Commission was the heightened vulnerability of Aboriginal women and children. Infuriatingly, the resulting legislation, with its aim of widespread removal of children, would do unprecedented damage to a society already under attack.

Friday 6 July 1906. Carlton Reach. Constable Hill, the two trackers, the prisoners, the witnesses, Toby and my grandmother made camp on the banks of the Ord River. A huge Kimberley full moon rose early, while the sun was still in the sky. By nightfall it was casting strong shadows. The sound of the river would be gentle and constant. Moonlight would glint over the surface ripples with the passage of water flowing west to Wyndham and then out into the sea.

They were one week and one hundred and four miles foot-march into an arduous journey. They camped away from the river to avoid the large saltwater crocodiles that inhabited the area and made all the cattle drovers windy with fear. Early the next morning they broke camp, crossing the Ord in the shallows. Pandanus and wild reeds covered the banks, obscuring any sign of crocodile nests. My grandmother told how she watched PC Hill shoot a bullock right by the river bank and then heave it into the water. He wanted a decoy in case any salties turned up looking for a feed. They crossed safely, making their way along the Ord on the west side, up towards Button's Gap. They camped at Sandy Beach before travelling on through Button's Gap, past the Mentinea Yard and out into the flat flood country. They broke away north from the Ord River as it wound its way towards the mangrove flats where it spilled out into the Cambridge Gulf. They passed through Pig Hole, Goose Hill, crossed the tidal flats, the Nine Mile, Six Mile, and finally camped at the Three Mile Well, just outside the township of Wyndham.

The Three Mile Hotel was a popular stop on the road in and out of Wyndham, a rough corrugated iron hotel with hewn-wood posts, rocks holding down roof tins, and plenty of places to tie a horse. In the Royal Commission several resident magistrates had expressed disdain for the Three Mile Hotel and what went on behind it. It was far enough from the main centre of Wyndham to be out of sight, but too close to stay out of mind.

Lines of chained prisoners were a common sight passing by the wayside house. Aboriginal women brought in as witnesses for trials would be released in Wyndham, often left to find their own way back to their country, sometimes hundreds of miles away. Many women in this predicament found themselves forced to camp around the Three Mile, waiting for a safe passage and vulnerable to whoever agreed to escort them home.

The children spent the last night of their escort unaware of what awaited them in the town of Wyndham.

The road to Wyndham is smooth and sticky in the midday heat of the build-up. In the distance huge thunder clouds hang over the landscape like giant floating jellyfish. The purple-blue masses of cloud rupture in places and whisper-like tentacles of rain evaporate in the sky before making it to the ground.

We drive across the mudflats, through the town and up to the hospital. When Nangala heard that my grandmother was taken from Argyle she said I must visit old Banggaiyerri. We walk through the lino corridors of the hospital and find the old man lying in a bed in a ward. He is wearing an old hat with his hospital-issue pyjamas.

Banggaiyerri is getting too old to be at home in his shack. He's busted his hip again and so has to sit in the hospital waiting for it to heal. He doesn't remember how it happened but recalls that for quite a few days his leg stuck out at a funny angle. He is looking forward to getting on his feet again so he can return to Frog Hollow. He was born on Argyle Station and worked as a stockman from the time he was able to lift a rope.

Banggaiyerri thinks he can place the story of my grandmother from a story he was told when he was only a snipe. He says he was born at the beginning of the century. He remembers when Hill was the copper at Wild Dog. He says there was only one 'half-caste' born at Argyle before him, a girl, and then there was a boy born after him. He reckons there weren't any more born on that station until his sister Daffodil was born in 1923. He says a house girl named Dinah was the mother of that first girl. He stops to think it over a bit longer, then he says, 'That one be your granny now. That girl was taken away.'

A nurse bursts into the ward and speaks over us as we are talking. I've brought the old man a bottle of cool drink and some chewing tobacco, and as I go to pull them from my bag he motions for me to wait until later. Our conversation is disrupted with the emptying of bottles and the administering of medication. Banggaiyerri slips a urine bottle under the blanket. He is easy with the medical treatment going on around him and he doesn't rush anything. When he's finished with the bottle he calls the nurse over to take it. While I'm watching all of this going on I'm thinking about how things have changed in Banggaiyerri's lifetime. Not only with the changes to the stations, but how the hospitals in the north used to be racially segregated. If I had lived through those times of tin and hessian-walled sheds and second-rate medical treatment, then I'd have those young nurses running around after me too.

After the nurse has gone Banggaiyerri gets back to business. He tells me that Dinah was a 'properly good-looking one', and she was brought into Argyle for one of the top stockmen, called Boxer. Dinah was described by M.P. Durack's daughter as a 'prize' for Boxer for having helped police track down some cattle spearers in 1900, and as becoming 'One of the much-loved universal mothers of the East Kimberley.' M.P.'s daughter, born fifteen years after my grandmother, described Dinah as childless but it is doubtful she would have known about a child removed well before she was born. Boxer, who was a Marban, did not stay with Dinah. She ended up living with Ulysses, another Durack faithful from the East Kimberley. They lived out their lives on Argyle. Dinah took care of other children after her own daughter was removed. She lived a long life in her own country, but died well before my return.

Banggaiyerri says he remembers Dinah's little girl and that she was a 'yella-fella'. He says she was 'bright coloured', just like himself. When I ask him who her father was he says with no hesitation, 'Old M.P. Durack was the father of that one.' He says Dinah's daughter was sent away all the way down to Fremantle. Then Dinah reared Banggaiyerri up like he was her own. He reckons she did that because she was missing her own kid. I ask him if the Duracks had any other children. He said he heard stories about different ones but he doesn't know for sure. I tell him that my grandmother always believed old M.P. was her father. Banggaiyerri says with a knowing grin, 'my word, he coulda been that kid's pop. That's what they all reckoned.'

Before we leave I ask the old man if I can take a photograph. He pulls himself up onto the pillows and looks directly into the camera. As I'm leaving we shake hands and I ask him to tell me his skin group. He smiles at me wryly and says he is Julima. This means, Miriwoong way, he is my son.

Tuesday 10 July 1906. Wyndham. The town of Wyndham swam at the junction of five big rivers. It was lined by not so much a bay as a muddy tidal delta. It flooded twice a day as a reminder that the moon ruled the oceans, and occasionally the town was washed away in storms that hit every Rain time.

The township was essentially a main street lined by tin houses and stores cobbled together along its length. Moving west from the inland route to the sea, the town of Wyndham was accessible only by crossing the tidal flats. The tiny main street separated the giant muddy delta of the bay to the west and the naked hill that rose up behind it to the east. From the back of the town a wooden jetty stretched out into the bay, forming a T-junction to nowhere—except when the state ships arrived to create a temporary lifeline and escape route. This back section of the town existed as either muddy mangroves or flooded embankments, depending on the time of day and the tide, and was where you could stumble upon saltwater crocodiles slinking in the murky waters like stray dogs.

PC Hill left camp late and arrived in town at around noon. He handed the Bow River prisoners and witnesses over to Corporal Goodridge, then sent the trackers back to the Three Mile to spell the horses and wait for him. Then he took my grandmother and Toby and handed them over to Resident Magistrate James Maloney. They had covered one hundred and forty-eight miles in eleven days. They were to be held at Wyndham until a passage could be arranged on one of the steamships heading south.

Nangala knew all about race relations in Western Australia. She was a young adult when the 1967 Referendum was passed and she became a 'citizen' of her own country—although voting would not become compulsory in the East Kimberley until well into the 1980s. She was there when her community started up a medical service against the wishes of the majority of the state, who preferred Aboriginal people to use mainstream services, even though it was widely understood that we were discouraged from doing so.

She was there when a big mob travelled all the way from Kununurra to Perth to march for Land Rights, when all the government people seemed to shout back 'No!' from every office tower she passed. In Kununurra, Nangala had seen the effect of the introduction of wages on stations in 1968, when most of the people had been dumped in town and the reserve was started up. She had lived in both Type One and Type Two government housing, tiny tin shacks with dirt floors that were hotter inside than out. She had seen the introduction of grog to the community as the Argyle Dam was constructed and large numbers of whites rolled into the crossing and began turning it into a town.

Down at the pub there are still two sections. There is the Saloon, where a strict dress code is used arbitrarily to keep Aboriginal people out. And around the side is what is called the Animal Bar, where the younger blackfellas get served. Inside, the Animal Bar is utilitarian, just a single pool table and locker-room style seating. From the straight line of the bar you can catch a glimpse of the Saloon, more salubriously decorated and air-conditioned against the humid tropical heat. Driving past the pub on a Saturday night, you need to be careful not to hit someone stumbling home.

In the early 1980s a diamond mine was established on a Dreaming site on a tributary of what is now Lake Argyle, but was then the Ord valley of my grandmother's country. It began a development boom in the area that is still resounding through the Kimberley today.

Having gone through a major slump in the latter half of the twentieth century, the northern regions of Western Australia are looking to boom again. While cattle is still one of the most influential industries in the region, the west is being crisscrossed by exploration teams in search of oil, diamonds, water — you name it. There is a sense of impending 'big' developments that echoes the century-old idea of the 'big' wilderness to the north. Aboriginal people have traditionally been marginalised from these developments. From having worked on cattle stations for tea and tobacco, to being rounded up and dumped on reserves once wages were expected to be paid, Aboriginal people still remain outside the main game of development in the East Kimberley.

The Kimberley does have huge potential, and Aboriginal people do want to engage in appropriate development for the future of the next generations, but the current hype smells a little too much like the old sell of developing the 'wilderness'.

It is a mixed message of open land for the taking with a minor back-beat of recognition of Native Title. Amidst the historical facts of exploitation and segregation, the newer visions of the future bump up against the resonance of older ideas. Future visions for these places can only include Aboriginal people if they include Aboriginal visions that reach to the future whilst recognising our ancient past. Amid positive stories of employment schemes, of new Aboriginal tourism developments and agreements with mining companies, the real task — of the real recognition of Aboriginal spiritual and cultural connections with these lands—is yet to be settled. For traditional owners this story is far from resolved. The Elders still speak for this place, sing for this place and dance for this place. Until this is really understood, places like Kununurra can still be described as frontier towns, 'the remote north'; it is how they are sold to the thousands of tourists that swell the region in the Dry. Until real negotiated outcomes result for the traditional owners though, it might as well be considered no different from when Nangala heard all those voices yelling 'No' from the office towers of the city of Perth.

Late one afternoon on my way to pick up Nangala and Namidge, I stopped for a young couple by the side of the road. The woman's foot was swollen and broken, and was causing her a lot of pain. I turned for the hospital, but on the way I almost came to blows with her husband. He didn't want her to go to hospital. We argued. When I stopped the car to sort it out, his wife asked me to leave it; she said it was culture, business, and that her husband was boss. She limped off to the park with him following.

I told Nangala about it when I picked her up. 'No,' Nangala said, waving irritably with her hand. 'That's not culture.'

Nangala works for culture. She speaks five languages and works to record language for the future generations of Miriwoong. 'Language, Jalyirri, that's culture now.' Nangala sings at all the ceremonies and organises people to help in identifying sites under the guidance of the Land Council so that mining companies don't harm sites, or can at least be made accountable for any damage they cause. 'Ceremony, Jalyirri, that's culture now.' Nangala is fighting to get back land for out-stations, and is involved in meetings about sharing out the royalties fairly from the diamond mine. 'Land, Jalyirri, that's culture now. And story. That's culture now. Mens beating womans that's not culture, that's grog, Jalyirri. That's rubbish culture.'

'Culture' has been described as the glue that holds the diverse peoples of the Kimberley together. But it is a glue that has had to weather policies of removal, enforced concentration on the outskirts of towns, the impact of grog and substance abuse, and increased migration of guddia as the potential development of natural resources is realised. There are stories of outright racism and conflict that inform the history and mark the present of this place, and stories of resistance and reconciliation that are equally remarkable.

When my grandmother was taken from her country, this part of the world was in flux. It is still in flux today.

Wednesday 11 July 1906. Wyndham Courthouse. The Bow River prisoners and witnesses faced the court. Resident Magistrate Maloney was presiding. It was a brisk walk for Hill and the white justice system. The women witnesses were compelled to give evidence against their own countrymen. The men answered 'yes' or 'no', depending on how good the translation was. There was no one to represent the defendants' case in court. They were all tried together as one. Three men received six months' hard labour. Three men received three months' hard labour. Three men received one months' hard labour. It was a lottery. Those who got one month were lucky. Those who got six months lucked-out.

Pop-up towns with flimsy constructions breed flimsy frontier politics. Money talked in a place like Wyndham. If there wasn't money in cows, they wouldn't have bothered to rebuild the town when one of the storms blew it away, or when one of the floods floated it away. As a township it hadn't been going that long when my grandmother was taken, but even then it looked old beyond its twenty years. A short-lived gold rush built this town in the 1890s, as it did many Western Australian towns, but there was still enough in cattle to keep the old hands at it, and new land was yet to open up near my grandmother's country.

The town's lifeline was the telegraph wire and the fortnightly cattle steamers from the south. Sometimes they came more often, or sometimes a boat coming in from Indonesia or Ceylon (Sri Lanka) made a stopover. Mostly these large boats avoided Wyndham, however, and stopped in at Broome, further west. The milk-run boats brought the mail, stores and passengers. These boats weren't stately, but they served their purpose. They would make their way into port at high tide and go belly deep on the muddy bottom when the tide pulled out. Tied to the jetty, they would remain stranded until unloaded of stores and reloaded with cattle, people and mail. They would sail on the high tide and escape south again.

Tuesday 17 July 1906. The SS *Bullarra*. My grandmother had never seen the sea before. It was a vast unknown plain.

The SS *Bullarra* arrived from the south, ending its long winding journey north in the Cambridge Gulf at the Wyndham jetty. Not one of the better class of ships, the *Bullarra's* main function was as a cattle steamer and cargo vessel. It was 1,735 tons of rust-streaked metal plate and was about to be retired. The *Bullarra's* passengers travelled in either Saloon or Steerage. The ship was unloaded in a flurry of activity. Cattle were herded through the town and onto the jetty from the Three Mile holding pens, to be sent south for the slaughter yards. Stopping at all ports along the way, the *Bullarra* would trail down the coast, dropping off and picking up supplies and passengers.

My grandmother and her brother were the only Aboriginal children travelling on the *Bullarra* for that voyage, entered on the shipping register as, 'Gipsy and Brofy, two Natives, Steerage'. They had reached the end of Hill's escort.

Five big rivers snaked their way across the land of the East Kimberley into the Cambridge Gulf. The Ord River flowed from my grandmother's country, spilling out into the murky waters surrounding the *Bullarra*. Crocodile tracks slithered across red mangrove mud, vanishing before the rising tide. The ship towered over the jetty.

As my grandmother walked onto the Wyndham jetty her tracks ended, slowly. Red-earth footprints lead a small way along the rough grey wooden planks, gradually fading, leaving no trace.

The jetty throbbed with the sound of the ship's steam engine. Vapour pumped through old pistons, hissing from the worn valves. Propellers churned, tearing the ship from its muddy berth. Ropes cast adrift, fell away. The *Bullarra* listed south. Pulling away from Wyndham port, my grandmother watched from the deck as her homeland slipped away. As the ship spilled out of the Cambridge Gulf, where the waters of the Ord River and the Timor Sea swirled in muddy currents, the mangroves, blue red hills, and the dot-like gum trees of the distant ridges slowly disappeared, leaving nothing but sea, sky and salt.

The Indian Ocean separated my grandmother from her homeland. In time her country would become flooded as easily as the Gulf waters flowed in from the sea at high tide and lifted the ship and carried it and my grandmother away. But, unlike the Gulf waters, the flooding of her country would not recede. This was no natural cycle. The moon would be unable to draw out the cycle of ebb and flow from the land to the sea. This cycle has been rendered impotent by a dam wall. The lapping waters of the flooding Ord River have smoothed into placid Lake Argyle. My grandmother's country would remain sealed.

Within days of my grandmother's departure, a fingernail was all that remained of the moon. As the ship moved south the nights became colder and darker. Eventually the moon disappeared, slipping below the ocean, leaving nothing but the night sky. My grandmother's life was now to follow another course, a course determined by others, based on non-existent fractions imagined within her blood, and new definitions of race that were marked upon her skin.

It's beautiful country, Miriwoong country. The deep red sands and the violent green of the trees and grasses are vivid in the Wet. That last time when Nangala was with us it rained a huge storm late in the night. Water poured out of the sky and onto the ground, filling up the rivers and the streams, washing into all the dry hot places, bringing life to the trapped and hidden parts of the land as we drove south-west out of Kununurra. Thousands of grasshoppers began their march along the creeks and roads before taking to the air, and frogs rose up out of the earth and sang. The out-door gaol of the police station in the centre of town was empty. The pub was closed. The roads were clear.

The rain has washed tracks clean from the land a thousand times since my grandmother's removal, but they have remained in other places—in the cycle of skin and memory, and in the people who were there to welcome a relative back.

My grandmother left this country as a child. It had become a dangerous home, but it was her home country, and I can see her in it—in the beauty, and in the violence; in the ranges that she travelled as she was taken from it, in the rivers she crossed with her brother as they made their way finally to the sea.

I have been to the stumps of the old Wyndham jetty where the two children last touched the earth of their country. At the back of the township, where the drain from the meatworks once fed the Gulf with streams of blood, drawing the crocodiles dangerously close to the bank, only the pylons of the old jetty remain. I jumped out, balancing on each one as I went, one bad judgement away from landing in the muddy, murky waters. This was the place of their leaving, but it was not their end.

Nangala told us that after so many children began to be taken, women sang songs to try and spirit the children back to their country. She sang that song for us on the Ord River, while kids ran around and surfed the diversion dam wall. The women who sang those songs sent their despair in their voices, flowing through the valley and out to sea.

But when my grandmother turned to face the mouths of the five big rivers, she had already been removed beyond the point of physical return. I wish she could have known that she would be remembered and missed from her country, and that the women had sung her return. When Nangala finished, she said very quietly, 'See Jalyirri, that's one good song that one—you came back.'

life lines

It is Saturday night in London. The underground swells with the perfumed bodies of expectant youngsters piling into Piccadilly Circus and Leicester Square. They swarm around the flashing coloured lights of the Empire Cinema and Discotheque to the competing sounds of African drums and Chilean flutes as bands of buskers vie for the tourist pound. Loud boy-men jostle arrogantly, half pissed, just waiting for someone to bump into them and provide the opportunity to start a fight. Groups of teenage girls and young women sway and strut, bantering loudly in the safety of numbers about 'pulling a bloke' amid laughter and drunken screams. This is the Leicester Square of the new millennium; the bright lights, the packed crowds and the gentle rain. Rude Britannia. The faded glory of the old Empire Cinema is bathed in a deathly shade of luminescent green. Neon lasers on its cheaply modernised facade syncopate in rhythm with the eager pulse of the crowd.

Away from the crowds, around the corner in the quieter St Martins Place, the old Coliseum Theatre has somehow managed to survive. I am delighted to find it, this tangible remnant of my grandfather's youth. It was a favoured stop on his nightly vaudeville itinerary as he raced about this city, just another young face out on the town in London in 1909. I stand beneath the decorative Victorian globe of the world that twirls above the city, mounted on top of the Coliseum roof.

I am trying to capture a sense of the life he had in this city. Opening the aperture of my camera I lean still against substantial walls, keep my hands steady, and let the light do its work. The crowds begin to slow, then fade, and finally disappear completely. Around me everything fades into the night; the crowds, the traffic, even the incessantly blinking neon lights. The overlapping strains of music from the buskers dim and become muffled. I imagine him here, at this very same spot outside the theatre. He is eighteen years of age and dressed to the nines. Having braced the crowds at Charing Cross Station he has sauntered through Leicester Square with his hands in his pockets. When he arrives at the Coliseum he pushes his way through the very same heavy wooden doors and into the auditorium with its intricate mosaic tiled ceiling.

With the click of the camera button the moment is broken. I am not sure what I am trying to photograph, but I want to document this place. The noise around me increases. The traffic picks up pace. In the distance I can hear testosterone-charged voices shouting over the constant din of the street. It is more than eighty years since my grandfather came here, but it is exactly the same street in exactly the same cold city. I imagine his frosty breath escaping in short excited bursts as he makes a ritual round of his favourite places, buoyed by the prospect of the decision he has recently made.

I have my grandfather's hands. He wears my hands in all of his photographs; holding cigarettes, clutching horse reins, grabbing spanners. They are always resting at the end of his folded arms. They are the same as my mother's hands; working hands. They are large, long fingered and steady. They are rough, lined and knocked about somewhat. Our tendons protrude too much and our veins are obvious through our skin. Our handshake is firm, but welcoming. We have a light touch, but at times the strength in our hands is surprising, as if it comes from somewhere outside us. These hands are an asset when it is time to grip hard and hold fast for dear life. They are a liability when really the right thing to do is let go.

I think I have an uncertain lifeline; it is forked. There is a point, not far along its path, where it appears to come to an abrupt end. But if I look carefully, I can see a feathery line in my skin that links this lifeline to another line that continues on. It's a lifeline to a lifeline, like an old railway siding running alongside a substantial road that continues into the scrub. I like to think of it as an escape route. A palm reader once told me, 'Hmmm … I see there will be a big choice to be made.' Long life; short life? Good life; bad life?

I know that my grandfather had to make a momentous choice in his country, at the beginning of his century. To leave or to stay? He seems to have made that choice gladly. He left. But even as I say this, I know I am being too glib.

The mythic story of 'Empire' was told so often in my grandfather's formative years that it became the new lifeline for millions of young men of his day. It must have been very comforting to be told with such certainty that you had an essential role in the world. Well-honed stories of exploration, discovery and adventure were just the thing to incite a young man to pack his trunk and book his passage to the other side of the world. I have no doubt that in 1909, as he was making his way around the streets of his city, my grandfather believed that he had been born in *the* centre of the world.

I look at my hand and I have to admit that all this business of destiny and predictions seems a bit dodgy. To project some idea of a preordained future onto your present seems a little unreal. I look at the fork in the story laid out in my hand and I think of my grandfather at eighteen years of age on the other side of the world. I can see that he is buying the myth, handing over his borrowed money for a ticket to the world of Empire. He's hardly even old enough to shave.

The winter of 1909 in London was one of the worst for decades. Miles of stone, brick and mortar lay frozen beneath thick washes of grey cloud. As night covered the city the gaslights were swallowed up in the dense evening air. Archival photographs show groups of children playing in the white-blanketed streets, the odd stray dog cutting a crisp silhouette against deep banks of hardened snow. The gaslights in the neatly curtained windows of terrace houses barely make an impression against the full strength of so much white.

My grandfather, with an eye for history, kept a sporadic diary of his last year in London. An entry records that somewhere near New Cross Station a young man tried to skip from the landing of a moving horse bus to the street. The heavy steel-rimmed wheels would have cut deep mud-slurry tracks into the road, freezing instantly and quickly covering with crystal white snow to leave slightly sunken, slippery valleys. The young man, not seeing this, landed badly, slipped, fell, and cut his imprint deep into the snow. Edward Alfred Byron Smith had indented himself in the cold crust of London yet again.

The sight of Edward—'Eddie' to his chums, 'dear old Eddie' to his sisters—crumpled in some corner of the city, was not an unusual one. An old-boy scholar of Westminster, and a clumsy one at that, he might have said *drat* or *blast* as he lifted himself from the street, pushing a questioning palm into the horse-shit and mud beneath the snow, to leave his hand's imprint on a New Cross road. Within minutes it would become snowed in, frozen, this mark of our shared hand. It would last some time before eventually melting, washing along the street, through the sewers, into the River Thames and out into the deep green Atlantic Ocean. I do not need to imagine that. The English seasons are extreme, and will freeze, and melt with each spin around the sun with ease, turning any past imprints into water and sludge, given enough time. Like the alternating actions of extreme cold and warm sun on gravestones, it will eventually flake the record bare. He would be gone by the time of the melting snow and the blooming magnolias; gone from London, and gone from England.

But, like most young city fellows of his age, my grandfather seemed not the least concerned with imprints, homelands or the past. No doubt his eyes were cast outward towards the future, towards Empire, and towards imagined imprints yet to be made upon distant shores. It would have been almost irresistible to a young English boy-man who had no idea of the realities of other homelands, or of the struggles taking place within them.

He pulled himself from the snow, rushed home to his New Cross digs to change, and made his way—hopefully a little more carefully—to the party of a bachelor school friend in fashionable Brixton. He was moving towards that imagined future of his. While our palm print slowly melted away, his lifeline's gamble was waiting to be wagered. But beyond the myths, the saving lies and desires for adventure, are the realities of everyday life. Other events in young Edward's life made leaving his homeland not such a difficult decision to make.

Saturday 2 January 1909. New Cross. Being a pipe man, I imagine my grandfather having a comforting puff on his water-filled china pipe as he wrote of the day's accidental occurrence. He was surely exhausted by another day of running around. Just before turning in for the night, he made a scratchy left-handed pencil entry in his new leather-bound Ruby diary: 'I fell off a horse bus. Went to W H Neagus's party at Brixton.' In the weeks that led to this night he had been busy stripping himself of unwanted possessions.

All that remained were the majority of his books that would not make the cut for the journey out and his large glass-panelled bookcase. These were the only things of value that he would have to leave behind. That is, things of material value, for there were other things of great value that he could never physically take with him, but equally could not leave behind, that formed part of his intangible link to these lands and their history.

Somewhere in his rented room in New Cross was a package that my grandfather would always carry with him. Tucked safely inside his trunk, or perhaps hidden under starched shirts in the bottom dresser drawer, were things that he not only valued, but knew were important to the society he lived in. I occasionally stole these treasures from his trunk and flipped through them myself when I was a small child. They were a small collection of certificates and official records about his family, the generations that had come before him, giving him the necessary links to fit himself in.

The doors to the archives of the Westminster parish are tall and foreboding. While the huge panels of wood call for a heavy knock, the intercom, buried in the stone wall of the Cathedral's shell, will get you further. I am met by a librarian at the gate who is welcoming, but economic. There are no grand gestures or extended hands waiting to be shaken here. He turns on his heel and I assume that I am supposed to follow. As I enter the dark stillness of the church archives the heavy doors groan shut behind us, and the sense of stone-cold history overwhelms me. I look quickly around, trying to take it all in. A maze of shelves stacked with cloth-bound books, the acidic smell of old paper, the dampness of centuries-old stone walls. It feels like an old dungeon, and I have to admit I rather like it. It meets all of my expectations of British history and medieval abbeys under one roof. The librarian guides me silently towards a tiny spiral staircase that curls up above the stacks of manuscripts to a small archive room on the second floor.

There are no relatives to greet me here. There are no people looking for someone returning to their homeland. There are no old women wanting to teach me the nuances of homeland culture, or how to throw a fishing line. There is no one to teach you the right way to say words, or the right relationships to observe while in home country. There is no system of extended family and skin to slip into. There is no homecoming like that. My English relatives have all died. My family is all that is left of this line. But there is information to be gleaned from archives. Written traces of ancestors and their stories to be pieced slowly together. Bones lying within graves to be tracked and paid respect.

After hours of searching the archives there is a grave on the other side of town that I want to visit. Outside, the church pavement leading me to the tube is covered with the names of other people's ancestors. In a city where space is a luxury, the dead and the living exist in close proximity. This is the London we are normally sold. The stiff-upper-lippers of the proper classes of the proper religion. But, out on the street, and into the tube, London teams with diversity. I move along in the crowd and down into the sunken stairwells of the underground that are filled with too many people. The bins at the entrance have been welded shut to prevent the planting of bombs, and there are no seats or resting places, so that we will all keep moving. In the heart of this city you are never encouraged to linger.

Television closed-circuit cameras are everywhere, watching for any suspicious activity. A bomb was recently found on Chelsea Bridge, not far from where I am staying. It did not have to detonate to make its point. In the capital of the old Empire, past actions have a history of coming back to haunt it. New laws have been introduced allowing police to search bags on demand for no other reason than that they consider you look suspicious. Drug busts at Earls Court tube station have been a lucrative result. But such powers are ripe for abuse, and the police are like a new set of turnstiles, added after the gate, picking out the poor, the odd and, in South London, where I am heading, the groups of young blacks.

For my part, I am conscious that I am a visitor in this city. There are others though whose ancestors have ridden the backwash of the waves of Empire, and this is now their home. London is no longer the centre of the world. A few times whilst travelling I have been stopped and questioned. The guards mistake me for Arabic, Moroccan, or anything vaguely Middle Eastern. It might be my imagination but they always seem surprised by my Australian accent. Outside a chippie in Tufnell Park, a Cockney newspaper seller informed me, very knowledgeably, that all Australians are blond with blue eyes.

England is not what it used to be, or so the old men tell each other as they wait at bus stops. I move closer to eavesdrop. The Empire version of whiteness, from which all other races were judged, has, today, been subverted. Fixed definitions from which cranial cavities were measured, skin colours classified and body parts severed for collections in British museums, have been challenged. But it is not to everyone's liking to see all the old ways tossed in the bin. The old men at the bus stop complaining about blacks and Asians taking over the country, or the difficulty of not being able to identify separate races any more, feel a betrayal of the future they were promised as young boys. As I listen I wonder if my own grandfather might have become like these men if he had not come out to Australia. Britain may be blurring the lines of racial intermixing, but that does not mean acceptance is automatic. Even after decades of engagement, with mixed-race couples walking the streets, trouble spots flare up and old Britannia waves the shadow of Empire from its inglorious past.

I've missed my station again, daydreaming on the tube, thinking over all these questions. It takes some getting used to, navigating the underground. Even when I'm above ground it is difficult to get my bearings by the weaker sun. The automated lifts are ancient and a worry. The stairs are more sturdy, but endless. Travelling first on the Central Line, then switching to the Piccadilly, I find my way to Brompton Road Station. A right turn out of the station brings me to the high Victorian gates of Brompton Cemetery. The cemetery itself is a crumbling beauty. At the beginning of spring, before the trees begin to sprout and the days are still short and dark, the cemetery is like a huge Gothic portal.

Following a central road I walk past the Celtic cross of Emmeline Pankhurst's grave, away from the numerous memorials to the dead of the Great War and towards the section where my grandfather's family are buried. Standing at the foot of their graves, in my first tangible link to my grandfather's family, I begin to feel something I have never felt before. The people lying here, in this place that is so foreign to me, are my ancestors. I also realise there is no one else to pay respect to them, and nor has there been for almost half a century. Suddenly, beyond the exciting hum of the city and the urgent drive of New Britannia, the London of the remaining stories of Edward's family seems a very sad and lonely place.

Sunday 3 January 1909. St Margaret's Church, Westminster. At Evening Service in St Margaret's Church, the poorer sister to Westminster Abbey, the parishioners walked over the tombs and headstones of past saints, sinners and clergy. They are buried in the walls, in the floor, in the grounds, under the streets, under train stations, under headstones, and even in the River Thames. Edward would have had no sense of amazement, as I have, when he walked the streets of this city, to come across some place of burial, or some story of a burning. I expect his step would scarcely have faltered passing the exact spot where a person accused of heresy had been bound to a stake and set alight. Londoners, it seems to me, like to keep their dead around them. They pile them up around their city in layers, both above and below the ground.

It was the first Evening Service of the year. Crossing over the murky, slow-moving Thames, my grandfather would have braced himself against the freezing winds sweeping north-west from the Atlantic. From the Embankment that runs along the river it was a quick walk across the corner of Parliament House, under the watchful eye of Big Ben, to the old church of St Margaret's. Walking through the church vestibule, he would pass by a neat rectangular marble plaque erected in memory of his father, Samuel Smith.

It was a memorial made by Samuel's friends. The memorial, and a fading sepia photograph, were my grandfather's most tangible links to the man that he himself had never known. On his father's memorial, kind words were chiselled in stone. Samuel's friends decided that Psalms 84:10 would do the job of summing him up. 'For a day in thy courts is better than a thousand. I had rather be a doorkeeper in the house of my God, than to dwell in the tents of wickedness.' The words of the plaque are remarkable, but tell me more of Samuel's 'many friends' than anything personal of the man himself. For my money, the photograph says much more. The photograph is rubbed clean in the corner from so much handling, well worn from careful study, as if it held some clue to the reason why a young man would die such a young death. Samuel, small mouthed and dark eyed looked unsteadily into the camera. A simple striped tie, just visible beneath his grey coat above his high-buttoned white collar, was chosen for the occasion. Ironically, the photograph is as old as he would ever look on this earth. It was not meant to be a grand image; his early death, and the fact that it is the only image to prove his existence, has made it special. It was taken in 1891, the year of Samuel's death, and the same year his only son, Edward, was born.

As my grandfather's father's body crumbled and decayed beneath the cold earth and grey marble in Brompton Cemetery, in stone tablet and in fading photo chemicals, Samuel was fixed at thirty-nine years of age. As my grandfather aged, his father remained constant in the photograph, another of the constants of Westminster life. And Samuel was not alone. There were five other Smiths, including Samuel's own father and brothers, in this single grave in Brompton Cemetery. Not far away were Samuel's grandparents and uncles, all of whom died relatively young, going back to the 1700s. They are all gathered there, the Smith family of Westminster, formerly of Kent. From the evidence that survives, they could best be described as amicable. They were the church wardens, bellringers, pewterers, civil servants, librarians and government messengers of their day. They lived short, quiet lives.

While the plaque and photograph were the everyday means through which Samuel Smith existed in his son's life, my grandfather was surrounded by other evidence of his family's quiet civility. There was a place reserved for Edward in a pew in St Margaret's, as there had always been for members of his family. He was expected to take his place in the civil service, as his father had done. He dutifully visited his grandmother and great-aunt, and kept up correspondence with the branch of his father's family that had emigrated to South Africa in the century before.

I wonder though, if he could see that the Smith family were on the slide. As they clung to the quietude of their urban patch, they held on to the best days of their past. They resisted the hype of the changing city in the new Edwardian age. They attended evening service dutifully, sat straight in their allotted pews and, I imagine, thought England's reign would go on forever. They were happy living out their lives in the respectable borough of Westminster.

But for Edward the colonial adventures of Empire were beckoning, the further from England the better and the greater the test of his skills. He was a young man with an eye on self reinvention, and London seemed to only offer more of the same. This future would be in another country. It would be a gamble, but adding up the years on the Smith family gravestones and calculating the averages, I see that he didn't really have much choice.

First rule of gambling—don't bet what you're not prepared to lose. The odds must have looked pretty even from where he was standing. To stay where he was, in this place where his father and grandfather had lived and died, was not attractive. The Smith family grave had one last plot to be filled, and in the cold flu-ridden winters of London, there were a good number of them competing for it, except of course Edward, who was busy making other plans.

St Margaret's Church is also where Edward and his sisters were christened. The day I decided to visit, every tourist in London must have had the same idea. Trying to stand still long enough to read the inscription was particularly difficult. Crowds of tourists literally piled through the alcove: in long lines we writhed like a giant centipede. I had to push my way against the crowd, holding out my hands blindly trying to carve a path through.

It is a sad little plaque really, stuck on the wall in a row with a few others. I suppose it is prominent in its own way, but in terms of leaving an impression on his city, it has very little to say about his life. But when I raise my camera to take a record of it for my mother, that unexpected feeling returns. It is the same one I experienced at the grave site, the feeling of an ancestral tug.

A short ride south on the Northern Line brings me to Clapham Junction. It is the nearest stop to Emanuel School, where my grandfather went to live when he was only six years old. It is the last stop before Brixton, which is no longer the white enclave that it once was.

At Clapham the remains of old industries are still evident. The lacy ironwork structures of the old gasworks tower up into the low-hanging sky. But gasworks jobs, and the families whose lives centred on them, are now gone, and the public housing has been transformed.

It is a racially mixed area with a good-sized black and Asian population. It is considerably run-down, but is filled with families with kids and has a good feel about it. Beyond the main corridor of the High Street, lined with derelict Victorian and Edwardian buildings, are the economic utilitarian blocks of housing estates. These giant concrete squares have replaced the patterns of streets of what was once a more human-scale city. They stand as monuments to an era of unchecked development amid inner-city decay. It is still an area of high unemployment.

The school itself is on the edge of Clapham Common. There are iron gates at the main entrance, and a bitumenised road that runs past the caretaker's cottage to the school buildings. Built of heavy brick, the main buildings were constructed with three wings, which from an aerial view resemble the letter E. Not all of the buildings of Edward's time still remain. The old spire and the detached infirmary for boys, where Edward had occasionally recovered from long illnesses, had been demolished. Even with these parts missing, the school is easily recognisable from the photos that Edward had kept.

The grounds, with their large expanse of grassed playing fields, create an atmosphere of country life. It is like an oasis in the middle of London, a world of well-tended gardens hidden away from view. By London standards it is a massive walled estate within the city, and in real estate terms it is probably worth a fortune.

Today children from all over the world are enrolled, and the sight of a stranger with long curly black hair, goatee and black vinyl jacket entering the yard during lunchtime is, quite rightly, enough to send a worried teacher scuttling for the headmaster.

When the introductions are made however, and my story of tracking is told, the staff are more than welcoming, if not a little intrigued. I am the grandson of an old boy and I get a grandson-of-old-boy escorted tour. I am taken to meet the school archivist named Marianne, who is very helpful and gives me stacks of old school magazines to plough through. As I am reading I hear the loud ring of the school bell and the clamour of children running up and down the corridors outside the library.

This is where Edward spent most of his childhood, within the walls of the stone school, and where the tracks of the railways ran either side of the school grounds heading south and south-west. He was a full term boarder with an anonymous bed and table to call his own on the top floor of Clyde Hall. Through the tall windows he could stand and watch the others playing cricket out in the yard. He could see the dayboys — those who went home at the end of the day — making their way down the school drive to houses in streets beyond the school walls. The archives tell me that boarders like my grandfather were getting fewer as each year passed. The school was gradually changing its status until, in 1910, it catered only to dayboys. I wonder how such a decision would have affected boys like Edward who, outside of Emanuel, did not really have a home.

My grandfather's mother, Kate Graham, was a different proposition to the Smith family she had married into. She was born in 1855 to Edward and Rosa Graham who lived in a fashionable quarter of Westminster. Whereas the Smiths were mostly reputation and community service, the Grahams were coffee house proprietors and successful small business people, financially very well off. They held shares in Harrods and the Gas and Light Company, and had a rather grand-looking house in Surrey. They knew how to make money, and how to keep it. When old man Graham, Kate's father, died, he left a comfortable lifestyle for his wife, and a handy inheritance put in trust for his grandchildren, Edward and his two sisters, Lily and Blanche. When Rosa Graham died the family fortune went to her son Alfred, bypassing her daughter Kate.

There are also Graham family graves at Brompton Cemetery, just around the corner from the Smiths. However the graves are not nearly as full of people, their lives not nearly as short.

Both families were originally from Kent, but ended up in the same parish in London — St Margaret's. The two families had lived close to one another when Edward's parents were children, and they had attended the same schools.

Edward was the image of his mother Kate; compact and dark eyed, with a prominent nose and soft, almost bruised, lips. Samuel and Kate had four children, but the eldest, Rosa, died when she was a four-year-old child. On the death of her husband, Kate was left to raise her two daughters, Blanche and Lily, and was in the final stages of pregnancy with Edward. She began to physically decline almost immediately, and did not appear to enjoy good health again.

Money had to be budgeted and spent carefully, and the Smith children were divided up. Kate had to share her children around the family, relying on the hospitality of her older brother, Alfred, who had not only inherited the bulk of the family money, but also Iron Gates, the house in Surrey. The girls went to Kate's stepmother, Grandma Graham at Lebanon Gardens in Wandsworth, where they attended the local school. Edward was sent away to Emanuel to live through the terms.

With her children cared for Kate wandered from hospital to hospital, seeking treatment for the illness that had set in after her husband's death. During school holidays the girls and Edward would reunite with their mother as guests of their uncle at Iron Gates, and this was the nearest they ever got to a family home. Surviving separately throughout the year, when they came together they tended to operate in their own separate spheres, spinning around the nucleus of their increasingly sick mother.

During school terms Edward's sisters wrote him very touching and affectionate letters that belied the awkwardness of their yearly reunions.

They were a family born of the death of their father, who existed only in fragments of memory and paper. Kate and her daughters could remember the first family, the one that existed when their father was alive. But for Edward the paper family was all he had ever known, and it revolved around one woman. As she moved around the country from women's hospital to hospice, the Smith children went about their duty, anxiously awaiting the next card or letter to assure them that she was still all right.

My grandfather was not the kind of boy to grace the Emanuel School magazine's more exciting pages, win any of its prizes for punctuality or sport, or receive special commendations for academic progress. His only entry would be as scorekeeper for the boys' cricket. On weekends, as he wandered around the drafty corridors of Emanuel, bathed in the icy baths under the stairwell and slept sardine formation in the neat, spartan dormitory, he at least had his mother's distant love as a consolation. It might have been the middle-class English way, but it strikes me as very sad. It is no wonder that my grandfather should find it easy to contemplate leaving his family; he had left them years ago when he was a small boy, and knew what it felt like to be alone in the world.

Thursday 7 January 1909. New Cross. 'Call on Gertie in evening but was not in. Looking out for her!' Edward was on the run again. Only two weeks left. He was preparing for his journey by day and enjoying the delights of London by night. It was as if he thought there was no such thing as theatres in Australia. He gorged himself on popular music hall repertoire and vaudeville. Gertie Gitana was a friend and a favourite, known for her rendition of 'There's an old Mill by the Stream Nellie Dean', a song I'm not familiar with myself. Edward caught her shows at the Empire, the Glasgow Palace and the Coliseum. She wrote him letters and he was keenly on the look-out for her. He was dining with friends and slipping from horse buses.

In archives I discover Gertie Gitana was the Madonna of her day. How well Edward knew her, I will never know. At eighteen he was only a pup, possibly an enthusiastic fan. Intriguingly though, she is the only woman who rates a mention in the diary he kept before he left home.

For all the changes that have taken place within London, it is still a city divided clearly by class. The tube stations may be universally grimy and run-down, but once you escape the tunnels and rise into the various boroughs, the differences are immediate. From Kensington to the East End is a long journey in more ways than one. The Nation of Islam is marching through the streets protesting against the killing of a black youth by four white policemen. General Pinochet of Chile is in town for an operation and has been detained for possible extradition to Spain to stand trial for the political killings of Spanish citizens during his dictatorship. The IRA are backing away from peace talks and the city is on jumpy alert for possible bombs.

A policeman stops me from taking photographs of the train station. He isn't interested that I am searching for a moment, catching elements of what was once here and is no more. He thinks I could be casing the place, looking for a suitable spot to stash a bomb. I explain that if I was, I wouldn't be standing on the platform waving my camera around. He checks me over and tells me to move off the platform. A boy asks his father what is going on as they pass me. The father assures his child not to worry: 'It's just one of those train spotters.'

I'm a tourist here, just another bit of the flotsam and jetsam of life that swarms through London, much as my grandfather might have been had he ever returned here after decades in the backwater of colonial Western Australia. And I'm a strange tourist at that, seeking something of a personal connection to a place that an ancestor once belonged to almost a century ago, in a city that he might barely recognise by the old buildings, but which is totally transformed from the place he knew.

London is more than an international transit terminal, but a transit terminal it still is. Political pariahs, refugees, returning relatives and the general swell of tourists push the city beyond its nine million capacity. Sometimes the lack of personal space is claustrophobic. Space between people, space between yourself and the street, space between the past and the present begin to pile up on top of one another. On the tube walls, in the leaflets handed out in the street, are constant offers to travel. You are urged to spend hard-earned pounds on holidays in Ibiza, Morocco, the Bahamas, or wherever is the latest destination for the hordes of tan seekers. Sun, sun, sun is the maxim. In some ways, this aspect of life in London may be little different from my grandfather's time. The pressure to leave can simply become the reason to escape.

Friday 15 January 1909. New Cross. 'Went to Coliseum … Gertie Gitana. Pack box … Sold cupboard to T.E. Davies … sent box to dock.'

Edward purchased his steamer trunk for fifteen shillings. It was a coffin-sized oak box resembling a pirate chest. He had his initials lacquered onto the front of it in big black letters—E.A.B.S.—Edward Alfred Byron Smith. He pasted his Royal Orient Mail Line details on the side, *Saloon Class, Voyage 20. The SS Orontes*, fastened a thick metal lock and set in motion his final week in London. Only seven days to go.

The London papers overflowed with the possibilities of the sea. You could travel First Class, Saloon or Steerage. You could choose the Orient Line, the Royal Line, the Royal Orient Mail Line, or any one of dozens of shipping companies, ships or passages. Turning to page two of *The Times*, cheap passages were on offer to Africa, the Amazon, Australia, Belgium, Bombay, Canada, China, Egypt, France, Greece, Italy, India, Japan, Malta, the Mediterranean, New York, New Zealand ... And of course it was more than just a holiday that was on offer. It was a clarion call to participate in the maintenance of Great Britain abroad.

A young man in white pants and a tight-fitting suit could choose almost any destination in the world as his place of reinvention. I don't know why he chose Australia. Perhaps it was part of a recruitment drive. Perhaps it was the sense of the unknown, of a place considered to be so different from England. Perhaps there really was a destiny written into his palm. Something must have caught my grandfather's eye about the Royal Orient Mail Line. It was some time in December 1908 that he spotted it. Perhaps it was the large type of their advertisement in *The Times*. Maybe the Fenchurch Avenue office caught his eye as he made his way back to New Cross. The next voyage was set for 22 January 1909.

I imagine that the carefully chosen ticket to his faraway place burned warm and bright inside his jacket breast pocket. It would have radiated an excitement and experience beyond the familiar. It was a measured chance, a plotted escape, and a secret pleasure. It is as if it acted upon his pocket watch in his waistcoat, pushing the second hand just that little bit faster. It is as if it acted upon his heartbeat, speeding up his internal clock, pushing him into imagined time. I imagine him then, time lost daydreaming on the underground, at vaudeville theatres, at the bus stop, and saying farewell to school chums and family.

In sending him to Emanuel School, Kate had entrusted Edward to the values of surrogate fathers. Emanuel guided its boys into useful service for England. It was not designed to produce candidates for Cambridge and Oxford, although a few of its boys went on to these institutions.

Predominantly, Emanuel boys were equipped for the world of Empire. Edward, who was a trained clerk, was capable of many other more practical vocations. A lot had been invested in him, and he had received an education that other boys could only dream about. At Emanuel he learned the simple value and enjoyment of knowledge.

Edward was not outwardly or obviously ambitious. He was the sort to create small evidences of himself in locked away places. Notes were written on the spines of books, small quotations at the bottom of pages in favourite books, occasional passages in Latin describing a particular summer's day or the cast of his slight shadow in the corner of his negatives. He was also deliberately secretive. Large wads of pages from diaries were cut out, names were assigned aliases, infuriating codes were invented, and details of people held within photographs were buried in small lists within loose pages of old books. He had lived most of his life in a place where privacy had to be guarded and protected. There is a trail, but it is not clearly signposted. You have to look carefully at what was kept and what was not.

I have brought my grandfather's photographs of his life in London with me. I suppose I am hoping they will reveal some hidden clue that is not clear to me in Australia. Clive James is right. Being in London is like walking around a film set. If Edward's photographs are like stills from some scratchy film, perhaps I will find the cohesive images that are missing. I lay each image out on the table in the archives room on the day I visit Emanuel School.

The oldest image that we have of him was when he was aged six. He is ready for school, this school. His small mouth is tight, leaving downward creases in his soft cheeks. He looks to me to be breathless, that is, not breathing, as if moving will betray something that he does not want anyone else to see. But his eyes betray him. He is terrified. His hair neatly parted down the middle, the tightly buttoned collar, the snug-fitting uniform, and the pointy ears scrubbed clean to shiny smoothness, signal that he is about to be sent away and he doesn't appear ready. He has his father's look of fear. It is as if he has practised it, copying that captured moment of his father at age thirty-nine. I am speaking of the photograph that was taken when his father had no idea that he was soon to die.

Apart from writing each other letters, he and his mother sent each other postcards, met briefly within the school term and spent family time together during the holidays. He gutted a pocket watch, the same one that he is wearing in his photographs of himself as a child, probably trying to see how it worked, and placed a small circular hand-coloured print of himself with his mother inside it. They stand together, trapped within the clock face. Perhaps it was an attempt to fix a private moment when he had his mother all to himself. Kate looks tired. Her hair is grey flecked. Her brow is lined. Her eyelids sit heavily over her dark eyes. Her finger is just visible at the bottom of the frame, blurred, twirling something at the end of a silver chain, maybe a cross, against an elongated moment of exposure.

Kate is sepia toned and untouched. Edward's tie has been clumsily hand coloured red. His hair and eyebrows have been hand coloured jet black. It is a home job by an unsteady young hand. He may well have coloured it in while sitting at this window. It is a touching image. Edward is taller than his mother. He is standing at her left. His hands are obscured. He may have his right arm around his mother's waist, or he may be helping her stand. Kate has a look of worn-out resignation on her face. Edward is again the image of his father in his final portrait, all fear and apprehension. It is as if they both sense that something so normal cannot possibly last.

Edward photographed his mother, his sisters, and Iron Gates, the Graham family home. He photographed his school, his friends, himself, the sports and the occasional park scene. He documented what was around him and what was important in his life. He photographed a school friend, Pol-Apol, a rumoured Indian prince, posing on his bike. He photographed himself on the same bike, in the same place, perhaps an experiment in movement, a slight blur across the frame.

He is a documenter who seeks to capture the moment. He sees through the viewer the framed moment of captured life, the proof of a moment of existence. He feels the moment of capture, the act of making an instant in time that will remain fixed, ageless, fragmentary, and able to be owned. His love of photography grew out of his love of the sciences. Edward was a whiz in the chemistry lab. I imagine he loved the chemistry laboratory of Emanuel School, certainly enough to sketch it and still have the drawing almost half a century later. He seems to have loved the rows of large thick glass bottles with heavy black labels denoting HCL, H_2SO_4 and N_2O_4. His collection of books from the turn of the century indicates that he revelled in the physical sciences and valued mathematics, not as a game but as a lingua franca to the other sciences.

For Edward, steam was interesting enough, but electricity, that was the thing. He was a child born of Newton, and Newtonian science was becoming the manual arts of his new century. He was caught up in the age of invention and technology. He wasn't a clubber or a mixer, but the school's photography club, like the school repertory group, was somewhere he felt he could belong. This team of pint-sized image makers who boasted in the school magazine about field trips where they 'obtained good negatives', met regularly through the academic year. They raised money selling glam shots of notable school sports teams and popular schoolmasters, to purchase new equipment to further their art.

My grandfather owned a huge unwieldy camera, a 1904 Seneca Bellows scientific camera. It collapsed down to the size of a large encyclopedia and opened out for use, concertina style, to the size of a giant typewriter. It took single shot five-by-seven glass-plate negatives, and he somehow adapted it, perhaps in his woodwork class, to take the newer celluloid-based negatives. It was a monster of a camera that seemed appropriate for Edward, who had altered it from something very Victorian and heavy into something modern and practical. It could shoot up to a pacy one hundredth of a second, but also had the longer exposures requisite for the lingering London light. He must have looked after it lovingly as it still works perfectly today.

As the years progress, Edward begins to move further left of frame in his school photographs, growing more distant, hiding behind others in the group, engaging less and less with the probing eye of the camera. In his photographs of his family, they are never all together in one group. There is one photograph however that comes very close. It is an image of him with his mother and Blanche, sitting in the back garden of Iron Gates. Edward is separated from his mother by a dog sleeping at his feet. Blanche, unsure of the camera, stands behind a chair. They are all still and quiet, and they look rather stiff. I wonder why Lily is missing, perhaps she took the photograph, but I tend to doubt this. In the Smith family history, someone always seems to be missing, through death or through choice.

When I look at other archival photographs of London in libraries I always imagine that I catch a glimpse of my grandfather in thick photographic emulsions painted on heavy glass negatives. I see him as the dapper young gentleman waiting for a tram, the lean young chap propping up a gaslight pole, the schoolboy with the bicycle, or the mystery man at the back of the crowd, head tilted to the left and hat swung down low over his right brow.

I see him in the audience of every major unveiling of memorials, window shopping in all the high streets, and strolling, somewhat stiffly, through all the local boroughs of his beloved Wandsworth, perhaps on his way from Brompton Cemetery to a lecture on phrenology or electricity. He moves steadily and determinedly once he knows what he wants to do.

It took a year blowing around London for him to realise that he was destined to be swept up in the movement of young men to the colonies, and to leave where he felt he no longer belonged. He traversed the city from New Cross to Wandsworth, Westminster to Fulham, Kensington to Chelsea, Brixton to Holborn. He travelled by horse bus, by underground, by open rail and by steam bus. He walked the river bridges as if they traversed nothing but another causeway, one of water, carrying barges and goods from city to port. The river flowed east to the ocean, to another highway of imagined sounds and smells.

In the spring of 1909 a very different photograph was recorded. Edward stands alone in a back alley of London. Beneath his shiny black shoes lie thick cobblestones. His creased white suit pants disappear beneath his long grey suit coat which, unbuttoned, reveals a casually falling tie. His Adam's apple sticks out above his tight high-collared white shirt. His hat dips slightly to the right, left hand on hip, eyes left. He strikes a deliberate pose; his new image, made for a new life and a new man. A pose for a young man about to take on the world, who needs to adopt such a pose when thinking of distant horizons. It was a nice try. In the photograph a group of children arm in arm behind him do not appear to be fooled. They don't seem to notice anything remarkable as they look confidently past him and into the same lens.

I have also brought a selection of his artefacts with me to London, but there were some items that were too valuable to risk misplacing in the course of travel. Wrapped up in a safe place within his wooden trunk, bound in a leather satchel, tied in string, were his most valuable mementoes. These are a collection of cards that his mother sent him when he was a boarder at school. I know these cards well. As children I took turns with my brother and sisters, delicately opening each one of these exquisite creations. They are markedly different from the photographic postcards she sent to him regularly, detailing the places she had visited, the trains she had caught, and the grim-faced hospitals and hospices that had become the fabric of her life.

These cards are special. Handpainted in watercolours, they open out like birthday cards to reveal concertina tissue paper in the shape of large butterflies, ladybirds, wild swans, bluetits, cloud banks at sunset, yellow baby chicks and pots of gold at the end of rainbows, around which leprechauns and elves dance. They are the sort of thing that a young boy in a dormitory wouldn't want other boys to see, and especially not to read. In increasingly fragile handwriting Kate wrote to her son: 'Dear Eddie, I hope to see you to-morrow, Friday. It does seem so long since I was with you, love Mother,' and when he was ill for some time in the infirmary, 'Butterfly sweet, when Eddie you meet, tell him to heal, and get strong … much love from mother.'

Back in the city the paper family that exists in the archives tells me that Kate's last years were not good ones. The illness that had plagued her since her husband's death was finally diagnosed as breast cancer. Having spread to both of her breasts it was rapidly consuming her whole body. Treatment in the early part of the century was rudimentary at best. The greatest hope for survival was a mastectomy, an extremely arduous and dangerous procedure. Having no other option open to her, Kate checked into the Chelsea Hospital for Women to go under the surgeon's knife.

The Chelsea Hospital for Women was a specialist gynaecological hospital for the treatment of 'diseases peculiar to women'. First opened in 1871, its charter was to 'provide treatment for ladies of limited means' whose 'social positions' and 'refined sympathies' precluded them from entering general hospitals for treatment. Poor but respectable women were also admitted free of charge if they had a subscriber's letter from a well-to-do family; otherwise they had to pay one guinea a week for treatment.

The hospital itself has a chequered history; problems in management and difficulty keeping staff culminated in an enquiry at the turn of the twentieth century into allegations of dangerous and experimental operations being performed on the poor and the desperate.

Kate became a patient around 1904, and the long periods spent in the hospital soon became a fundamental part of her life. It appears she endured several operations aimed at removing the cancer from her body, but without any success. Spending so much time in the wards, my grandfather must have come to know the route to the Kings Street building, by horse bus and underground, like the back of his hand. Visiting hours were regulated and strictly controlled. Only two visitors were permitted, for one and a half hours at a time, on Wednesdays and Sundays. With three children eager to visit, it must have been difficult to ration the time that Kate spent with her small and disparate family.

I can imagine Edward pacing the backstreets of Chelsea between the hospital and the bridge, and the hospital and Brompton Cemetery, trying not to jump to negative conclusions but knowing that it was unlikely he would have his mother for much longer. I can imagine the unmitigated sense of helplessness Edward and his sisters must have felt as they visited her after each operation and witnessed her slow and painful deterioration, or her morphine-induced haze. The fear of cancer is something we can relate to today. Cancer is an invading power that transforms the life of the sufferer and the families that love them. After all those years of suffering and operations, it must have seemed unjust that there was no recovery, or window of remission.

Having survived her little daughter Rosa and her husband Samuel, Kate Smith passed away late in the night of 7 November 1907. She was fifty-two years old. Her death left two daughters and sixteen-year-old Edward to keep any semblance of a family alive.

Kate's grave stands alone. She was buried in New Wandsworth Cemetery, away from her husband and child. It is almost as if she was exiled from the Smith family once Samuel had died. It is a short train ride from Waterloo Station to Earlsfield Station, and I make a point of going there to place flowers. On my way there on the tube I am conscious that I am doing this for my grandfather, that after almost ninety years one of us has come back.

Alighting from the railway overpass, the walk to the cemetery leads to an open expanse of rolling green lawn broken uniformly by the shapes of white crosses and angels carved in stone. It is a newer cemetery than Brompton, each plot evenly spaced from the next, neat and prim, as if they are all sitting up next to one another in hospital beds.

The railway line that had run past Edward's dormitory window on its way to Brighton now took him to his mother's grave. There was no record in the Ruby diary of his visiting her before he left, but I know that he went there. The photograph of himself with his mother trapped in the carved out watch face tells me that he did, that he would, that he probably spent hours there, alone and quiet, on late afternoons.

Her grave is in a lovely spot, high on a rise in the cemetery, overlooking the railway line and the sound of the trains singing along steel tracks into the city. Untended, grass had grown over the grave, obscuring it. When I remove the overgrowth, lilies carved in stone relief are revealed, along with a reference to the little child Rosa. It was not until this moment that I had known of this first child. The lilies, engraved within an oval crest at the top of the headstone, had darkened and wept down the front of the white marble facade. Beneath them was the body of Edward's mother, and the words in memory of her first daughter, who had died well before what I thought of as the first family—Edward's mother and father and three sisters. Rosa is not mentioned on her father's grave, even though she is buried there. The plaque on her mother's grave is the only way of knowing that this little girl had taken her mother's place beside her father, marking the beginning of a sequence of family tragedies in the years to follow.

As Edward stood on the rise by his mother's grave he could see the traffic on Earlsfield Road and busy movement at Earlsfield Station. Wandsworth Common, where he had made many of his negatives, and Emanuel School where he was raised, were only a short walk away. In all the years of Kate's moving about the country from sick bed to sick bed, she had never been so close for so long. When she stopped moving she stopped altogether.

In the same month that his mother died, in the winter of 1907, my grandfather left the dormitories of boarding school. There would be no more cards, no more letters, no more photographs and no more affectionate notes. The paper family dissolved and blew away in the wind. With no immediate family to live with, Edward found himself private lodgings in town. Boarding was a situation he was well used to; one way or another he had been a boarder since birth. He found a boarding house in New Cross which he forever referred to as his 'digs'.

In the year leading up to Edward's decision to leave England, he began to drift around the city. His father's gravestone had already begun to deteriorate from the cold winds of London, its lettering peeling away. His mother's grave would do the same. It was only a matter of time.

Friday 22 January 1909. Tilbury. *Leave London for Australia.* Just as his ticket held within his waistcoat pocket had burned brightly, speeding up time so that the departure date raced closer, I imagine that the torn, used ticket slowed down time, stretching out the sea voyage through new territories and oceans. His remaining family moved on in London real-time, anticipating his quick return. But he was sailing out beyond the equator, beyond their stars, and into a world within a different time, both in physical distance and in unfamiliar culture.

He had two pounds in his pocket for the voyage, and seventeen pounds waiting for him in the Western Australian Bank. His trunk was packed with provisions that reflected the variety of his interests, as well as things he thought he might need. He had new suits and leggings, putties and stockings, books on chemistry and conjuring, and, of course, his camera and chemicals. He brought the cards from his mother, studio portraits of his sisters, photographs of school chums, diaries and letters, a Bible given to him from St Margaret's, and a collection of plaster figures that someone had sent him from India when he was a child. When I read through the long list of shirts, nightshirts and underclothing, it seems as if he must have bought out the store.

I don't know what he thought he was going to do in Australia. He had some unusual skills. He could operate the props, trapdoor and curtain from his experience with repertory theatre at school. He had become adept in stagecraft and could even operate the limelight at a pinch. He could strip a Fiat motor car, drive, set up electric circuits and was a budding electrician. He could shoot, develop and print his own photographs using the older dry solarising technique, as nimbly as he could slap up a wet plate neg. He had passed his clerk's exam, and studied the classics; he wrote and spoke in Latin and even had passable French, which he'd practised on a school excursion to Paris. He had a doctor's certificate proving his perfect health.

He was a young man of many contradictions: a city-bred lover of the arts, a man of science, a quiet boy who loved the theatre but who had dreams of starting up a farm. He was just eighteen. He was just a kid with too many choices. But the Colonial Club he belonged to was ripe for kids like him. Maybe he just flipped a coin. Maybe it had nothing to do with destiny and a great deal more to do with chance. Either way there is no doubt that he would never have guessed the direction his life would take. Some people can make such guesses and be fairly close. They stay within the lines. I do not know for sure the various scenarios he imagined for himself as he caught the *Orontes* from London, but I am sure it wasn't the one that he eventually took hold of, or that eventually took hold of him.

My grandfather's last dark winter in his homeland was the last time he tasted the dry frosty air, smelled the acrid crackle off the frozen electrified rail cables, and felt the burning sting of the cold Atlantic winds chapping his lips. While my grandmother had watched her country slip away from her in horror, my grandfather set sail from his with great excitement. I think for him the city of London was easy to love, but it was just as easy to leave. And while he appears to have left it easily, it remained indelibly marked on his heart.

On that cold grey day at the Tilbury docks, the deep green of the Atlantic met the grey of the River Thames. In the distant horizon curtains of rain dissolved into a colourless haze. I would have found it terrifying. I am a land lubber. I hate the sea. If I were on that deck, my hands would be gripping the rail for dear life. I may share my grandfather's hands, but there is much of him that is different from me. Edward was a young man seeking adventure; he had his new pose, and a new image of himself. He was setting off into a new future, to a place that I know very well.

It's my last night in London. I'm going for a walk. I have no idea which way is north, south, west or east. There are no stars, only cloud, but even if there were, I could not read them. They are not my stars. I find myself at the Chelsea Bridge over the river Thames. I have no idea where I am, but it seems strangely familiar. That feeling overcomes me again. It is like when you first wake up and see things with great clarity. My footsteps have walked in my grandfather's footsteps and created a sense of connection, but also a sense of his loss.

London isn't my city, but it was my grandfather's. He was born into death just as he was eventually exiled by it. I don't think that he would have seen himself this way. I don't think he was a man particularly given to thoughts of death. As the dead closed in around him he looked away from them, and forward to his imagined new life. But if Nangala is right, then the dead are a busy lot, and they will take the time out to watch a young relative slipping and falling towards his imagined future. They may even be watching another relative, years later, tripping over the threads of his distant past.

In the distance the stacks of the Chelsea Wharf blow smoke out into the low hung clouds, almost as if they are marking the sky. I am out in the world, and I begin to notice small things: women pushing prams, old women walking their dogs, fishermen tying off their boats. I turn to go back towards Brompton Road, and my soft shadow, born of this softer, northern sun, follows me along the heavy paved streets, reminding me of grandfather walking these very same streets. As I walk back to where I am staying I pass a stand with newspapers from around the world. I buy a copy of the *The Times* and, I have to admit, I feel a little less out of place than when I first arrived.

II

BORDERLANDS

captive souls

St Stephen's Day, 26 December 1906. Gypsy from Argyle Station, along with her brother Toby, was given a new name. The baptism was a ritual of renewal as well as destruction. Their older names and skin names were replaced with English names and they were forbidden to ever use their language again.

Their new names were sanctified in the name of the Father, the Son and the Holy Spirit. In the name of the Father, the inmates of the Mission walked across baked clay in crocodile lines over the dried creek bed and up past the more substantial Swan Boys Orphanage where the white boys lived. In the name of the Son, the children took their place in the Church of St Mary, built in the shape of a cross and surrounded by gravestones and even more crosses. Inside the darkened church the filtered sunlight streamed through stained-glass windows illuminating depictions of biblical stories and projecting a 'pious light' onto the gathered parishioners. In the name of the Holy Spirit, my grandmother walked with her brother towards the marble font at the head of the cross-shaped church. A hand was cupped. Water was poured. The sign of the cross was made. Gypsy was renamed Jessie Argyle. Her brother was renamed Thomas Bropho.

She had been held at the Swan Native and Half-caste Mission in Middle Swan for almost six months. Her mother would have been fresh in her memory. The country that she was taken to must have been as strange to her as if she had been taken to some other land across the sea. I don't know why they called her Jessie. The Aborigines Department that had effected her removal left her with the church authorities to mould and shape. Before long she would come to know this place as her new home. It would be her home until she was old enough to be sent out to work as a servant to white people.

The Swan Native and Half-caste Mission had been operating in the village of Middle Swan for at least seventeen years when my grandmother and her brother arrived. On the morning the SS *Bullarra* docked at Fremantle, the children were met at the wharf by the missionary Miss Jenny, who ran the Mission along with her sister, Effie Mackintosh.

Perhaps given a coat or something warmer to wear, the children were taken by steam train on the long journey to Midland Junction. I can't imagine what they made of the train, of its steam, its size and its thunderous noise.

Built on a pastured ridge, in cleared bushland, the Swan Mission grounds sloped gently towards Jane Brook, which swelled with paperbarks and reeds. Beyond the brook, hidden by the paperbarks and accessible by a muddy track, were the much more substantial buildings of the Swan Boys Orphanage and St Mary's Swan Parish Church. Although possibly the first establishment at the site, the Swan Native and Half-caste Mission would always be the poorer of the two institutions, hanging on at the fringes and beyond view.

It was winter in the south when my grandmother arrived, and she and her brother were placed in the dormitory with thirty or so other children. Being infants they were able to stay together for a time. It was Mission policy that when boys reached the age of seven they were transferred to the nearby Swan Boys Orphanage with the white boys. The girls remained at the Swan Mission House.

The children at the Swan Native and Half-caste Mission had come from all areas of the state, and their removal to the Mission coincided to some extent with the colonisation of Western Australia. As the colony spread from the South-West through the Midlands to the Gascoyne, out to the Goldfields and eventually into the Kimberley, the names of children being removed from these areas reflected this expansion. Children were renamed Cue, Gascoyne, Linden, Argyle and Menzies. The names were registered at the Mission in parallel with the growth of towns and stations of the same names as white settlement spread and more children were scooped up by the police. With the rapid expansion in the north, from 1905 onwards the population of Swan Mission was increasingly made up of Nor'wester children like my grandmother.

Children who were removed from their families learned to form special bonds with other Mission children, bonds that were to last a lifetime for my own grandmother. Separated from family, country and homeland culture, the children of Swan Mission survived by adapting as best they could. But that isn't to say they lost all sense of an Aboriginal framework of belief, respect and belonging.

Where you came from and who your people were became especially important to children taken thousands of miles from their homelands and people. In your own country, rules of belonging were clearly defined and understood. With the disruption to this constancy the children held all the more defiantly to their sense of country. Skin defined you within your own culture, and as the missionaries worked to wipe any sense of skin from the children's minds it became even more important to know where you were from and who else was from your region.

Out of the pain of removal, Mission children learned to claim as extended family people from country in the same general direction as theirs. Skin was replaced by a sense of your country, and those from similar country became your countrymen. In broader terms the children divided themselves into Nor'westers and Sou'westers. It was a system the missionaries tried to replace with a sense of belonging in the church, but while some children no doubt acquired a sense of the God of the Christian church, they were also aware of other spiritual and cultural belonging linking back to their homelands.

Nor'westers were kids from Carnarvon and further points north, including those from the Goldfields to the north-east. Sou'westers were mostly Noongar kids from the south-west who had been removed from their specific homelands but still remained within Noongar country.

My grandmother was taken from the new world order of the guddia in the East Kimberley to the new order of the missionaries in the south. Children from different Aboriginal countries were forced together under a singular fixed ideal of a Mission education that was supposed to equip them for a world of servitude and piety. They were influenced by their home cultures, by other people's home cultures, by the church, by their removal and by the situation they found themselves trapped within.

The Mission was supposed to be their new family, their new homeland, their new culture. It was supposed to be a place of Christian teaching and obedience. It was this, but with the addition of the children's own different senses of belonging, the culture of the Mission became far more complex, dynamic, and even contradictory than the missionaries were able to realise. The children might have prayed to Jesus daily, but at night they feared spirits that dwelled in the fertile Noongar country outside the dormitory windows.

Swan Mission received subsidies from the state government on a par with other white institutions of the time, marking it out as unusual compared with the New Norcia Mission to the north, which received far less for the children in its charge. Nevertheless, the children still had to contribute to the working life of the Mission to make it a going concern. When Thomas Bropho turned seven, he and my grandmother were separated. He was sent across to the Swan Boys Orphanage to sleep and to receive schooling, but would return after his three hours at school to help with the chores around the Mission. The same went for Jessie and the girls who lived their entire day at the Mission House. The younger girls had to learn to sew, cook and serve dinner and, as they became older, to care for the younger children. They had to tend the orchard, milk the cows, feed the stock, collect the eggs, and generally help run the place.

After a long day's work the children were locked into the main dormitory. Single beds stretched in rows down either side of the long red-brick building that cut west from the main Mission House where the missionaries slept, meals were prepared and lessons were carried out. It was a place of planned repetition designed to breed well-mannered, hard-working, obedient children who would take their place — and that was never expected to be too high a place — in white society. They did learn, but not beyond what they had to know to be good workers. They ate well when the Mission was doing well, and sang for their supper, literally, to raise funds to keep themselves afloat. The place was small enough not to be overwhelming, but large enough for the children to separate into groups of Nor'westers and Sou'westers.

It was the kind of place that was greatly affected by the staff who ran it, and for some of my grandmother's years there, there were some staff members who were particularly good. Sadly though, for some of those years there were staff members who were particularly bad.

We're heading through to red earth country. As you leave the city of Perth the sky, which to most city dwellers seems endless, opens out beyond belief. Heading north on the Great Northern Highway, Noongar country gives way around the town of Geraldton into Yamatji country. Heading up to Geraldton the country rolls out gently between small, mostly dry, river valleys. The road follows these valleys for the most part, occasionally rising onto winding ridge roads until it opens out wide into vast plain country. The trees that mark the road of the Wheatbelt plains are a testament to the power of the westerly winds from the coast that have forced them to bow at right angles to the north-east. As you move out of Geraldton the sky unfurls itself even further than you can imagine, and the earth transforms from soft red clay to iridescent red sand plain country. This is the beginning of Yamatji country and the beginning of the country that my Uncle Gordon worked as a stockman, the Shark Bay area, when he was a young man just out from the Swan Mission.

It's the kind of country where you pass other cars only rarely and you can roll your arms on the wheel, lean forward and sense the vastness enveloping you.

My Uncle Gordon loved this place. It wasn't his country, but as a child growing up I always believed that it was by the way that he spoke of it. When he retired he boarded with our next-door neighbour in the city in order to be near our family, but he always seemed like a man who was made for bigger spaces than that house, our street and the city allowed. Uncle Gordon was a giant of a man, with hands like leather that made my mother's chipped blue tea cups look like thimbles. He walked slowly but comfortably defiant, as if he was used to walking long distances without having to turn a corner, break for a street, or watch for minor nuisances such as cars. He let the world rush around him and walked as though he was still out in red earth country, the country that had remade him into a solid stockman with a dry sense of humour. If there is any country that he's returned to since he passed away it's this country.

I've come to Carnarvon to see Uncle Gordon's brother Bob. Turning into the driveway of Bob's timber and fibro home, I'm surprised by the spitting image of Uncle Gordon sitting in the open window of the kitchen. Seeing Bob like that at the window transports me back to when I am nine or ten years old. I am sitting in the dirt of our driveway, in one of the grooves in the grey sand that was an excuse for a driveway, of the red-brick state housing house that I was reared in. It is barely dawn, but my feet are covered in black dust and I am digging, digging, something I was always in trouble for doing, as the magpies chortle and the crows in the tuart trees drone. I look up and am startled breathless by the sight of my Uncle Gordon Dorey staring down at me from six foot five. A huge bear of a man, he is silently laughing, almost crying with laughter because he has done it again. He has snuck up on me real good, and I can just hear the sound of my own breath filling my lungs involuntarily. 'Shit,' I say, and he stops and looks reproachful, shaking his giant finger and tsk-tsk-tsks me as he sneaks through the gap in the picket fence, slips onto our back verandah and through to our kitchen for his morning pot of tea with my mother.

Bob is sitting at his kitchen table; he's a big man like Uncle Gordon and he wears the same trademark white singlet that Uncle Gordon always wore. After we've become acquainted and caught up about family, he is mulling over the questions I have shouted to him. Bob is going deaf. A cool breeze lifts off the bay, filtering into the heat of the kitchen. His grandchildren are playing outside the window, cheekily jumping up to see what all the shouting is about. He is trying to answer my questions about the Mission, but his mind turns first to his own stories, to how he ended up at Swan Mission.

There were three Dorey brothers: Fred, Gordon and Bob. They were living at Esperance with their mother, Dora, in their camp. Their father, Richard, worked clearing land and carting wood around Esperance to feed his family, and was often away on trips out along the railway line for days at a time. Then Mrs Dorey fell ill while her husband was away working on the railway and he returned to find she had passed away. The authorities were already involved. Official enquiries were made, telegrams were signalled and police reports ordered; the outcome was that in 1911 Richard Dorey boarded a steamer from Esperance to Albany with his three small boys to place them, paid for by his own wages, in the Swan Mission.

Over the years their father continued to pay for the boys' maintenance at the Swan Mission. He was operating under the impression that the Mission was a kind of school. There were no other schools they could have attended, being black, and having visited the Mission and met with the Matron, their father had every reason to think he had done the best he could by his sons. My grandmother was an older girl by then, and she cared for the three Dorey boys when they first arrived; when younger children came in, it was expected that the older girls would take responsibility for them. At first, being so young, the Dorey brothers slept in the girls' dormitory in the Aboriginal part of the Mission.

The boys hadn't been at Swan Mission long when letters from their father arrived carrying the money he scraped together from working at Southern Hills Station, Norseman and Esperance. A couple of months later Richard Dorey received a reply from the Mission. It made its way from the hands of one officer to another until they found him working alone out in that dry, hard country. The telegram advised him that Fred, his oldest boy, had died of meningitis. Bob thinks it was around this time that his father disappeared and they never heard of him again.

Bob is looking out at the bay remembering his father: 'I had some photos of him. He stood about six foot. I think he must have just gone rabbit trapping around South Australia and then that was that.'

Bob moves away from this memory and into others that crowd around him. He can see the font and the piano in the church and remembers the calling of his name, Robert, as the water pours down upon his head. I imagine he can feel the well-worn and mended denim against his skin, and the taut wire fence as he escapes from the dormitory and sneaks down to the vineyard to pinch grapes from Houghton Wines to have a feed. The orchardist has heard them and is out in his tin lizzie searching for them. They are running through the fence, away from the headlights framing the orchardist's legs as he searches under the vines for them. Back to the dormitory. My grandmother is helping them back in through the window and shooshing them as they laugh at the grape stains running down the front of their nightshirts.

He remembers the things that a small boy remembers. There was too much church. He remembers gramophone record nights, and fist fights to see who would win, just for the fun of it. His brother Gordon stands up for him, already a giant; his fists, tight and boulder-like, rule the playground.

The best times though were when the children headed down to the river. 'We used to go down the brook and used to catch these little trouts we used to call 'em. We used to get a dozen or more and cook 'em in the fire. They had an old chook farm there and we used to steal these eggs, bury the eggs in the coarse sand of the brook, light a fire on top and cook them that way—beautiful.'

Then the memories fade and get caught on the wire like the clothes that he would have to wash out before breakfast, before the Superintendent cottoned on to the tricks they had pulled stealing grapes from the vineyard the evening before.

Uncle Bob says he hasn't thought much about the Mission, or Jessie Argyle, in a long, long time. He takes time to try and remember more about those days. When he does remember, the clarity seems to surprise him. He can picture my grandmother fighting like a boy with Lily Clatworthy, another girl from the Mission. It's no holds barred and she kicks up the dust behind her, eyes steady, mind on the job. She is good with her fists and she doesn't let the blows through. She keeps one eye out for any sign of the matron; if she sees her coming, she will be the first to disappear.

Bob remembers it is suppertime and all the children are standing in the dining room with their heads bowed, and Jessie is standing at the head of the table, beside the new matron, ready to sing grace. She has an impressive singing voice, low and deep like a baritone. In the school choir she sings the low notes and her brother, Tommy Bropho, sings the high. These contrasting images of my grandmother — of determined fighter and angelic singer, don't surprise me. She was becoming an 'old girl' at the Mission.

Bob belongs to that older generation of men who worked hard all their lives and never expected to do anything else. They have a way of seeing the world that is based on respect for other people. They may not agree with everything you say, might even feel sometimes that my generation has had it far too easy, but they give you the chance to have your say, and are pleased that at least some of us want to hear about their lives, to really understand what it was like within their living memory.

Seeing Bob reach over for a photograph of Uncle Gordon that I've brought with me, I can see my Uncle Gordon in his white singlet reaching for the copper jar to get the money to send me down the shops to buy his brown sugar. His leathery hands are dropping coins into mine as he laughs, recalling the words, 'brown sugar'. For all I know he could be thinking about Nellie Lyndon who he almost married, but the joke is lost on a child. Instead, Uncle Gordon tells me that as a young man he worked as a stockman. Alone in the bush that surrounded the station, he'd lie flat and perfectly calm, waiting for the ants. When the ants begin to crawl all over his arms and his legs, he doesn't move. He barely breathed as he allowed them to crawl all over his face and chest, he just lay there and they didn't even bite him. One day, he said, he would tell me the secret, how to lie still, because he knew that I couldn't—that I had to run rather than walk—and that I would run all the way to the shop and back to hear the secret. But he would just say, 'Later on, later on,' and hide his copper jar and get dressed, then come over to our house before catching the bus into town.

It strikes me now that one of the worst things about getting old must be the loss of people to talk to. I mean people who lived through the same experiences as you so you don't have to spell everything out. My visit with Bob has tired him out. He might look like he could pick up the back of a small truck without effort, but he's well into his eighties, and this country, where he's worked his life through and which will see him out, has also worn him down.

We agree to keep in touch. As kids follow the wagon down the street, in my rear-view mirror I see Bob's hands waving from the window. Reawakening other people's past is a tricky business. Sometimes they've just put these things aside as they got on with life. Sometimes they've closed doors on them.

Swan Mission, 1911. When my grandmother first entered the Mission, the Mackintosh sisters who ran it were considered to be women dedicated to their work. The children were comfortable with them and referred to them as Miss Jenny and Miss Effie. They were both old women then, and after they retired to the hills in 1907 they still received visits from children who had been at the Mission. From 1908 to 1910 the day-to-day running of the Mission was entrusted to a Reverend F.J. Price and his sister, Lucy Price. Reverend Burton, high up in the Anglican Church and responsible for the Swan Boys Orphanage, took on the overall responsibility of the Mission when the Mackintosh sisters retired, and a Mrs Sweetapple was appointed as a teaching assistant. The Mission had grown over the years and by 1910 was running ten acres of land to help support itself. The buildings were often in bad condition and in need of repair.

In 1910 the Colonial Secretary requested the removal of 'half-caste' boys from the white Swan Boys Orphanage, and Thomas and other older boys, who had been sent to the orphanage since 1907, were returned to the Mission House. They were to sleep in a different dormitory attached to the main building.

The Prices took a photograph of Thomas Bropho and Mary Magnet when they took over the management of the Mission in 1908. Thomas and Mary are sitting on some dead tree trunks by the banks of the Swan River. They're dressed in their best Sunday church clothes looking out into the distance and Mary is holding someone's wristwatch. The clock face is huge in her tiny hands. The thinned-out bush surrounding the river frames them against the southern winter sky. The caption on the back of the photo reads, 'It is quite a triumph to get pictures of them, they are so wild and shy. Tommy and Mary are full-blooded aborigines … they are very funny and naughty, but so affectionate.'

The Dorey boys entered the Mission in 1911, not long after it had been rocked by twelve months of scandal, beatings, escapes and falling living standards. In June 1910 the Prices had been replaced by a Mr and Mrs Coulston, who took over as superintendent and matron of the Home. A woman named Miss Ott took over as teaching assistant from Mrs Sweetapple. From that point, the number of children trying to escape from the Mission increased dramatically. Previously, escapes had occurred from time to time, but under the new matron and superintendent, they escalated rapidly and Swan Mission soon became the focus of public scrutiny.

A Noongar boy escaped in 1910 and made it to a camp where relatives took him in until he was found and brought back to the Mission, whereupon Mr Coulston reported that the boy had 'Learnt a salutary lesson.' In 1911 three girls escaped from the Mission and managed to make it all the way to the town of Gingin, almost a hundred kilometres north, before they too were brought back and punished.

The *Sunday Times* ran an article in May 1911 with the headline, 'Swan Native Mission Management by Muscle'. The article described how the Swan Native and Half-caste Mission was

> … situated only a hundred yards from the orphanage, but it has by
> no means so pretentious an appearance. It is a rambling collection of
> ramshackle buildings no doubt considered quite good enough for
> the juvenile blacks and half-castes.

It went on to detail the corporal punishment of inmates by the Reverend Burton and, in particular, how he had hit young Albert Corunna with 'a heavy bang to the side of the head.' Albert had been taken away from his country in the Pilbara in December 1906, and was baptised on that same St Stephen's Day as my grandmother and Thomas Bropho. Albert Corunna later escaped and never returned.

Reverend Burton was soon replaced by the Reverend J.W. Armstrong as the overall manager of the Mission and the Swan Boys Orphanage. Fortunately for the children, the Coulstons also were not to last long. In the year they spent at the Mission they were the cause of numerous escapes, and had meted out harsh punishments.

The Mackintosh sisters stepped in briefly as emergency caretakers until a replacement couple could be found to manage the Mission. In July 1911 Mr and Mrs Jones were appointed as superintendent and matron. They were to be in charge of the Mission for the remainder of my grandmother's time at Swan, and beyond to the Mission's eventual closure in 1920. Following the period of great turmoil, the church set about changing the Mission's poor image, and in James and Letitia Jones they seem to have found the complete opposite to the Coulstons.

The Jones appear to have been hard-working, dedicated, God-fearing people who were prepared to take on the hard work of running the Mission for low pay. James Jones was originally from Wiltshire in England and had set out from his home county as a young lad intent on seeing the world. He'd worked all over Western Australia and in various jobs in Queensland. Letitia Jones was a trained nurse with a kind face in photographs, and a relaxed manner of engaging with the camera. They'd met when James Jones came rolling through Albany working for her father in the timber industry, and married soon after. They already had two small daughters by the time they began working at Swan Mission.

Changes were immediate. Soon after the arrival of the Joneses the authorities set up a fund to replace the old dormitory, which was in bad repair. The children started going on excursions to the river, to the city and into Midland Junction. Bob Dorey remembered the Joneses as decent people who made sure there was plenty to eat, but who also made sure you did plenty of work and went to plenty of church too. 'We used to get all our clothes sewn up, never used to wear raggedy clothes, they had machines and all.' Like my own grandmother, he remembers old Mr Jones' deep singing voice and how he loved to train them in the choir, and his thick bushy eyebrows and handlebar moustache.

The children soon became attuned to the regular rhythms of a Mission life of work and prayer, and within a short time of James and Letitia Jones' arrival, escapes decreased. In that period the new girls' dormitory was also completed. Photographs were taken of the sturdy new walls lined with iron cots down either side of the corridor of highly polished jarrah floorboards. It looks like a hospital ward. Kapok pillows sit on crisp cotton bedspreads with neat tassels that the girls would have sewn and embroidered themselves, and you can just make out the high and wide, heavily barred windows separating the neatly hung pictures of Christ.

The Joneses allowed the children to head bush on Sunday afternoons to hunt, cook food in hot ashes and scout the country. The inmates loved this chance to get out into the bush. It seems to have been some kind of recognition by Mr Jones of the children's culture, and they appreciated it. Beyond Mr Jones' desire that the children really understand the Bible, and that they really embrace Christ; beyond the repetitious rhythms imposed by these desires, the children were also operating from their own rhythms—watching for *jennuks* (bad spirits), and checking out each new inmate to see where they belonged; to see if they were from their home country.

Of the many people who managed the Swan Mission, Mr and Mrs Jones were the only ones that my grandmother remembered fondly. Among the people I have spoken to from the Mission and the stories that have been passed down, the Joneses were remembered for being solid, fair-minded people. My mother tells a story of when she once met them, years after they had left Swan Mission, on a visit with my grandmother. The Joneses had a small farm in the Perth hills and my grandmother was given a tour of the orchard and enthusiastically invited to sample fruit from every tree. She wasn't allowed to leave until she did.

I decide to try and track the Jones family down. I know that it isn't possible for either Mr or Mrs Jones to still be alive, but I am curious about what happened to them. Registrar-Generals' records in the archives lead me to death dates. Obituaries in the newspaper lead me to the married names of their children. The Joneses' deaths, their children's marriages and their addresses begin to link up as a paper trail, and I begin building my own files on the people who entered my grandmother's life. Shipping records and biographical indexes take me back in their story to when their ancestors arrived here, to the journey that would bring the young Mrs Letitia Jones, and the not-so-young Mr Jones, to the Swan Mission to answer their Christian 'calling'.

Tracing them back, I want to go forward and track them across electoral rolls and through telephone books. A good thirty calls later, some distant family are revealed. This branch of the family has photographs of the Mission and they give me the contact details for a woman whose name I recognise. She was the youngest daughter of the Joneses, who the children in the Mission referred to as 'Baby Jones'.

In a well-tended suburb of the city, widowed, and not exactly sure of what I want of her, was the woman I will call by the name my grandmother used, Baby Jones. Baby Jones is eighty-six and she looks well for her age. The child of missionary parents, she grew up in the Swan Mission separated by a brick wall from the girls' dormitory where my grandmother and thirty or so other young children slept. She has agreed to give me her time and to tell as much as she can about the Mission. She agrees for me to use a tape-recorder so I won't forget the details of what she has to say.

Baby Jones' story is carefully filtered by her fear for her parents' reputation. She is guarded because there is much talk in the newspapers of the Stolen Generations. She doesn't like that term. She doesn't think it represents the real situation as she sees it. As we talk I realise there is a bigger stake here. Baby Jones became a missionary herself and worked in other countries, and I believe is worried that all that she has worked for is under threat. In some ways, it is. It is the fate of all of our histories to be scrutinised by later generations. But as she becomes more relaxed and realises that I am not here to attack her, that I am genuinely interested in her history, she shows great pleasure in remembering the many Aboriginal children of Swan Mission who she claimed as her friends.

She remembers back to the time when her limbs were wiry and supple and she ran without fear of anyone or anything, where the world of childhood seemed as natural as breathing. As a child she had shared the same air, played in the same orchard, hauled up gilgies from the same creek, and looked for love from the same woman as the Mission children had. Washing with the Mission children, eating with the Mission children and being punished with the Mission children is how she describes her upbringing. They were friends of her own age and she remembers them with a great sense of affection.

'Oh dear,' Baby Jones says, as she looks at the photographs of the children that I have brought with me. 'That's Tommy Bropho, my coachman.' Each morning Thomas had taken her in the sulky, over the river, beyond the brickworks and the grounds of the Orphanage, to the state school where the white children received their education. Each morning, barefooted, but without a stitch out of place in his heavily mended clothes, Tommy took the young Baby Jones to a place where he was not allowed to go. If she is aware of the obvious difference between her privileges and Tommy's situation, she does not mention them.

Baby Jones is peering at the images as if they will somehow begin to move. But the images don't move easily for her. It is a long time back that I am asking her to remember. The names have a bit of difficulty coming to her, even if she recognises their faces. 'Ah, this is Bob Dorey, he was my little friend.'

Baby Jones remembers her adventures with Bob Dorey. She remembers how the Mission creek would flood in wintertime, right up to the horse's chest as they tried to cross the river, and how they'd hunt for gilgies every weekend. Out of school, and after chores, they were free to roam the grounds, dig for roots and bake fish in ashes on the river bank. She remembers 'Ception (Conception) and Chattra Benjamin milking the cows, filling the pails for the day. Queenie Magnet is watering the vegetables. Thomas Bropho is gearing up the horse and buggy and the Parfitt girls are getting sulky, 'jumping the traces'. They'll be brought back into line by her mother, Mrs Jones, she says with a knowing smile.

After a slow start the memories come flooding in. Dion Dirk is checking the chicken coop for any eggs to feed the little children and Mrs Jones is keeping an extra special eye out for little Mary in case she fits again, due to her epilepsy. When she tells me this it jogs my own memory of a story my grandmother told about Mary fitting in the dormitory, and how the older girls learned to look after her so she did not swallow her tongue.

Baby Jones remembers learning to milk the cows and polish the floors, which were always kept so shiny you could see your face in them. She can see her father, an older man, who had travelled the world from the age of nineteen. His bout of malaria, which nearly killed him, turned his hair white for the rest of his life. And she can remember my grandmother, Jessie. 'I can remember her quite well. When you said her name, yes, Jessie Argyle, I could make a mental picture of her. I can see her quite plainly, what she looked like. She used to have long hair, fair skinned she was, and very sturdy.'

She sees them sitting outside on a summer's night. The Mission children are all gathered in the evening dusk. Mr Jones plays his gramophone, seated in his wooden chair in front of the children who are sitting barefoot on the grass in neat rows. The strains of the 'William Tell

Overture', the 'Huntsman's Chorus' and the 'Ride of the Valkyries' waft out over the orchard and settle in the paperbarks that strangle the creek.

Baby Jones says she loved her time at the Mission. It gave her some of the happiest memories of her life. She believes there was really no difference between her upbringing and that of the Aboriginal inmates. She says she ate the same food, cleaned as they did, played as they did and attended church as they did. To her it is a story of racial harmony and equality.

Baby Jones does not seem to realise that she was not one of them. Simply by having her parents, she was not one of them. She got to keep the name her parents had given her and live the choices in life they would make for her. When she turned sixteen she would not be sent out as a domestic servant.

Baby Jones is surprised to hear that Uncle Bob Dorey is alive, and a little defensive as she asks, 'And what was his story?' A moment of relief sweeps over her face as I tell her he remembered her parents fondly, but not the people before them. Uncle Bob had remembered Baby Jones with affection too.

But Uncle Bob has his own memories. They are of a different place, though it is locked within those same grounds and occupies the same space. For him, the Mission is viewed from a perspective which could never really be called home. It is a place out-of-country. This is not to say that Baby Jones' version of her life at Swan Mission is invalid.

In tripping over the threads of the past you have to respect the experiences of witnesses; you cannot confuse one telling of a story as the only telling. In the battleground of the Mission where hearts and minds, cultures and races were up for grabs, stories of friendship are always welcome. But they aren't the only narratives that affected these children's lives, and to ignore the story of servitude that was set out for them is to ignore too big a part of the picture.

The children were trained to serve God and Jesus, to serve the white people who had taken them from their homelands and replaced skin, country and family with the wafer-thin pages of the Bible. Their lives revolved around lessons, work, survival, and the slow movement towards their exodus into a world that they had only made small excursions into since leaving their home countries. Mr Jones schooled them in the books of Revelations, Mark, Job and all the others that go to make up the story of the one, singular, omnipresent God.

Swan Mission, 1915. My grandmother was sleeping at the end of the dormitory hall. It was nearly her time to leave the Mission. The hanging pictures of Jesus looked less directly upon her, replaced by the eyes of Mrs Jones when she peered through the observation window that was just above my grandmother's sleeping head. Baby Jones was sleeping on the other side of that same wall in her mother's room.

It was a hot airless night and you could smell a rainstorm coming. You can feel the intensity of a summer storm as it sucks the life out of the air, draws your blood close to your skin and you can't help but hear your heart beating. As the heat builds to a soupy pitch it inhabits every pore of your skin.

It was a long, late summer when the storms began to roam up and down the coast, building slowly and dreadfully. They would cross into a river valley, stream east from the Indian Ocean and crash themselves into the hills that surrounded the city before blowing themselves out. This storm was different though. It came straight from the north. It travelled overland from the north-west, strangely picking up strength as it headed south towards the city. In the dormitory the children tried to sleep as torrential rain drummed upon the tin roof and then subsided. The storm, it seemed, had passed. But instead of a cool change it brought a dense humid atmosphere and the sky suddenly became alight with globular lightning.

Through the barred windows the children could see these strange small balls of light floating against the shifting shape of the hills, sending down beams of lightning like searchlights; searching, striking, igniting. Trees in the distance burst into flame as the wind began to pick up again. This time it became louder and stronger until the sounds of thunder could not be heard over the howling wind.

Outside, even the largest trees of the orchard began to lift into the night. Silhouetted against the milky night sky they floated off as sheets of rain started to fall and the building began to sway and lift. Mr Jones had tried to reach the girls' dormitory but was stopped by the sheer suction of the storm. Unable to open the door he made for the window above my grandmother's bed just as the entire building collapsed.

Mr Jones and the boys worked quickly by the light of hurricane lamps as the storm continued, their bare hands pulling at the rubble, guided by the sounds of the children crying. My grandmother lay crushed, pinned to her bed by the other girls, who were trying to jump from her bed through the matron's window. As the building swayed they leapt for the window, where Mrs Jones pulled them through to the safety of the main building. My grandmother was trapped and gasping for breath as she watched bum after bum fly over her head.

In the first light of the morning the flattened mess of the dormitory was all that was left. Girls wandered in a daze while Mr Jones and the boys worked in lines to remove the bricks one by one. The orchard had disappeared, the trees flattened. The river had begun to swell from the torrential rain, but the air was still, and the sun, just peeking over the hills to the east, was piercing.

My grandmother came upon Mary Benjamin who was sitting holding up her hands and flicking the fingernails from her crushed fingers. A pile of rubble buried the bed of a young girl named Elsie. By pure chance the barred box window frame above her had come down first and shielded her from the falling debris. It had saved her life but broken her legs and ribs. My grandmother came upon Dion Dirk, who grabbed her and tried to head her off from going towards the verandah. He couldn't speak, being deaf and mute, so he motioned with his hands in a chopping motion — head, stomach, legs. Molly, one of the younger girls, was dead. When the building collapsed she was cut in three.

Molly's coffin was carried across the brook to a service at the cross-shaped church, and then consigned to an unmarked grave.

Decades later Swanleigh, the school that now occupies the site of the Mission, listed all their names on a sheet of brass on stone, at last marking the fact that somewhere in that small courtyard cemetery lie forty-four child graves of those that did not survive the Mission.

This was the first of the blows that would signal the slow end of the Mission from 1915. The second blow came in the form of a government man, who would make himself real in their lives soon enough. The 'Chief Protector' would no longer exist in the form of an imaginary God, but in a man who set himself as the earthly judge and controller of Aboriginal lives. My grandmother's last years at the Mission were spent in preparation for her leaving. The records of her exact leaving of the place that shaped her from a child to a woman have been destroyed after being damaged by water, which regularly inundated the area. Of the records that remained, her age fluctuates wildly across the pages.

The dormitory was rebuilt. Instructions in Bible study no doubt continued. My grandmother moved into the final stages of preparation for the 'new world' that she had been removed from her 'old world' to serve. At sixteen years of age women were no longer subsidised by the Aborigines Department. From the age of sixteen to seventeen women were prepared for service by working at the Mission. In their seventeenth year, they were sent out into a network of Anglican Church connections to white families considered suitable by the Mission.

It was some time in 1919, piecing together the fragments of records, that she left the Mission grounds for the family that had been chosen for her. She had been taken from the northern Ord River valley to the southern Swan Valley, and was about to make another journey into the Blackwood valley of the then deep south of Western Australia. She was being sent out into a world where it was believed, literally, that 'God made the white man, God made the black man, and the Devil made the half-caste.'

reinvention

The *Orontes* Ocean Liner dwarfed the Fremantle docks, snared and tied into place on 25 February 1909. Edward Smith, 'Ted' to his shipboard pals, was a new chum looking out over the tiny port town from the deck of his home of the last three weeks. As the ship wound its way south they had passed through the Suez Canal, down the coast of Africa, through the seas of the Middle East, across the humidity of the equator, and into the dry heat of the south-west of Western Australia. Edward's immediate future upon landing had been organised ahead. He had anticipated his arrival, I am certain, with a great sense of urgency. Jack Bayly, a schoolmate from Emanuel School had made the journey out with him. Together they stepped into the frame of the colony on the edge of Australia. They had travelled all the way from Wandsworth together, and though each went their separate ways in search of work, being old friends from London they were never far apart in their first years in the colony.

Within hours of setting foot on dry land at Fremantle Edward was working. He hadn't even the time to cast a look at the city of Perth a few miles to the east. He was off the boat and into a car, a seventeen-year-old baby-faced white boy driving wildly out into the Wheatbelt. This would have been exactly what he had come for, to get out into the Australian bush and taste something he had only ever read about, only ever seen in pictures or in drawings in his school atlas. Never mind it was in the middle of a February heatwave, he wanted to be away from the death and cold of London, and Western Australia was nowhere like London. At least, it was nowhere like London at first glance.

Had he taken a short time to look, even just a day's breather to see the city of Perth of 1909, he might have been struck by how much it resembled his old borough of Wandsworth. He would have seen a city being developed with new Edwardian buildings, that offered roughly the same shops and the same produce as London. Around him people in the streets would look greatly like him, and it was English they were speaking even if it had a peculiar twang. He had travelled half the world around to a little Wandsworth-by-the-sea; a cleaner, warmer and essentially younger Wandsworth. A Wandsworth that looked as if it had been cut with giant scissors out of a London grid map. There were arcades and tea-houses, theatres and newspapers, and similar buggies, charabancs and cabs.

This new Wandsworth was also being electrified in the form of crucifix poles dotted with nails and crisscrossed by wires sweeping electromagnetic energy across the heart of the city, along its busy corridors and into the newly established offices and shops. But, of course, this was not what he had travelled all this way for, and so he had brushed the city aside and headed towards the interior of his dreams.

Edward had been employed to check up on some properties on behalf of a squatter on holiday in London, someone he'd met through a friend, and to report on the state of business. Within days he found himself burning off bush in Three Springs, two hundred miles to the north of Perth, counting sheep in Bunbury a hundred miles to the south, laying fence lines in the Newcastle district fifty miles to the east, and taking work clearing land at the 300 Mile North Camp, three hundred miles to the north-east of the city. If Perth was little Wandsworth, he wanted nothing of the city, or of the towns and churches.

In one of his first diary entries he took a roughly sharpened pencil and wrote himself a list: 'Wallabies, Kangaroos, Parrots, Snakes, Lizards, Ants.' Then he drew a sharp line through it and wrote again. 'Chicken, Guinea fowl, turkeys, pigs, cows and bulls, sheep and horses.' Joseph Banks he was not, but he was awake to the differences he saw around him in the landscape. In those first months he drove a borrowed T-model Ford from the south-west to the mid-west, from Bunbury to Mingenew, from Midland to the 300 Mile North Camp, from the sale yards at Subiaco to the wharves of Fremantle. He turned eighteen years of age out on the road somewhere in the north-east, halfway to the 300 Mile North Camp, and after another week's work, headed south again to check on other properties. He lived like this, fuelled it seems by the brilliant light and the warmer sun, and the distance of his family, until the winter set in and the work began to slow down. Then finally, after the outdoor work had dried up, and within a few months of his arrival, he found himself drawn back into city life again.

In Perth, Edward stopped. He paused. He took time to look around and, it seems, this time he liked what he saw. That he felt he had made the right leap, the right choice, and that for the first time in a long time, life looked pretty good. After all that hard work in the bush, respite in an inverted patch of home was probably quite welcome. Edward picked up work here and there, driving trucks in the city and in Fremantle. His friend Jack Bayly was living in the city too. Jack was staying at the Royal Hotel, and Edward, needing to stay somewhere, moved there as well. When he got bored with the Royal he moved to the Orient; when he got bored with that, he moved to the Prince of Wales. He developed a pattern of living most people would envy. After a few days work of solid driving or loading, he would take a few days off. He would go fishing on the Swan River in the middle of a working week. He took boat rides with Jack Bayly on a Tuesday, and walked the streets in the evenings, claiming favourite spots for himself. Possibly he saw in the brashness of a young colonial city, a place ripe for a young man ready to embark on a little reinvention. I think this was one of the happiest times of his young life.

London wasn't the only place where an opportunity could present itself to a young man in tight pants and a snug jacket. There was something kind of roguish, maybe even reckless, in the way he could work at manual labour, pop off to the theatre, indulge in a little fishing, and still look to his future prospects with expectations of a fine time. In a place like Perth he could work driving a truck, fencing sheep in the hinterland, loading stores at Fremantle, and still live in the middle of the city. He could look to the east from the window of his hotel balcony and see virgin bushland burning in the distance, a constant reminder of all that land, more than any young English lad could imagine, that appeared to be just out there, waiting. Opportunity, it seemed, for a hard-working young white boy, floated on the breeze with the smell of eucalyptus and the acrid-sweet ash dust wafting in from the distant fires beyond the hills.

Edward Smith could have applied for the public service, a life of slow advancement, of climbing the public service ladder, of setting his chin to the daily grind. He was a trained clerk and young men from the mother

97

country had little trouble finding good positions. Instead, he chose a more flexible life, the chance of free time and good prospects.

Enjoying their leisure time he and Bayly caught a few shows at the local theatres, and by the time the winter rains had properly set in they had picked up casual stagehand work. Edward began shifting his digs around town again, moving from theatre to theatre, from lighting to props manager, from trapdoor operator to ticket assistant, from set builder to operating the limelight for the new program of silent flicks. At the Royal Theatre they worked on 'My Partner Jack' and 'Maggie Moore Struck Oil'. Their theatre contacts in London were helping them make headway in the colony, and a friend of Gertie Gitana's contacted Edward for work on the production of 'Sailor Jack'. Edward's diary contained notes on stage directions and cues for when he was to fire the pistol sound, when to make the train whistle and when to raise the curtain for the Third Act.

Eddie and Jack were two young lads about town. They even had their own business cards made up, 'Smith and Bayly, Theatricals'. Before long Edward landed a job working at the local vaudeville theatre in Guildford, a hamlet of houses and shops east of the city on the upper Swan River. The theatre wasn't much more than a large tin shed with a stage, but nevertheless it was a theatre, and for a young lad whose main experience had been repertory at school, it would have been good work. When that fell through Edward moved back to the city, operating the limelight on a 'Jack and Jill Panto' for the leading J.C. Williamson Company. In between nights working at the theatre he drove carts and loaded stores for transport from Cannington on the outskirts of Perth to the city.

The theatre. The country. The fresh clean river. Getting his hands roughed up on good, hard honest work. Fishing on workdays with this new city as a backdrop. Catching all the latest shows from the loft of the lighting rig or from the pit of the props department. Living the bachelor life. The warmth of a close sun. The so-called working man's paradise. It was all so alluring and while it might have had a physical resemblance to Wandsworth, it was so unlike the life he'd left only months before.

Back then my grandfather still carried his prayer book with its private note written to himself. On the inside cover he had transcribed the ten commandments to the 'Clues to Success': 'Honesty, Industry, Temperance, Civility, Punctuality, Economy, Perseverance, Courtesy, Observance and Attentiveness.' He still believed in all these traits. He still believed his future would be lit by a dry, clear blue sky and the sharp unforgiving light.

All he had to do was wait until he was twenty-one years old and his long-awaited fortune, his grandfather's inheritance, would arrive. Then he would begin. Then he would start to build. He would take his plans out beyond the smoking hills that rimmed the city and start making real headway in his life. He was so young. 'Honesty' he would retain. 'Industry' it seems never left him. 'Temperance' would be a constant companion, only ducking out once or twice in his entire life. 'Civility' was ground into his soul. 'Punctuality' was worn into him from years of routine and regiment at the Emanuel Boys School. 'Courtesy' was something he was not short of. 'Observance' and 'Attentiveness' would be sadly lacking, in regard to his own wellbeing at least. 'Perseverance' would be sorely tested. 'Economy' would be his downfall.

By the end of that year he had worked on productions from 'Farewell Spy' and 'The Belle of New York' to 'The Term of His Natural Life'. He had no immediate plans for anything, no pull towards home and no plans to change what he was doing for the time being. To have made definite plans before his inheritance arrived would have gone against the spirit of adventure and youth. For Edward the colony seemed to be booming, its prosperity boundless. He was waiting, marking time most enjoyably. He might have thought of himself as fitting into the surroundings of Western Australia, but in many ways he was still a Londoner at heart. His address book was filled entirely with London addresses. He kept slightly irritated notes about the lateness of the English mail off the boats, and about the papers that arrived well after the latest gossip from London had already circulated through the colony.

Edward settled more permanently into a room at Smith's Chambers, a lodging house in Barrack Street. He began to discard his over-planned wardrobe and began to fill his trunk with new objects and new images. The light cleared out the musty dank from the oak planks of his trunk, now covered liberally in thick brown boot polish. This new light required a turn on the dial of his camera away from the open lens appropriate to the softer light of London. He was toughening himself as his skin was toughening in the heat and light. The aperture was tightened, squinting the landscape clear against the light, seeing in upside down negative for miles and at a lightning speed. If only he had taken the same care and looked a little more sharply at the path he was treading for himself. But I can say that with the benefit of hindsight; I can see the wrong moves ahead.

Edward could have left Australia at any time, but he had become fond of the city of Perth and of the hills, beyond which, he believed, lay his fortune. He had only been in the colony a year and a half in 1910, and he had tried out all types of work. The winters were more like an English summer, and in a photograph taken in his nineteenth year he was dressed somewhat lightly for such a cold, cloud-filled day. He was proud of himself. I can tell by the way he stood. He is turning from boy to man, from new chum to worker. His callused hands are a trophy of his honest industrious endeavours, the more appropriate suit, the looser fitting pants, the high ankle leather boots, are much more geared to his new life.

The cobblestones of London were replaced by the dirt, mud and gravel of Western Australia. The brick walls of London were replaced by jarrah pickets and chicken wire. The wrought-iron gates of Westminster were replaced by loose-hinged pickets opening onto front yards of bungalows with all-round verandahs. His skin was tanned. It was leathery from so much outdoor work. He looked out from under his narrow-brimmed city hat, a confident young man able to turn his hand to most things with success. But there are some positions that are not worth trying out, that are not suited to a man with a family history of illness and early death.

When Edward began work in the Infectious Diseases ward as an orderly it perhaps started out as just another one of his jobs to keep him afloat and fill in time until his inheritance arrived. The diphtheria outbreak of 1910 was severe. The epidemic took a heavy toll and with the increasing influx of migrants from all over the world, many new arrivals were succumbing to the deadly virus. Within weeks of beginning this work, he fell ill himself.

There were no antibiotics to ward off infection. His family's susceptibility to illness made him an easy target and he was in bed for weeks hovering between unconsciousness and violent pain. He could barely eat. Breathing became difficult. The iodine drops and acid that were the standard treatment did little to remove the membrane that was growing surely and steadily across his windpipe. The feather treatment—plunging a feather into the throat of diphtheria patients to break the membrane on a regular basis so that they could breathe—was found to be aiding the regrowth of the infection. Finally, when it looked as though Edward might be heading for the morgue, it was decided to operate, to try to cut the membrane and infection out of his throat. It was a new procedure in the colony.

The operation saved his life. When he came to, he must have sensed the tear in his throat, felt the thick plug of blood that had to be swallowed regularly, and the burning of infection that was common in these early operations. He was bedridden. I imagine he listened carefully to the reports that were made on his condition. The rhythmic sound of his own swallowing would have been as natural as the sound of his breathing, heavy and slow. One of the nurses caring for him decided to contact his family in England on his behalf. A response came quickly from his sister Blanche. Perhaps the seriousness of his condition was not properly communicated, because it was a strangely chipper letter that arrived across his hospital bed. It told of an intended holiday to Colchester, and that she had expected to have heard from him sooner, congratulating her on the birth of her first child, Jack. Blanche told him that she had once had diphtheria, when he was away at school. She said she hoped by the time her letter reached him he was better, and that the illness 'only reminds you of a very bad dream.' She thought it very kind of the nurse to write her of his condition, and 'good' of the hospital authorities to keep his job open for him while he was ill, 'that shows that you give satisfaction.'

What Blanche was not told, and perhaps Edward did not even know himself at the time, was that he would never be the same again. His vocal cords had been severed. At first he could say almost nothing and he would have feared he was a mute. Eventually he would be able to manage a whisper, but that is all he would ever be able to speak. Blanche had ended her letter with hopes that he would soon return from his adventures, and that he would be able, perhaps with luck, to make it back home in time for Christmas. Home. How could he ever return home? He had left so self-assuredly. He had tossed his coins, landed a double-header, and laughed in London's face. Now, he could only manage a strange gargling noise at best.

By the time his inheritance money finally did arrive, the day he turned twenty-one, he had lost a great deal of his shine, of his desire for a wide open future, of his youthful dreams of adventure in the outback. Instead, the timing of the inheritance found him back working the limelight in darkened theatres, working the props and the curtains where you did not need to speak. In a colony filled with young boy-men, where manliness was a necessity of colonial survival, a whispering, squeaking voice was not an asset. It would have proved harder to gain work, to talk your way into new situations, to be seen as capable and not 'handicapped'. Night work in the theatres made it possible for him to live quietly while he adjusted to the new limits on his life.

He still looked out beyond the hills, but gone, it seems, was the boy who thought nothing of driving three hundred miles into the bush to burn off some land, or to manage stock, or to organise a team. Instead, he looked a little closer to the city, just far enough to be away from the crowds, but not so far that he would not be able to fall back on old habits if the venture didn't work. He appears not to have realised that in a colony like this one, you don't need a voice if you have money—it will do your talking for you. He was about to learn something of this as he passed through the doors that money could open, into the businesses in which he would be welcome, and in the form of the nice people who would help him spend his nice big pile of cash, perhaps a little too eagerly.

It had been a great muddle from the start. When Edward's grandfather died he had set up a trust for his three grandchildren. The proceeds from the sale of a couple of houses in London, the disposal of stocks and shares and the sale of personal items, were to be evenly distributed when the youngest, Edward, turned twenty-one. Edward's grandmother, who outlived her husband, had not been happy with the arrangement. She had never wanted either Blanche or Edward to receive any of the inheritance. If she had had her way the entire amount would have gone to the eldest, Lily, with whom Grandmother Graham had a close relationship. Lily, it seems from the correspondence written by Blanche, would have been happy to receive it, but Kate had ensured the money would be equally divided three ways in her will.

In the weeks leading up to Edward's twenty-first birthday, letters began arriving from London, and letters were in turn sent to London from Perth. Uncle Alfred Graham had been placed in charge of the disbursement of the estate, and was handling it badly. Blanche wrote of her problems with the family, but asked him not to tell Uncle Alfred she was in communication with him. Uncle Alfred wrote giving Edward advice contrary to what Blanche had said, and in favour of Lily. Edward sent back letters, as both had requested, and appears to have kept his mouth shut. It was a very tense experience of hinted allegiances and frayed relations. He not only kept his mouth shut about the correspondence, but also about the loss of his voice.

When all was not said but most was done the final figure that lay waiting for Edward in the Western Australia Bank was more than four hundred pounds. His weekly wage at the time was somewhere just over a pound; he had come into the equivalent of eight years' wages. The baton was being handed to him a little too late perhaps, but nevertheless handed and received. Just as they had finished executing his grandfather's estate, Grandmother Graham passed away, leaving everything she had to Lily. The lines had been well and truly drawn in his family.

Blanche was hoping that Edward would return for the funeral. But instead he sent his condolences, and hid behind the thousands of miles between them and his lost voice. She wrote him loving letters hoping to kindle enough interest that he would return to see his nephew, Jack, who was too young to talk, but who, Blanche was sure, would recognise his expatriate uncle through the many photographs that she kept of Edward about the house. The letters continued. They spelled everything out in large longhand as if they were speaking across distant telephone lines. Eventually they would have to face the fact that Edward did not want to return, and with the knowledge of that their letters became more strained, more distant, and were exchanged less often.

Finalising the accounts, Edward's Uncle Alfred provided a final balance sheet for the total sum of four hundred and thirty-eight pounds, taking the opportunity to offer his nephew words of advice: 'This is a very nice sum and should be of lasting benefit to you if as you say in one of your letters you know the value of money and are anxious to pull-up and make headway—now is your opportunity.' He advised Edward, probably quite wisely, to leave the bulk in the bank and draw out only what he needed. Uncle Alfred also forwarded Edward his father's watch and chain, with seal and key attached, that had been handed to Alfred by Blanche when their mother, Kate, died. Alfred hoped that Edward would be able to tell them some good news of his plans when he next wrote.

A final letter of family advice arrived from his aunt, Lily Smith, his father's sister. Lily, matriarch of the Smith side of the family, had waited patiently until the heightened emotions of the negotiations were over to offer her words of advice. She was not interested in actualities, or the plans Edward was making, but more concerned with his need to keep a calm head. Aunt Lily warned Edward of 'how easily money could slip through one's fingers, if one will let it.' She hoped, most especially of all, that he would treasure his father's watch and chain as she could remember the day the watch was presented to him at Westminster Hall. She recalled 'how he looked so splendid in his uniform,' and how they had all been so proud of him.

The watch and chain was no ordinary gift. The old-fashioned seal was centuries old. It was Edward's father's grandfather's: Thomas Smith's seal. Thomas Smith was born in 1700, and Aunt Lily reminded Edward of his duty as the last Smith heir to hold true to his mother's love. 'How little your dear mother dreamed where her boy would be when they reached his hands.' Then she warned him, less for the thought of the money than for the young man, the only son of her favourite brother and sister-in-law, who was perilously far away, 'Eddie, my boy, I trust for her sake you will do your best and keep to a good path through your life. Please don't yield to any sudden temptations that the possessing of a large sum of money may bring.' Aunt Lily was a canny old girl and probably knew full well, even as the ink was drying on her letter, that she was probably wasting her breath.

Of all the investments that were available to Edward, of all the directions that his inheritance could have taken him, it found him pursuing the dream of owning a farm. Nineteen twelve was not a good year to be thinking about farming. A cashed-up Edward decided to go into business with Jack Bayly. Within days of receiving his money Edward purchased the lease on a farm property near Keysbrook, south-west of the city on the base of the rocky slopes of the Darling escarpment. It seems in this early stage of his new venture, as he set about planning how to spend his inheritance, that he was mindful of his uncle's advice, keeping most of the funds in the bank and using only what he needed to get things up and running. This farm was to be the big beginning, the first dipping of his toe in the bright future he had always imagined.

In reality however, he had not leased a farm, but an almighty hole. This large hole was to be the focus of their youthful attentions as Edward and Bayly set about filling it with a large portion of Edward's inheritance, christening the farm with the auspicious sounding name, Walgin, a Noongar word meaning rainbow. The nearest railway siding, Balgobin, on the Perth to Bunbury line, was no more than an hour's train ride from the city. I don't know if he sighted this property before he leased it, but I don't believe it was a con. I suspect it could have been a viable prospect if you understood more about the fundamental properties of the soil. With a rural crisis just around the corner, probably nothing could have saved it from going bad.

Edward might not have looked it over before he purchased it, but he and Bayly certainly searched over every inch of territory once they had finally settled in. Edward set about photographing his newly purchased future, capturing himself standing in a farmer-like pose with his new pitchfork; Bayly and he lounging in front of the old shack that passed for a house on their brand new deckchairs; Edward looking out over the waterfall in colonial pose, hand to eyebrow, shadowing the light, gazing into a virgin landscape fed by the stream at his feet. Edward may have sought a life away from the city, away from the realities of the loss of his voice, but he was not camera-shy. If the loss of his voice left a gaping hole in his life, there were other ways to fill it, and a large sum of money could form a nice wall of comfort from the outside world.

While Edward and Bayly may have been playing with the fun of becoming the young lords of Walgin, Balgobin, they were not completely amiss in their ideas of farming. They made careful plans, measuring paddocks, deciding which trees would have to be pulled, where the vegetables would be dug, where the chicken coops would be built, how much livestock they would run, whether they needed a horse and cart and what tools they would need to buy. Such decisions were to be expected. A farm, a commercial concern such as theirs, would warrant such consideration. But there were other considerations, other, let's say, peripheral concerns, that it seems were impatiently taking shape in their minds. They began wisely, browsing the aisles of Bairds department store for practical tools. They bought all the necessary items: a level, a hacksaw, a file, a large blade, some brushes, a hatchet, some brackets and bolts, and an all-important hurricane lamp. The next day they continued with their commonsense approach. They went back to Bairds and bought locks, bits, a clothesline, grease and a soldering iron. They walked across Barrack Street to Walton Jones the draper and bought a looking glass, two mugs, plates and a wash up—all respectable objects for their venture. But within a short space of time they began to wander along different aisles.

On the Monday they bought two brand new suits from 'Patten The Clothier' and followed up with a year's subscription to the *Sunday Times* to be delivered, by rail, to the siding of Balgobin. On the Tuesday they bought a spring cart and hired a pony, and then proceeded over the next week to fill the cart with little extravagances. Firstly, they ordered customised stationery, not just pads and pens, but special seals, stamps and notepaper embossed with their names and the name of their farm. Armed with their special seals and official papers they began the business of issuing instructions, notes of orders to purchase, notes of issue by rail, notes of intentions to lease. They were now 'Messrs Smith and Bayly, Walgin, Balgobin, Western Australia, the World, a Planet, in Space'.

In case they might wish to come into the city from time to time, they paid up the rent on their boarding rooms in Wellington Street, handing over seventeen weeks rent in advance to old Mrs Efford, the landlady. They bought two of everything. Two beds, two cots, two tables, two chairs, two chests of drawers, two pairs of gumboots. They bought enough food to last a month; bacon, cheese, cordial, sardines, salmon, flour, butter, coffee, apples, oranges, syrup, mustard, onions, curry powder, rice, worcestershire sauce, more salt, more sugar, kero, saucepans, billy cans, cutlery, tablecloths, a baking dish, bread tin, teapot, jugs, brooms, flyswats, lamps, washboards, and tubs. Edward was again busy with his lists.

When they were finally ready they moved out to the farm for good, well, so they told themselves. The first few months of that season were spent industriously enough toiling on the land, laying down seed, fencing off their livestock and clearing the bush. At Balgobin siding they posed with a giant load of firewood they had cleared and loaded onto their new spring cart for transport to the city. Edward stood astride a forest of cut timbers piled three men high, almost as high as a steam engine, his arms cut and bruised, his face beaming. In Serpentine, they became friendly with the Middletons who ran the local store and had a property at Keysbrook called Hillside, where they now swapped their vegies and eggs for seed, milk and bacon. It was the life, or so it seemed, until the heat set in, and the work became, perhaps, a little slow and repetitive, and then the little trips began.

At first they conducted their pleasure trips to the city alternately, Edward staying behind to look after the farm while Bayly went into town for necessary supplies. When cooking on the open fire was no longer practicable, a Metters stove was purchased and transported on the train. Having a kitchen necessitated a homely atmosphere, and so lino and a large dining room rug were purchased. A little colour was found lacking. Perhaps to give a certain sense of home pride, flower seeds were purchased for a garden, and wallpaper, and new pillows, and pump sprays for insects, and wash tubs, and …

Within two months Bayly's short trips to the city had extended from one night to four. Perhaps it was due to lack of water, or perhaps pests or disease damaged their vegetable patch, but soon they stopped eating from their own produce, and their food began arriving, as if by magic, by mail.

They ate well for men just starting out on the land. Instead of the odd sheep's head, they ate steak. Instead of tinned, salted corned beef, they ate bacon fresh off the bone. Now when Bayly made his extended trips to the city, Edward joined him. Not surprisingly the farm began to deteriorate, so they did what any young empire builders would do, they employed a local casual worker to care for the property while they were away. A realisation must have occurred to them. Why waste time tilling the land when you could employ others to toil for you? It was time to enter the world of property management and capital, of partnership and enterprise. It was time to be men of business. Before this change of plan they had not done too badly by their labour. That summer they sent a good harvest of peas to market, but the proceeds were nowhere near enough to sustain the costs of the farm. The idea of working a farm may have seemed grounded in raw honest fundamentals, but it would never be a fast track to a fortune. In the city, walking the streets in their new suits, patronising the theatres and the backstages where they had recently worked, it appears they were missing the comforts and excitement more than they cared to admit.

With Walgin holding on by a thin thread, Edward branched out on his next business venture. It might have been advertised in the *West Australian*, along with the numerous adverts for mediums, palm readers, phrenologists and export quotas. But Edward came upon 'Rockdale' through one of those 'rock solid' friend-of-a-friend deals that just couldn't go wrong. Rockdale was an egg farm on the outskirts of the city. A friend from the theatre had arranged the deal and brokered the handover. There was money to be had in eggs.

Edward set to work on another list. Traipsing around the Rockdale Egg Farm in Belmont he was noting the sheds, the fowls, the tools, the house, the curtains, the fences, and even the number of bolts and nuts. The farm at Balgobin was losing money at great speed, but he persevered. Bayly stayed on at Walgin, part time, and Edward spent his time between the two farms, doubling his enterprise, shuttling between the city and the hills. It would be just like when he had first arrived and roamed the country looking after his employer's interests. Voice or not, he would make the headway that he had promised his uncle he would. All it would take was hard work, and he was not afraid of that.

With the chook farm Edward had forked over most of what was left of his inheritance. He had enterprising ideas: to be a partner in a large poultry farm close to the city, to split his energies between the two farms, to double his profits so to speak, to spread his assets. He threw himself enthusiastically into repairing the sheds at Belmont, selling his eggs at market each day of the week, then heading out to Walgin on the weekend to take over from Bayly.

His silent partner in the scheme was a Mr Rockliffe who, on putting up a third of the costs, was to receive fifty percent of the profits. For Edward's role as farmer and partner, and for the sum of one hundred pounds, he was to receive a wage of three pounds per week from the venture, and fifty percent of the profits also. They bought the farm from a Mrs Robbins who, Edward had been assured, owned the property outright and was keen to sell to the two gentlemen for the agreed sum. Meanwhile, the partnership with Bayly was one based upon the future earning of Walgin, where Bayly had signed and delivered, as his part of the bargain, a large paper containing the letters 'IOU' followed by a considerable sum.

In the ensuing months, taking him from late 1913 to midway through 1914, Edward did indeed work solidly and, to all outside appearances, profitably in his ventures. By this time he was not only a partner of Walgin at Balgobin, and of Rockdale at Belmont, but he appears to have branched out into an extraordinary business adventure, promoting a comedy vaudeville act, William Lennard and George Dumville from London, in some kind of deal with William Anderson's Companies.

I don't know how he kept up the pace he set himself. He was putting in time on the land, catching trains about the patchwork of networks that serviced the city and the South-West, and doing the odd stint of promoting, in addition to working the occasional night operating the limelight or the props pit for some extra cash. When he wasn't working he was entertaining friends in his rooms at Smith's Chambers, and even managing to catch one or two of the cutting-edge science lectures hosted by the Museum.

The pain, the suffering, the lost time of months in hospital, and the shocking blow of the loss of his voice were ameliorated by keeping himself busy, and by the comfort of his inheritance. He was beginning to feel like his old self and had written home to Uncle Alfred, to Aunt Lily, and to Blanche about the great success of his new path. He sent them photographs of his farm at Balgobin and some pictures he'd taken when he and Bayly made a day trip to the Serpentine Falls in a borrowed T-model Ford. He was proud of his achievements, and I am glad, after all that he'd been through in his young life, that he got to experience such a moment of satisfaction.

I don't know if there was a first blow. It seems more like there were many blows that rained down on him like a hailstorm. It seems as if the slide from prosperity was more like a flood, starting gently with the swelling of a creek and ending terribly, sweeping away everything familiar. I do know that as 1914 came to a close and as Europe began to erupt in ties and binds of allegiances and fears, Edward's own world was about to collapse. Blow one: the letter from the solicitor is probably where and when it began. Rockdale may well have been owned on paper by Mrs Robbins who had sold the farm to Edward and Rockliffe, but the original owner, Mrs Cook, had yet to receive payment for it. Mrs Robbins, it seems, was nowhere to be found. Blow two: the farm at Balgobin failed, just at the time when the rural market was beginning to dive and properties were harder to sell. Blow three: the invoices for all those nice things that had been purchased to outfit his ventures, for the steaks that arrived by train, the wallpaper that gentrified the dilapidated cottage, the tools that helped them clear the underdeveloped land, and the cart that was used to transport all these things, began to roll in. Blow four: the deal with William Anderson's appears to have fallen through.

He had stretched himself too thinly. His plans were not bad plans, just badly executed ones, on top of which he had been caught up in wider economic problems beyond his control. After all had been sold off, after he collected the debts of friends who had borrowed from him and all the farm creditors had been paid, he was back where he started when he first set foot in the colony, only now he was voiceless, and there was no prospect of an inheritance arriving as a lifeline. Edward walked away from the dream of his own farm forever. He remained good friends with Jack Bayly, but he never went near the theatre industry again. As he moved back to the city, letters from his family congratulating him on his great successes washed back from the shores of England. He must have hit the lowest point of his life.

Balgobin no longer exists. The siding where Edward and Bayly had stood so proudly on top of their huge haul of jarrah and wandoo has long gone. It didn't last longer than the few years they were there trying to farm Walgin. The sign was probably just painted over and used somewhere else, wherever they were opening up another timber siding, where the railway lines were cutting deeper into Noongar forests. There is a giant camphor laurel standing at the turn-off from the South Western Highway to one of the last remaining rail lines, less than half a mile west, that still passes through this area, heading on into the South-West. This tree was only a sapling then, planted in the schoolyard that sprang up for the children of a small community that only thrived for a short period of time. The school, and the families, soon shifted further towards the more prosperous Serpentine district where the plains were more fertile.

As I drive up to where Walgin had been, the roads dive off in all directions in new subdivisions of land that have been marked out in the hills. It is gravel strewn, rocky country. Today people move out there seeking a quieter lifestyle. They have horses, but they don't appear to entertain thoughts of making the land work for them. Looking at the soil it is obvious to me that it would not produce. The myth of Empire had been so strong in both Edward and Bayly that they appear to have projected all their faith and will onto the land, expecting it would sit up and obey.

Where Edward and Bayly had removed the taller jarrah trees, smaller ones have taken hold and reclaimed the hills, along with a thick growth of banksia and low scrub. It seems they left no tangible mark. There are no sheds or fences or remnant outlines of vegetable plots. Any foundations have been eaten out by termites.

By 1915 Edward had gone, Balgobin was probably gone, and the Great War was well under way. Like thousands of others, Edward waited in line at one of the recruitment centres, keen to enlist and fight as a 'son of the Empire'. But he was rejected, found unsuitable for military service on account of his 'defective voice'. His fingerprints were taken and stamped on a Medical Certificate of Unfitness. An exemption badge was soon issued. By this time he had had enough of making big plans for his future, of seeking his fortune, and of any notions of headway. He did not respond to his family's letters of congratulations about his venture into farming. Eventually he did what most young white men without plans, or ties, or prospects have done in Western Australia since colonisation; he packed his trunk and headed north.

In 1921 Edward was working on the wharves at the port town of Derby. For two years he had been chief engineer of water, which sounded a lot better than it was. He once drew a sketch of his workroom and lodgings. I imagine it was a long hot day in the tropics. I can see him sitting on the low hill just behind the pumping station, perhaps pausing to take a drink from his water bottle, or maybe to watch another group of Aboriginal prisoners, chained at the neck, making their way through the town under police escort. Welcome to Derby. Edward took out his charcoal pencil and sketched the latest port stop in his life. A small wooden shed tacked onto the pumping station, a windmill sticking at odd angles, some vegies in a rough vegetable patch and, in the distance, the wharves leading out to the ocean with the wooden poles standing high above the mudflats.

When he first arrived in Derby he began working immediately, saving his money, adding up the long columns of numbers each week, eagerly watching as his bank balance began to grow again and replace something of the money he had lost. Eight years' worth of salary had slipped through his fingers. It was going to be difficult to ever make that up.

His work involved pumping water on board state steamships making their way up and down the coast. He worked six days a week and in his spare time he helped to load wool, lumped bags of coal, and helped moor ships at high tide, holding them fast before the massive thirty-foot tide disappeared, leaving the hulls stranded against the pylons. He made notes about what he borrowed from friends and what he returned. He made small cryptic entries in the margins of his Engineer's Diary, and little drawings of seascapes, of a woman with a parasol that looked like Daisy Bates, the well-known amateur anthropologist and journalist, of unusual pump engines and chemical equations. He made another list of his possessions. It was a very short list. He took a few shots with his camera, but either ran out of glass-plate negatives or simply didn't want to document where he was.

Of the images that he did record in Derby, the ones that survived, they were not all that optimistic. His collection of photographs of the town included blurred men on the steps of the hotel, himself working on a windmill and tall sloping ships against the wharves. There were also images of Aboriginal prisoners standing silhouetted against the sun, West Kimberley men awaiting their own fate locked in a spider web of heavy steel chains shining through the heated lens of the camera. Derby, generally speaking, was the sort of place to eat into the will, just as the heat and humidity ate into the thin layer of silver halide spread on a glass negative. It was only a matter of time before it began to eat into Edward.

For most of the time that he worked at the wharf his boss was a man named Jack Campbell. Major Jack Campbell was a decorated returned officer, and he looked every bit the old boy's old boy. He was the sort of man you expected to see in a colonial backwater like Derby. He was wide around the girth, a solid pigeon-breasted, stout-looking man who was fond of a wide-brimmed canvas hat. He was a military man in the way he stood, in the way his eyes held the camera and the way that he carefully shaped his broad moustache.

Edward became friends with Jack Campbell and his wife and their little son, Bertie. In Derby there was not a lot of single men's entertainment, and it was a welcome break to be invited to their home for the occasional family meal. However, Major Campbell and his family soon left Derby for a position closer to Perth. He had been appointed superintendent of a relatively new government-run settlement for Aboriginal people. It was considered his military experience would be an asset. He had been appointed to the Moore River Native Settlement near the Wheatbelt town of Mogumber.

Not long after Campbell left Derby he wrote Edward a letter offering him the prospect of work. It seemed Campbell did not like the farm assistant at the Settlement, and he was engineering to replace him with someone he trusted. The offer went like this: 'Dear Smithy. Just a line. I think I can procure a permanent job for you at this Settlement, the job is assistant to me and Mrs C, if you would care to take it on.' The sell went like this: 'You get your house, servant, wood, light, the house is a small cottage, two rooms, verandah, kitchen and store room which you could make very comfortable for yourself.' The nod went like this: 'Keep this to yourself, don't let anybody know, because the department is supposed to advertise the job.' The wink went like this: 'I told the Secretary that I had a man if I could get hold of you.' The warm handshake: 'Mrs Campbell and myself would be glad to have you. Kind regards from us all and love from Bertie, Chin-Chin.'

Edward must have regarded the letter with some caution because he took some time in answering. He had made compulsive decisions before and had paid for them. He had, at least by the middle of 1921, learned to take a breath before leaping at another fork in his lifeline again. Edward took the time to weigh up his circumstances. It was time for another list:

2 shirts, 2 singlets, 1 fashion shirt, 4 pairs socks, 12 blanket slips, 4 collars, 2 white pants, 2 white coats, 1 khaki coat, 1 pr boots, boot brush and chamois, 1 looking glass, 1 soap, 1 razor, 1 plate, 1 soup plate, 1 cup, 1 knife, 1 tea spoon, 1 cup and saucer.

His list confirmed what he already knew; that he was a man of very meagre means. He had managed to save just over eighty pounds since 1909. It was not an untidy sum, but it had taken him almost a decade to accumulate.

I can imagine him alone in his two-windowed cottage, perhaps late in the evening, sitting at some small square wooden table that may have doubled as a workbench, with maybe only one single chair, holding his bankbook under the dim light of a hurricane lamp and wincing. It would most likely be too warm to sleep no matter how hard he had worked that day on the wharves. It may well have been one of those exhausting lucid moments when the heat of the night matches the heat of your own blood and you can just hear it, pumping constantly inside your ears, thickly rushing through your arteries towards the place where thoughts of the past rush in and out like the tide beneath the wharves.

As I look at my grandfather's trunk now I remember the sense of it as it lay buried beneath piles of newspapers or Emu Export empties on the back verandah of our house. In a way my childish imagining was true—he *was* buried in the trunk. But there are no dry bones waiting for me as I open the lid. Instead, there is the haul of a lifetime of hoarding. Old envelopes labelled with past addresses and dated postage stamps are filled with receipts, old letters, small notes and lists. The more official documents signposting his life are tied in string and bound in large acidic paper bags. Old porcelain water pipes and dry wooden ones still smell of deeply seeped fine rub tobacco. Capstan and Log Cabin tins are filled to the brim with the trinkets of travel. Small glass spearheads from Derby, Aboriginal message sticks and a beautifully carved boomerang that was made in Noongar country.

There are small pockets of space where he has tacked on an extra secret drawer, or glued solid a crack that began to form in the oak as it acclimatised to the Western Australian sun. His camera is still here, wrapped in his black photographer's cape. It is the same camera that snapped his family, his school chums and that weaker London light of Wandsworth. It has been well protected. There are a few screws missing here and there, but nothing too drastic. Its bellows fold out neatly, and still bring the city into focus. But you have to know how to work it. It's not simply a case of pointing and clicking the aperture open. As the negatives no longer exist I have to make them myself. It is a long and slow process, but it can be done. He has all the chemicals to do it still in his trunk, but they have since lost their potency. I have to apply my own techniques to make his camera work, but when it does it makes an impressive image.

His documents are buried in his trunk, hidden in the crevices that were added on here and there, or slipped within the large brown envelopes that have begun to yellow and fall apart. What is not here are the stories of the people who will help me with the leads and threads of his story, and who will guide me in putting the pieces of this earlier time in his life back together. They are like the camera that he has left behind. They come from another era, but if you take your time with them, and pay attention to the details, be patient and show the respect that is deserved, they can help to bring the past to life.

in service

Nineteen fifteen marked another important turning point in my grand-mother's life, and in the lives of all Aboriginal people in the state of Western Australia. It was the year that Mr A.O. Neville became Chief Protector of Aborigines in the Aborigines Department based in Perth. It was a government department that had received little interest from previous administrators, but Mr Neville took his role of 'guardianship' over the population of Aboriginal people in Western Australia very seriously. He was an ambitious public servant who had plans of moving up the ladder.

He was arrogant and officious, a prodigious organiser of files and documents, and a man who never appeared to question his own sense of superiority. By 1915, the 1905 Act had already brought great hardship to the Aboriginal peoples of Western Australia, but under Mr Neville the Act would enable an unprecedented level of control over all aspects of the lives of those in the state's Aboriginal communities.

Immediately upon entering office, Mr Neville began reorganising. He reorganised the previous administrator's plans for government settlements in the South-West so they would become a reality. Under Neville's guidance the Carrolup Native Settlement, two hundred and forty kilometres south-east of Perth, and the Moore River Native Settlement, one hundred and thirty kilometres north of Perth, were established in 1915 and 1918 respectively. No longer relying on missions, the Department would use these settlements for the incarceration and management of the Aboriginal community. Immediately upon their creation, Neville stopped sending Aboriginal children to places such as Swan Mission, and as each older child became an adult and went out to work, the population of the missions dwindled.

Under Neville's regime women found they could not leave their places of employment of their own choice. They could not leave for fear of arrest and imprisonment—without trial—in the new settlements that were being erected away from view in the mid-west, the south and the north. Women who were sent to bad positions with overbearing mistresses or their lecherous husbands had little or no redress. Even a good position could go sour because of a personality clash within the confines of white homes. Sometimes women would not be paid, and if they complained they were sent packing to the settlements.

Mr Neville also began to reorganise the files that were created to manage his Aboriginal charges. He sent out circulars to police enquiring about employment permits. He investigated the numbers of women in employment, and called up their bank accounts for inspection. He instigated new regulations of employment, collected a loyal team of workers around him, and began to reshape the old system of general files into a new system of 'personal' dossiers and administrative files. As each individual was brought to his attention their name was recorded, a number was assigned and paperwork began to accumulate to document their lives. But that was only the beginning. In time Mr Neville would come to use these files, not only to document, but to manage, direct and control. By 1921 he was turning his attention to my grandmother. 'File No. 1261/21—J. Argyle Personal File' was brought into being and began to grow. It linked up with previous Mission files, previous removal orders, and started Mr Neville's narrative of my grandmother's life.

When my grandmother's file first arrived it was a bit of a shock. It's one thing to find out there were administrative files kept on the community. It's another thing to realise the extent to which the Department watched and controlled members of your own family. My grandmother's file is as thick as a telephone book. It tracks her from soon after she left the Mission almost up to the end of her life. This is just her personal file. Any one personal file does not exist in isolation but links up to other Aborigines Department files, police files, Health Department files, Crown Law Department files. Together, they are the bureaucratic manifestation of the wall of silence that limits real dialogue about Aboriginal history in this country. These are not the voices of Aboriginal history, but they hold clues to our history. They are double-edged. If they did not exist, then I would not have access to this information that has helped me piece together my grandmother's story. But if they had not existed, that would have meant that the culture that created them also did not exist. This would have been far preferable. But as this culture did, and still does, exist, the files can be made useful in Aboriginal hands.

The language contained in them about our families and our communities does not reflect how we see ourselves. This is how others have seen us. While they give me some details of my grandmother's life, their reading of her tells me more about the people who constructed them than it does about her. In our own community's hands these files are used to link up with lost family and to make steps to reclaim what was taken.

My grandmother's file was one of the earliest of those files that survived to be released to Aboriginal family members. That was in the late 1980s, over twelve years ago. Since then the release of personal files has become more common, but it is a slow process. There are so many thousands of such files that the waiting list is long. They variously bear the stamps of the Aborigines Department (1905–1936), the Native Affairs Department (1936–1954) and the Native Welfare Department (1954–1972), but they all represent the same thing—the power the state vested in government departments for the control of the Aboriginal communities of Western Australia.

I have sifted through hundreds of administrative files; there are literally thousands that have survived. But there is no guarantee that a particular file will be found. Hundreds were destroyed over the years and many files that remain are microfilmed copies of originals that no longer exist. Many were incinerated in forty-four gallon drums at the back of administrative offices. Some that do survive bear self-explanatory names such as '*Removal of half-caste Children General File*' and '*Children on Nor'West Stations to be Removed*'.

To consider the voices within these files as representing the views of all whites would be wrong. They are the voices of a small team of people in the Aborigines Department connected to a wider network of police officers and protectors. But there are other voices within the files. There are letters from employers, letters from the general public and letters from our own people, often complaining about their treatment.

My grandmother, and many of the women who passed away before the release of these files, would have had no idea of the extent to which their lives were tracked, recorded and monitored. They knew they were being watched and tracked, but to actually see the volume of paper, the lines of type, and to hear the powerful voices of ignorance within them is something that has to be experienced.

For those who have accessed them the language and attitudes have not been surprising, but have been distressing nonetheless. Sometimes it is the use of such labels as *prostitute* and *harlot* that sticks in your throat. Sometimes it is the strangest things. My older sister Jess was named after my grandmother. The thing that Jess couldn't get over, as we sat around the kitchen table as a family and pored over the file when it first arrived in the mail, was the fact that my grandmother wasn't even allowed to buy her own underwear. A departmental officer was required to buy it for her because her wages, like the wages of almost all Aboriginal women, were controlled and held in trust by the Aborigines Department. Of all the things that were carried out in the name of their 'protection'—the imprisonment without warrant, the removal from country and family—the lack of control over what colour underwear my grandmother could wear seems unimportant. But Jess was right, it was so absurd as to be frightening. There is a sexual intimacy that is breached when men in suits and hats pop off with someone else's money to buy their knickers, petticoats and shimmies.

For my grandmother, Chief Protector A.O. Neville would come to represent the constant cycle of control and entrapment over her life. From 1921 he would be the main controller of her life as it was tracked across the pages of her file. He will revisit her story again and again. In retracing her journey out of the Mission, the file leads us to the family she first worked for—the Sherwood family of Bridgetown.

The road to Bridgetown traverses Noongar country. Heading south from the city of Perth, I'm passing through the coastal plain of the Swan River, ridging the escarpment that snakes its way parallel to the winding coastline, and moving inland through hill country where the land becomes nestled in folds of rock, wooded hills and lush valleys. I am passing through the lands of the Whadjug, Bindjareb, Geneang, Wardandi, and finally to the border of Bibulman country, curling into river valleys that increase in frequency as I make my way deeper into the south-west of Western Australia. As a Nor'wester I'm an outsider here. I was born in the south, but Noongars still speak for this place. It's been smoothed flat, cut into paddocks, cleared and woodchipped, but it is still Noongar country, still retains its elemental beauty. There are stories of thousands of years of connection and care, and decades of post-contact transformation and misunderstanding that are layered into the valleys of this land.

It's springtime and the light that filters through the trees is mesmerising and electric blue. I'm heading to Bridgetown. As the groves of marri and jarrah and the clearings of moodjar trees fly past me, I am moving deeper into the south of my grandmother's story. I'm moving closer to her beginnings in these southern lands of once quilted pastures, giant trees, freshwater valleys and white authority. It's a region of mixed histories, of wealthy farmers who originally took up the best lands, of poor whites who worked orchards, dairy farms and small cattle ventures, and the Group Settlement Scheme of utopian working-class experiments. Nowadays it is still mixed, with poorer families escaping the city existing in pockets of the less-developed parts, and incredibly wealthy areas of vineyards, tourist ventures and intensive agriculture. It's booming once again, as it did in the 1920s when railway lines skirted the rivers and valleys that followed the lines of Noongar Dreaming tracks and song. The roads that have replaced the rail lines are smooth, well marked and wide.

It is a good long drive that takes you south past the smaller regional towns relying on dairy, fruit and the tourist dollar, until you reach the intersection of what is the border of three Noongar countries in a deep well-wooded valley. To the west is Wardandi country, stretching all the way from the hills and valleys to the sea. To the north is Bindjareb country, extending along the coastal plain and the freshwater estuaries, rimmed by an escarpment. To the south-east is Bibulman country, curving in an arc along the coast, hugging the ranges of the inland valleys, the giant timbers and the freshwater rivers of the Blackwood. Welcome to borderland country.

As I head inland I am heading up, away from the sea, higher and higher into the hills. It doesn't feel as if you're climbing higher from the sea, even though the air becomes cooler and denser. The valleys and winding roads become deeper and the forests that remain grow taller and taller, stretching to the sky and enveloping you in a filtered leafy world of undergrowth. I feel as though I am descending. I feel like I am going back in time as I drop into the filtered light of the valleys, the rivers and the remnant forest.

I have travelled all over this country. The logging tracks and disused railway lines take you away from the four-wheel drives hauling caravans and the car loads of families heading for the resorts that have sprung up, pushing up land values and changing the landscape. The logging trucks can be heard a long way off, giving you plenty of time to get out of their way. They fly past down the rich red clay roads, carting away the stands of jarrah and karri from the heart of the forest, leaving a deceptive curtain by the roadside to hide the gutted interior.

The disused train lines are even more hidden. They are overgrown and rotted now, but they once formed the backbone of the development of the south. They cut their way along routes followed by pioneers, who traced older Noongar routes, laying down the corridors of western development over Noongar trading and migration runs. The railway sidings of small timber towns that once dotted the landscape are gone, but some of the names remain — Yornup, Wilgarup, Bibilup, Quilergup — places of camping and water gathering that became sidings, then work sites, then when the work dried up and the rail lines receded, disappeared like ghost towns. In 1919 my grandmother was sent here to work, straight from the Mission. That is why I've come back.

The Old Rectory where my grandmother worked as a servant still stands at the southern end of Bridgetown. When I arrived it was unoccupied but had recently been sold. There was talk of it being used as a Bed and Breakfast. It is a short drive from the centre of Bridgetown — or maybe a ten-minute walk — up the main drag of Hampton Street, across the bridge over the Blackwood River and then right along the Brockman Highway. It is a large house.

I am guided in my visit by a photograph that my grandmother kept from 1920. The bleached light of the silver gelatin emulsion of the photograph mimics the mists that shrouded the bungalow when I visited. Upon the distant hill that forms the northern barrier of the town, and over the bridge and surrounding hills to the south, are orchards of apples intermixed with the remnants of stands of gum trees. The rough dirt driveway to the house matches the faded texture of the corrugated iron roof of the house. Wide long verandahs open out around the shaded windows of fourteen good-sized rooms. The verandah draws the visitor to the central heavy double glass doors, swinging in towards the dark polished interior of the Old Rectory.

The house has not changed much. The large double glass doors are the same. The room that was my grandmother's is still tacked onto the front of the house. The hills in the distance are less ordered than they once were. The brook that runs by the house is just flowing, still tapping the run-off of the winter rains. There are no other houses nearby. It is in a very secluded spot. The pool that the brook will form in summer is not visible yet, but I can see where it will form by the shape of the bank. As I walk around the back of the house I can see the remnants of an old orchard. My grandmother told stories about this place, which makes it feel eerily familiar.

Bridgetown, 1920. Photographs of the town reveal a small rural community set deep within the recesses of the southern forests. It exists in these archival images resting silently within an unusually cool and misty valley along the Blackwood River. Connected to the world by a main road over a north–south bridge, it holds the assurance of a fortress. Relieved of its giant timbers, the valley slopes have been transformed into a quilted pattern of orchards, paddocks and vegetable gardens. Order has been placed upon the land by industry. Over time a good-sized town with an even better reputation has materialised.

Further back in time I want you to picture the images that have not been recorded and the history that is little talked about. The colony was moving inland from the southern coastal regions of Busselton and Augusta. Almost overnight the land had been claimed and pegged. Equally as swiftly the original Noongar people were removed, in body if not in spirit. Moving forward to 1922 we see the trains that carried out the timber and fruit produce and also carried the Noongar people of the south to the countries of strange Noongars to the east and the north, and to the government settlements that were built in these other people's lands. The Bibulman, Wardandi and Malngin were transported in overcrowded special carriages to camps and settlements built on old ceremonial grounds of the Yuat and the Mineng.

Against the ideal image of a rural idyll bathed in the light of dusk, with columns of smoke rising from the well-made chimneys of small houses neatly placed in rows leading off from the main street, cooling and settling over the town in a blanket fog between evening mist and sun-touched air, came outside reminders of violence. As the sun slipped over the lip of the valley and Bridgetown settled into a age-old cycle of quiet rural existence in 1920, some of the results of the Great War in Europe were making their way home. Perhaps some of the returned soldiers had attended the Empire

Day celebrations of 1918 when the local headmaster, Mr Roberts, had explained the red, white and blue of the flag of Empire thus:

> ... the red symbolising the blood of heroes, who had laid down their lives for their country, the white for the purity of the motives which actuated the Empire's policy, and the blue, the boundless expanse of ocean over which England had for so many centuries held undisputed sway.

As 1920 ended and the decade of the teens drew to a close, the people of Bridgetown prepared to celebrate the return of the men who had survived The Great War.

The memorials that seem old to us now were yet to be built in every town and every square of the country. As was the practice, committees were formed before the first of the men had even returned. They laid the plans for the plinths, the gardens and the parks of remembrance to be filled with lists of names of the one-third of men who had gone and would not return. Men from Aboriginal missions had also gone to war. Those who survived did not return to saved jobs and celebratory memorials. These men truly did return to the same life as before the war, a life of surveillance files and settlement camps, of forced labour and arbitrary imprisonment.

As a young woman, my grandmother would have watched from her room at the Old Rectory as the train passed and the men returned. She went on with her life, just as she had done for the past eighteen months since leaving the Mission. Her room was at the end of the front verandah, not far from the large double glass doors that opened onto the rooms that the family inhabited. It was in a good position. It received the last rays of the sun as it slipped over the valley wall on misty afternoons. It looked out onto the road and onto the tracks leading to the patchwork of southern towns that she had yet to visit. These names would become familiar to her. Like the new name given to her on arrival at the Mission, these towns often had English names imposed over other, older Noongar names. Some were renamed after Noongar sites, but sounded strange and twisted through the bad translations of a language thousands of years older than the English which tried to replace it.

In the following years my grandmother would come to know the length of the journey by train and the cost of a second-class ticket between these places. She would know the slow rattle and clank of the wheels crushing roughly laid track from newly hacked timbers of the forests that the railways cut their way into. In 1920, my grandmother was a servant to the Sherwood family of Bridgetown. That was her place in the scheme of things. This was all she had known since leaving the Mission at the age of seventeen. She had left all that she had known of her thirteen years there for a family she had never even seen, but had been trained each day of her life to serve.

The Sherwoods were well-respected members of the Bridgetown community. Having been residents in the district since 1907, they were considered almost pioneer stock in a town with such a recent white history. Arthur Hay Sherwood was the bank manager for the Western Australia Bank. Mrs Dolphin Sherwood was the daughter of the Chief Inspector of Police in Perth, two hundred miles north, and mother of a large family. Arthur and Dolphin had moved their six children—Tom, Corinth, Jack, Constance, Enid, and the baby of the family, Betty—from the cramped premises of the bank in the main street of Bridgetown to the more comfortable sprawling Old Rectory just over the river. Dolphin had lost two children at childbirth and with the birth of their youngest daughter Betty their family was complete.

Dolphin Sherwood considered the state school was a little rough, so she sent her girls to the local Catholic school for their education, despite the fact that they were Anglican. The family was not particularly religious, but Dolphin prided herself on being practical. A convent education was considered a more suitable preparation for life. They were a tight-knit family, woven into the fabric of the town and each other's lives. Far from wealthy, they were modestly well off, were well liked, and keenly linked into the town's established families: the Wheatleys, the Hestors and the Allnuts.

At nineteen my grandmother's life followed the path that the missionaries had laid out for her as a domestic servant. Little white girls called out to be dressed by her. Clothes had to be ironed, meals had to be prepared and floors had to be scrubbed. This was how she was supposed to be fulfilling her purpose as a black child 'saved' from the 'depravity of the northern camps'. That is what her personal file would have us believe. But she was doing much more than that. She had survived the removal when many children did not. She had survived the Mission when not all would.

As the last summer of the teens were coming to a close, preparations for the turn of the decade, the oncoming twenties, were well under way in

Bridgetown. The exceptionally large Royal Show of the previous month was still a major topic of discussion in the town. Newspaper editorials talked of the dark cloud of the war lifting from the world, signifying the coming decade of the 1920s as the decade of peace. The Soldier Land Settlement Scheme would take its first shaky steps into the yet-to-be-cleared lands and remnant forests of the South-West, as poor whites moved into the area to try their hand in Noongar lands. As with all turning points, even those who had no reason to hope began to. The turn of the decade was like any other transition—fleeting. There was the build-up to that moment of the passing of one year to the next. Distant sounds of people no doubt erupted at midnight as they gathered together to sing 'Auld Lang Syne', and the sounds of their lives caught on the breeze. None in the household my grandmother worked for could have guessed what lay ahead for them in that new decade.

My mother Betty is riding up front with me and my partner Lauren on the bench seat. Mum has had a few beers by the time we pick her up. She rarely drinks, and certainly not during the day, but obviously needs to calm her nerves today. She is smoking frantically, which she was also planning to give up but never has, as we turn from the city and head towards the better part of town that she hasn't visited in decades. My mother hasn't seen any members of the Sherwood family since she was a young women in the 1950s. She calls them 'the Sherwoods'. She tells me how as a child she used to go with her mother to their home in Swanbourne on New Year's Day. For years it was a ritual that my grandmother was the first visitor through their front door in Swanbourne on New Year's Day. It was considered good luck for a black person to be the first through the house. If other visitors turned up they would have to enter through the back door until my grandmother showed up. My mother laughs as she remembers, but I am not sure how to react. When she sees I am troubled she says, 'Oh they were just English. English people do things like that!'

My rusty old station wagon is a little conspicuous as it cruises slowly along Circe Circle, one of the more eloquently named and expensive streets of the suburb, past Hollywood-like 1930s bungalows with well-tended gardens and neat lawns stretching all the way out to the road. If we don't find the house soon I know someone is going to call 'Crime Stoppers'.

When we finally arrive my mother becomes more animated as we head up the driveway to knock on the door. I have brought a tape-recorder, some cake and the Aborigines Department personal file that was kept on my grandmother.

In a spacious back room of her home, Betty Sherwood, now Mrs Davies, and my mother get into the serious business of collapsing the long years of the past. The tape does not work properly. The cake that we brought along was a little unnecessary. Mrs Davies has baked. The tea tray and pot are already prepared, and my nervous hands seem huge trying to hold delicate china cups. But the stories are flying around the room pleasantly as my mother and Mrs Davies jog each other's memories and add bits that the other had forgotten. Mrs Davies makes sure that we're all topped up with tea and cake. It is a nice visit. Many of the stories that I'd heard as a child are retold and repolished, and I am interested in the bits Mrs Davies can add.

Everyone is on their best behaviour. Lauren is an old hand at afternoon teas, but I must admit I am feeling a little restless. I want to get to the meat of the stories about my grandmother. Learn anything they may know about her that goes beyond how she played practical jokes with them as children. Perhaps my impatience is just youth. My mother is happy to let the afternoon, and the stories, roll on. But there is another guest at the table, one that I would like to be heard. I have put my grandmother's personal file near the teapot, and no one has asked me what it is. It contains letters from old Mrs Sherwood to the department about my grandmother. It's sitting there and it seems everyone is aware of it, as if it might stand up and start speaking out of turn at any moment and break the gentle flow of the stories that everyone is enjoying telling, and that I am listening to and taping, feeling a little like a spy.

Mrs Davies passes around the tray of cakes, commenting that she is baking for my mother the way my grandmother had baked for them. It is a surreal statement that cuts across time and speaks volumes in what it implies. My grandmother was her family's 'servant' and I am ambivalent about how I feel about that. This word that unites our two families, that is the reason we are here today, is never actually spoken, at least not by either my mother or Mrs Davies.

I want to know what it was like in Bridgetown in the 1920s and have my list of questions ready to go when Mrs Davies sends one my way. She asks if I have seen the Rectory in Bridgetown, and politely offers me more cake. I have seen the place where my grandmother worked for her family. It is too big for any one family, surely, but it had once been her family home.

'Yes,' I say. I tell her how I walked around it and peered into it. How I imagined my grandmother there, polishing the boards, peeling potatoes, mopping floors, washing the children's clothes.

'Oh, yes,' she agrees, but Mrs Davies is disappointed. She believes that I haven't seen anything at all that was important. She asks me if I can also see Jessie playing cards with the family in the lounge room, or singing songs to the children as they walk along the brook. She tells me that when she was only little she'd sing out to her in the mornings, 'Jessie Jessie, come dress me,' and my grandmother would go and help her with her clothes. She would cuddle her, make a fuss of her, and be genuinely loving. I have to admit I hadn't imagined this. She wants me to. And she's right, the relationship of a young servant to a family is more complex than the pages of files would have you believe.

'But your mother was pretty strict too,' my mother suddenly intervenes. 'She used to make my mother take all her clothes off at the doorstep after she'd been to the pictures. She reckoned they were bug houses. There was no getting past her.' Mrs Davies has to agree. Different memories of the past hold each other in check.

Mrs Davies passes around family photos, handing us one of her parents. Mr Sherwood, Arthur, looks as I had imagined he would, diminutive, proper, suited and calm—a bank manager to the core. But Mrs Sherwood, Dolphin, is not the southern belle Dolphin that I had imagined at all. Instead, I see a solid Dolphin McKenna, of Celtic Scottish roots and upbringing—a firm woman, born of firm women, wide and sturdy. It was taken around the time my grandmother came to work for them, when the size of the family had outgrown the bank quarters, and six children had become too much for her to manage on her own.

Mrs Davies remembers the day my grandmother first arrived at the Rectory. She was so anxious to see the little girl their mother had told them about. She had been told that a 'coloured' girl from the Mission was coming to care for them, and had wondered what colour she was going to be. At fifteen years of age my grandmother was sent by train, a full day's journey from the city. 'She seemed so little and frail then,' Mrs Davies recollected. 'Yes, frail is the word. And shy.' My mother almost coughs up her cake at the thought of my grandmother ever being shy, or frail for that matter. 'Jesus,' she laughs, 'must've changed a lot by the time I came along.'

I hand around the photographs of my grandmother and I am pleased at how it genuinely means something to Mrs Davies to see her image again. She has a photograph of Jessie somewhere in the albums, and promises to dig it out and send a copy to us.

When it is time for us to leave I pick up the file from the table. It remained unopened. My mother is pleased she got to see Mrs Davies again and I have learned a little bit more about my grandmother's story. Opening up the narratives of other people's stories where your family's past crossed with theirs is a revealing business. It reveals the historical power plays that separated black and white in this country, and the small fractures that people were able to effect in this facade. It also reveals the boundaries that remain unchallenged, seemingly reinforced by their formation in past generations when segregation was considered acceptable and desirable, and power imbalances seemed natural—if you were white. But opening up these narratives also reveals the narratives of tragedy, love and friendship that manage to cut across these more dominant boundaries, if only fleetingly.

My grandmother kept in contact with the Sherwood family over the years, but she entered their lives as their servant, with all the rules and inequality that the term implies. Mrs Davies told me of when she was young 'Miss Betty' Sherwood. She was the baby child of the family and would call for my grandmother who would come and comb her hair, cuddle her and sing to her. She sang me one of her favourite songs that my grandmother sang to her.

There is a happy land far, far away.
Where we get bread and scrape three times a day.
Bread and butter we never see.
No sugar in our tea.
While we are gradually starving away.

I recognise it immediately as the Moore River Settlement song. It is so strange to hear this song being sung by Mrs Davies as a childhood reminiscence. I've only ever heard it on the lips of older black women who had been at the Settlement, who sang it as a kind of bitter irony, not a lullaby. My grandmother had not been to Moore River in those early years when she worked at Bridgetown. Mrs Davies' childhood memory of my grandmother singing this song is of a later time, after my grandmother had come to know Moore River well and had been sent back to work for her family again.

The thought of my grandmother singing this song of bitter resentment at how people were treated in the Settlement as a lullaby is a wry reminder of her wicked sense of humour.

Jessie would tend to Miss Constance, Miss Corinth, Miss Betty, Tom and Jack—all the Sherwood children. The second youngest of the family, Enid, Betty's sister just above her, suffered with epilepsy and they had to be on the look-out in case she had a fit. When my grandmother came into their house to do the work that she had been trained for at the Mission, she had previously had little to do with whites, or white families.

I can see her, now that I think of it, my grandmother, in that same photograph of old Mrs Dolphin Sherwood. In an odd way, my own grandmother came to resemble this first white woman that she had been sent out to work for. There, in that photograph of Dolphin, is the image of an older Jessie Argyle, sturdy and solid. It's as if my grandmother had been so young and impressionable that, like a sapling planted too close to a taller tree, she could not help but bend to the light around the branches of the taller tree. But, while my grandmother's environment was shaping her like a sapling to look around it and seek out the light, there was also less obvious growth. Beyond the camera's gaze were deep roots searching out softer soil, underground watercourses deep under the dry earth, and thin seams of fertile ground being tapped, followed and surveyed. So while Jessie Argyle was looking around her and making a place within this family, she was also making space for herself, learning to grow beyond what was to be seen on the surface and what was expected of a servant.

Mrs Sherwood instructed my grandmother in the right way to serve, from the left to the right; the right way to embroider, without leaving a trace from the stitching; and in the right way to polish the floor, on your hands and knees. My grandmother had already learned these things, as well as how to pickle fruit, how to grow food and prepare it, how to sew, how to write her own name, and, of course, how to read the Bible. She had learned all this in the Mission, but under Dolphin's guidance she was to hone these skills.

In the first few years away from the Swan Mission it was usual practice for young girls to return to the Mission during holiday times when the white families they worked for went on trips, or visited their own families, or simply no longer required the services of their maid for the summer.

Sometimes my grandmother would accompany the Sherwoods when they made summer holiday trips up to Cottesloe Beach. Many families chose Cottesloe as their summer getaway and many brought Aboriginal servants with them to mind the children. On their days off women like my grandmother gathered together at the Cottesloe jetty, swapped their experiences and addresses, and began a network of women that would form my grandmother's community in the coming years.

On some breaks in the first few years out, when the Sherwoods had no need of my grandmother, she would return to the Swan Mission. At the Mission she would be regarded as a 'Big Girl', and charged with taking care of the smaller children, who were no older than she had been when she was taken away. She would take them under her wing, as older girls before her had taken her under theirs, and to these younger Mission children she became like a visiting aunty, someone to look up to and look out for when their time came to be sent out to work.

When this Mission 'holiday' ended, Jessie would be sent back to the Sherwoods to take up her position again and re-enter the life of their family, leaving her own extended Mission family behind. It must have been difficult to be shifted from the bonds of extended family to another family not your own. I have no doubt that my grandmother cared for the Sherwood children because she kept in contact with them all her life. But each house that a domestic servant found herself and her labour bonded to was also a space of rules and lines and boundaries that differed from house to house. It was a space where a servant could be welcomed and treated well, as I believe that first family had treated my grandmother, or where she could be brutalised and raped, as had happened to a number of women. In so many other houses, friends of my grandmother's, women I knew as aunties, had very different beginnings as domestics.

Nineteen twenty had seen another summer of storms rip through the coastal plains, but the valley of Bridgetown, nestled inland from the sea, was never really threatened. My grandmother covered up the mirrors against the threat of lightning, and kept an extra close watch upon the children as the warm nights came and the air began to turn sour.

Jessie and Tom, one of the Sherwoods' sons, developed a Huck Finn sort of friendship in the grounds of that house on the edge of town, stealing fruit from orchards, playing tricks on visitors—kids' stuff. On some days, in the cool of the afternoon after the children finished school, Jessie would disappear with them into the orchard to pick fruit, or they would head down to the creek where she would teach them how to catch gilgies, and how to build a fire and cook them in the ashes. Young Betty loved to go to the orchard with Jessie and while they were picking fruit they would all talk amongst themselves and enjoy the cool relief.

One day, Jessie was minding the girls in the orchard while picking fruit for Mrs Sherwood, who was having tea with a visitor. It was an afternoon like any other. Young Enid Sherwood said she wasn't feeling very well and decided to go back to the house. Jessie sent her off with the instruction to go straight there, not to stray. No one really took a lot of notice as the little girl headed home.

An hour or so later, as they were making their way back to the house, having stripped a couple of trees of fruit, they could hear Mrs Sherwood calling from the back door for Enid. Mrs Davies recalled the sound of her mother's voice calling, 'Ni-ni, Ni-ni,' and then the sense of puzzlement in her voice that grew into a panic, as the child did not respond. My grandmother, hearing Mrs Sherwood, hurried the other children along the path up to the house.

The two women, my grandmother and Mrs Sherwood, were no doubt feeling very anxious. The house was turned upside down as they looked for Enid from the kitchen to the lounge, through the children's rooms, the guest rooms, the dining room, Jessie's room, out the back, along the front, on the road to the bridge and back in the orchard. They couldn't find a trace of her.

Mr Wheatley, one of the town residents, had been going past the Old Rectory in a buggy and hearing the commotion stopped to see if he could help. He began his search down at the brook. From the house they heard Mr Wheatley call out. As they ran to the brook they saw him wading into one of the muddy pools that remained from the winter creek. He lifted Enid's lifeless little body out of the water and carried her back to the slippery muddy bank.

Betty Davies was six years old when it happened. She was too young to understand the gravity but her memory of the sense of enormity of the event stayed with her all her life. Her mother and Jessie were mortified as Enid was fished from the shallows and laid out on the ground. All the rest was a blur.

Betty Davies can remember her mother carrying Enid home. Everyone followed slowly behind. Mrs Sherwood washed her little daughter clean of the choking mud. Jessie helped her to lay Enid out. Together they worked quietly, putting her in clean clothes. She was placed on her bed, just as if she was sleeping. When Mr Sherwood came home from the bank, he took Betty by the hand and led her over to the bed to say goodbye to Enid. He lifted her onto his knee beside her sister, and it struck her then, when she was so close, that something was wrong.

Mr Sherwood was holding Betty and telling her not to cry. She touched her sister's hand and realised she was unnaturally cold. It was still hot and humid outside. This was when Betty sensed that her sister could not speak and she became even more alarmed and afraid. Her father tried to calm her down, but she was too upset.

In a private room of her house, Mrs Davies has kept a small purple suede handbag and a neatly cut lock of Enid's curly blonde hair. Her mother had saved them. She has kept them near her all these years. 'Apparently she had dropped the purse on the bank near the brook,' Mrs Davies says. 'Enid had somehow dropped it and gone in after it. Years later, when we used to speak of it, Jessie told us how Enid's hair was floating in the water. She was the only one of us with curls and they were floating.' When I ask Mrs Davies about the epilepsy, she is reluctant to acknowledge it. There was an inquest. It arrived at a verdict of accidental death with, 'No one to be blamed'. The report in the press hinted that the child had fitted and drowned.

By the time Enid's body was carried north by train to the city for burial in Karrakatta Cemetery, the papers had dealt with the story and moved on to the forthcoming visit of the Duke of York. While the parents and grand-parents kept vigil over the body of the child in Perth, Jessie stayed behind to care for the children. When Mrs Sherwood returned from the funeral she was never to be the same again—neither was my grandmother. It was not as if blame had been apportioned, regardless of the court's verdict, but it had been shared, it seems, between my grandmother and Mrs Sherwood, in their own bond of responsibility. Within months Mrs Sherwood, my grandmother and the remaining children left Bridgetown, leaving Mr Sherwood to sort out his next posting. Dolphin couldn't bear to stay at the Rectory any longer. They moved to Cottesloe beach, where they were only five miles from Karrakatta Cemetery.

The grave is in the older part of the cemetery. Mr and Mrs Sherwood, and many of the other Sherwoods, have since joined Enid. Crops of headstones, marble angels and porcelain roses trapped within glass bubbles lie beneath the dry grass. It is patrolled by wardungs, kulbardies, honeyeaters and watched over by sentinel kookaburras. Children's graves stand out like reminders of fleeting life amongst the more substantial plinths and stones of crosses, grey vines and virgins. Young death. Nearby stone angels cast angelic glances towards the sky, framed on either side by tall thin palms. Here my grandmother had stood with Enid's mother, sisters and brothers. My grandmother had also stood here alone, apparently walking the five miles on foot on her weekly day off.

In 1922, as plinths and monoliths sprang up all over the state marking the losses of the Great War, this small unremarkable grave wed my grandmother and this family in their private grief. Within six months the family had settled in the Wheatbelt town of Pingelly, only an hour's train ride from the city. Within months of this shift Mrs Sherwood and my grandmother's relationship had cooled. The reclaimed pages of the file show that Dolphin wrote to the Aborigines Department asking for another girl.

> I'll be glad if you will send on the little half-caste girl as soon as possible. I do not want a black girl … Jessie will go the day after the other girl arrives and says she would like to go to Geraldton or Carnarvon as soon as she leaves me.

They were difficult months. My grandmother was ill for some time. She underwent repeated treatment in the Perth Hospital for an unspecified bone disease in her leg. When she finally returned to the Sherwoods, it appears that she just didn't care any more.

My grandmother had been with the Sherwoods for over three years, but her leaving was mutually agreeable. This was the beginning of her years on the road, being moved from place to place, family to family, from relative safety into certain danger. The Department put Jessie under the watch of the police. Jessie was seeing a Noongar man just out of prison. She was staying out on the town. The life of servitude that she had been trained all her life to fulfil was a bitter pill. Her leg was getting worse. She learned to hide the pain rather than end up being sent to the Settlement where she would be tended by a horse doctor if she was lucky.

My grandmother was taken away from her family and placed in a Mission. The Mission had raised her and sent her to what seemed a substantial house. The house had crumbled with the death of a child. She had been claimed on behalf of the imagined white blood within her veins with the imagined blood of Jesus. I don't believe that she had any idea what she really wanted. I don't for a minute believe that she thought the life she was leading was what she wanted for the rest of her life. As my grandmother moved from house to house, from town to town, from mistress to mistress, I believe she became increasingly disillusioned. As more and more regulations were created to curtail her freedom it must have seemed like there was nothing but service and limitations, drudgery and interference, scrubbing and control, on the horizon ahead.

isolation

I am driving down the Mogumber West Road. My old Valiant's steering swings wildly as I fishtail through the wide stretch of burnt orange gravel that swells and corrugates in piles left by sheep trucks, harvesters and heavily loaded farm utes. I am approaching the bend where I once piled my car in a swirl of dust and rocks, swerving to miss, of all things, a goanna standing in the middle of the road sticking its blue tongue out at me. On that occasion the car spun out of control and the wheatfields and gum trees blurred into a wild pastiche of colour. There was nothing I could do. I just had to sit and wait, gripping hold of the steering wheel to see what was going to happen as time stretched out, elongating each second.

I slow down, click the car out of overdrive and let the needle drop below fifty miles an hour as I pass the tree that nearly took my life. It's the sort of place where you wouldn't be found for hours.

I don't know how many times I've travelled this road since that mishap. Not many people travel down this road nowadays. It joins the siding of what was once the town of Mogumber, a collection of workers' cottages, a wheat loading depot, a pub and the shells of a schoolhouse and post office. The newer highway and the cleaner, shining roadhouses are away to the west. Large farms run off from side entrances along the fenced paddocks of wheat and sheep, blistered by patches of sandy white soil that mark the beginnings of the coastal plain leading west to the Indian Ocean. It's not rich farm country.

People drive past the turn-off without looking, as they head north to larger Wheatbelt towns, or on through the Mid-West into the North-West, and then much further north to the Kimberley.

Eight miles west of the turn-off though, about halfway to the main highway, is a place that has touched the lives of almost every Aboriginal family in this part of the world, and certainly the lives of the Yuat Noongars, the traditional owners of this region.

I don't really know what to call it any more. It is a place of such significance, of such sorrow, of death, of birth, community and alienation. It conjures up a strange sense of belonging in me, even though it is not my country. Thousands of our people from all over the state have been imprisoned here, or passed through here. Hundreds have been born here. Hundreds have been buried here.

As you head west along this straight but undulating road, the sky opens out wide and clean. Clouds roll past in hues of pink and grey, shadowing you as you climb the next hill, lip the next valley, and follow the odd gentle ridge that leads you to the remnants of the Moore River Native Settlement. The Moore River, snaking its way from the gentle hills to the east, gradually closes in on you as you head west towards the sea. At a point its pools, streams and small waterfalls skirt close to the road. This is where we turn off, to the place that was once a traditional Yuat meeting place, then a farm, then an unhealthy government experiment: the Moore River Native Settlement, a government-run detention centre from 1918 to 1950. Thirty-two years of incarceration and control.

First turn on your right will bring you to the Settlement. The white bosses are gone. Today it is an Aboriginal-managed heritage site. I've worked here myself, trying to help restore a sense of Aboriginal meaning to this place. It is run by Noongars who understand its complicated history of desolation and misery, but it is also a place many people remember as their home.

Second turn on your right is the old Settlement cemetery. Here long days of cutting overgrown banksia and saltbush by hand revealed the remnants of one of the largest Aboriginal burial sites in Australia. Rusted iron crosses lean this way and that above tiny mounds of earth and the remains of crushed shell and jars that once held flowers. Almost all the graves are unmarked. Most of the people buried here are children under the age of five.

The first time I visited here, I shot a film on a third-hand super-8 camera I bought for ten dollars. Run the film and you can see the faint, scratched names of people bleeding through the rust of the few remaining crosses. A gentle wind blows a necklace that someone has strung over a relative's grave. Some white bailer shells, bleached chalky by the sun, remain where they were placed on a grave. The people of coastal country believe souls leave the body and travel out under the sea. Sheep skulls buffed white shine against the thick blooms of everlastings incidentally scattered among the graves.

It is a powerful site, resting on a ridge beneath the parade of clouds that stream above us. On most days, if you stay long enough, you can see eagles riding the warm air currents. Their giant wingspans shadow the earth as they spiral high above the cemetery.

Many people who have visited the cemetery have spoken about the effect this place has had on them. Some have said they've heard the sound of children crying as they leave the cemetery gates. Others have returned to make peace with their own past or to make sense of what happened to relatives here. They come back for their mothers, for their fathers, their grandmothers, sisters, brothers, uncles and their cousins. Sometimes people make the trip here searching for links to living family.

It is an isolated place where many lives have crossed and rubbed up against one another. The Mogumber West Road was once little more than a track, but it was well worn by the thousands of people who found themselves forced to walk it, or were placed on the back of sulkies and taken down it to the Settlement. Some were brought in bound, sometimes dragged behind horses for having tried to escape. This is our history. It is a shared history that thousands of other Aboriginal people endured through the years of segregation, separation and imprisonment.

But these are not the only stories of this place. It was also a place of communion, of the making of bonds, and of the strengthening of culture and community. To many it was a prison, but for some it is their birth country. It is a place that stands testimony to their pain and anguish, but also to their determination and ability to survive.

At the heritage office there is a display of black and white photographs, almost two thousand, of the marriages, the picnics, the workers and the trackers, of babies and their proud mothers, and the funerals. It is a tough and complex place. I come here because this is where my grandparents' histories crossed.

I remember that day when I swerved to miss the goanna and landed stuck in the piles of gravel at the side of the road. In that elongated moment when I lost control of the car and my life, I had no idea what the outcome would be as the car spun around. One minute the straight road, the next second a blurring landscape and, almost ghostlike, the image of my grandfather standing alone in the Wheatbelt landscape of the Mogumber Siding flashed into my mind. Later, after laughing a little too loudly, I got out of the car, took my shovel from the back, and began digging the car out of the three feet of gravel it was buried in. It struck me as strange that I had thought of him in that moment. Pausing from digging out my car from the side of the gully I looked back towards the Mogumber Siding, but there was nothing there, not even any sign of a train siding.

I imagine my grandfather here on this road in the heat of February when he first arrived in 1922. I imagine him from the photographs, from the diary entries, and from the files that I've researched about his time at the Settlement. I can see the train that used to stop at the siding to drop off supplies and pick up the mail. Edward Alfred Byron Smith hops out of the train and is helped by the railway guard to load a large wooden trunk onto the back of a horse cart. Edward shakes hands with a young Tommy Bropho, sent from the Settlement to meet him, then climbs onto the back of the cart. When the train leaves the siding, heading northwards to the coastal town of Geraldton, it dwarfs the small cart making its way slowly out along the Mogumber West Road towards the Settlement.

It was sand plain berry time when Edward arrived. The bobtail goannas were a sure sign of it. They cross the gravel road from one ribbon of trees to the other seeking out the bounty of berries that fall upon the white-grey sand plain floor. They move slowly, too obstinate to get out of the way of even a slow-moving horse and buggy. Edward Smith was thirty years of age. His thirty-first birthday was creeping up on him. It was nearly thirteen years to the day since he stepped off the *Orontes* ocean liner in Fremantle and marvelled at the brilliant light of the southern continent. It had been ten years since he had even bothered to write to his family in England. They had not heard from him since well before the Great War.

Looking towards the Mogumber sky he would have seen the late summer sun that had blinded him on his arrival. That clear, sharp Western Australian light that cuts deep shadows in the earth, burns skin, bakes the air bone dry and turns straight lines any further than a hundred yards distant into a shimmer. On days like this the waxy leaves of the river gums and red gums lining the road shine like thousands of little mirrors twisting and twirling in the late sea breeze, reflecting the heat and light outwards into the land.

The ride from the station to the Settlement is long, slow and hot. Sitting on the tray, his legs most likely dangling from the back of the cart filled with sacks of flour, tins of jam and boxes of powdered milk, he may well have decided to have another cigarette. He'd shelved the pipe except for special occasions and had picked up the habit of rolling his own. The wooden trunk that he'd brought out from London looked somewhat knocked around from being dragged around the state. It still carried all his worldly possessions. It was not supposed to. He was supposed to have made headway in the world of Empire by then. He had the same field glasses, the same books, some picture frames, some prints, his camera and an assortment of single men's amenities: a shaving mirror, a razor, his pipe, some tobacco, a few tools, a cup, a plate and some working clothes.

I wonder if he paused and reflected on all that he owned, just for a split second, remembering the English boy just shy of eighteen, checking his neatly folded new clothes, his tightly packed books, his leggings and pyjamas, and catching the train to Tilbury docks. That boy, clean skinned and hopeful, was somewhat unrecognisable in this thirty-year-old. His possessions were filled with the red dust of the North-West, and no doubt they had already received their rough lines and dents through overuse. If I know anything about him, the trunk was just as neatly packed as that clean-skinned young Englishman's. In his lists that he seemed compelled to make, tallying up items, he was meticulous in detail. He had not had that trait knocked out of him, even after all the failures he had endured.

It is a long road that leads you out to the Settlement. It gives you time to sit back and think while you swelter under the February sun. A good time to pick over your life as you draw in the flavour of tobacco and watch the wheat fields and goannas drift by. I can see him as he passes the tree with which my car almost collided. He is spinning in his own blur of uncertain fate. I know this is not the future he had planned for himself. I know that his life was again at a point where he was ready to flip a coin, catch the first boat that came along. My grandfather had no idea what was in store for him at the Settlement. I have imagined him along this road dozens of times, riding the back of that cart, making this new start in his life. He had already experienced a great deal, but was about to enter another world, to cross through the Settlement gates and enter a history that most whites have managed to ignore their entire lives

The Moore River Settlement is nothing like what people expect. Today there are only a few buildings left of what was once the Settlement compound. The main road still runs north–south on a ridge road that leads nowhere but to the fall of a cliff. From the top of the compound road the remains of the church stand defiantly against the heat, the cold and the winds that hurl their way up the river valley from the Moore River. Tellingly, the gaol is still there. On hot windy afternoons the giant pines, which were saplings no taller than Edward's waist when he came here, bend and sing above the dirt road that leads to where the Big House once stood overlooking this outpost of empire.

The superintendent's garden, once fenced, weeded and lush, has survived as a collection of giant Japanese pepper trees and remnant hibiscus hedges. Standing on the edge of the cliff that falls down to the Moore River valley, you can see breaks of river through the tops of the river gums that line it. Closing your eyes, you can hear the water, faintly, at just the right time in the late afternoon when the sea breeze reaches the compound. To the west, you can see the foundation mounds of what were once the camps—tiny one-room squares of raised earth that mark the homes of hundreds of displaced people alongside the compound in which their children or other family were forcibly kept. The rusted remains of the Settlement pump house plunge into what was once the river bank, but is now a muddy grassy expanse. The water level has dropped as a result of the watercourse being so overused.

On my way up to Mogumber I usually call in on Granny Bella Bropho. Granny Bella always sits on the porch of Aunty Gladys' house in Saunders Street. She hasn't been back to the Settlement in years and has no desire to do so. Her supple black skin is framed by her long, straight snowy-white hair, and her brown eyes are clouded over blue with the cataracts that she will never have removed. We always sit here for a long time, just catching up on what's been happening since I saw her last, who's back with who, who's out of gaol, who's passed away—when the funeral is. We sit on the porch and I ask her questions, or just listen as Granny talks about her life, tapping her walking-stick on the cement, sometimes stopping for a cup of tea brought out by Aunty Gladys or her grand-daughter Pauline.

The occasional police van, the *munach*, passes by very slowly. There are only half-a-dozen houses on this semi-rural street but they are all black houses, and even though we are a good ten miles out of town, and the bus only passes on the main road once in the morning and returns once again at night, the police will drive past three or four times on any given day. This is the Swan Valley where Granny has lived a good portion of her life with her husband Nyinda, Thomas Bropho, my grandmother's brother. They raised their large family here and at other Noongar camping places around the city before the houses began to encroach. Saunders Street is the longest that Granny Bella has ever lived in a house. She has mostly lived in camps and stayed close to her country. She takes great pride in that.

Granny takes as much time as she needs to tell a story. There is no rushing her, and when she says, 'Har, I seen so much, I know everything,' no one who has met her would ever doubt her. 'Old Smithy, Old Captain Smith'—Granny almost laughs when I ask her about Edward's time at the Settlement—''e was 'armless. We use to be able to push 'im around.' Granny laughs and pokes my arm with her cane. 'Oh, 'e was all right for a second boss.'

I ask her what Edward's nickname was, and she is so old, so slow and deliberate in her movements, that it is like slow-moving footage, moving frame by frame. This is how she lives her life now, and so when she speaks, there is not a word out of turn, or a waste of intent. 'Well. Whisperin' Smith, we used to call 'im, because he could never raise 'is voice over a whisper. He just used to squeak … like a mouse.' She pauses for a moment. 'Some peoples said it was the gas from the war. Some said it was shrapnel from a bomb, 'e never talked of it.' It's a story I often ask her, because I like to hear it, and because it is a story that she likes to tell. No one seems to have known about the diphtheria.

I've brought some photos of the Settlement, as I usually do, but Granny's eyes can't see much today. Some days her vision is clearer, like on the days she can spot a rellie in Gillie Park from fifty feet. But when they're no good, like today, I describe the photos to her. 'This one's up at the compound,' I tell her. 'Oh … right,' Granny says, as she leans in closer as if hearing me better will make it more real, make her more able to see what can't be seen through the blue haze of the clouds covering her eyes. 'Here's Nyinda, working at the bakehouse, baking the bread for the Settlement.' Granny nods, that's right. 'Here he is again with an emu that he shot with some of the trackers.' I am shuffling through a pack of prints I recently made from my grandfather's glass-plate negatives, some of the earliest images of the Settlement. There are photos of Edward and Major

143

Campbell on horseback, views of the compound vegetable garden, and portraits of the nurses and attendants taken against the side of the newly built girls' dormitory. Edward is dressed in white cotton pants and white tunic; he stands awkwardly at the end of a group shot of staff members; everyone is in white, they seem to shimmer, seem to lift from the sand plain beneath them. I wonder how many of them wondered what the hell they were doing there.

'This one here is Nyinda reading for a funeral service, when that cemetery only just started up. And this one's at the sewing room.' All the women are working barefoot under the gaze of the sewing mistress. Granny worked in the sewing room before she was married; she used to work 'sewin' up the mans' pants.' She tells me how the girls used to sneak comics in, take the needle out of the machine, and put the comics under the foot of the Singer and read them quickly, as they pretended to continue to sew, before the sewing mistress found out. If you got caught you'd be punished severely. But it was worth trying to break the boredom.

Once, when Granny was just a young girl, she answered the sewing mistress back. It was just a moment of cheekiness from a girl who usually did what she was told. She was marched over to the Superintendent and they punished her harshly, way beyond the seriousness of her 'crime'. Granny had all her hair shaved off and was placed in the Boob — a tin-walled prison barely large enough to lie down in — for two weeks on bread and water.

'This one's taken down at the camps.' About a hundred people face the camera — men, women and children from the compound. They sit in a semicircle, the trackers wearing discarded military uniforms, the children in ill-fitting calico shifts. It is early in the Settlement's history — the river bank behind them has not been denuded to supply firewood and frames for campies' houses. Beyond them are the tracks that lead to Chalk Cliff, the traditional ochre mine south of the Settlement. Campies brought the ochre back to whitewash the hessian and bits of salvaged tin they used to build their camps.

'And this is another one, taken the same day.' It is the entire population of the Settlement — compound children, adults from the camps, trackers and staff. I can just make out Granny at the very back of the group shot. 'Here you are Granny,' and I hand her the photo to hold. 'What ... where is that one taken?' Granny is suddenly very alert. Everyone is lined up in rows against a large wooden building. The white nurses, the matron and

144

the superintendent, and a man visiting from the Aborigines Department. 'All the women and men are lined up for a photograph, and it looks like … yeah, it's the office, Granny, do you remember that day?' 'Yeah,' Granny says, 'they was always makin' a fuss when anyone come up from Perth for a visit, cleanin' it up and hidin' the dirt … Har!'

The next image in the series looks almost identical. Everyone is in pretty much the same place except that for this photograph, Edward has used the time delay. As you scan the photograph closely you see hundreds of people in rags and calico dresses, or in pants tied with rope. If you look a little closer, amongst the children that look blankly towards the camera and the girl who has placed her hands upside down over her eyes to make masquerade goggles, you will see Edward Smith sitting in the dirt. The other staff sit stiff-backed in a line at the top of the steps, a separate line from the inmates. A small baby has broken away from a group of children and is crawling in front of the scene, but my grandfather does not see. He's too busy turning his good side to the lens, his white colonial suit, his work boots shining in the sun. His hat is tilted low, casting a shadow over his eyes. He looks towards the church, at something that has caught his eye out of frame. That's the problem with the photographic image. It is a captured, framed moment.

But even in this simple moment, there are the elements recorded in the image that say much more. Edward's white suit is the suit of an overseer, and it is not harmless. His boots are unremarkable except that in a place like this they stand out. Most of the people in this photo are barefoot, and everyone with footwear is white. There are no ties, no fine shirts, no expensive belt buckles, but it does not take much to see the obvious differences in privilege, between those who have power and those who don't. Those who can walk out of here of their own free will, and those who, if they attempt it, will be brought back by the black trackers and possibly whipped, have their head shaved and be placed in the Boob.

Edward might have been all right. He might have been a pushover, but he was still a white man in a place where white equalled boss equalled power. Even if he was a second boss, in charge of the farm side of things, in charge of the sheep, the growing of vegetables, the gathering of wood and the fencing of paddocks, he was still a boss. Edward might have had to defer to the superintendent, to the first boss, and he might have only spoken in a whisper, but the trackers didn't need more than a whispered instruction to act.

But although the people here were certainly poor, and they were certainly trapped, they had lives that went beyond the Settlement boundary. The white uniform meant a great deal within the official structure but there were other things that went on there, within the camps and the compound, that no starched white suit had any control over. There were things that happened in the land, on the sands of the coastal plain, flowing out along the river valley, that the staff had no idea of, or power in which to intervene. People's lives were controlled. They were physically incarcerated, but there were important matters of spirit, of culture and business, that escaped the white bosses.

A Silver Chain nurse arrives and Granny Bella tightens up. She doesn't like any fuss, or anyone she perceives to be interfering in her life. She has had enough of that. Granny's sugar is bad, but she is not in the mood for a nurse this week, and so she answers, 'Yes Sister' when she has to, and 'No Sister' until the nurse has gone. Granny has nothing personal against the nurse, she knows her by name and sometimes likes to talk. But Granny Bella has her own way of dealing with the systems of authority in her life. It is an art form she has had great practice at for many years. Sometimes you have to kick up and fight. Sometimes it is best to let them think that they know what they're doing, to 'crack dumb' and get on with your life. And just sometimes, every now and then, there is room for a little movement, for some common ground, of some kind, to be carved out.

Edward traded his shack on the Derby wharves for the second boss's cottage at the Moore River Native Settlement. He shifted his attentions from the management of water to the management of people, crops and ration stores. The wages were nothing great, but they were steady. The cottage was hardly a home, but it was better than sharing a bed with an oil pump. The work was solid and constant. Each day he was responsible for organising the work teams of men to go out collecting firewood for the Settlement. He would take his pocket diary from his white staff jacket and regularly note the names of those camp men and older compound boys that would have the job of walking all day beside the cart, running to and from the bush, loading old branches, stumps, fallen trunks and driftwood for the return journey. It was hard, back-breaking, dirty work, but it was work, and while far from eager, Aboriginal men took any work that was on offer for a few sticks of tobacco, or an extra ration of meat to feed their families back at the camps. He also made notations of Noongar words he was learning from the men, simple directions in language that he could use when they were out working in the bush. The speaking of traditional language amongst the Settlement population was discouraged by the public servants in Perth, but for the white staff working at the coalface on the Settlement, a bit of language amongst the workers was no great offence.

When Edward wasn't on the work teams, leaving the men in the charge of Tom Bropho, or the third boss, or one of the trackers, he would oversee the fencing of paddocks, or the weeding of the vegetable garden, or the maintenance of the Settlement buildings. Once a week, on a Thursday, he would open the store and have rations distributed amongst the Settlement population of the camps. Just like Pension Day. Everyone would line up for weekly rations that were not fit for more than a few days, and barely enough to keep a working body active, but which supplemented the food that could be got from the bush — kangaroo or emu, or even the odd stray sheep that managed to wander from nearby properties.

At the close of each day Edward would report to Major Campbell, who ran the Settlement like a military camp, and provide statistics of food that had been consumed, what needed to be ordered and what was in need of repair. He would then see to the mail, heading out to the Mogumber Siding, following that same long road that had brought him here carrying all that he owned on the back of the dray. If he was unable to go himself, it would be one of the men, a trustee or a tracker, who would go in his place. There would almost always be another passenger to bring back — young women sent in from service for the most minor misdemeanour, or men unable to escape the compulsory net of the Department as it began to wind into full motion its new Settlement scheme. There were even whole families removed from towns for the slightest of reasons, or for no reason at all beyond the fact that the white townspeople didn't want them there.

The sheep that had required tending when he first arrived had been sacrificed in the need to keep up appearances for the visits of the Departmental Secretary, Mr Copping, and for the simple fact that there was not enough money to feed the growing number of people sent by train from all parts of the state. The situation was becoming dire as the winter of 1922 descended and an epidemic of flu was making the rounds of the camps. Moore River was a fake town, segregated from the world by a thin line of race, and Edward would have realised that it was running on the

147

credit of the land, and on the credit of the unpaid labour of the trapped inmates. Who better to realise the failure of an idea, of a venture embarked upon with no hope of success, than someone who had already failed spectacularly.

I imagine he was in no great rush to move on, but equally had no great desire to stay at the Settlement, or remain in his role as second boss. He had come to like many of the people that he was responsible for. He could not bring himself to lord it over anyone. It was the superintendent who had that role. Edward was not ensconced in an overseer's office. He worked with his hands as the men worked with theirs. He was freer than the inmates, ate better than they did, and could leave when his heart desired, but he, unlike many of them, had no place to go to. He did not have his own sense of community then. He was liked by many of the inmates and had got to know Thomas Bropho well. Men who worked with him found him affable and, unlike most white men, not keen to act the boss or cause trouble for people. Some hoped that he would stay on because he was easy to get around, but they guessed that he wouldn't because it was thought that no one in their right mind would have stayed if they didn't have to.

The Settlement was a place where every detail was noticed, where work was sometimes a break from the monotony of poverty, where rumour and myth were the stuff of daily brawls, and where allegiances were defended and claimed. The entire farm, from the compound to the camps, from the river to the plains, was watched and noted by the trackers, by the superintendent and by the inmates. There were strict boundaries to be adhered to and locks to be placed over the windows and doors of the dormitories at night. Not for inmate protection, but to prevent their escape. Escape attempts were not uncommon, and punishments were harsh.

It was a prison for people guilty of nothing more than being the wrong race in a white world. It needed no fences, or gates, or lights from watchtowers at night to contain its charges. It was bounded by those lines on the map keeping black from white, and white from black. It existed in a landscape that supported this regime, where an escaped inmate stood out in their own country more sorely than a crow at a picnic, recognised by whites of the town as both out of place and needing to be placed somewhere out of sight. Moore River was that out-of-sight place.

When Edward was at Moore River, he himself could not have felt out of sight. As he rose from his bed and began his day he could not have missed that he too was being watched very closely. He could not have missed the lines closing in as he became responsible for how much someone ate, how easily they worked or how trapped they, too, might feel. He could not have missed that the mail that arrived for inmates was opened and read by the superintendent as if the place was a prisoner-of-war camp and the inmates were completely without rights. And it was not only the inmates' letters that were scanned for critical comments they might be making, or any call to agitation that might be coming through from outside. There are instances in the archives of individual staff mail similarly being read. Edward traded his shack by the wharf at Derby, surrounded by the desert and the heat, for an equally lonely house surrounded by a people he had only ever before watched from a distance, who now also watched him every moment of his working day.

I imagine the solitary second boss's house was actually a comfort to Edward in a place where one was never quite alone. Even the other white staff, the Major, Mrs Campbell and the nurses, were not averse to a little spying on each other, a little prying on what one had that the other didn't, or which one was in or out of favour with the inmates. There are files full of letters of accusation, of petty jealousies and of falling out of favour with one another. The inmates realised this vulnerability and often managed to exploit and manipulate any tensions between the staff. One of the nurses was reprimanded for starting rumours amongst the inmates. After several instances were drawn to the superintendent's attention, this nurse was replaced. The inmates decided they did not like the new nurse and a group of Elders from the camp wrote and signed a petition saying they wanted the old nurse back. It made the incoming nurse feel even more isolated in this isolated place. It might be all very well for public servants like Mr Neville to sit in his office in the city deciding how things should be run, but it was a very different matter when you were alone in your cottage at night, surrounded by a population of people who didn't want to be there.

I imagine that in times of staff upsets and clashes in personalities Edward reassessed why he was there. He'd received the cigarettes that had been promised by Mr Campbell in his letter offering him his job. He'd been saving his money as he had been promised he would be able to. He had a quiet little cottage, with a girl from the compound to cook his meals and clean his room. But it couldn't have been a life you saw for yourself for any great length of time.

In September 1922 Edward handed in his notice to Major Campbell and packed up his trunk. His reference from the superintendent says he left of his own accord. He had been at the Settlement for eight months. The period of exile from the city appeared to be over, and Edward had made enough money to return to Perth. He had started writing to his family in London again.

Whenever I come back here to Moore River I always pay my respects at the cemetery. Before I head back into the city, I make my way down Mogumber West Road to the cemetery turn-off and drive up to the ridge where the memorial stands to the more than four hundred people buried here. I always come before dark. No self-respecting marda-marda would be found sniffing around a cemetery after dark, and especially this cemetery. The wall of remembrance at the cemetery entrance was created by the old Mogumber Heritage Committee years ago. It rises out of the earth like a giant bailer shell patterned with the hundreds of names of those buried here. The trees that were planted as part of the memorial have grown into shade trees that cover the site almost completely. Like most Aboriginal sites, it is not an obvious statement. It belongs here. It's subtle. You have to know its significance.

A Noongar family was once driving through here on their way to Moora. It was getting late so they decided to pull over to the side and stop for the night before carrying on the next day. When it's dark out here you have no way of seeing where you are. They thought they were pulling into an abandoned road-workers' camp, the kind that road workers leave by roadsides all over the state. That night they saw lights hovering around them. They heard footsteps around their car, and what sounded like a child crying. They had a look around and realised they were camped at the Moore River Cemetery. They didn't stay long. The Noongar managers of this place see these lights all the time. They've considered light inversions. They've considered reflections off the plains. They've considered whether it was someone playing a trick. They're not those sort of lights.

My grandfather was awoken from his sleep at 10.30 pm on 24 March 1922. Ranjal, one of the Moore River trackers, was knocking on his door. Someone had been seen 'walking with fire sticks, 2½ miles away in direction of Elbow. No one missing from the Camp.' The next day Edward sent Ranjal out to check and see if he could track whoever had been down in the direction of Elbow, the bend of the river near the cemetery, so late at night. Ranjal found nothing, *minyan*, not a peep, not a print.

When I leave this place I pick up some dirt and toss it over my shoulder as I pass back out the gate to remind the spirits of this place to stay where they belong—in this place, not following me as I make my way south.

When Edward came into this place riding that cart along Mogumber West Road, I imagine him looking back over his shoulder and wondering how he came to be here. When he left I imagine that he was looking gladly out to his future again, a little more aware of the subtleties of the lands that he had flung himself into as a young boy-man in tight pants driving wildly out into the landscape. It's that sort of place. It makes you realise that there is more to these countries than the story of triumph and Empire that swept young lads like my grandfather out into the colonies. Edward had entered into histories that most white people manage to avoid their entire lives, Aboriginal histories, and I believe he left transformed by his experiences.

prohibited areas

East Perth is a shadow of its former self. This new inner city redevelopment is a little like the redevelopment of London's East End — over-the-top, exclusively expensive and a little gaudy. To be fair, it had become a bit of a shadow of its former self long before the redevelopment was considered, but its shadow was clearer then. It still had something of the style of its working-class roots in the disused factories, boarded-up houses and shopfronts that have since been knocked down, cleared and replaced with shiny chrome, polished steel and glass. These older roots have been almost completely erased by the neatly paved streets, faux Federation street lighting, and three or four-storey townhouses.

There was always someone to visit in old East Perth. There are still little pockets of it that retain just a hint of its former self, but they are well hidden. The few remaining older houses in East Perth are surrounded. They are an island of Federation simpliciity in a sea of modern villas. The old centre of East Perth, which existed for much of my own time in this city, retained a sense of the original Claisebrook Creek which was a traditional camp site and hunting ground for the Noongars of Perth. In the 1940s and 1950s it was a place where people would camp, when they had to get out of the centre of the city as quickly as possible before dark, needing a place to kip that was outside the Prohibited Area.

In the later 1990s it was still there, the sense of old East Perth: the foundry works in Glyde Street, the Boans Furniture Factory, St Barts Old Men's Home, the Metropolitan Gas Works, the towers of the Electricity Supply, the laneways, the old East Perth pub, the building that used to house the SP Bookie next door to the pub, the Taxi Cooperative's head-quarters, the old horse stables served the Gloucester Park track, and the flame and peppermint trees that once lined the streets.

Super-8 films that I shot in the mid-1990s have become, even in a few short years, archival documents of old East Perth in a city that likes to tear down any sense of its history. Against the same electric-blue Western Australian sky that greeted Edward Smith, small pockets of clouds race across the top of the old East Perth railway bridge. The faded Swan Lager sign straddling the tin roof of the pub fills the screen. Pulling out of frame reveals what remains of the small townscape that existed here for most of the twentieth century. In the buildings that remained, only the diehard businesses had stayed. There was an unwanted bootmaker, a film distribution unit (where they still rolled the film reels by hand for delivery to some of the older cinemas in the city), an almost empty sandwich shop and a bric-a-brac shop that never opened, but retained its window displays of bakelite appliances as if it was part of a museum exhibition.

I was lucky I got in when I did. When they decide to pull something down in Perth they don't waste their time about it, and they don't like to leave traces. Within weeks of filming, the pub was transformed into a sandy patch. The Taxi Cooperative was next to go, followed by the Gas Works, the electricity towers and finally even the streets themselves disappeared. Almost all the old East Perth street names were changed with the redevelopment. There is the odd original street that has survived, like Brown Street, but far many more have disappeared under the tunnel that now cuts through what was then East Perth. Others have been sunk into the fake inlet that replaces the original creek.

To be fair, something did have to be done about the river. It was heavily polluted from years of neglect when it was used as a drain by factories, the old gas works and the old power station. When you neared the stands of bamboo that had taken hold like cancer and strangled the remaining water that flowed from the underground streams that fed the creek, they smelled like rotten eggs. But instead of returning it to its original form, the developers widened it to create an exclusive marina; a kind of long sculpted puddle in which the new residents can park their expensive boats.

The beginnings of the Claisebrook Creek used to run at the back of Saunders Street, near the Old Boans Furniture Factory, which has been converted into a series of modern minimalist apartments. Even in its crumbling state, East Perth was full of life and gave a sense of the original underground watercourses that ran all through the city, emptying out into the Swan River and linking up all the original swamps and freshwater lakes that have since been drained and transformed beyond recognition. Saunders Street was destroyed when they widened the brook. It was turned into a car park, but the original fig trees still mark the edge of what was its bank. Most of the original houses were knocked down in the 1960s and 1970s when East Perth entered its tail spin and they bulldozed most of the old tenements to get Aboriginal tenants out of the centre of the city. They were just beginning to build state housing homes in distant suburbs, and the policy was to sprinkle us all, salt and pepper fashion, into the outlying white neighbourhoods.

My grandmother stayed in East Perth in the 1920s, as did dozens of other Aboriginal women who worked in the city or were in town for medical treatment. They boarded with an older woman named Anna Fielder. Anna's house was at 15 Saunders Street. Anna was an ex-Swan Mission woman who married an Irishman, Gerry Fielder. The Aborigines Department made women stay with the Fielders because they believed that Anna was keeping an eye on them and thus they wouldn't stray while in the city. The Department had no idea. The face that Anna showed to the Department, and the experiences she shared with younger women like my grandmother, were worlds apart. Anna Fielder was sharp. She knew how to play the system to gain as much freedom as possible.

My grandmother told my mother stories about staying at Anna's. I happened to mention one of these stories to someone working for the East Perth Redevelopment Authority. The next time I went down to East Perth I noticed they'd renamed one of the old streets after Anna. Fielder Street is not far from where she used to live, and although it was essentially by accident, I'm glad that she's got a street named after her. To be honest I think she'd laugh her head off about it.

Anna Fielder rented derelict buildings all over this suburb. She once told her landlord she'd only pay half the rent on account of the rats that occupied the other half. She didn't see why she had to pay rent on behalf of rodents. If anyone deserves a street named after them in some recognition of the working-class families that used to call East Perth home, it's probably Anna. I'm sure my grandmother would have approved of her old friend being given such an honour, and would have also seen the funny side to it.

Though the area's gone swanky, if you head west into town on a Friday night when the lights of the Trots turn the East Perth skyline into a summery milky haze, you can easily imagine these old girls walking down the rows of fig trees that were once Saunders Street. If they've won a packet of money on the horses at Belmont or at cards, Jessie Argyle will be heading into the city to meet up with her best friends—Bertha Isaacs, Clarrie Layland, Dolly Wheeler—while Anna Fielder will be tucking her stash of cash under her hat so that her husband Gerry doesn't end up spending it down at the local Kaiora Wine Bar.

My grandmother and women like Anna learned to make what they could of the time they had because they were well aware they didn't have the final say over what happened in their lives. They shared the same philosophy. Take what you can while you can, and never look a gift horse in the mouth

The Department was watching Jessie Argyle closely in 1924. The file that documented her comings and goings and who she worked for and how much she earned and whether she was 'behaving' herself was growing in volume. Jessie was receiving regular telegrams from Chief Protector A.O. Neville telling her that she was in grave danger of being sent to the Moore River Native Settlement if she didn't settle down and work hard in the positions they sent her to. It was their standard threat. It was predictable and it was frightening. Her workdays were long and hard. Her bad leg, that had inflamed soon after young Enid Sherwood's death in Bridgetown, grew worse each year. Jessie served her time with various employers. She knew what her mistresses would do if she let them, they would rule her life and think nothing of it. They would write letters, make phone calls and send telegrams to the Aborigines Department complaining about her performance.

A friend of my grandmother's from those days, Alice Bassett, referred to this feeling of being constantly watched by white authorities, even within the confines of cottages and houses, as living in a place where 'the walls had eyes'. The Aborigines Department was under funded and understaffed but Mr Neville was obsessed by his charges and used every employer, policeman and magistrate as his eyes and ears. He was the wrong man in the wrong place at the wrong time. I've read thousands of the departmental documents that he created, nurtured and wielded as his mechanism of control of our communities. His exceptional adherence to procedure, his ability to sniff out and follow a trail of insubordination, and his blind faith in his own 'calling' to 'save' the Aboriginal people of the west was our greatest burden.

My grandmother knew the man well enough from the many times she had already been through his office in East Perth, and had good reason to distrust him. Every Aboriginal Elder I've met who knew Neville disliked the man. They were not wary of him out of a naive misplacement of blame for their troubles, as some historians seem intent on claiming. These Aboriginal men and women lived the realities of his personal intervention in their lives.

All the women who knew my grandmother and who had to do the same work she did in white homes spoke of her skill at sewing, her abilities as a cook and her knowledge of 'the drill' of housework. All these women knew 'the drill' backwards and took pride in the work they did as domestic servants and the small petty intricacies that were demanded of them as they polished, cooked and served for white families. It was what they were trained for. It was what they were taught in place of the education that was supposed to be provided to them in missions and government settlements. Some employers acknowledged this hard work. Most of them didn't.

Many of the white women that Jessie and other women worked for did not see or imagine their employees having lives outside the households in which they worked. These black women were bonded labourers. They lived in the homes of the people they served. They waited on the mistress and her husband, their children, their relatives and their guests. They lived in the streets, suburbs and towns that were made up of these white households, often hundreds of miles away from their own relatives, and from the companionship of other women like themselves. It was an intimate space into which women like my grandmother were sent. There was no more intimate space than the home. But it was not their own.

Hundreds of women worked in the homes surrounding Circe Circle, or running along Stirling Highway, or backing onto the Swan River, but equally as many worked for not-so-well-off farmers, or the wives of policemen, or the families of furniture sellers, or corner shop owners. Aboriginal women's wages were so low that almost anyone could afford to employ them. These women were in constant demand. The production line of the removal of Aboriginal children led to the creation of a cheap Aboriginal labour force. Tracking my own grandmother's movements across the pages of her file reveals houses and dwellings far removed from the imagined mansions and manor houses that people generally associate with the sort of family that could afford to employ a servant.

These families owned the space, and for some people, it seems they thought they owned their servants too. Who Jessie saw, what she spent her money on, where she went on her day off, what time she made it back in at night, the state of her clothes, the size of her body—they made all this their concern too, in their letters to Mr Neville, who gladly received this information and stored it up on my grandmother's personal file.

If Aboriginal women were sent to a good family who treated them and their work respectfully they counted themselves lucky. For my grandmother, I know from her own letters pleading not to be sent to the Moore River Native Settlement, that this was a major threat employers used to keep her in line. Those women who had not already been sent there, heard about it from other women who had, and they feared it. Most of the employers Jessie worked for knew she had a fear of the Settlement. If they were unhappy with my grandmother's attitude they'd suggest in their own letters to the Department that she should be given some time there to teach her a little respect.

Jessie had been in and out of hospital for years. She had travelled from town to town by train, to wherever the Department sent her to work. On some days the pain in her leg was so bad she could not work. Most of the women she worked for thought she was malingering. One mistress wrote to the Department recommending that the Settlement was the only place for 'a girl like her to teach her a lesson.' It is strange how Moore River is so absent from people's minds today, when employers in 1924 were all too well aware of it, and all too aware that it could be used as a threat to make their servants work.

After Jessie left the Sherwood family, her working life followed a pattern of disruption. She lived under the constant threat of incarceration at the Settlement and her wages were regularly cut or withheld without recourse. It must have seemed a recurring bad dream to be trapped in households with controlling mistresses and without any sense of escape. In the summer of 1924 her leg had become so bad that she was sent to the hospital in Perth for treatment. As they did with all Aboriginal women who were in the city on business, or for medical treatment, or between jobs, the Department ordered her to stay with Mrs Anna Fielder of East Perth.

Anna Fielder knew the lot of domestic servants well. She was also adept at keeping the Aborigines Department, in particular Mr Neville, at arm's length. I suspect that the Chief Protector had never inspected Anna's place himself or he would never have allowed her to board Aboriginal women. If ever Neville had contact with Anna it would be by mail or when she dressed up and went into the Aborigines Department office, put on the dog and conned him into thinking what she wanted him to believe. She'd managed to keep him in the dark for years.

Claisebrook Creek flowed past the back of Anna's Saunders Street house. Perth Hospital was a short walk away. The local East Perth football team was known ironically as 'The Royals', it being one of the poorest areas of the city.

While my grandmother recuperated, making daily trips to the hospital to see the doctor, Anna Fielder made sure that she learned the ropes of how to survive the Department and the city.

In 1924, just as today, there were few places where Aboriginal people could go in the city without being noticed and watched by the police. But there were some private spaces, small holes in the net, where people could get together without incurring trouble. These were the pockets of black spaces, meeting places; the White Seats opposite the Perth Railway Station, the Government Gardens at the foot of Government House on the Esplanade near the river, the dugout behind the Aborigines Department, or, in later years, the Bull Paddock at the bottom of East Perth.

The lessons that women learned as girls while in the Mission, of looking out for girls younger than themselves, continued in the outside world. There were hundreds of domestic servants working throughout the state. At any time there were dozens working in the city of Perth. When free of the confines of the homes that they were sent to work in, these women kept an eye out for each other. They kept in touch by mail. They waited on their days off at places where they knew other women would congregate. They would gather until there was a group large enough for them to feel secure and they would head into the city together.

Anna's house became one of these places. If women were employed at a house in Perth they soon learned through the grapevine who was staying where, who was in town for medical treatment and when Anna Fielder was setting the table for one of her marathon poker games. Anna was a cardsharp and a gambler, and she liked to be regarded as knowing a thing or two about horseflesh. Between cutting the deck, dealing the hands and tapping her clay pipe clean on the table, she filled in her younger charges on the finer points of managing the Aborigines Department.

Sitting around Anna's table Jessie learned that the money the Department took from her wages was used by the Department to pay for everything from her medical treatment and boarding at Anna's, to train fares for places that she was sent to against her will. The Department set up 'trust' accounts the women had no control over or access to and they deducted money from it as they saw fit. In 1924 the Department was taking fifteen shillings a week out of my grandmother's twenty shilling wage and using it to finance their management of her life. The five shillings Jessie received was what the Aborigines Department described as pocket money.

My grandmother learned that the government medical officer, who was the only doctor at the hospital she could see, and who wasn't thought to be that much chop, was paid for with her own wages. The medical treatment that many Aboriginal women thought was part of the conditions of the job, as recompense for low wages, was paid out of their own accounts, controlled by Mr Neville. The clothes that they had to request from the Department, and even the train fare for their incarceration in the Moore River Native Settlement, was paid for by their own sweat. They were even paying for the people who escorted them on the train.

Anna didn't care when women came and went from her house. As long as they paid their bills, ate the food she prepared for them and didn't leave a mess, they could do as they pleased. For her part, Anna kept Mr Neville out of the way with glowing reports on the women who stayed with her, leaving them free to enjoy the time they spent out of the watchful eyes of their employers. The women were free to catch up with family, see their boyfriends, head off to the Government Gardens, take in the pictures, go for a swim down at the river or head out to the camps. Their time was their own.

If, however, they didn't mind a game of stud poker after dinner, or a turn at the horses on a Saturday, well that was all right too. By day Jessie would catch up with other women around town, or meet up with Dinah Sutton and Nellie Lyndon down at Government Gardens. When someone bought a box brownie, the women began recording their own lives in the city. They took photographs of themselves in large groups at Government Gardens, or down by the river. They took photos posing in the back yard of Anna's house, or out on the front verandah, and down by the Claisebrook Creek. They never took photographs in the street. There were never any white onlookers watching from somewhere in the background.

These were images that were taken carefully, of private and intimate gatherings away from the scrutiny of strangers.

They secluded themselves within the wide open spaces that the city offered. They spent their hard-earned money on tiny two-by-three inch prints, and circulated them amongst themselves. They captured their moments of freedom in the city, secreted them away in their belongings and took them back to their places of service as reminders that they weren't completely alone. They had their own family of women like themselves and the city became their place of reunion. Mostly the women couldn't get served in white shops, but at Con's Cafe on Adelaide Terrace they were served if they agreed to sit in a back booth, which was curtained off from the other customers. It was a kind of a compromise. At Con's they could have a cuppa in peace. The whites in the cafe would have no idea they were sharing the establishment with black servants. Sometimes Jessie would gather with some other women and head down to Cottesloe beach where a good number of other women worked, or back to Anna's place for a game of cards.

While her leg healed my grandmother began to work the system as Anna taught her. The Department was loath to give women cash out of their accounts. They preferred to give them redeemable government coupons that would be exchanged for goods at city stores. Instead of being able to hand over their own money, they were forced to hand over ration coupons as if they were receiving government handouts. Anna taught my grandmother how to request a coupon for clothing, and told her which places in the city would let you cash it for money. She learned to pretend to borrow money from other women, to plead with the Department to pay the imaginary debt, and once the Department had reluctantly agreed to pay the other woman, split it with them on a day out on the town. She learned how to deal cards fast and clean, to watch her cards closely, and to always pay and collect on her real debts.

White City was known as 'Cooee City' or 'Ugly Land' to regulars who frequented the rides, the stalls and the contests contained within its carnival atmosphere at the foot of the city. It was run by the Ugly Men's Society, a charitable institution, and was basically an amusement park at the base of William Street, right on the Swan River. Jessie had been going to White City with other women on their days off. There were wooden slides, boxing tents, dance floors, games of chance, and alongside was an open-air picture theatre in summer. It was a drawcard for any Noongars in the city as it was considered a good meeting place, avoided as it was by the more conservative and self-righteous citizens of Perth who would not want to be seen in any establishment that welcomed Aboriginal people, or was considered rough.

At White City the women would catch up with friends who'd got out of Moore River, watch Jackie Layland boxing or riding the broncos, and enjoy the cool evening breeze wafting off the river and through the city. It was time of relative freedom for Jessie after years of being shunted around the country by the Department. She was a young woman of twenty-four, growing in confidence and getting around town with other young women.

Edward Smith was boarding with Jack Bayly and his wife Rachel in Norfolk Street, North Perth. He was thirty-four years old, still spoke in a whisper, but when he went out on the town, he dressed like a London lad heading out to Leicester Square on a Saturday night. He didn't drink, was a hard worker and, after Moore River, had built up a steady circle of black friends who he would meet up with down at 'Cooee City'. I can see how he would be eager to leave the young couple he boarded with to enjoy their own company, and after grooming himself meticulously, would walk through Hyde Park, down Lake Street, across the Horseshoe Bridge and on to White City.

Maybe he was just heading down to White City to chase up someone who owed him money. Maybe he was heading down to pay back a small loan. There seems to have been an endless amount of lending and borrowing going on between the lads he knew. Maybe Edward was thinking that, at thirty-four, it was time he found himself someone to settle down with. Maybe he had spotted Jessie Argyle in a group of women from Anna Fielder's as they lined the boxing tent to watch the Noongar boys try their luck. Maybe she spotted him and decided that he looked good in his carefully cut suits. They may have been introduced by Amy Mippy, whom Edward knew from his stint at Moore River. Maybe she asked Amy to introduce her to the shy white man who seemed at ease around Noongars.

There are different versions of how Edward and Jessie came together. Some old fellas are emphatic that they met at Moore River when Edward was second boss and Jessie came into the Settlement for a short time and was assigned as his servant. That version believes that it was the scandal of their 'affair' that saw him leave the Settlement, and saw her sent out into the country by the Department in order to be kept away from him. But there is no mention of their first meeting in Jessie's departmental file and Edward's diaries of this particular summer are missing. Another version claimed they met at White City. What I do know is that when he fell, he fell hard. What I do know is that they used every spare moment to spend time with each other in the city. What I also know is that it would not be long before Edward Smith would enter most definitely into Jessie Argyle's departmental file and, more importantly, they would each become the most important people in each other's lives. By the winter of 1924 his diary is filled with talk of her, of meeting up with her at the railway station, of taking her to the pictures, or to tea at the Grand. When they met I don't know, but if I had to lay money on it, I'd bet that they met at White City, and that they cut an unusual couple there.

Edward called Jessie 'Cully' and she referred to him as 'Miff' or 'Squeaker'. He bought her presents of shoes and bags and introduced her to his friends the Baylys. Edward, 'Eddie' from Emanuel School in Westminster, London, met up with 'Cully', Jessie Argyle, 'Gypsy' a Miriwoong woman from Argyle Station. They were both of marrying age. He was a wiry suntanned Englishman with a kind face and a cheeky way of turning his head when she took his photograph. She was a good-looking solid woman who didn't waste time, who did as she pleased as long as she could get away with it. She was disarming, quick-witted, and in control, and he was all vaudeville and magic tricks and had seen a bit of the world.

They went on a picnic in the hills with friends. They photographed each other and sent each other small cryptic messages on the backs of the prints. They spent a day at Serpentine in the hills, walking through valley country, sitting at the base of waterfalls, drinking fresh water scooped from the stream. They're young and strong. They're standing together arm in arm in a stream while a friend takes their photograph, looking for all the world like there is nothing wrong with them being together, and as far as they're concerned there isn't, any fool can see it.

They were crossing boundaries of race without care, going places where they would have been noticed and discussed. They were having the time of their lives in their first six months together. They had both travelled a long way from their homelands. They were not supposed to meet. The society in which they met did not approve of mixed-race couples. They were not *allowed* to meet as far as the Aborigines Department was concerned, and they were about to learn that the hard way.

In the following months, when Jessie had to return to the country to work, they would meet in the city at least once a week, and two and sometimes three times a week when she was working in the city. Edward would take Jessie out to 'tea' at one of the many tea-houses in the city, perhaps overcoming the problem of being served by using one of the larger establishments such as Boans or Albany Bell's. They would take a walk to the Government Gardens by the river before heading back into the city to the Grand Theatre. Then they might head down to White City where the buckjumping and boxing drew everyone. They stayed together as long as Jessie could get away with it. Her employers didn't like her staying out at night and even though it was her time off, they would complain to the Aborigines Department. When Jessie felt that one employer was getting too involved in her life she would, contrary to the wishes of the Department, find herself a job elsewhere—until the next people became troublesome, when she would find another family to work for. Jessie was doing anything she could to stay in the city, but what she didn't realise was that all those complaints from employers were adding up on her file.

After being sent out to work in different country positions, Jessie decided that the only way to be free of employers in rural areas would be if they didn't want you working for them. It appears she began her own campaign of resistance. There were instances in her file of employers trying to short-pay her. The Department ignored her letters of protest and so she withdrew her labour. She decided to engage in a go-slow campaign, cleaning only what was necessary, refusing to do anything that was not essential. She decided she would work at three-quarter speed if they were going to pay her three-quarter pay, and each time an employer complained it was documented and entered into her file.

Telegrams and letters were sent complaining that 'Jessie would effectively cure one of having a coloured girl', and these letters resulted in further warnings from the Department. In one instance my grandmother called the Department's bluff and ran away from her employer. When she was threatened with being sent to the Settlement, Jessie went out and found her own jobs in the city. She would stay with Anna Fielder for a week or two, have herself a good holiday in the city, and only let the Department know where she was after having found herself a place to work. The Department was incensed, but was loath to remove a woman from employment—it made too much money out of them. The

Department charged a fee to employers to employ Aboriginal people. It was in part a money-making exercise.

In early 1924 Jessie began working for some people in South Perth. It was a bad call. This family decided to move to the country and, as she was their servant, and considered a part of their household, they wanted to take her with them. They had the Department's blessing, but not Jessie's, and she took herself back to the city without anyone's permission. She found another job in the city and settled in, but the complaints began again. She was being watched, and her times of coming and going were being noted. A visit was paid to the Department by a particularly interfering employer. Words were said about her staying out every night. This employer's recommendation was simple: 'Send her to the Settlement.'

Jessie tried to stay one step ahead of them, to play right down to the line, to leave a little time for them to forget her last encounter with them. Then she would try it all over again. She had won a few hands, but they were playing for the game. They were playing with the knowledge contained in the file that they kept on her. They kept every letter, every telegram, every scrawled note or hint of gossip and every note that she herself had written them, recorded every telephone conversation in neat type, and every interview to which she had been summoned to answer questions, and every judgement made upon her performance. Jessie was betting as if each encounter with them was a new gamble, as if the table was laid clean with a fresh cloth. She was playing as if the deck had been cut fairly, to see who would make the first deal, sifting the cards back and forth, tossing them out fair. But the Department's deck was an old one. It was large, detailed, precise and meticulously marked in their favour. When the cards were dealt and the play began, they had already seen her hand, long before she even had a chance to play a card.

The Department decided it was time to collect. It decided to collect by taking my grandmother's liberty as payment. The file was opened again. More telegrams were sent to the new superintendent of the Moore River Native Settlement, Mr Brodie: 'It is considered twelve months at the Settlement will do her good.'

Aboriginal women were only supposed to be under the charge of the Department until the age of twenty-one, however the wording of the Act was vague enough that any Aboriginal person of almost any age could be moved around the state at the will of the Chief Protector, without any legal redress.

On 30 April 1924, Edward came to East Perth to say goodbye. Amy Mippy was down from Moore River waiting with Jessie to escort her back to the Settlement. Edward saw her off on the ten o'clock train and went back to his lodgings and began to pack his things. He must have imagined there was a momentous year ahead because he went out and bought a new Radio Press Wireless Handbook and Diary. It was already May so he took out a pencil and crossed off the months of January, February, March and April immediately. Then he wrote his first entry: 'Cully left Perth for Mogumber with Amy Mippy.' He was being methodical. He paid his board, packed his belongings and decided to kiss Perth goodbye again.

Edward's ship slipped quietly out of the Port of Fremantle and swung north-west. It moved away from the coast, taking him far from the city. He was moving away from the South-West where he arrived in 1909, from Jessie, the Department, and from his old farm. The ship headed west out to sea, and then turned full north. Edward had made the arrangements in Perth. He was heading out into his own exile, past Geraldton, to Shark Bay—sandalwood country. He had lined up a job through a friend of a friend. He was to work for the Creeds of Hamelin Pool, carting wood, wool, tin, food, anything from the Bay, where the lighters left the state ships and beached to unload their cargo. His run would include Hamelin Pool Station, Nanga Station, Talma Station, and all the camps in between for as long as it took.

He knew that this time Jessie would not get off lightly. He had tried to intervene on her behalf, and had been warned off by the secretary of the Aborigines Department, Ernest Copping. Edward had come to know Copping from his time at Moore River. As Neville's responsibilities now focused on the North in the form of his new role as head of the new Department of the North-West, Aldrich and Copping had taken over responsibility for Moore River. Edward had even photographed Copping in a group shot with the superintendent, Major Campbell, in 1922.

Edward and Copping had kept in touch over the years. Perth was a small place and people knew each other through friends of friends. Edward no doubt thought that his friend may have shown him some leeway as he tried to persuade Copping not to send Jessie to Moore River, but Copping didn't listen. Instead, Edward was warned that he could be imprisoned for cohabitation and sentenced to three months gaol. Edward was told that he was the cause for Jessie's imprisonment. His request for

Jessie's freedom was only to make her imprisonment seem more important to the Department. No action was taken against him. He looked for a way out of it, and thought he saw a loophole, or so I believe. Money.

He seemed intent on amassing enough money to set himself up as a solid marriage prospect. Then they could not stop them from being together. There had been other mixed marriages, such as Anna Fielder's, but these were uncommon and had generally been approved before Neville came to power. Edward seems to have thought that if he proposed marriage that would prove he was not the 'low type of white man' that Neville assumed any white man must be if he was attracted to an Aboriginal woman. It is true, money talked in a frontier capital like Perth, but my grandfather was forgetting the even more powerful concept of race in deciding the lines of what was deemed acceptable in wider Western Australian society.

Hamelin Pool is now a lunar landscape compared to its former self. The sandalwood that once forested this peninsula has been completely harvested. The remaining spinifex and orange-red soil stretch for miles over sand dunes, ripples of sand covering over the tracks of kangaroos, snakes and other small animals that survive there. On a clear day you would swear that you could see the ocean as the heat mists rise off the sand creating the illusory effect of distant floating water. Spinifex clumps and huge anthill mounds shaped like fertility figures dot the landscape between the rise of one dune and the fall of another. By night the stars are clear and focused. You can see the Milky Way in all its glory stretching across the night sky as the Southern Cross swings around the South Celestial Pole. The night sky, clear air, the sound of the wind off the ocean, the dry heat of the middle of the day. This is what Edward escaped to.

The base camp where Edward worked from the winter of 1924 and all through the dry summer of that year is surrounded by powdery red sand and low clumps of coastal scrub. Tourists pile into the region to see the dolphins at Monkey Mia, but it is also station country, as it was when Edward made his way north. The beaches stretch for miles, crisp white sand that shifts and changes with the moderate tides. In 1925 the only way in and out was by boat or by plane. Edward crisscrossed the spinifex dunes in his truck, watching the mirage ocean float in the distance, and sleeping out under the stars on the back of the vehicle. The bush turkeys that he shot from time to time for food are now nowhere to be seen. The area that was once his base camp, where he watched the sky for a hint of rain and the hills for a sign of company, has disappeared. It's probably around here somewhere, hidden under one of these shifting sand dunes. It's beautiful country. It draws you into yourself through its simplicity and subtlety.

The early morning light reveals the myriad animals that still exist in this harsh and wide open landscape. Kangaroos, snakes, small birds and the odd goanna leave their nocturnal signatures. By early morning, once the breeze strikes up, the tracks will simply disappear, just like Edward's camp.

It wasn't so much a base camp for him as a turning point. The long quiet evenings gave him time to think about how he was going to handle his next move. He could sit and read Jessie's letters over and over, and study the photograph that she had sent him from Moore River. He could just as easily have travelled further on to another country. State ships were regularly heading north to Ceylon, Manila and Hong Kong. I believe that this was when he decided to stay and make his own claim for himself and for Jessie.

Jessie's letters began arriving within weeks. They moved from hand to hand, snuck out of the Settlement by a visiting priest, or with other women being sent out to work, or a man going to the hospital for treatment, which was rare. The letters would travel safely within warm coat pockets or calico bags thrown over shoulders, along the road to Mogumber Siding, and down the tracks by train to the city before finally being posted north to Edward at Hamelin Pool. They would be carried by steamer, be off-loaded by lighter and sorted at Shark Bay, before making their bumpy way along red dirt tracks, past the sandalwood cutters, the sheep farmers and the salty bores, into Edward's camp. They snuck past the superintendent's censor, behind the Department's back, and safely into my grandfather's care.

Then Edward would reply. He would have mail taken down by one of the Yamatji men going south to visit relatives, or with a friend to hand on to Jack Bayly or other trusted friends in Perth. From there Jack, or whoever had been entrusted with the letter, would hand it on to one of Edward's mates who visited White City, and it would be passed around until someone was heading back to the Settlement.

Edward kept neat notes of the transactions in his diary, 'Wrote letter to Cully. Gave it to Russell to give to Jimmy Holt to take down for Jessie.' The letter would travel back out along the train line, along the Mogumber

West Road and into the compound. Hidden safely on someone's person, it would pass right under the superintendent's nose again, while he opened all the other letters that had arrived by mail, checking for anything suspicious, any hint of trouble, and arrive safely into Jessie's hand.

Sometimes it would take weeks for a letter to arrive. Sometimes two would arrive on the same day. Sometimes a reply to a letter sent weeks before would be stranded in Perth while a second, sent asking after the first, would arrive ahead of it. They were jumbled and furtive communications.

Edward settled into the rhythm of Hamelin Pool. He worked long hard days carting stores and produce to and from the coast and the stations. He worked on his truck, mended the constant punctures, helped to dig out camel teams that became bogged, andkept a constant watch on the horizon for any sign of rain, noting it in his diary along with short personal notes to himself. 'Missing Cull.' It was hot, dry work, but it paid well and he kept himself tight, saving, amassing another sum of money, living rough, sleeping on the truck, under the truck, in the feed shed, spending money only on his cigarettes, taking no time off to head into Carnarvon or Shark Bay. He was just working, working each day.

It seems that Ernest Copping was playing a double game with Edward. Jessie's departmental file allows us to see beyond what Copping told Edward as he locked my grandmother away. Copping was also a friend of Edward's boss up in Hamelin Bay, and he was writing to Edward in Shark Bay, sending him notes about what the 'old man', Mr Neville, was up to in the north; about the death of an older inmate at the Settlement that Edward had known when he worked there in 1922, and snippets of gossip from the city, but there was never any mention of Jessie. He sent Edward a parcel of books to read.

Edward requested that someone be released from the Settlement to take up work with him on the Shark Bay run. Georgie Merritt's release was approved by Copping and he was sent up by boat. Edward had known George from his own time at Moore River. It wasn't much, but any chance to get work away from the Settlement was eagerly taken. Not only did it get people out, but it gave them a chance to get money together to help their family members who were still locked away.

Copping advised Edward that he was sending George up to Hamelin Pool, but gave no news about Jessie, even though it was Copping who would determine how long she would be kept at Moore River. For any news, Edward knew he had to rely on his own mail run.

Edward's lists had ended. He was no longer a man who needed to make long tallies of small personal items to sum up his life or make sense of himself. He knew what he wanted and had perhaps decided that the only way to get it was through hard work.

Jessie worked at the Settlement, was locked up at night in the girls' dormitory, worked by day in the sewing room, and braced herself to survive a freezing winter at Moore River. Edward set himself to work in Yamatji country, carting away the sandalwood and huge bales of wool, and loading the stockpiles of goods that filled the white sandy beaches onto the lighters that plied the waves between land and the steamers just beyond the breakers. He shot the odd bush turkey for dinner, shared a fire with work mates, and watched the sky as the new airmail run operated by Major Brearley made its way up the coast towards Carnarvon, droning just above the sound of the waves and wind.

Had he taken time to stop and look at himself, I believe he would have seen a glimmer of that same boy that had disembarked from the *Orontes* in 1909, heading bush to take on whatever lay beyond the hills that rimmed the city, his imagined future lying in that vast expanse of country. But now he had a very different motivation. The expanse no longer contained his imagined future; it was now a personal past. Those dreams had not been realised, but had been replaced by something else that was larger than himself—his commitment to someone else.

He could so easily have hopped on a boat and not turned north, but east to Sydney. He could have just moved on. He could have simply returned to Perth and ignored Jessie, forgotten her, and no one would have questioned him. He could have avoided any contact with blackfellas. Edward could have decided not to return to White City; could have stopped looking towards the White Seats and kept his eyes straight ahead and his ears closed if he should ever have to walk through the train station, in case Jessie or one of her friends should see him; could have decided to close that chapter in his life. But the fact was, Edward was in for the long haul.

The Settlement, 1924. It was overpopulated. It could be a dangerous place. People had come from all over, from Malngin country at the furthest tip of the East Kimberley, to Mineng country at the southern start of the Bight. They were all thrown in together, without any thought for the cultural boundaries that existed well before colonisation and areas of separation and exclusion.

Granny Bella Bropho was put in Moore River with her sisters and mother in 1922, while Edward was working there. When they shifted her from Carrolup, it was the second time she had been forcibly moved by the Department. The first time, when Granny was taken away from her family, they placed her in Dulhi Gunyah Mission near Perth. It was not much different from Swan Mission. It was run by the Aborigines Inland Mission, and was mostly filled with Noongar and Wongi children.

Granny Bella was at Dulhi Gunyah a few years and could remember Mr Neville coming up to the Mission in 1915 to check it out. She could remember his manner, brisk and officious, as he passed the open gate that she and the other children were swinging on as he entered Dulhi Gunyah and made his way up to a meeting of all the white benefactors and Miss Annie Loch, the missionary who ran it. They knew nothing about Mr Neville then, except his name, and decided to rhyme Neville and Devil together into a nice chant to greet him on a later visit when he came marching up to the gate. They soon learned that he was a man to be feared, and kept these games to themselves, staying well clear when he came back.

Soon after, Neville removed the government subsidy and Dulhi Gunyah was closed. All the children were placed in Carrolup Settlement, where Bella was reunited with her mother, old Granny Clara Harris, who'd ended up there after being cleared out of the South-West. Not long after that though, it was Carrolup's turn for economic rationalisation. Bella, her sisters, her mother Clara and the entire population of Carrolup were transported in specially ordered carriages to Moore River, where she was to spend the rest of her childhood.

Edward left the Settlement in 1922, but Granny stayed there for more than ten years straight until she was married. When she was a woman with her own children she still spent time moving in and out of the Settlement. Granny can see all those old people pass in front of her cataract-clouded eyes even as we sit on her verandah and look out over the Swan Valley: the trackers, the bosses, the women in the sewing room, the children in the compound, the camps where she would go after she married Thomas, my grandmother's brother. They were all real for her. Granny Bella says it's like the ground that exists below the city, that no matter what is built on it, it remains Noongar land.

Granny Bella can remember the nights. 'That's when the fights used to start up. There were a lot of north girls there, north people would be Carnarvon up. It used to be the Nor'west girls against the Sou'west girls.

Ooooh they'd fight over anythin' at all. It would start up over the talk. They'd talk about one another, then that yarn'd get around, and there you are, there's a fight. You'd hear them talkin'. "There's goin' to be a fight in the dormitory tonight." Then when the doors shut they'd pull the beds all back and they'd get into it.'

There was no way out, so there was nowhere for the anger, the frustration and the hunger that fed it, to go. There were some good fights too, and I know my grandmother was in them because no one could give such a good right hook as my grandmother — able to knock a person clean flat and across a room, without having had any practice. Granny Bella can laugh about it now because there is distance, and the fights were just a part of daily Settlement life.

My grandmother worked in the sewing room. There is a well-known photograph of the women working at the Singer machines. The week's work is piled high on the shelves that line the wall: shirts for Fremantle Prison, pants for Claremont Asylum, shimmies for Moore River children. In the middle is Dinah Noble, and behind her Aunty Bertha Isaacs, and behind her, hiding from the lens, barefoot and head down, Jessie Argyle. The superintendent, Brodie, didn't like my grandmother. He let his feelings be known in a report to Mr Copping at the Department.

> With reference to Jessie Argyle … Jessie has a pretty good opinion of herself … She is employed in the Sewing Room and for a native is fairly satisfactory … She is a bit of an agitator amongst the other girls.

The Settlement had changed a great deal since my grandfather was there in 1922. The biggest change was the new superintendent. Men who had worked under the old superintendent, Jack Campbell, found him to be a military man who operated as if he was still at the front. Most of the women that I spoke with didn't have much to do with Campbell. They came under Mrs Campbell, the matron, but they didn't think that Campbell was as bad as Brodie, who everyone hated.

Jack Campbell spent his last night alive at one of the dances held in the church. Within the confines of the institutional life of the Settlement, the dances were a chance for people to let their hair down and were something to look forward to, but they were fairly sporadic, sometimes happening two weeks in a row, sometimes only every two or three weeks, depending on the mood of the superintendent.

The evening Mr Campbell died he had been drinking. He floated into the dance in an unusually good mood. He danced with a few of the women, which was uncharacteristic, then scooped up the violin from old Ben Jeddah and played a lick. He played the hymn 'There is a Happy Land', and everyone was surprised at how good he was. He was gone before the dancing ended, driving to Perth on business, but he never made it. His car ran off the road near the railway tracks.

Most thought it was the drink. Some of the older Noongars thought his death was inevitable after he stripped the flowers from one of the many moodjar trees that surround the Settlement. These are sacred trees. *Wadjellas* call them Christmas trees, because in December their usually subtle green foliage explodes into a rich golden-orange glow, unmistake-able in the land. Campbell took these blooms and hung them around the Big House for Christmas. He even had them sitting in the middle of the family's Christmas dinner table.

Granny Bella remembered it, and told me how the campies waited and watched, knowing that something was going to happen. When his car ran off the road, everyone believed that this was Campbell's punishment for desecrating the moodjar trees.

It happened just before Jessie was sent to Moore River, while Edward was still in Perth. He attended Major Campbell's funeral and paid his respects to Mrs Campbell and their two sons.

Some of the old people used to call the moodjar the Sorry Tree. Noongars know to give it more respect than to cut it, and Nor'westers soon came to realise it was a tree to be reckoned with. When the previous superintendent, Mitchell, the one before Campbell, was looking for a new site for the cemetery, he had the sense to ask the people of the Settlement where would be the best place to bury the dead. The old cemetery was located at Elbow, just off the Mogumber West Road, between the road and the river. It had been located there because it was close to a traditional Yuat burial site. There were six Settlement people buried there between 1917 and 1920 when the Bandys, whose farm was adjacent to the Settlement, objected to the cemetery being so close to a watercourse.

The watercourse was an access path that ran from the road to the river. Such watercourses were used by farmers to access water for their stock and were considered as a common, cutting through any private land that was deemed necessary for all users of the river.

Superintendent Mitchell asked Neville to approach the local Roads Board to have the watercourse included in the original Moore River Settlement Reserve because he hadn't seen anyone use it since 1918. To his knowledge the Bandy brothers always watered their stock further down the river. However, the Bandys were incensed that the Roads Board were considering releasing the watercourse, and complained. It seems that some farmers camped there with their stock on the way back to their properties, and they didn't like the idea of being camped so close to a cemetery. The Roads Board supported the farmers, and the old cemetery had to be shifted. Mitchell complained that the Bandys didn't even really know where the reserve was, and were continually trespassing on Aboriginal Reserve Land when they watered their stock, but in the end the Roads Board won out and the cemetery, including the bodies already buried, were earmarked to be shifted.

Old Moses, one of the oldest and most knowledgeable inmates of the Settlement, set Mitchell straight about the moodjar tree, and so the new cemetery was placed on a high stand of moodjars, a few miles south of the compound. It was close enough that people could visit during the day, but far enough come night-time, when spirits might wander. Mitchell wrote to Neville asking that

> ... a sufficient number of Banksia of the vernacular mungite trees be left growing inside the cemetery so that the superstitions of the natives may be decently recognised. The native timber inside the cemetery will give rest to the spirits of the dead, 'who will not be as likely to wander'.

The moodjar tree is part of the cycle of spirit, death, rebirth and renewal that was at the centre of Settlement culture.

Mitchell was smart enough not to carry out Neville's request that the bodies of those buried at the old cemetery be exhumed and shifted. Repeated requests for those bodies to be shifted were ignored because Mitchell knew that he would lose the respect of the inmates if he pressed the matter. He couldn't expect the inmates to exhume bones, and if he did it himself, he knew that he couldn't guarantee his own safety. Years later when a dam was being dug some of the remains were exposed and were duly covered over again. The dam site was shifted.

The first person buried at the new cemetery was a baby girl. By the time Jessie arrived in 1924, it had been in use for three years and more than fifty people had been buried there. The favoured method of burial by the Department was the 'plank method'. This involved wrapping the body in a blanket and placing it on a plank that could be reused. It would not be until 1926, after the inmates ripped timber from buildings to bury old Mr Mippy, an Elder of great respect, that the Department conceded it would have to supply timber for the purpose of coffins for burial.

Granny Bella remembered the plank method with disgust: 'They'd sew them all up in a hessian bag, stitch them all up. They never had a coffin to put them in, they reckoned there was no more boards to make a coffin. They'd stitch 'im up in a bag, the shape of his head, down around his arms. It's wicked! We had to follow 'im three miles out to the cemetery, all standing behind looking at that man all the time while 'is head just moved all around.'

There were only a few crosses at the cemetery. Those few that existed had been scraped together from bits of rough timber found in the scrub. The practice was to place a jam tin at the foot of each grave with the name of the deceased painted on the side. This was before coffins were provided.

Life in the Settlement was bleak. The church dances were one of the few chances for enjoyment. Women made their claim on dance partners for the night: 'Alley Owns Him' ('He's mine'). Dresses for dance nights were run up in the sewing room from bits of saved material, between the making of clothes for the prisons and hospitals. Special tobacco was rolled in the ashes by old girls who'd spend the night chewing slowly and deliberately and watching the proceedings. Dance steps were practised at lunchbreaks by younger inmates.

Ben Jeddah and Charlie Bullfrog were brought over from New Norcia Mission for the violin and squeezebox music, and someone would accompany them on a tea-chest drum. The church pews would be pulled back and the floors swept for the one night of the week, or the fortnight, that everyone looked forward to, from the camps to the compound. Tommy Bropho had returned to the Settlement after working in the Wheatbelt in 1923. He and Bella would marry at the same Settlement church later in 1926. Granny Bella could remember Jessie and Tommy singing together. 'Her and Tommy used to sing together at the dances. She'd sing in a low tone and Tommy could go high.' Jessie's eleven months at the Settlement had one consolation, my grandmother was reunited with her brother who she would only have seen sporadically since he left Swan Mission.

On dance nights, some of the older men, the Boolya and the Marbans, used the night as a cover to go down the back of the Settlement where there was a grove of young pines in a perfect depression in the earth. They too would be dancing, but they would dance business. They would sing for their own country, and for the country that surrounded the camps and the compound. They would be heard by those who knew to listen for them, beyond the pines to the moodjar trees. Old people from the Settlement days speak of spiritual battles between Marban men from the North and Boolya men from the South. There is a giant moodjar tree in the main area of the camps. A hollow was cut out of it and everyone knew that Marban men used to catch people's spirits and place them in the hollow of that tree. Granny Bella used to call it the 'Boolya Tree' and sometimes the 'Sorry Tree', because you could hear the weeping of people's spirits trapped in the tree. The only way they got out was to get a Boolya or another Marban to sing them out of that tree.

There were women's dances also, and Granny Bella could remember the women's dances held down on the flat near the camp site. 'The women, they'd dance on one side, and the men all on the other side. They used to do the snake dance, paint themselves up with all the colours, and do the snake dance.' But that was away from the church. Back at the dances the couples would take the floor and hurricane lanterns would hang from the ceiling, illuminating the room ringed by the wallflowers and the old girls, all watching the younger ones dancing.

Everyone would be dancing to the beat of the tea-chest, low and resonant, and the high fine violin. It was a release from the grinding poverty. It was a chance for people to meet up away from the unending daily routine. It was a chance to escape the sense of being trapped and confined, if only fleetingly.

The church still stands, but few people ever visit now. If you stand in the road and and look back over it as the sun sinks in the river valley, you can imagine it alight and filled with a momentary sense of freedom. The lights would go out when the superintendent decided they must be put out. The women and children would be locked away as the people from the camps descended from the compound, down the chalky white hill to the river flat where fires would be restoked. Some of the campies preferred a good game of cards after the dances.

The next day Jessie would be working the Singer sewing machine again;

pushing the treadle, spinning the leather belt with her feet, back and forth, back and forth, running the pants long and straight, biting off the thread with her teeth and folding the finished clothes for the sewing mistress, who was watching closely. If Jessie was not at the machine, she would be on the needle, embroidering, hand-sewing collars, mending, stitching and talking low. The women would be whispering to one another, in case the sewing mistress heard and disapproved.

Superintendent Brodie was yet to commit the infamous tarring and feathering of a young Noongar man, but he was known for having women beaten until they urinated on the floor, being held down by trackers as they were hit. He was another ex-army man in a line of military men who were placed in charge of people they knew nothing about and generally had little respect for. There were some people, usually nurses or special teachers, who inmates came to have friendships with, but, for the most part, the divide between black and white was rigid and strictly enforced.

More and more deaths were recorded as the living conditions took their toll. Women who were sent there to have their children suffered under the poor hospital facilities. Children formed the largest number of those buried in the Settlement cemetery. Children died of simple preventable illnesses. They died of colds that developed into pneumonia. They died of dysentery that could not be controlled. They died of malnutrition, unable to get enough nutrition from their mother's milk because their mothers had gone hungry throughout their pregnancies, leaving them weak and open to infection. These were hard, fragile years. The poor sanitation that was the result of overcrowding only increased the risk of disease. These diseases ran rampant through the weakened children, unable to keep warm in winter or cool in summer.

The hospital was feared by everyone in the Settlement. Granny Bella had a fear of it. You would start with a cough, and then it would sink down into your chest. The sick would be taken to the hospital, which was not much more than a room with bricked-in verandahs for a ward, to isolate them from the rest of the Settlement. Many people lost their lives from treatable illnesses such as diarrhoea and gastroenteritis, but overwhelmingly death was caused by simple respiratory illnesses that developed into bronchitis and pneumonia. When someone died the women would know what had to be done and would start out looking for wild flowers, blossoms, leaves and woolly bush to make wreaths, to give the dead some sense of dignity. There would be a priest sometimes, but often as not it was

Tommy Bropho who gave the service, carrying the cross out in front of the congregation, the whole Settlement population making the long march out to the cemetery. They would march silently along the dirt track that led towards Shannaway, over the hill and down through the groves of banksia and moodjar, to the hill slope that faced north-west.

In the eleven months that my grandmother was at the Settlement twenty-four people died: fourteen adults and ten children under the age of fourteen. They died of untreated asthma, heart failure, epilepsy, dropsy, chronic bronchitis, pneumonia, convulsions and congestion of the lungs. That was an average of two Aboriginal deaths in custody every month, but in fact such statistics mean little when considering the reality of these tragedies. Death seemed to visit the Settlement in waves rather than in any orderly manner. In August 1924 there were four burials in the space of four days: two baby boys, a middle-aged man and an elderly woman. There were three more deaths in the following month of September: a nine year old girl, a twenty-five year old man and a seventy-five year old woman. In November there were another four deaths in quick succession with two elderly men and two boys aged eight years and two years dying needlessly. Of the nine children under the age of two that died in the time that my grandmother was at Moore River, one lived only eight days and another only seven days. These statistics were well known to the Department but were conveniently glossed over in the investigations into Moore River during the 1934 Royal Commission.

In fact these were not unusual ages for babies to die at in Moore River. It is a reflection of the level of wanton neglect of administrators like Neville who, in spite of such high levels of mortality, actually continued to send Aboriginal women to Moore River specifically to have their babies. Women knew how bad it was and would try to go full term without being found out by the Department. These poor women would turn up at country hospitals at the last minute in an attempt to avoid being sent to Moore River. In later years the matron of the Northam Hospital complained to Mr Neville that this was almost a common practice. Northam Hospital reluctantly decided to tend these women. Some women who were still working would try to hide their pregnancies. They would bind themselves and continue working, hoping that they could delay knowledge of their pregnancies. An aunty once told of how she lost her child this way. She was so desperate not to be found out, having also endured the shame of rape, that she bound herself so tightly that the baby was born prematurely and died. She was not more than an child herself at the time and had no idea what was happening to her.

In the women's dormitory one pan was left in a corner for thirty or forty women who were locked in until sunrise. Many of the women didn't make it through the maze of cots in time. It was bad, but it was not the worst that the Settlement would be. That was yet to come, as years of over-crowding and the effects of government thrift made conditions even more deplorable. To survive, people just kept their heads down, and kept a lookout for Marbans and Boolya, keeping on side with both. When people got out, going to work on properties sucker bashing or shearing, they always tried to get work for their relatives, to get them out too. If women tried to run, the chances of getting away were very slim. The trackers generally caught them before they had reached Mogumber Siding. Many women tried to run but were brought back tied by ropes and thrown in the Boob.

My grandmother had a different plan to get out of Moore River, and this time to stay out for good. Jessie wrote her letters to Edward in secret and snuck them out when a chance presented itself. She also wrote to previous employers, asking them to write to the Department to request her as their servant. Nothing came of it, until late 1924. She seems to have worked out that if you were able to bring in money, there was a good chance that they would release you. Employment was going to be her ticket out of Moore River.

Mrs Sherwood to wrote the Department from York asking if Jessie could come back to work for her family. Edward had organised some months earlier for a letter smuggled out from Jessie to be passed on to the Sherwoods. But it had not worked on the first attempt. Superintendent Brodie seems to have wanted to teach my grandmother a lesson for her 'agitation' in the sewing room. So another letter was smuggled out by my grandmother, this time by a visiting priest. It took Brodie two months to respond to the Department's request that Jessie go to the Sherwoods. Finally, after complaining about her, he replied, 'If there is a position that will have her, I say, let her have it.'

Mr Copping laid down the terms and had Brodie read them to my grandmother, making it absolutely clear that if she strayed in any way he would be seeing her again very soon. Jessie was ordered to go to the country and stick at it. If she did not stay and began to wander back to the city, she would be returned to Moore River immediately.

In late January 1925, Edward loaded up his possessions again. He'd received a letter from my grandmother saying that she was getting out of Moore River. Other letters he had sent her were probably still strewn around the state, but I don't think he would have cared. The letter that arrived telling him of Jessie's release came so late that he only had a few days to get back to the city if he was going to be able to meet her before she left for her position with the Sherwoods in York. Edward quit his job and made hasty plans to get back to the city. The boat was not fast enough for him so he made arrangements with the airmail run for them to pick up a more substantial load at Shark Bay—he and his trunk.

The telegrammed instructions from the air service were clear about what had to be done to secure a ride with the mail run. He stayed with the Hamelin Pool postmaster after the long trek from his camp. At dawn he lit smoke fires along a straight stretch of beach where the plane was to land. It floated into Shark Bay, plucked Edward and his possessions from the beach and powered on over the Bay, along the coast and south to Geraldton. Here another stop was made before taking off again, laden with more mail for the city of Perth.

It took a good solid day of flying. As the sun began to drop to the west, Edward took out his pocket diary and made a note: 'Passed over Mogumber, 6.00.' The plane would have created a fuss as it passed above the Settlement, droning slowly as it slipped south, but Jessie would have had no idea that Edward was on that plane. She was getting ready for her own journey. Three hours later Edward landed at Perth Airport, a strip of grass by the river, and the pilot, Major Norman Brearley, drove him home to Jack and Rachel Bayly's place in North Perth.

Jessie was still locked inside the girls' dormitory at Moore River. She was about to leave the Settlement, but there were no assurances that she wouldn't be sent back again. She had been there for eleven months and only managed to get out a month early through her own efforts. Eleven months is a long time in a place like Moore River.

dangerous love

Edward was waiting on the platform of Perth Station for the eleven forty-five from Mogumber. He had been scouting around town, catching up with anyone from the Settlement down at White City, hoping for any scrap of information. A letter had arrived from Jessie, a month old. It had travelled all the way from Mogumber, north to Hamelin Pool, and back. In it Jessie asked him if he could buy her some shoes. Somehow, with only three days notice, he was able to buy them and get them up to her at the Settlement just before she left. He wasn't wasting any time. Jessie had no shoes during the time she was at Moore River.

When women finally got the signal that they could get out of the Settlement, they didn't wait around. They would grab what they could, take the dray out to the siding, and leave that place as quickly as possible. When my grandmother left she did basically the same thing. She left with someone else's suitcase.

Edward and Jessie didn't have much time. The day after leaving for the city, Jessie would be off on the train to York, back to the Sherwoods, away from Moore River, the city, and Edward. The Friday she arrived they hit the town. The next day, Edward took her to the Grand Pictures, then out to lunch, and saw her off on the four o'clock train to York. They had to bide their time. They hadn't seen each other in almost a year, but they had to be cautious, to think through how they would deal with the Department and plan their approach.

The Sherwoods lived in the bank residence in York. It was two storeys high and in the centre of town, just opposite the Palace Hotel. It was only an hour from the city by train. Jessie was weak and thin, and had nothing to her name bar the clothes she wore on her back, her new shoes and the case she had 'borrowed', promising afterwards in a letter to the Department to replace it when she earned money again. The woman who owned the case had complained to Mr Copping, the Deputy Chief Protector, and he had contacted Jessie to ensure that the debt was made good. Mistake one. Getting caught thieving someone else's suitcase.

Mrs Sherwood wrote to the Department requesting that Jessie be given money to buy some clothing as she was without any, but they held out, waiting for my grandmother's account to grow again. A month later, my grandmother wrote a letter to Mr Copping begging for some clothes, saying she was 'ashamed' when people visited the house. They sent her two white aprons and two pink dresses, picked by them, bought with her money.

It was at this time, while they were keeping their relationship out of the eyes of the Department, that Edward took some work around Keysbrook for his old friends the Middletons. He caught the train out to fix their truck. A little drive was in order to try it out, and he carted stores for them for a week, camping out around the Peel Estate region and even visiting his old farm, no doubt thinking back over his life.

He began writing Jessie letters as soon as she left Perth and her replies were quick. They no longer had to rely on smuggled letters and hidden correspondence. They could use the post like anyone else, without any fear of censor. Edward had amassed funds from his work at Shark Bay that he felt made him a good prospect for marriage. He met Copping and talked it out with him, mentioning Mrs Campbell, the old superintendent's wife, as a referee. He had set his mind to it. He was not short of work. He was being offered work all around town fixing cars, from the *West* in the Terrace to the WA Charabanc Company.

As Mr Neville was running the Department for the North-West, day-to-day decisions fell on the administrative staff, Mr Copping and Mr Aldrich. However, although Mr Neville was focused on the north-west of the state, he wasn't too busy, it seems, to have paid my grandmother's file the occasional visit, just to keep an eye on things.

Edward made a note in his diary: 'Determined to go to York next Saturday', and was good to his intention. He took a room at the Palace Hotel, just opposite the Western Australia Bank building. From her second floor window Jessie could look across the street to see Edward's room and balcony opposite. Betty Sherwood remembered my grandmother telling the children about Edward, and seemed to delight in sharing a secret about a stranger involved somehow in Jessie's life, taking a room just opposite, engaging in secret meetings.

Jessie didn't want Edward to see her hanging out the washing and so young Tom Sherwood was pushed into doing it, though he only agreed if he could wear a dress and hat so none of his mates would see what he was doing.

I believe that Edward thought he was making the right move this time. He decided that, as the Department had been so obstinate, he would approach Mr Sherwood, Jessie's oldest employer, and make known his intentions to marry her. The Sherwoods were a well respected family in the community. They had known my grandmother for years, and their opinion might be able to sway the Department. I imagine Jessie and Edward thought that if they had the support of a bank manager who could vouch for them, they might be able to convince the Department.

On his first night in York, Edward and Jessie walked the streets of the town together, unbeknown to Mr and Mrs Sherwood. It didn't take long to cover the entire length of the town. They were making plans, certain they were doing the right thing. They parted and Edward returned to his room. Jessie whistled to wake one of the Sherwood children, who dutifully dropped the key to the front door from a second-floor window so that Jessie could sneak back into the house while Mr and Mrs Sherwood slept.

The next day, Edward called on Mr Sherwood in the early evening to 'interview' him about marrying Jessie. Not all of Edward's old English habits had been erased by his southern life. He had prepared his approach, was well dressed and, from where he stood, had good prospects. As he fronted up to the door he could have had no idea that it was going to go so badly. 'I remember him coming,' Mrs Davies recalled on the day that we visited her, 'but my father didn't know how sincere Mr Smith was, and he told him to leave Jessie alone.' The interview had been cut short. Edward was sent packing without a clue as to why the Sherwoods would react the way they did.

The support Edward and Jessie hoped would enable them to win over the Department was clearly not forthcoming. Edward stayed around

York the next day, bored and waiting. He and Jessie weren't able to see each other until the Sunday evening. He hung around the stables all day, taking the odd walk around the outskirts of town, across the suspension bridge and back. When he finally got to see Jessie, it was only briefly, and the next day he was gone, back to the city alone, after paying up his account at the Palace and catching an early train.

It was then that my grandmother began her trips, every two weeks or so, for treatment at the Perth Hospital for the mysterious 'bone disease' in her leg. As the Department had considered her a malingerer, her leg would have received no attention in Moore River. I believe she decided that her leg would be her cover, a way to bend her circumstances to her favour. She would turn her disadvantage to her advantage. Mrs Sherwood was suspicious, but Jessie knew that when they saw the doctor's reports they would have to believe her. I imagine that she had weathered the pain in her leg so long it had become a part of her, so much so that she had not, until then, seen its potential as a means to get back to the city.

Edward and Jessie began writing to each other every week and seeing each other on the odd occasions that she made it to the city. He would wait at the train station every Saturday and if she did not make it that week he would head off to White City to catch up with whoever was in town: Sam and Wally Isaacs, Bill Bodney, Fred Mead, Millie Long, Cyril Parfitt. Jessie asked Edward to buy Tommy Bropho a birthday cake and send it to him at Moore River for her.

The Department it seems had, in the meantime, finally worked out that Anna Fielder was giving them a false impression about what went on when women boarded with her, and so women were no longer allowed to stay.

Mrs Mulvale had been a nurse at Moore River. Her boarding house was originally in West Perth but soon shifted to Maylands, where her small timber and fibro home opposite the Blind School was designated the new government boarding house for Aboriginal women staying in the city. Mrs Mulvale was making a killing. Apart from the money she earned from women boarding in her home, she received money as an official escort for Aboriginal women in the city. She watched the women with the eye of a policewoman and, what was even more attractive to the Department, she had a telephone and could keep in regular communication. Gone was the freedom of being able to stay out all night in the city, play cards until the morning or wander back to East Perth as the city slept. Instead, Mrs Mulvale's required a careful negotiation, a planned approach to claiming the small freedoms that the city offered, along with avoiding its traps in the form of uniformed officers who would report anything unusual to the Department.

When Jessie went to the city from Mrs Mulvale's, she and other women boarders would make out they were heading out for a walk, or to visit friends, or perhaps for medical appointments, and then stay out as long as they could stretch the time without getting into serious trouble. They would gamble on the number of minor warnings they would have to receive from Mrs Mulvale before she would involve the Department, and thereby curtail their activities. It was a ludicrous situation of control for a woman like my grandmother who was twenty-six years old. But she and the other women knew the arbitrary nature of the Department in deciding when to punish them for minor offences, and so they simply had to watch their step. It worked in their favour that Mrs Mulvale was often on escort duty, accompanying people from the railway station to the Department, and from the hospital to the train to Moore River. On days when they knew they could take their time returning, the women could meet up with others who worked in the city. Inevitably, they would make their way to White City. So, for the next year White City, in the safety of the crowd, was where and how Jessie and Edward would meet.

My grandmother continued her work for the Sherwoods as the means of staying in line with the Department's ruling that she remain in a country position or be sent back to the Settlement.

Jessie's trips to the city were necessary. The problem with her leg was the best kind of cover, because it was true. She actually did visit the resident medical officer. Ideally she should have been hospitalised, but that could have meant being sent to Moore River to 'recuperate', which was something to be avoided at all costs. However, her lifestyle was taking a toll on her health. Instead of slowing down she appears to have simply kept up the pace. She was working overtime, making long train trips, running all over the city and sometimes taking risks by mixing in places that would have brought the unwanted attention of the public and possibly the police.

Mrs Sherwood was doubtful that my grandmother's leg really required treatment. She believed that my grandmother's habit of finishing her work up in quick time to make it to the train to Perth had more to do with Edward Smith who had come calling months before. She informed the Department of these views, writing to Mr Copping that 'Jessie seems anxious to be with that man Smith who writes to her.'

The Department immediately wrote to my grandmother for an explanation. Jessie was obviously rattled at how they knew about Edward. She sent off a quick reply: 'Don't think I am shamming just to get back to Perth because I really like working in the country. I wouldn't work in Perth now if I was to get two pounds a week.' The Department was busy with other administrative matters, including the decline of the new Department of the North-West that Neville had been running, and she was overlooked for the time being.

Edward and Jessie continued writing to each other regularly. Edward would make cheerful little entries in his diary about receiving a letter from Jessie, and noting when he posted her a reply. They were very regular, mostly weekly, but sometimes twice weekly.

In March 1926 my grandmother's leg had become worse and she was making preparations to visit the medical officer in Perth when a letter arrived from Edward. Having had to smuggle letters to each other while Jessie was in Moore River, they seemed to believe that the censorship that existed then, was no longer a threat. However Mrs Sherwood, suspicious of Jessie's involvement with 'that man Smith', intercepted one of Edward's letters. It was addressed to my grandmother at their residence, but Mrs Sherwood opened it. She obviously didn't like what she read because she immediately telephoned the Aborigines Department and posted Edward's letter on to Mr Copping.

With her leg in great pain and with the knowledge that she was in deep trouble, Jessie acted quickly. She arranged for her personal mail to be henceforth held at the post office in York so that Mrs Sherwood could not intercept another letter. When she arrived in Perth for medical treatment, Mrs Mulvale was waiting at the station and escorted Jessie straight to Royal Perth Hospital. There would be no side trips to warn Edward, and it was too late anyway. Edward was already being interviewed by the Department. Copping could have sent Edward down for six months imprisonment for cohabitation. Strictly speaking, cohabitation implied they were living together, but the Department chose a loose interpretation and used this clause of the 1905 Act to enforce overall segregation of any kind. Copping could have sent Jessie back to the Settlement for another year.

Mrs Sherwood didn't know what she was dealing with. She had interfered in my grandmother's life in a way that could have been devastating. Many employers seem to have acted in this way, as if they were an extension of the state with the power to open people's mail, report them to authorities, and have a say in what they did outside their employ. Perhaps Mrs Sherwood was acting out of a sense of benevolent paternalism for a woman she had known since she was a sixteen year old child straight from the Mission. Perhaps she had responded to what she perceived as the immorality of an illicit affair. In the eyes of society at large, the society of which Mrs Sherwood was a respected member, Jessie and Edward were not just a man and a woman, but a 'white man' and a 'half-caste'. Their relationship was illegal in the eyes of the general Western Australian community, and under the statutes of law enshrined in the 1905 Aborigines Act.

They were extremely lucky. I don't know why Edward wasn't imprisoned, or why my grandmother wasn't immediately sent back to the Moore River Native Settlement. There were other cases at the time that were being tracked under the detailed card system kept by the Department to monitor their charges. There was a completely separate category of cards for 'cohabitation' in the Department, for the tracking of just such relationships.

I imagine that the reason they escaped this time had something to do with Edward's friendship with Copping. It could also have had something to do with the fact that the Department was under transition. Mr Neville was about to return to the Aborigines Department from the Department of the North-West to again manage it the way he had designed it when he set up the huge system of personal files and card indexes. Copping would soon be seconded to another department.

So, instead of imprisonment, Jessie and Edward escaped with a final admonishment by Copping in his office at the Aborigines Department. They had escaped punishment, but they were severely warned to stop their relationship.

Instead of breaking off their relationship, they simply became more careful. Edward began writing about Jessie in secretive references to 'my friend' and using his nickname for her, Cully. Jessie's visits to the city became rare. They still wrote to each other every week, sometimes twice a week. Edward still went out to White City and caught up with any news on the black grapevine. He waited every Saturday for the train, but she was rarely on it and when she was, they rarely stayed together for long. Jessie heeded whatever was said in Copping's office and stayed away. Edward threw himself into his work.

A photograph was taken for the papers. The new tramlines were stretching from the centre of the city out across the river to Victoria Park and along the Albany Highway, extending the older lines that used to run a small way into the Victoria Park area. The welding team was captured, mid pour. The weld box over the track spat fire as men worked with shovels around the plant and machinery. The welder was placed at the centre of their work, a small train carriage with gas bottles on the back and tubes of metal wound into valves pumping the gas to the weld not two feet from the operator. Edward Smith stood at the centre of the picture wearing long, thick cowhide pants and gloves to protect him against the heat and sparks as they flew up from the tracks.

It had been a hot November, filled with storms that met him each day as he worked on the tramways, each night as he worked a shift at West Australian Newspapers on the printing machines, and every other evening as he worked at the Vic Park Markets for his old friends from Keysbrook, unloading produce and helping to clean up afterwards.

There was little time for Edward to strike his customary pose for the newspaper photograph, but he had managed it anyway. Edward was located at the centre of the weld as men worked with shovels of rock, tar and sand around him. He turned his head just so, dipping his hat a little over his brow. His eyes were on the weld as he worked the molten steel. Thankfully, his customary fag was nowhere to be seen. The gas bottle was just beside his head.

It could have been the image that captured the moment. Perhaps it was the moment just before the weld split and the flame flared. Perhaps he was too tired to be keeping watch, or too concerned with the camera and unable to protect his face in time. Molten metal flew up into his face, across his left cheek, just missing his eye, taking away a good amount of his scalp and his hair.

He lay in bed for days with headaches and in pain. Almost immediately, Jessie came to the city to see him.

My grandmother recommended her trips to Perth. After almost a year of working for the Sherwoods, I am certain she was tired of the country. She had paid her debts, avoided trouble since the episode of the letter and had done her work as she was told. But after Edward's accident she returned to her pattern of making regular trips to the city whenever she was able to get away.

Edward and Jessie had been seeing each other for nearly six years, but this was not respected by the Department, nor it seems by Mrs Sherwood. I imagine both believed they were against this relationship 'for her own good', but my grandmother was the best judge of what she wanted to do with her life, and legislation and state-sponsored informing by employers was not going to stop her. Mrs Sherwood again began making complaints to the Department about Jessie's trips.

This time, Mrs Sherwood seemed all too aware of the possible trouble she was causing and was recommending that Jessie be sent back to the Moore River Native Settlement for 'keeping late hours, bad company, and being beyond control.' The Department most probably would have sent her back to the Settlement had they not had their minds on other more pressing issues of their own: staff, budgets and internal disputes. I'm sure Jessie expected she would be sent back, that they would be good to their word and to Mrs Sherwood's recommendations and send her on that morning train north. But the landscape of her file was beginning to change.

Mr Copping was beginning to fade from her file pages. There were changes taking place in the Aborigines Department. With the Department of the North-West collapsing quickly and Mr Neville about to return, the ownership and management of the files used to control the Aboriginal community were in dispute. There was a fight over who controlled the information because the more files that a department was responsible for, the more staff it required. The more staff that a department had, the more status and money it received. In Neville's intermittent absences the Aborigines Department had allowed staff from the Colonial Secretary's Office to handle issues of accounts and various other matters. For this the Colonial Office needed access to the files. Having received them, they were keeping them.

While this farcical bureaucratic war raged on in memos, telephone calls and interdepartmental spats, Jessie and Edward were relatively free. Mrs Sherwood's recommendations were not acted on, but my grandmother had had enough. She found a new position in Darlington. The departure from the Sherwoods was by mutual agreement.

By 1927 Jessie and Edward were seeing each other and writing twice a week, meeting in the city on her night off and even making the occasional trip together to the hills with Mrs Campbell and her children. Mrs Campbell had been well liked by many inmates of the Settlement when she was matron and remained in contact with many of the women. Since Jack Campbell's death in 1923, Edward had remained a friend of the family and would often visit Mrs Campbell with my grandmother. A photograph was taken of Mrs Campbell, Jessie, Edward and the two children standing together in a clear stream in the hills. The cool waters are tickling my grandmother's bare feet as she stands, leaning easily against Edward, who always looks younger in photographs when he is with her.

Nineteen twenty-six had been a good year in their lives. Mr Neville no longer had complete control of the files, and so he was not able to control Jessie's earnings. In a stroke of luck the Department, managed by newly assigned government clerks, let my grandmother keep all her wages for the first time in her life.

After leaving her position in Darlington where she had worked for over six months, my grandmother began working for the Sharpe family in Guildford. It was a big old house that needed two maids to run it. My grandmother was treated as just a hired servant by the family, and I assume that after the measure of control that Mrs Sherwood had tried to maintain this was a welcome situation. Jessie was working in a house with children, under a woman who seemed to regard it as none of her business what my grandmother did on her day off. Edward had recovered from his burns and had a permanent job at the *West Australian*, working the electrics of the printing press. They were catching up with whoever they liked in the city, going to the pictures, to White City, to Anna Fielder's for a game of cards, or catching up with blackfellas down at Government Gardens. Sometimes they spent time with Edward's crowd, friends he knew around the city, taxi drivers and workers down at the Perth Railway Station.

However, Mr Neville was about to re-enter their lives. His mind was refocusing on the city. I can see it in my grandmother's file, and in so many of the files at the beginning of 1927. There is a sudden resurgence of monitoring of accounts and employer permits, and Neville's signature begins to appear on almost every piece of official correspondence.

There is also a new file he created, where he set out his ideas to reorganise the city, to restrict the numbers of Aboriginal people freely walking the streets. Jessie and Edward were not to know this, of course, but for Jessie and Edward the reality of racial segregation was already understood. When the Prohibited Area legislation was introduced in March 1927, this understanding was made real again. After six o'clock at night, a five kilometre square surrounding the city centre was made illegal to Aborigines.

The city was a place of meeting, of the crossing of railway lines, of rivers and creeks linked by corridors of black spaces. It was a place of alleys, of certain cafes and picture palaces that would serve Aboriginal people and others that would not. It was a town large enough to slip through if you had to, but small enough that you could seek out your own kind.

For Mr Neville, however, it was not a city for everyone, and it was within his powers to control access to it by Aboriginal people. He already had the power to decide who could and could not marry, or where you should work and for how much. He could determine your relationships, distinguish a right match from a wrong one. He could draw upon the resources of his files and informers, make his judgements and decide people's fates, all from his office chair. Neville was back in control. His newly devised Prohibited Area scheme would soon be replicated and enforced in country towns and reserves throughout the state. He would have the power to define boundaries, not only of how Aboriginal people interacted with each other, but how Aboriginal people should interact with whites. He was still involved in a minor scuffle for control of his files but had managed to retrieve enough of them to enable him to once again stamp his own particular autocratic and officious style on the management of Aboriginal lives.

The Chief Protector waited. He wore down his opponents and won back control of the files. Within a short time he had control of the trust accounts again, my grandmother's and everyone else's wages. Jessie was back to receiving only five shillings from her twenty shillings a week. Jessie was twenty-seven years old. She was already working for half a white woman's wage for the same work. Now three-quarters of that was again deducted and held in trust by the Aborigines Department. Mr Neville knew that his files were the means with which to fight a battle, to control a people financially, to amass information about them and use it against them without redress. He used this information devastatingly, to decide if a child should be removed from their parents. He used this information pedantically, as with the management of domestic servants staying at Mrs Mulvale's. He also used this information politically, against small groups of Aboriginal people gathering under the formation of the Native Union.

There was a new movement afoot in Noongar society. The Harris brothers were old Swan Mission men who were well known and respected in the Aboriginal community. They were just beginning the process of starting the Native Union, a proposed unified indigenous voice from the South-West. Bill Bodney, who my grandmother had known well from the Mission, was also a key member. A major target of the Union would be Neville's policies.

There is a well known photograph that was taken for the *West Australian*. The men of the Native Union stand on the steps of the government offices ready to meet with the Premier to make their view known that the Aborigines Act was destroying their people. They approached the situation honestly and calmly, ready to discuss these issues openly. They weathered the patronising Western Australian press, and expected the government to meet them and take their grievances seriously. They wanted the government to investigate their claims of oppression under the control of the Aborigines Department and the Aborigines Act. However, the Chief Protector, A.O. Neville, used his files to undermine the men's complaints. Instead of face-to-face discussions, the men were discredited by the files Neville had constructed on them. The Union's solid work and heartfelt pleas were shot down before the men were really given a chance to be heard.

Neville was certainly back in control. He was a bureaucrat, in a personally powerful position within a lowly department. He claimed his own territory, making the supposed 'saving' of the Aboriginal community his personal crusade. Neville was about to launch himself on the public. Having taken back control of his Department, he was keen to place his stamp once again on the 'Aboriginal problem' as it was generally perceived in the white community.

Ironically, by this time his Settlement scheme had clearly failed. In his absence the Carrolup Settlement had closed and Moore River was over-populated. Neville had planned for them to be training grounds where blackfellas would learn white-right from black-wrong, and go out into the world to function as a cheap labour force. Instead, they had become dumping grounds. And yet, amidst the violence and the poverty, an increased sense of black community cohesion had been created. Community exists beyond country; damaged, but linked by blood, by skin and by claimed kin, it rises up out of what has been taken, and makes new culture.

In 1927, wanting to ensure that Aboriginal affairs were firmly under his control, Neville determined that it was a great nuisance to have 'half-castes' cavorting around the city in full view of white people. White City was a place of amusement and carnival. Neville did not like to hear reports that young black men were beating white men in boxing contests on the doorstep of the city. He was sensitive to the general community's expectation that he was responsible for the way Aboriginal people behaved in the city. It was no good to have black men winning the buckjumping contests over white men, and to have black women watching such spectacles.

This was, of course, exactly why White City was so popular. In the ring you could take out a man in a fair fight, then return to the camps in glory with a purse of money. It attracted both a black and a white audience. There was no other place like it in the city.

The Prohibited Area declaration was made on 9 March 1927, under section 39 of the 1905 Aborigines Act. From the moment of its proclamation Neville was in constant contact with the police to ensure they acted according to the letter of the law, and compelled any Aboriginal people not on lawful business to leave the city. What constituted 'lawful business' in Neville's mind certainly did not include what was taking place at White City.

The police were frequently called upon to remove Aboriginal people from White City, but they did not like Mr Neville wasting their time. In the main they ignored his constant requests, although they did patrol White City more often, and Jessie and Edward would have been aware of the increased police presence.

As Mr Neville explained to the Commissioner of Police in April 1927, the establishment of the prohibition was mainly on account of White City—which only occupied a small section of the vast Prohibited Area—and its attraction for 'half-castes'. Neville lamented,

Some of these places are also becoming resorts of half-caste girls, leading to them living lives of prostitution. It is precisely in the interests of these young people themselves that action has been taken.

In looking over his handiwork he commented with a sense of self-satisfaction, 'It is really a provision which we should have obtained many years ago.'

The police were told to look out for cohabitation between white and black. In the summer of 1928, police provided a summary of their patrols in a report to Neville which found that,

> The resort was visited by large numbers of Aboriginals and half-castes both male and female … They were well dressed, kept to themselves collectively and on no occasion did I see any attempt by white persons to enter into conversation or fraternise with them.

They gave great detail, almost glowing detail, of the four pound and five pound purses on offer to any young men wanting to take their chance in the ring, black or white, and found no problem with this. They noted, interestingly, that,

> There is also about 5 or 6 girls between the ages of 18 and 23 that often visit this place of an evening. They are extremely well dressed and their conduct and behaviour are exemplary and I have never seen them in the company of white persons and are well known to be in domestic service in the city and suburbs.

Neville never seemed happy with the reports that he received from police patrols, preferring instead to believe the gossip and complaints of disgruntled employers of the women who visited White City. In fact any white person in a minor position of authority seemed to feel that they had the right to question Aboriginal people's presence in the city. Train conductors, theatre usherettes and shopkeepers became Mr Neville's accomplices, and women like my grandmother and her friends increasingly found themselves being asked to account for their presence and prove their lawful employment.

Neville was very clear about what he thought of those women who visited White City. In one of his regular communications with the Police Commissioner Neville stated,

> The decent girls do not visit White City. There are a certain number of them who go there mainly for the purpose of inveigling some

white man to accompany them somewhere else. These girls keep late hours and are a constant source of worry not only to their employers but also to the Department.

In closing, he repeated to the Commissioner of Police that,

It is my desire that neither half-castes nor aboriginals be permitted to frequent the White City on any pretext what so ever. It is simply debasing the natives, and the contests lower the status of whites in their eyes.

My grandmother lost her job at the Sharpes in Guildford. They were only keeping one maid on for the winter, and as Jessie was last on, she was first off. Even though it was Department policy for women to stay with Mrs Mulvale, my grandmother moved back to Anna Fielder's at 100 Royal Street, East Perth. She was now unemployed and, due to the new boundaries, living inside the Prohibited Area. Just sleeping in the spare bed at Anna's was an unlawful act. When Neville realised she was not where she was supposed to be, he ordered her to Mrs Mulvale's in Maylands, where her money was drained dry paying board at the rate of one pound a week.

When Jessie had access to her own money, she was fine, but as soon as her hard-earned money was being managed on her behalf by Mr Neville, her account would quickly slip into the red.

I believe my grandmother was growing increasingly tired of these petty controls on her life. She was losing most of her wage to the Aborigines Department who now forced her to stay in a boarding house that charged more than she earned. Without work coming in she was racking up debts even though she was not responsible for her own funds. She began to stay out late for as long as possible. Thanks to Mrs Mulvale, Neville was well aware of what was happening. My grandmother was not alone, of course. All the women resented the Department and its control over their lives. Neville wrote to the Police Commissioner in early 1929 complaining that,

It is constantly being reported to me that the girls are out until midnight and after, and I appeal to you to assist me in putting these matters right. A mistaken sense of leniency only results in the unfortunate natives coming to grief.

In reality, the factor by which most women judged their grief was the extent of Mr Neville's involvement in their lives.

Neville was a hopeless administrator, too focused on minor details, on matters that he should never have been concerned with, like the purchasing of women's underwear and shoes, when there were larger issues at stake. When there were people dying at Moore River due to the neglect of his department. He must have had an idea of how hated he was, but appears too arrogant to have admitted it, and he continued on, planning, messing and meddling with other people's lives.

Before long Mrs Mulvale was recommending in her notes and telephone conversations with Mr Neville that Jessie be sent back to Moore River. My grandmother's bank account was almost cleaned out through paying Mrs Mulvale for crowded accommodation. Finally, my grandmother found her own work, just out of town. Her pay was docked to meet debts that were owed to Mrs Mulvale. Moving from one employer to the next once again became a habit. My grandmother found work in the city at Dilhorn, the grand residence of the Ledger family. It was a two-storey Victorian mansion overlooking Loton Park, a small patch of tennis courts and gardens next to the Perth Oval in East Perth. It was a good position and they gave her a good reference before letting her go for the winter. At Clackline she found herself stranded, working for a woman who realised that my grandmother simply didn't want to be there and subsequently complained about her to Mr Neville. When she couldn't stand Clackline any longer she went back to the city, necessitating another stamp in her file, another call for retrieval, and the Chief Protector taking a closer interest in her. It was becoming a tired and bitter cycle.

On almost any Friday in the spring of 1929, Edward Smith could be found waiting at the Perth Central Railway Station for the afternoon trains from the country. During the day he worked the printing presses, preparing the machines for the different print runs of the various newspapers that were the mainstay of the city's grapevine. He'd been working at the *West Australian* off and on as a mechanic since 1925, but by 1929 he was a fully paid-up member of the Printers Union. He was a proud weekly wage earner and, I imagine, he was as happy a man that summer as he could be. His Friday nights were always spent waiting for Jessie.

The railway station was their weekly rendezvous point. He noted it all down in his pocket diaries: 'Wrote Cull. Cull coming in by train, tonight!' He never wrote more than he had to. He had to be discreet because they were still being monitored by the Aborigines Department, who used the police as their eyes and ears. Being a Friday, he would often borrow the work car, on which he also did repairs, or the car of his old pal, Jack Bayly. Edward boarded with Jack and his wife Rachel and their two children at their home in Norfolk Street, North Perth, and had stopped his roaming life. The city that had sparked little interest when he arrived fresh off the boat in 1909 had finally captured him. It had changed little since he first arrived, and still bore a resemblance to Wandsworth. It had become busier and faster, and for him, after what he'd experienced, it had become a harder place.

The city would have hummed constantly around him. Throngs of pedestrians hurried along the pavements that lined the narrow streets as shops began to shut and the lights began to blink into life. Over the distant blue hills the sun would cast a purple haze against the fading cobalt of the approaching night. He knew this patch of ground well. Taxicabs lined the south side of the Horseshoe Bridge in a crescent, leading out towards Wellington Street. Edward knew most of the taxicab drivers by name. They all knew him as 'Whispering Smith'. Those who knew him well enough got away with calling him 'Squeaker'. His voice had never returned and he had resigned himself to being somewhat of an oddity. Stories abounded about how he had lost his voice.

There were those who believed that Edward was a returned soldier. One story went that he was gassed and left in no-man's-land for a day or two before they found him. By the time they came to patch him up the gas had eaten right through his vocal cords. Another story placed him in the middle of a hailstorm of shrapnel as they were charging German trenches. He should have died instantly; the hot metal hit him front on and became lodged in his throat, burning his larynx.

People who knew him well have told me these stories in deadly seriousness and with the complete belief that they were true. I've searched for a record of military service, but there is none. Unless the story is even more covert than I can imagine, and has been squirreled away in a file marked 'Top Secret', then I am sure the defective voice on his rejection papers was due to diphtheria.

I don't know if he helped some of the stories along himself; maybe he embellished the truth a little. Maybe the people he knew were prone to a little exaggeration. It's true, he would have cut an unusual figure in the streetscape of the city, and would have made a good hook for spinning a yarn. There were probably people he didn't want to explain his affliction to, with whom he simply feigned a disinterest in discussing it, letting their imaginations fill in the gaps of his silences. In the years just after the First World War afflicted men were not uncommon on the streets of the city. In the Perth of the 1920s it wouldn't have been the done thing to ask a bloke you thought was a returned serviceman how he caught the shrapnel, how he lost his leg, an arm, an eye, or his voice. It was better to discuss such things away from earshot, to speculate and fill in the details yourself.

Edward was thirty-eight years old in 1929. He was fit for his age and had retained his wiry frame. When not at work covered in grease, he was meticulous about his appearance, especially when he took my grandmother out. His years spent working in the theatres around the city came in handy when he was preparing for a night out with Jessie. The scars from his welding accident were permanent and deep. Before heading into the city he would apply a thick layer of theatre make-up across his scar, comb his hair over the place where it had been completely removed from the front of his skull, and affix one of his hats at its customary tilt.

I suspect he enjoyed the anonymity that the city offered, and that he particularly loved the city at night, where he was able to pass his injury off without notice. He was always out in the city after sundown. If he wasn't waiting at the train station for Jessie Argyle, he would walk the streets of Perth, from north to south, east to west. He could have jumped a tram into the city from the top of William Street, but preferred to walk down Norfolk Street into Hyde Park, along Lake Street into Northbridge, over the Horseshoe Bridge that crossed the railway lines and down William Street to the river and the town jetty.

In all his photographs he looks well groomed, neat as a pin, and his photographic pose is struck as carefully as ever. He had been a manual worker for almost twenty years but dressed as if he worked in the Terrace as a broker. Those expensive suits he had bought for himself and Bayly with his inheritance seem to have lasted well. He had been in the colony for two decades but still spoke with his Westminster accent, which people described as sounding 'like the men on the radio'. Because of his whispering voice, people had to lean in carefully and pay special attention to what he was saying. It puzzled most people the first time they met him, as if he was somehow having a lend of them, or there was a joke being played on them. Some people whispered back, thinking there must be some good reason for the hush.

Perhaps these circumstances added weight to the other story that circulated about him, that his manner, dress and speech would also have lent credence to. A lot of people thought he was a remittance man, a wayward son of Mother England who had committed some folly and been paid off and sent out to the colony to hide the family shame. They created imagined stories of broken love affairs, a disinheritance, a youthful indiscretion that saw him banished from London to the wilds of Western Australia. It seems to be a story he was happy to let float around.

Work, and Edward's ability to attract accidents, had taken its toll on his body. He was well past the usual marrying age, a little too old for a man in 1929 not to have settled down with a family and a house in the growing hinterland of new suburbs. He was a long way from where he had imagined his life would lead him, but I don't believe there was anywhere else in the world he'd rather have been on a Friday night than waiting at the train station for Jessie.

They often bought fish and chips which they ate, safely concealed within the parked car that Edward had borrowed as they waited for the late summer's night to fall so that they could walk the dimmed city streets without drawing attention. It seems they would just sit, watching, enjoying the seclusion and each other, eating their fish and chips wrapped in the previous day's newspaper as the workers of the city made their way to the train station or along the streets to the tram stops to take them home. They were not allowed to be together, to be seated so close to one another, to share the same food, the same desire, the same car seat. They knew the risks, but they chose to be together anyway. They were caught in this situation not of their making; unable to marry, unable to be together on the streets after dark.

There is an image of Jessie Argyle that was taken in 1929. It is part of a series of photos that my grandmother took on a day off when she and two other women from Moore River, Bertha Isaacs and Dolly Wheeler, headed to the hills outside the city. They photographed each other by a stream. They posed seated on stock fences in the bush. They took images of each other standing alone in the landscape. The image that stands out the most for me though is the one of Jessie on the train tracks.

As the tracks disappear towards the city below, Jessie stands defiant and steadfast. It looks to all intents and purposes as though she's setting herself to rob a train. She looks confident. But, she has no reason to be confident. She is almost thirty years old and still being referred to as a 'girl' by the Department. She has no money of her own and only receives five shillings a week for six days work. She has been working as a servant for almost fourteen years and is receiving the same money in her hand as she did when she first left the Mission at the age of sixteen. However, for all this, she looks free. In that moment, there is captured the sense of someone who has a life of their own.

But control over her life was the last thing she had. Mr Neville decided that what my grandmother needed was a distant country position and Jessie found herself sent out, away from the city, into the central Wheatbelt, the South-West and finally the Goldfields. Her leg was still giving her trouble, but there was no way that she would be allowed to come back to the city for good.

Yundamindra Station was a cook's position, stranded miles from anywhere. She was contracted to stay for twelve months, but she left when she thought they had tried to short-pay her. Mr Neville was not pleased. She was sent to Quairading Hospital to work as a domestic servant. Mr Neville's warning was clear; if she did not stay twelve months in this position, she would pay for it, and she knew what that meant. A few months into the job the matron struck her across the face for disobeying a command, and my grandmother left without hesitation. I cannot imagine someone striking her and not being struck back.

I imagine she was expecting to be sent back to the Settlement when she arrived in the city. She knew she would be expected to stay at Mrs Mulvale's boarding house but she had no money left in her account. She hadn't followed Neville's orders to stay in her country position, in fact she had acted unlawfully by leaving without her employer's permission.

Show Day, 1929. Jessie was about to disappear. Another long year, after all the other long years, had taken its toll and she was back at Mrs

Mulvale's, but only for a short time. She was looking for work, but there was none. The Depression was just about to bite and it was the worst possible time to be out of work. Mrs Mulvale had been writing to the Department complaining that she had not been paid for the last time my grandmother stayed with her. They informed her that Jessie had no money in her account, and that Mrs Mulvale would just have to wait. When my grandmother couldn't pay her debt, Mrs Mulvale told her to leave.

She was not allowed to go back to Anna's. Neville would not allow it. If she wasn't able to stay at Mulvale's, then she knew what would happen; she would be sent to Moore River again. Everyone knew how much worse it was getting at Moore River and women were even more desperate not to be sent there. More than a score of people were dying in custody there every year. On top of that, my grandmother's leg was troubling her again, and she was unwell with a respiratory illness.

I don't know how the fight started, but it was a mean one. It was bare fisted and rough. My grandmother put one of the other women staying at Mrs Mulvale's in hospital. The next day, Jessie Argyle disappeared. The Department was furious to find out that Mrs Mulvale had been going to turn her out on the street. Mulvale was in a favoured position, being paid good money by the women for the privilege of being watched by her. In return, she had acted as if she ran an ordinary boarding house, and when payment was late, had tossed out a bad debt. Mr Neville acted immediately. The police were alerted to look for Jessie on their patrols, but there was no sign of her.

Five days later Jessie Argyle turned up at the Department in the city. She knew they had been looking for her. Her illness was worse. She was taken to hospital with chronic bronchitis. She was also in need of some dental work as a result of the fight. When she left the hospital she disappeared completely. She had no intention of returning to Mulvale's, to the Settlement or to any other place to wash, cook, clean and scrub for white strangers.

Jessie ran to Edward. He had moved to a place of his own in East Victoria Park. They would spend the next two months together. The Department seems to have had no idea where Jessie was. In January my grandmother went in to the Aborigines Department to face Mr Neville. She told him that she wanted to marry Edward Smith. Mr Neville agreed to consider her request, but asked her to send this man Smith in for an interview. Edward met with Mr Neville and followed up the meeting with a letter on 21 January 1930 asking for permission to marry Jessie Argyle in accordance with Section 42 of the Aborigines Act. Mr Neville wrote in her file that he understood Smith to be 'a respectable man', and that it would probably be a good thing if they were to marry. Neville wrote again almost immediately stating, 'I hereby grant you permission to marry Jessie Argyle, an aboriginal of Perth.' It was a complete about-face. After so many years of enforcing a policy of segregation, Neville was allowing this particular black and white couple to marry without objection.

A.O. Neville was halfway through his twenty-five year rule over the Aboriginal people of Western Australia. Mixed marriages were rarely condoned, so why did he approve Edward and Jessie's marriage when the Department had worked for ten years to try to keep them apart? I believe the decision was due to his growing interest in the ideas of biological absorption as the means to physically assimilate the Aboriginal community into the white community of Western Australia. He was formulating plans to manage men and women like my grandparents, black and white, as a means of breeding Aboriginality out of the Aboriginal community. Gradations of skin colour, calculations of caste, imagined portions of 'native blood', and hard-line assimilation policies were to be the tools of his proposed absorption. I believe Mr Neville allowed them to marry as a means of testing some of the new theories he was about to launch upon the public.

When my grandmother was interviewed by Mr Neville in January 1930 she was two months pregnant. There is no mention of her pregnancy on her file. I do not know if she informed Neville of her pregnancy when she asked him to allow her to marry Edward. He made no record of it in his deliberations. Neville had sent other women in similar situations to Moore River to have their children, women who had given him less trouble than Jessie Argyle. Some of these women found themselves separated from their children soon afterwards, and sent out to work again. A different path was being cleared for my grandmother by the Department.

My grandparents probably had no idea as to why they had suddenly been allowed to marry. My grandmother and grandfather just wanted to be together, and it seems that they rushed out of Neville's office as quickly as they could and booked themselves a church.

Jessie and Edward were married at St Bartholomew's Church on the hill in East Perth in January 1930. There were no fences then to keep people out of the adjoining cemetery, no expensive shiny apartments reflecting the water back onto itself. Mr Neville's signature was scratched onto their certificate, along with the signatures of friends and well-wishers who actually witnessed the wedding. It was not a lavish affair. They would have been crowded in the small church for the ceremony which entered them into the 'bonds of matrimony'. Edward slipped a ring on Jessie's finger and she slipped a ring onto his. And I would bet good money that they hoped they were finally free of Mr Neville and his meddling department. They probably thought their rings, like their certificate, represented an institution that would shield them from all they had been forced to weather. But then, they probably knew that any such thoughts were just wishful thinking.

III

BORDERLINES

glendower street

Sundown at Hyde Park, North Perth, rings out with the calls of the hundreds of birds that flock to its oasis. The twin lakes of this now central city park are surrounded by English plane trees, date palms, jacarandas and a row of Moreton Bay figs. Once it was a wetland that formed part of the massive freshwater underground and flood valley system upon which the city of Perth now stands. In its original state the wetlands would regularly overflow along ancient watercourses to East Perth and out into the Swan River. The underground watercourses still flow beneath the rows of expensive double-storey town houses that ring the wetlands, but they have been subdued by so much building and overcrowding.

By day the park is a haven and an escape from the nearby city. People come here to power walk, to stroll as a family, to picnic, to sunbathe or to just rest beneath the shade of the trees. There are many regulars; it is not only locals who claim the park as their own and return every day to reacquaint themselves with it, to walk around it, seek out others that they know and unwind within this world away from the world. By night the park is left to the birds who find sanctuary within it, to the men who sometimes use it as a beat, and to the police who patrol the streets around it, moving on any prostitutes who have made their way too far north from the city into what has become a very wealthy and desirable suburb. It is officially within the boundary of North Perth, but only just. Hyde Park sits at the junction of the small enclave of Highgate to the east and the salubrious rise of Mount Lawley to the north. The city, only a few kilometres away, is visible in the mirrored glass of the skyscrapers that rise above the roofs of the houses. But the city is silent against the noise of waterbirds making their way to the islands of the twin lakes.

The wetlands were cleared, drained and replanted at the turn of the twentieth century. Hyde Park seemed a more substantial name to the colonists for the transformation from 'Third Swamp' into an English garden. Even so, the clearing, draining and replanting could not completely transform this fertile freshwater haven from its significance as an essential site of human interaction with the natural world. The deep depression in the landscape, the cool earthy smell of the water, the canopy of trees and the islands of reeds still retain a sense of the original Noongar camp site and meeting place, Boodjamooling. Noongars met at the centre of the wetlands.

The overhead tree branches shield the lakes, flowerbeds and walkways from the harsh Western Australian light, and bear witness to all that happens beneath them. Each year the leaves become filled with the stories that they hear winding their way around the tracks that circle the park. They grow until they can no longer carry the weight, wither and fall to the earth to rot, filling the gardens below and joining the silt of the lake beds. Each year the captured stories become layered into the park's being. You can feel them in the fleshy smell that the park never loses, summer and winter. Each story, captured in the branches and collected in the leaves, creates another ring of history around the trunk of the tree's skin and becomes another earthy layer in the park's foundations. These stories amass and rupture the tarred surfaces of the pathways ringing the lakes as the tree roots break through the surface of any substance that the city attempts to lay over them.

At sundown when the birds strike up I can hear my own family history singing its way through the branches of the trees. I can hear the sound of my grandmother's voice singing deep and loud over the park. I can hear the sounds of women walking from the tram stop to her house at 69 Glendower Street, just opposite the park. I can hear the sounds of my mother creaking open the back gate and dropping her bike as she returns from laying a bet for my grandmother at the SP bookie's, and the voices of men and women dancing in the back yard to the sound of old-time country and western being played on a mouth organ. Being here also reminds me of the Aborigines Department that watched the women and men who visited. It reminds me of stories I have been told since I was a child, of the children my grandmother fostered and cared for because their mothers were unable to.

This park watched them all and silently recorded their history. It recorded their lives through the Depression, the war and into the 1950s, and then it lost us for a while until I came back as a regular visitor. When my mother and grandparents lived in this neighbourhood it was the sort of place where people grew pumpkins in their back yards, kept chooks and geese, and in summer the Bulwer Street Circus would set up just down the road. The park appears in many photographs of our extended family. We still judge the date of images by the size of the trees and the changes taking place in the park that forms a perennial backdrop. It grew as my mother grew from the child that needed to be held, one hand each side, by Jessie and Edward, as she took her first steps, and later the young woman who used to run through its darkened interior.

The Department and police were also watching the house. Each year, just like the rings of the trees, my grandmother's personal file continued to grow its own layers of story: surveillance reports, correspondence, threats, and letters from informers.

My grandparents moved to Glendower Street, North Perth, soon after they married in February 1930. As the news spread that Jessie had married old Whispering Smith, women and men came to visit from White City. It became known that Jessie Smith's home was an open house and that all were welcome. While Edward worked at the *West*, my grandmother's house became another black–white meeting place in the city. There were few Aboriginal people who lived in houses so close to the city in 1930. The prohibited area ended at the centre of Newcastle Street, five minutes' walk from 69 Glendower Street.

It was the beginning of the Depression. Jessie was pregnant. Women came to visit to wish her luck, and just as many came in need of a place to stay. My grandmother felt obliged to help people who were in less fortunate circumstances than herself. A friend who was too sick to go back to work was staying for a week or two. Women whose children could not accompany them to work were leaving them with Jessie to care for rather than having them placed in the Settlement. Men and women were gathering at Glendower Street of an evening, having a drink, playing some cards, getting together just outside the Prohibited Area. Well before the birth of my mother, my grandmother began her extended household of women and children.

This is not what Mr Neville had in mind when he agreed to their marriage. My grandmother was supposed to sever connections with her

Aboriginal family and friends, act white and fade into the suburbs.

In February 1930 the clerk in charge of the Aborigines Department, Mr Taylor, wrote a memo to Mr Neville complaining that he had,

> ... received verbal reports that a number of our half-caste girls are making Jessie Smith's home in Glendower Street, Perth, a general rendezvous ... There is no question that Jessie consorts with these girls as she has on occasion come to this office with them and I consider this woman to have anything but a good influence on the girls. I understand that as many as four and five are at the above address at meal times at night.

Three days later the memo was acted upon. Mr Neville wrote to my grandfather with the first of his threats.

> I desire to draw your attention to Section 21 (b) of the Aborigines Act, which reads as follows: Any person who — Without the Authority in writing of a protector permits or suffers any aboriginal or any such half-castes as aforesaid to be upon or in any house, ship, boat, camp, or other place in his occupation on or under his control, shall be guilty of an offence against this Act. I am informed that your home has become a rendezvous for half-caste girls, and that one is even staying there. Please note that this cannot be permitted. You will remember that prior to your marriage I warned you that if such became the case it would be necessary for us to take action in the matter.

Edward decided to keep his response low key. He wrote to Neville in March stating his case for not being prosecuted, and playing for time.

> In answer to your letter of the 1st inst. I deeply regret if I have been responsible for offending against any section of the Aborigines Act. I am sure that your informant has conveyed to you a wrong impression, and that, she herself has placed a wrong construction on the facts. The true facts of the case is as follows: Five girls have visited my wife at different times; to wish her luck and happiness, which is only natural. They have stayed or made a (rendezvous) of my home for a

limited time and left soon after tea. During the short period they remained, their behaviour was excellent. With reference to Mrs Elsie Oakley. She remained at my wife's request, as she was in bad health. Although I informed her that I thought it was wrong, Elsie has returned to Mrs Mulvale's establishment at Maylands today. It is not my wife or my intention to encourage any of the girls under your care to visit our house, without your consent.

Mr Neville was not accustomed to receiving written responses to his threats. Most Aboriginal people who received such letters in the mail knew all too well the power that Neville could wield over their lives and did their best to avoid trouble. Neville seems to have left the situation alone for a while.

On 24 June 1930, exactly nine months after the fight on Show Day in 1929 when my grandmother put Lily Clatworthy in hospital and disappeared from Mrs Mulvale's for five days, my mother, Betty Smith, was born. It was a violent birth. My mother was born breech; leg and arm, shoulder and knee. The stress of the birth was such that the doctor warned Jessie never to have another child as the risks were far too great.

As my grandmother recovered and my mother was taking her first breaths, Edward was again being threatened with prosecution under the Aborigines Act for 'suffering' Aborigines under his roof without the permission of the Chief Protector. At first he ignored the letters, but then the police were involved. As my mother was taking her first blurry look at the world, Mr Neville was requesting police action against the alleged 'goings on' at Jessie Smith's house. If convicted of allowing Aboriginal people into Glendower Street without permission, it could be six months imprisonment for Edward and the Settlement for Jessie and Betty. If Neville had any notion that Edward, Jessie and Betty would become the role model of a well-behaved mixed-race nuclear family, he had chosen the wrong couple.

With the arrival of my mother, they set about creating their home. Their house in Glendower Street was gradually filled with modest possessions—a crystal radio set, a polished oval dining table, some kitchen chairs, a Singer treadle sewing machine, a lounge suite; a baby's cot—all the objects expected of newlyweds beginning their family, all bought on tick. The house was rented. It was a brick and iron Federation workers' cottage in a poorer part of North Perth. Red brick, tin roof, bullnose verandah, jarrah floorboards, two bedrooms, a sleep-out, lounge room, kitchen, back verandah and a rear laneway. It had an outside toilet backing onto the laneway, a tall picket fence enclosing the back yard, a low front fence leading up a few steps to the verandah, and it had electric lights.

To the casual observer, it was nothing special, but to my grandmother, I'm certain, it was everything. For the first time in her life she had her own place. This was not some mission house or Settlement dormitory, some white mistress' house or the home of a friend. It was where she could shut the door on the Department, so she told my mother. It was where she could welcome her own mob, other women like herself looking for a place to stay in the city without fear of the Aborigines Department.

For all these very good reasons I had always thought of it as Jessie's place. But I missed the importance of the house for Edward too. This was the first home that he also could call his own. It was not someone else's house to board in, a men's hostel or a dormitory, or the home of a relative where you were welcomed to visit but not to stay.

In this house they had each other and, more importantly, they had their daughter Betty. In this house they had their own family, including their extended family of Nor'westers, down-on-their-luck wadjellas and anybody that they damn well liked. This house was where they stopped moving, stayed firm, and faced the world.

Only two weeks after my mother's birth, the Department again began threatening prosecution. Mr Neville wrote to Edward stating that,

> I am informed that half-caste girls are, or have been, again frequenting your home. I would draw your attention to my communication of the 1 of March, informing you that this could not be permitted, and now desire to repeat this warning which I then conveyed to you. Will you please also note that I will not issue any further warning in this connection, but proceedings may follow any further breach of Section 21 (b) of the 'Aborigines Act', which section I quoted to you in my letter.

Mr Neville was worse than a dog with a bone. Ensconced in his office with his staff, busily typing memos and taking notes, I imagine him enamoured with his own sense of importance.

Edward tried a conciliatory approach, and it was noted in my family's file:

> Mr. Smith called to see me and expressed regret saying that he would do what he could to stop the practice. The trouble was that it occurred while he was out. He thought, however, that now that Jessie had a child to look after there would not be so much trouble in this regard.

Mr Neville had my grandmother figured all wrong. She wasn't going to stop seeing her own mob. Edward was appeasing Neville in an attempt to avoid trouble. Older women I know call it 'cracking dumb', dealing with powerful forces by agreeing with them, lulling them into a belief that you are not a threat while continuing to do what you wanted to do anyway. It was how the community generally avoided trouble with Neville, but it was a lottery, and once he was on the trail, he was hard to shake.

There were fifteen thousand blackfellas estimated to be living in Western Australia in the 1930s, and there were three staff members in the Aborigines Department. But, of course, they used the police, the magistrates and, as in my grandmother's case, informers, as their eyes and ears. If you managed to bluff them, to keep them from turning the dangerous and powerful wheels of injustice at their disposal into action, then you did stand a chance.

However, as was the case in many other parts of the world, in the early 1930s there were forces at work in the wider Western Australian community that were becoming harder to ignore. Our identity, our living conditions and, most importantly, our rights became the subject of daily newspaper opinion and myth making, which only increased the pressure on Mr Neville and the Department to ensure that people like my grandparents toed the line.

But this wave of public fixation with race and caste must also have been very satisfying to Mr Neville in his campaign for public support for his plans of biological absorption of Aboriginal Western Australians into mainstream white society. He had been active in the press, publishing letters under the disingenuous pen-name of 'A.O.N.'. Buried in the editorial pages, beneath the layers of bad news of the growing Depression and massive unemployment that showed no sign of slowing, Mr Neville tapped into a racial prejudice that seemed to be welcomed by the wider community as a distraction. But for all the problems that were faced by whites in the Depression, they were more often tenfold for Aboriginal people.

My mother Betty still lives in the same state housing area of Scarborough where she raised my older sister Jess, my brother Terry, myself, my younger sister Beverley, and my foster-brother John. She loves it by the sea, where she came when she left the city over forty years ago. In the neighbourhood in which she raised us children, my mother was well known for being the centre of family gatherings, for being a hard worker and a gatherer of people.

Our house was always filled with people: other kids from the street, women dropping in for a cup of tea, gatherings of adults on a Friday night for a beer, some music, and far too many stories that got more interesting, at least to me, as the night went on and the brown bottles of Emu Export piled up on the back verandah. As a child I collected beer bottle labels and coasters instead of stamps. I had a very large collection. For my mother, it was a chance to let her hair down after a long week working early mornings and long afternoons as a cleaner at the local high school, and then coming home to care for us children.

On these nights when our uncles and aunties would gather there was a great sense of community, of a shared history that had its roots in the house my mother was born into in 1930, in which her own mother raised her within a collective of aunties, uncles, foster-brothers and neighbours. My mother was an only child, but my grandmother ensured that she was surrounded by an extended family of support and connection.

As for our own neighbourhood, I don't want to paint some picture of a suburban idyll. As with any working-class neighbourhood where marda-mardas like us, and Anglo-Indian, Greek, Italian, Czechoslovakian and English migrants were thrown together, there were occasional differences of approach to all kinds of things. Generally everyone got on well, although that is not to say that sometimes things didn't get a little rough, or that the police weren't called to our street from time to time. While people retreated behind their windows with faces lit blue by flashing lights, minor problems, usually of a domestic nature, were usually easily sorted out.

On nights when the stories were flowing thick and fast and the house was filled with laughter, my mother was at her happiest. Those days are long gone, I must admit a little regretfully. Many of the old aunties that used to call in for a visit have passed away. The neighbourhood in which everyone seemed to know everyone else has long since been replaced by private villas and expensive real estate, but there are just enough of the older residents still around for my mother to want to stay, 'where I know people.'

My sister Beverley and I have brought my mother back to Hyde Park. It is the first time she has been here in years. Perth is certainly one of the most spread-out cities in the world, but it is a little surprising that my mother has stayed so far from the city centre for so long. As we walk around Hyde Park she seems amazed at how large the trees have grown, how small the park seems compared to her memory of it, and how many of the houses in her old neighbourhood have been bulldozed to make way for the newer apartments and town houses flooding the inner city. My mother spent her entire young life close to this park. She ran around it, climbed all over it and once, accidentally, found herself swimming in it. Normally my mother has no trouble talking about the past, but today she is very quiet as we lap the park. I can see that her arthritis is causing difficulty, a legacy of all those five o'clock starts in winter, and she is leaning, maybe a little hard, on my sister as we round the lakes and make our way over to where her house used to be.

We've brought her back because we thought it would cheer her up. She is one of the last of her generation of inner-city dwellers that called this place home, and with the many losses she has suffered in these last years of people who had been mainstays in her life, we thought a little trip back to the place her stories revolved around would do her good.

But it's not that simple. I believe my mother stayed away from here so long because she knew it would be like this, that change was inevitable. She loved her life in the city with her mother, her father and her extended family. By freezing the frame on her memories there, she allowed them to live on past her mother's and father's deaths, supported in this by the many friends that she kept from those times, and by the stories she told. In this way she kept all these people and events she had been witness to alive.

As in the old neighbourhood of Scarborough where we children were raised, in her old neighbourhood of inner-city Perth, houses had been pulled down, families had moved on and lost touch, people had died. Walking around the back of the block that was once my mother's home at 69 Glendower Street, but which is now a Greek Orthodox Church, my mother laughs at the thought of their old place becoming consecrated ground. When we came upon a little cottage that still remained from when she was a child, she is suddenly pleased. 'There you go,' she says to us with a hint of defiance, 'the buggers didn't get rid of everything.'

All places have their time for the people that live within them, and their experiences are made real again with the retelling of their stories. We sing these stories of dead relatives, of past friends, bringing them to life as a means of making sense of the movement forward into our present. Ancient Greeks used to call this feeling of the spirit of a city, or of people's interactions with their places of living, the *tyche* of a place. When I tell my mother this she laughs, rolls her eyes at my attempt at 'putting on the dog', and says the only Greeks she ever knew were the family of her best friend, Mary Mallis, who lived down in Lake Street.

My mother just calls these feelings about the past her memories, and she has told them to us because it always pleased her, and because she wanted us to know our past, and to have respect for it. My mother's stories are simply of the people she loved in the place that she loved, and central to all the memories, just as she was central to my mother's life, is her own mother, 'Mum Smith' as she came to be known in her neighbourhood opposite Hyde Park.

In the early 1930s my mother was just a child, but as my grandmother's constant companion she was a witness to everything that happened in the neighbourhood, on their travels in the city and in her own small and increasingly overcrowded house. All the women who came to visit loved young Betty and commented on how my grandmother was always looking out for her, sometimes maybe a little too closely. Some women believed that my grandmother was a little too controlling, a little too protective, but they reasoned that it was because Betty was her first child. 'You're always a little hard on the first child,' they would say from their own experience, and think nothing of it. But I wonder if there were also other factors at work here.

When the letters first arrived from Mr Neville threatening action if she did not stop seeing other Aboriginal people, I expect my grandmother gave a large sigh and thought, 'Here we go again.' Except that now the threats were not only to herself, but to her daughter as well. My mother remembered that my grandmother hated Mr Neville and that she had her own way of dealing with overt threats from the Aborigines Department. *Step one*: crack dumb. Act as if there was no problem, and no need for trouble. *Step two*: make it seem to all intents and purposes as if you are complying with what the Department wants. When replying to any questions, simply lie. *Step three*: hide behind the cover of 'normality', that is, what the Department considers 'normal', 'white' and 'respectable', but do what the hell you like, see who you like, and be yourself. *Step four*: keep the Department out of your life at all costs. If they take hold of your life, shake them loose as quick as you can. *Step five*: extend your network of support to neighbours around you that you can trust.

From as early as my mother can remember, my grandmother told her, 'Keep yourself clean, your house clean, and your body clean and they can't point a finger at you.' It was advice that she always followed herself. It sounds vaguely like a motto from one of those colonial instructional films popular in the 1950s, *Mr English Goes to Town*. But these films were aimed at training and preparing black populations for assimilation into the white communities. My grandmother's advice was a strategy for surviving the prying eyes of the Department. In 1930, any real progress in Aboriginal rights was two generations away. As a woman who had experienced being taken from her country, being raised in a mission, seeing children and families dying in Moore River, being ordered around the state by a white public servant, and being imprisoned when his orders were not obeyed, she had no conception of white society as anything but a dominating force over the lives of Aboriginal people. Live so they can't 'point a finger at you' my grandmother would tell young Betty, adding, 'Once they get their bloody hooks into you you've had it, they'll rule your bloody life.'

This is why my grandmother's house is a site of contradictions. It was kept spotlessly clean as if at any moment a missionary, a government official or a policeman could turn up and demand an inspection. But it was also an open house to anyone who wanted to stay, for as long as my grandmother wanted them to.

The nuances are ones of intent and action, perception and reality. Mr Neville intended my grandmother to marry a white man, settle down in a suburb, isolate herself from her community and raise a little white girl with no connection to community. My grandmother wanted him to think that was what she was doing, while all the time she did as she pleased, and raised my mother in a community of extended family.

In the 1930s my grandmother referred to herself as a 'coloured woman'. She raised my mother to see herself as a 'coloured girl' with 'coloured' relations. She raised her daughter as part of the Nor'wester community living in the South-West.

My grandmother's community was truly multicultural, a community of Noongars, Wongis, Yamatjis and Gidjas, and various other Aboriginal peoples from all over the state who had been removed to the South. A community of peoples strengthened by claimed connections of country, marriage between groups and shared histories of segregation and manipulation by the Aborigines Department.

My grandmother certainly saw the world in terms of *them* and *us*, *they* and *we*. *They* constituted the Aborigines Department and white society at large. *We* constituted the large, varied, multiracial, eclectic, poor, generally working-class 'underclass' that had survived the Aborigines Department and the racism of the white community. This was the 'Coloured Minority' that Mr Neville was intent on 'breeding out'.

In marrying a white man though, my grandmother was entering into contested territory. The 1905 Act was clear about what penalties would befall Edward if he 'suffered' Aboriginal people. The Act was also clear about how it could still control my mother's and grandmother's lives, without any redress from my grandfather. My grandmother had married a white man, and often said to my mother that, 'They want me to live like a white woman and that's what I'm going to let them think.' But she did not have the rights of a white woman. She could be removed under Section 12 of the Aborigines Act to any part of the state at the Chief Protector's bidding. My mother was classed as a 'quarter-caste' and under some clauses of the Act could be considered to be white, although in reality many children even fairer than herself found themselves deemed 'Aborigines' under the Act. These arbitrary and absurd notions of what constituted our community were soon to change though, and with these changes my mother's status as an Aborigine, under the Act, would be clearly defined. But these were external definitions, impositions. For my family, their own sense of community overrode these outside judgements.

For my mother the stories of this time are not about struggles with the Department, which is testament to my grandmother's ability to shield her from what was taking place outside the house, even while making her aware that there were outside influences to guard against. My mother was aware that her upbringing was, in part, determined by these outside influences and that she had to pitch in to make the system work. My mother remembered that she 'started doing chores' from the time she was five, 'standing on a soapbox.' But mostly for my mother the house exists as a series of memories of people. 'There's that many people who used to come and see Mum and either visit or stay. People would say, "Oh, we'll take you up to Jessie's."' As life in Glendower Street settled into its rhythms of comings and goings, of children staying, women playing cards, men and women staying while in town from the country, my mother watched, listened and learned.

In the early 1930s the effects of the Depression were hitting everyone, although Edward's work at the *West* was constant and brought in a good regular wage. Unfortunately, there were still debts that had been accumulated in my grandmother's time as a domestic servant, staying at Mrs Mulvale's boarding house and catching trains all over the state, and to keep the Department at bay, Edward was making regular payments off that debt. There were also their hire-purchase payments on all the goods they'd bought for their house. But they had regular money, and compared to some in the street, they were doing all right. When considering life today against those early years, my mother remarks, 'It was a battle for the average woman, black or white, to bring her child up then.'

Even before my mother was born Jessie had taken on the children of a friend, Cissie Forrest, who was ill with TB and knew she was dying. My grandmother tried to keep Cissie's children, but was forced to hand over the older boy. She raised the baby girl for a time, but eventually the Aborigines Department stepped in there too and had the girl removed to the care of the Salvation Army Girls Home.

This is when my grandmother began her regular trips around the city with my mother. Jessie and her baby daughter went everywhere together. They would travel down on the train to Cottesloe where Cissie's children had been placed to visit them. They would travel to visit Daisy Corunna where she worked in Claremont, and Nellie Lyndon where she worked for Captain Courthope in Fremantle, and anywhere else within easy reach of the railway line and able to be travelled in daylight hours. They could not risk getting caught in the Prohibited Area after nightfall. They travelled down to East Perth to visit Anna Fielder, or headed across town to the railway station or Government Gardens to meet up with friends who were still working as servants, and then back to Glendower Street in time to get dinner ready for their regular five o'clock dinner.

Apart from entering new territory by marrying a white man, my grandmother had also entered the difficult situation of being a black mother in a white neighbourhood. Having worked as a servant in white homes she was not unaccustomed to this, but having actual neighbours of her own was a new experience.

To cope with this situation her strategies included making friends with the white women in the street, a strategy which coincided with her *step five*—creating a trusted network of friends and neighbours—which saw her extended community of marda-mardas grow to include white families, as well as the white men who were seeing friends of hers. Race is the great divider, but class was the common bond that eased the crossing of the dividing line. Being, ironically, in a better position than some whites in the street, my grandmother was able to help out other families, providing food when she could and minding kids when needed.

In Olive Biggers, the woman who lived just across the vacant block that was next door to Glendower Street, Jessie made a good friend.

My mother got on well with the Biggers' children, and remembered how Jessie and Mrs Biggers 'were very good friends, and used to visit each other. Mrs Biggers was short and round, like Mum. They were like peas in a pod only Mum was coloured and Mrs Biggers was white. They'd just sit down and have a cuppa in between their work or cooking, share things that each one needed. She was a lot like Mum that way, her house was an open house. Some nights we'd all gather in our back yard with whoever was staying and Mrs Biggers and all her kids, and if there wasn't enough food, Mum and Mrs Biggers would head off to the park together. Oh, I knew what they were up to too, and that I'd have to clean up whatever they brought home. They used to head down to the water's edge with some bread, just like they were feeding the ducks. They were feeding the ducks all right. They'd wait till they spotted a really plump one, and then they'd slip it some bread with a safety pin hook in it and, *whoosh*. It was that quick I tell you. One minute the poor duck is in the water looking for a feed, the next thing Mum would have its neck wrung before it had time to take a breath.'

Against the background of threats of prosecution, my grandparents worked on *step two*: making everything as normal as possible. On weekday mornings Edward set the fire and each night cleared the fireplace for the next day. Betty would set the table of a morning, lifting the heavy plates up to the table that she could just see over, while Jessie cooked breakfast and readied the house for the day. My mother loved summer nights when they'd 'be lying on the grass looking up at the sky. Mum would be sitting in her favourite old chair. You know I don't know how that thing survived as long as it did. Dad used to be sitting on his old crate, and there'd be Aunty Bertha Isaacs, or Aunty Elsie Gardiner, and Dad would be telling me about the stars, y'know. I used to love those nights like that.'

Ensconced in his office with only his secretary, Miss Stitfold, and Mr Taylor as his co-workers, Mr Neville ruled over the amassed information used to control his charges. The meticulously kept records of the card system were alphabetised by name. The volumes of personal files were cross-referenced to thematic files such as 'Removal of Children', 'Punishments', 'Alcohol Related Matters' and, increasingly, 'Cohabitation'. Whispered rumours were carefully recorded, date stamped and signed off. Any sign of trouble called for the actioning of a file, the sending of letters to the Police Commissioner and the eventual use of the police. Be it a simple matter of removal, or the cancelling of a family's rations, it was all within the easy reach of Neville's office staff.

Thomas Bropho was thirty years old and had three children in the early 1930s. At Northam town camp with his wife Bella, he was a long way from Argyle, and a long way from achieving the justice that he had begun to fight for while he was still at Moore River. Thomas was a clever man, good with words and able to inspire large crowds of people. He had the 'gift of the gab', a skill he had honed while lay preaching at the Settlement. Although a Nor'wester, he had been accepted and trained alongside elder Noongar men at Moore River in Noongar culture. He married a Busselton Noongar woman, and he knew Noongar country well, could speak lingo, and while he might have preached a good sermon, he believed solidly in Noongar spiritual ways. Noongars knew him by his language name, Nyinda. Living rough and working hard were not new to him, but he longed for equality and a more prosperous future for his own children and for Noongar families like his own.

As the Depression bit hard, and more and more people found themselves without hope, Nyinda began to look for something better, but hadn't quite found the way to bring about change. Like the men of the Native Union, who he knew well, he wanted more than just hand-outs and small gains. At Moore River he had rebelled against a tracker who was about to whip a woman, and disarmed a violent confrontation by hiding the superintendent's gun. He had headed petitions to the superintendent about living conditions, and with Oscar Little was responsible for the words to the hymn 'Happy Land' that would come to be an anthem for the black experience of Moore River. But in the 1930s, while he hoped for a better future, he and Bella's chief concern was for their children's survival.

Living in the country regions had become perilous. White townspeople resented the swelling numbers of Aboriginal people in camps around towns. This was particularly true in the district where Thomas and Bella were working. Throughout the 1930s the Northam town camp had swelled. The camp was located on a creek bed, not far out from the town heading south-west. It was a traditional camp site where Aboriginal women had been going for centuries to give birth to their babies. By 1933 tensions were increasing with the harassment of camp people by whites and *bungee* men (white men looking for sex) coming out to the camps.

All over the countryside, as the work dried up Noongars were forced to settle on the outskirts of towns. Those who could make it to the city stood a better chance of cobbling together a living, and so Bella and Thomas decided to bring their family to pick grapes in the Swan Valley. The system of rations that white workers could rely on was less than certain for Aboriginal families, and when it came their way, it was not enough to feed a family. Granny Bella remembered the arbitrary and controlling system of rations. 'They would only give you rations if they thought you was worthy of it. The rations was meant to last you two weeks, but if you used it all up and went back to the ration place the next week they'd say, "Ooh, you got rations last week," and they wouldn't give you any. So you'd just have to go away and battle yourself to feed your kids.'

As Bella and Thomas were making their way to the Swan Valley, the people of the Northam camp were being rounded up to be placed on a train for removal to the Moore River Native Settlement. The reason for this, according to the authorities, was an outbreak of scabies, but when the camp people arrived at the already swelling Settlement, it was found that few people had any such skin problems. It was a ploy designed to rid the town of its Aboriginal population. Section 12 of the Aborigines Act allowed for any person deemed to be Aboriginal under the Act to be removed from one part of the state to another at the minister's pleasure. In that meticulous manner of Neville's, a Section 12 was typed, dated and signed for each one of the more than eighty people who were forcibly rounded up by police and herded into rail trucks for the journey to Mogumber.

Bella and Thomas were determined not to return to the Settlement. Even though, on the outside, the value of Aboriginal rations was between 2s 2d and 2s 8d, almost a quarter of the ration for whites, there was at least a chance of work, and if you avoided the authorities, some measure of freedom.

William Harris, who had been the key figure of the Native Union, had passed away, but there were younger men and women who were thinking

224

about how to overcome the position that their people had been placed in. While Thomas lived with his family in and around the camps of the city, from Guildford to Swanbourne, and worked at anything he could get, from grape picking to the bagging of fertiliser that scorched your lungs at Cresco's fertiliser factory, he was attending political meetings held on the Perth Esplanade. These open meetings focused on unemployment, union representation and the need for better conditions for the poor.

Mr Neville discouraged the employment of Aboriginal people around the city and maintained surveillance of those living in camps in Perth. The police estimated there were one hundred and fifty-four Aboriginal people living in and around the metropolitan area in the early 1930s, but the figures were most likely much higher, as people avoided contact with the police. Neville called on the police to make regular inspections of the camps and to list the names and origins of those people who were found in them. People from the country who were on rations would have their rations cut unless they returned to where they had come from. Thus they were faced with deprivation in the city unless there was work, which there often wasn't, or returning to country towns, where they weren't welcome, to live on less than nothing. In the country they could supplement their food by hunting rabbits, which many did, but resentment and harassment by white townspeople was endemic.

As Thomas jumped trains to get around the city, avoiding the police and the Department, he made regular visits to my grandmother's house. When he visited, he would catch up with other people staying there, like Carrie Layland, Bella's niece, and tell them what had been going on at the Esplanade in the political meetings. He was always gone before Edward returned. Mr Neville began watching the house again, and wrote warning Edward,

> Now that Carrie Layland has left your home I shall be glad if you will
> please note that no native or half-caste people whatsoever are to stay
> at your home without your first obtaining my consent. You will not
> be warned again.

My mother was only young at the time but could remember the tensions that would build in the house, usually around the threats that arrived in the mail from Mr Neville. 'Mum and Dad never had arguments, he always gave in to her, she always had her way. But for a while there he was really tetchy about Tommy Bropho coming. Tommy used to come and have a cup of tea. He'd be selling props around the town, you know, like big wooden sticks women used to prop up the clothesline. He'd leave his props by the back gate and come in. Mum would always go and pick through Dad's clothes to give to him, and she'd run up a bill down at the shop. One time Dad came home and he said, "Where's my shirts Jessie? Tommy Bropho's been here again hasn't he!" Then the grocer's bill would come and it would be, "What, you running up bills for Tommy Bropho again?" Dad used to keep the money in a cabinet in his workroom. No one put money in banks, never keep it long enough. It was like his room in the house, where he could have time on his own. When Mum wouldn't stop running up bills for Tommy, he put a lock on the cabinet. But Mum got cunning. I was standing there watching her and she got Dad's screwdriver and undid the hinges. She looked at me as if to say, "Don't you say a bloody word, Betty." But Mum was just like that, she couldn't say no to people. She'd always give someone a feed, or help them out if she could.'

Aunty Eileen Harwood hasn't slept for two nights straight. Our visit has stirred up memories of the past. It's mealtime. While Aunty Eileen stirs the tuna curry that she's cooking for us, she's calling out stories about 'Aunty Jessie's'. Aunty Eileen hasn't talked about those days in years. Her tiredness is not stopping her swift well-honed movement as she squeezes lemons and sprinkles in more Keen's curry powder after a taste test.

Aunty Eileen worked as a cook in the 1930s at the Avro Hospital in Subiaco. She was Eileen Gentle then, before she met up with Uncle George Harwood in the 1940s at my grandmother's house, when he came down to Perth after a long and meandering journey from his home town of Broome. It's not that she hasn't thought about those days, or about the homeland she was taken away from as a child, but in Canberra, where she and George have settled, there aren't many people from home to discuss the past with. 'This brings all the memories back for me, Stephen, talking like this, true.'

Aunty Eileen is cooking for us like my grandmother used to cook for her when Aunty Eileen, Aunty Alice Stack and all the other girls who were just young women then used to gather at my grandmother's.

While tea is cooking she comes back to the table to join Uncle George, Lauren and myself as we're going through the photographs I've brought with me. 'Here, see, there's me, Glamour Girl they all called me.' She laughs and holds the photographs to her chest. 'They all called me Glamour Girl back in them days.'

Aunty Eileen was taken away from Moola Bulla in 1933. She was thirteen years old, but had been known to Mr Neville since she was just a small child. On one of his tours of inspection to the Kimberley in the late 1920s, Neville made a note of Aunty Eileen and other young girls for future reference—those he thought suitable to remove when they were old enough. He made a note of her age and her parentage, and guessed at the imagined fraction of Aboriginal blood in her veins.

He made her stand against one of the feeding depot buildings while he took her photograph. In the photo she's a happy little kid looking straight into the camera and smiling. By the time she was thirteen, she was on a boat south and would never see her mother again.

Mr Neville was clear about why he wanted to remove girls. If they stayed in their country it,

> ... would simply mean that they would be married off to some native, and continue to procreate their species without being given any chance in life whatever. I am of the opinion that it would be better to bring these girls South and give them a chance in employment in suitable positions found by this Department. Prior to being sent out to work they would undergo a period of training at our Home at East Perth ... Failing that, the only thing to do is to leave them where they are, but I am afraid their fate would be to mate with full-blood husbands.

He reduced the context of their story to a few lines in one of his files specifically dealing with 'half-caste' children earmarked for removal. The file is a poignant collection of documents, two hundred and sixty pages of real people's lives being broken apart.

Aunty Eileen remembers the boat trip, and the arrival at Fremantle. 'We got off the boat and Matron Campbell was there to meet us. We caught the train to the East Perth Girls Home, and that's where Aunty Jessie came looking for us.'

The East Perth Girls Home was set up in 1930 by Mr Neville as a place where Aboriginal women would receive domestic training before being sent out to work. Initially it was run by Mrs Grace Campbell, who had been matron of Moore River Settlement.

The Home was intended to replace Mrs Mulvale's boarding house; it could accommodate more women, and as an official government institution could be brought under the legislative boundaries of the Aborigines Act. By 1933, when Aunty Eileen arrived from Moola Bulla with Rosie Gilligan and Alice Stack, it was the only place in the city where Aboriginal women were permitted to stay, although it fell just inside the boundary of the Perth Prohibited Area.

Aunty Eileen had been happy at Moola Bulla. She was born and raised there, felt free there surrounded by her own people. She names people she remembers, and smiles when she tells how they called her Poodlum, 'Because I had curly hair and I was cute.' She is critical of government interference in her life. 'We don't know our ages because they don't identify us. We weren't born as human beings. You might as well say they thought we was like a dog or a horse. We were in East Perth Girls Home for twelve months to get our training, but we didn't need any training. Mrs Woodland taught us all that up in Moola Bulla, about housework and cooking, all the domestic.'

Meanwhile my grandmother and mother would still go visiting. They'd catch the number 22 tram into the city and take the trolleybus out to East Perth to visit Anna Fielder. They'd visit the few other places in East Perth where Noongars had houses, and eventually end up at the East Perth Girls Home, which is where Aunty Eileen Harwood first met my grandmother. 'Aunty Jessie knew about us, you know, people talk and word gets around. Well, she came to see us. She came looking for any North girls that were taken away. Aunty heard we were there and she came down with Betty, her little girl. Betty was only really little then, like a little kid. But we weren't allowed to see her because the Native Affairs didn't allow us to see Aunty. They didn't like her. They thought she was a bad influence. But see, we were from the same country. Alice Stack, she was from Turkey Creek, and Aunty Jessie, she was from Argyle Station. We all had our skin names, like we knew our skin groups then, and her and Alice, well they knew all their uncles and other relations. Jessie was married to a white man, old Squeaker, Aunty called him. Pop Smith, we called him. They had a blue with Pop Smith, the Native Affairs, that's why we weren't allowed to go. But we used to go. It didn't stop us.'

Aunty Eileen hasn't talked about these stories for years and Uncle George is quietly watching his wife, a little worried that she'll overdo it, because she's into her seventies now. But Aunty is enjoying herself. In between huge servings of 'whip-crack' hot tuna curry, Aunty Eileen is telling us about the Glendower Street days.

'We were at that home for twelve months training and any time we got out, off to Aunty Jessie's. Both Alice and I went to work together. We were just domestic and cooking and all that. Our first job was out at a farm in Beverley. On our holiday, we used to come back to the Home, and we'd catch up with all these other girls and go to Aunty Jessie's place for cards. We used to play cards all day, every day sometimes, and all the coloured people used to go to Aunty's. It'd be, "You going somewhere?" "Yes, we're going up to Jessie's to play cards," and we'd all stay there too. Aunty was a champion card player. She used to play the mouth organ for us too, and Christmas time the girls would give her money to celebrate the New Year and she used to cook for us. We used to make our own party, nowhere else for us to go them days. We weren't supposed to talk to anybody, especially a white man. They had funny ideas because you're coloured.'

The 1934 Royal Commission into the Treatment of Aborigines was headed by local Magistrate H.D. Moseley. The Commission was set up to investigate

> ... the social and economic conditions of aboriginals and persons of aboriginal origin, with special reference to— the inclusion or exclusion of different classes of persons of aboriginal origin, in or from native camps; proximity of native camps to towns; physical well-being of aboriginals and any suggested measures for amelioration; disease amongst aboriginals and measures for their treatment; native Settlements; employment of aboriginals and persons of aboriginal origin; missions; trial of aboriginal offenders; Laws relating to aboriginals and persons of aboriginal origin and suggested amendments; the administration of the Aborigines Department generally; and, allegations which have appeared in the Press since the 1st day of July, 1930, relative to the ill-treatment of aboriginals in Western Australia.

It was quite a mouthful. As with the Roth Royal Commission in 1904, Aboriginal evidence would be taken by Moseley, with the difference that this time the evidence was given voluntarily, by Aboriginal people coming forward to state their case.

Mr Neville proceeded to comb his files and plan his strategy. He searched back into his archives to compile evidence that would take him two days to deliver. While Neville prepared his staff and his office for the Commission, Thomas Bropho and other Aboriginal people began to muster themselves to give evidence about the conditions that the community suffered under.

Eleven Aboriginal people came forward to give evidence to the Royal Commission: Norm Harris, Sam Isaacs, Alf Mippy, Mary Harris, Mary Warmadean, John Egan Snr and John Egan Jnr, Melba Egan Jnr, Dave Nannup and Thomas Bropho. None of them gave any support to Neville, the Department or the current state of affairs. They were keen to relate their stories of government repression to a member of the bench.

Thomas Bropho spoke eloquently of the need for proper education, training and employment for Aboriginal youth, without suffering the stringent management and control over their lives. He believed that Aboriginal children 'ought to be given a chance in the world', to which the Commissioner, Moseley responded, 'There is a good deal of common sense in what you say, and some day all these things may be done.'

Other witnesses spoke of the terrible conditions they had suffered at Moore River, of the poor food, lack of freedom, excessive punishments and the overt power of the Superintendent and the trackers. They spoke of witnessing ill treatment of women with children in Moore River, and Mary Warmadean described how, 'I have seen a lot of awful things at the Settlement.' They spoke of being forced to sign agreements against their will, and they spoke of being chased out of Northam by police when they tried to return after the mass removal to Moore River.

Neville attended the Commission throughout its proceedings, made copies of evidence given by people and put his staff to work digging up any dirt on them they could find in his departmental files. When an Aboriginal witness gave evidence Mr Neville not only repudiated them in the Commission proceedings, but took the liberty of producing their personal file. Neville's singular plan of action was to cast aspersions on people and, after damaging their reputations, hand in their personal files for the Commissioner to flick through at his leisure. It worked. These documents were not available to the people they were written about. The accuracy of their contents was never subject to scrutiny. On his personal notepad Neville scrawled notes and questions and rebuttals that he would pursue, along with various doodles when he was bored. There were population figures for Aboriginal people in Western Australia, with comparisons to other states, as well as various lists and statistics of costs and accounts and the numbers of children that had been removed by his Department since 1930. The removal of children was to be a chief focus of the Royal Commission.

Now that we have access to these same departmental files that Mr Neville was using, it is easy to see that he was misquoting his own evidence, misrepresenting the actual number of children removed from their families and, in particular, misrepresenting his style of administration.

What he did not mention to the Commission was that under him, conditions for Aboriginal people had deteriorated rapidly. At Moore River, which was never meant to hold more than two hundred people, the population had reached five hundred, and living conditions were near to rock bottom. Neville also neglected to mention that by the end of 1934, one hundred and sixty-four people had died in custody at the Settlement. Of these, seventy-five were children under the age of fifteen years, with most of them under the age of seven. Neville's policy was to remove children six years and over. Since 1930, the beginning of the terms of reference of the Royal Commission, fifty-four people had died in Moore River, twenty-two of them since the Northam people were placed there. In 1932 alone, twenty women had tried to run away.

It was Mr Neville's single-minded belief that biological absorption was the key to 'uplifting the Native race', and he had become blinded to any other means that we might have chosen to employ to 'uplift' ourselves. Neville made his views clear to the Commissioner.

The Commission will learn during its peregrinations how numerous these cross-breeds are, but particularly in the South-west and coastal towns in the North. There are half-castes married to aborigines and their progeny. There are three-quarter caste blacks married to other aborigines or quarter castes and their progeny. There are the off-spring of a white woman by a half-caste father living with a half-caste woman. There is the union of a full-blood aboriginal with a white woman and their off-spring. There is the Asiatic admixture, and Afghan and Negro admixture, complicating matters generally. They have, like other cross-breeds, an inherent dislike of institutionalism and authority, yet above all things they have to be protected against themselves whether they like it or not. They cannot remain as they are. The sore spot requires the application of the surgeon's knife for the good of the patient, and probably against the patient's will.

Biological absorption was to be the tool that Mr Neville planned to wield, scalpel-like, 'for the good of the patient'.

My grandfather looked like any other white worker in the city. Each day he rose early and lit the kitchen fire in the grate that he had methodically prepared the night before. Sometimes he made breakfast for himself and his wife and 'egg'n'soldiers' for his daughter before he prepared himself for the day and headed off to the Terrace, to Newspaper House. He would wheel his bike out to the back lane and ride off down Primrose Lane towards the city. As he headed down William Street he'd pass the milkman making his final deliveries, and ride past the crates of potatoes and cabbages stacked outside the corner shops in Brisbane Street, which were just beginning to open. The first trams were already moving, half full and silent, carrying sleepy workers into town.

The night shift would be coming off and the morning papers would have already hit the street. He didn't have to bother buying a paper, there would be plenty left over at work, test-run papers he could browse. Working the day shift meant he was on the afternoon run of the printing presses. Turning off St George's Terrace into the laneway on the left side of the building, Edward descended into the bowels of Newspaper House to begin his day.

He would have read about the gathering storm as it was printed across the pages of the newspapers that ran off the printing presses he maintained. Between 1930 and 1934 there were more than six hundred articles and letters in the press concerning what should be done about Aboriginal administration and management in Western Australia. He must have worried about his family's future, about the way that people would perceive them, and whether the Department would act on its threats against him.

Certainly he was lucky to have work in 1934, but I doubt he saw it as lucky that his family, and families like them, were the subject of a Royal

Commission, and of the bitter political divisions played out in newspaper editorials. From the time of his marriage to Jessie and the birth of their daughter, stories focusing on the 'Aboriginal Problem' had been building in volume and hatred.

Edward never brought home fellow workers from the *West Australian*. I imagine that this was the one time in his life when he was glad for the lack of a voice, when his uncommon silence was not a disadvantage, but a blessing. There were no doubt 'experts' within his own ranks, among the men who drove the trucks or sold the papers in the street, who hung around the delivery bay having a cigarette on their breaks, and the men who worked alongside him preparing the presses. Experts with theories and solutions they would be only too keen to share. He tried to keep his work and home life separate, but he could not screen out what was going on. With Edward's access to the latest breaking stories, the household at Glendower Street were all too well informed of the wider world existing outside their home.

Unlike his work mates, the rooms in Edward's house were piled with mattresses for women and children, and for men unlucky enough to be both out of work in the Depression and black at the time of the 1934 Royal Commission.

In that February, Neville took time out from his involvement in the Royal Commission to write to the Commissioner of Police.

> I am informed that the home of Mrs Jessie Smith, nee Argyle, is the resort of half-caste girls, and is also a place of assignment with white men encouraged by Mrs Smith. Mrs Smith's husband is, or was, employed by the *West Australian* as a storeman. I have previously warned Jessie, who is herself a half-caste, that her husband would be proceeded against under Section 21 (b) of the 'Aborigines Act' if she continued this practice. In order that action may be taken if necessary I shall be glad if an eye could be kept on the premises, with a view to ascertaining whether the facts are as stated.

Edward had tried to persuade Jessie to get some of the people to leave the house so that they could avoid trouble with the Department. He was worried that if things escalated, he would be imprisoned for cohabitation and Betty and Jessie would be taken to Moore River. Jessie refused to budge.

As Mr Neville made his way to the Royal Commission, tucked somewhere amongst his personal prompts and notes to himself was a list. At the top of that list were the names Jessie Argyle and Edward Smith. They were not directly mentioned in evidence but, it appears, formed part of Neville's statistics and evidence for his argument that such unions, between black and white, were a means to an end of achieving biological absorption. What he neglected to mention was that in reality this planned 'solution' was not leading to the kind of assimilated families he desired.

The climate of fear in the community caused by the Department's control, police surveillance and the threat of imprisonment, spilled over into acrimony. A Noongar woman whose daughter had been removed by Mr Neville decided to let him have a piece of her mind and, in the process, brought trouble for my grandmother. There is a ring of *Peyton Place*, or perhaps *Harper Valley PTA*, to the note, but the writer was deadly serious. The note was addressed to Mr Taylor, the department clerk.

> Well, Mr Taylor, our daughter was taken away from us because she was supposed to be carrying on with those awful white men, so your pimps said so, and yet your girls can go to Jessie Smith and carry on with white loafers and bludgers, ex-gaol birds as well. If you don't believe it go and see for yourself ... I got Gaol for the same thing, yet that's been going on for years at Smith's, go and see for yourself if you don't believe me; so if that is allowed at Smith's we should be left alone.

It was this letter that prompted Mr Neville to make the time to write to the Police Commissioner. The Police Commissioner duly provided his report.

> re Mrs Jessie Smith ... regarding the above named person, I have to advise that the following report has been received in connection with this matter—'I report having made inquiry and giving supervision to the residence of Mrs Jessie Smith of 69 Glendower Street. I cannot obtain any information to support the alleged complaint. Mrs Smith had a dark girl, Minnie Prosser, living on the first occasion of my visit. The house has been very orderly each time I have visited the vicinity

and I have not seen any other person there beside the girl Prosser and Mrs Smith and her child.'

Mr Neville wasn't satisfied.

I received information yesterday which indicates that the position is not as reported by your officer. I am told that coloured people are coming and going to this residence continually, and that moreover it is being used for a clandestine meeting place for immoral purposes. I should be much obliged if a close watch could be kept on the premises with a view to action being taken to put a stop to the present state of affairs.

Another report was drafted for Mr Neville.

I report having given further attention to 69 Glendower Street, the Home of Mrs Jessie Smith. I have ascertained that Minnie Prosser was married to Michael Pittard on the 9th April at a Church in North Perth and is now residing with her husband in Busselton. Pittard is a white man. Mr and Mrs Smith and child are the only people residing at 69 Glendower Street at present. I still cannot find anything to uphold the complaint. The result of my inquiry is that the Smiths are law-abiding citizens. Some of the neighbours, white people, call and have a game of cards in a friendly way during the evenings. I am of the opinion that the complaints made are of a malicious nature.

Mr Neville underlined the words 'Pittard a white Man', to be followed up further.

What Mr Neville did not know was that Police Constable Tompkins was one of the white neighbours visiting my grandmother's for a game of cards. What Mr Neville could not imagine was that my grandmother had created a network of support, from the grocer to the drycleaner, from the butcher to the taxidriver. She helped people in her own neighbourhood, and they helped her. In an ironic twist for my grandparents, Neville was not prepared to lose face over a mixed marriage that he had sanctioned, and so at that time, while the Commissioner was making his deliberations, my grandparents enjoyed a reprieve.

Sifting through the State Archives tells me more about the people who watched my family than it does about my own family. Our communities have been documented in departmental files, police files, by government photographers and would-be ethnographers. Until the early 1990s when Aboriginal people such as myself started documenting our communities in film, there was an estimated six thousand hours of material created *about* our communities, of which perhaps ten hours actually involved some Aboriginal input. It is the same with the images that were taken to document our communities in missions, in Settlements and in camps — they are not the images that we would have chosen to represent ourselves. To see us as our communities wanted to be seen, you have to come into our houses, our back yards, our streets and see what records we have left of ourselves.

Laying out my family images from the 1930s across the table before us, what do we see? We see my grandmother, Mum Smith, sitting in her old lounge chair propped up against the sawtooth wooden picket fence in Glendower Street. Wally Isaacs and Mack Hanson, two good-looking young black men dressed in white shirts, flank my grandmother as my mother, aged five, inadvertently flashes her gigantic white bloomers from where she is nestled in the grass at the foot of my grandmother's giant twenty-one stone frame. The camera has caught my mother unawares as she squints a cheeky (*kurra warra*) grin for the camera. My grandmother's wedding ring is shining defiantly on her left hand. Wally and Mack each have an arm around my grandmother's shoulders and are resting their hands comfortably on the fur collar of her oversized golfer coat. They're calm and relaxed, looking directly into the camera like some Bonnie and Clyde re-enactment — Mum Smith's Boys.

There is a series of images of my mother with children in Hyde Park. In one picture she is with the Biggers children, the twin lakes shining clean and open in the background. The lakes are yet to be cast in the shade of the plane tree that stands behind them, that seems too small compared to its gigantic self of today. They have my mother's old cane pram in the frame, which she has grown out of; it has been commandeered by a marda-marda baby that looks as if she is about to point a finger and demand, 'What you lookin' at?' They look like inner-city kids ready to take on anyone questioning what they're doing in *their* park.

There is a series of shots of groups of people, old women, young women, older men, younger men and heaps of kids. Someone has a piano accordion. There is my grandfather standing by his 'summerhouse' that he built every summer in the back yard. Rough timber poles frame an old canvas tent where Edward sleeps to escape the heat. An old water tank rests on its side as a chook shed and his newspapers are stacked to the side. He has little spots of his own about the yard; a seat he's made out of old bits of iron next to his tulip patch, a handmade pitchfork next to his sunflower patch that will eventually take over most of the yard. My grandmother sleeps on the back verandah, and my mother, although she has her own room to go to, is still young enough to bunk in, top to toe with my grandmother, when someone like old Sarah Low needs a place to stay.

Moving away from the house are a series of images taken when the family went to the beach. They'd load up a neighbour's truck and head to Naval Base beach where they wouldn't be disturbed. Secluded in the dunes, old Sarah Low, my mother, my grandfather, Marjory Coin and some neighbours are waiting for my grandmother to finish taking the photo so they can eat. Edward is playing the fool, wearing some kind of poncho and a tea towel on his head, sipping a cup of tea. Food is laid out on the crowded blanket and a cloth covers the hot damper from the camp oven.

My grandmother is photographed with my mother, half submerged in the rough surf. My grandmother came to love the sea. From the highway that had once transported her from her country, the briny sea became a haven which buoyed her twenty-one stone. When they came to the beach she always let the children use her as a diving board. They would stand on her shoulders and leap off into the sea. Eventually Edward would be called to dig her feet out before she was completely submerged in the rising waves.

In one of the images of Naval Base in the 1930s my grandmother and my mother are swimming together in the shallows. Somehow light has managed to get into the darkness of the camera's body and has left whimsical trails swirling around them. They're looking at each other and smiling as if they have no cares at all, as if they're completely free and the world will simply leave them to themselves.

But they are not left to themselves. Most of the people that I have mentioned from my grandparents' images also appear in the official state images of people incarcerated in Moore River, of men having mug shots taken by the police, of women lined up to have specimen shots taken for passing anthropologists. Photographs are powerful evidences. There is a great difference between a state-created image and a backyard gathering;

between being ordered to line up and look into the camera, and the calm relaxed moment with friends that you *want* to record.

The car headed east out of the city, along the Swan River following the railway lines, then north to the Moore River Native Settlement. They tried to hire a taxi but no one would take them that far, so my grandmother turned to her extended network in the neighbourhood. Mr Bill Gartrell, who ran the drycleaner's in Fitzgerald Street, saw how upset Jessie was and agreed to drive her to the Settlement. My mother had only ever heard my grandmother refer to Moore River as 'a place God started but forgot to finish.' She didn't know why they were headed there. She just knew that she was headed somewhere bad, and that my grandmother was very anxious.

News about the appalling conditions at the Settlement were widespread in the community, and in late 1935 it was at its worst. It was a good three-hour drive north into the Wheatbelt before they turned west at Mogumber West Road, made their way through dried-out fields for twelve miles and then hooked a left into the Settlement.

My mother remembers the day vividly. 'At first when we got there it was real quiet, like not a soul was around. Then all of a sudden these kids came running towards the car. These kids looked scared and desperate, and they were really poor. I mean, you could see they were poor, and I was really scared to tell the truth. Mum looked me straight and said, "Don't get out of the car. Don't move from here." Mum disappeared into some wooden cottage with all these kids following her. She wasn't long, but when I lost sight of her I got worried. Next minute she came running out with these kids under her arms, put them in the car and we took off.'

It was a remarkable story. A friend of my grandmother's was sent out to work by the Department, and had been moving around with her two children for some time before they found out and informed her that the children were not allowed to accompany her. She had reluctantly agreed for them to go into Moore River, but when she learned from Jessie how bad it was, she asked my grandmother to do something. My grandmother said, 'We've got to get them out of there,' and that's what she did.

When they finally returned home that night my mother was shocked at how sick the children were. 'These two little kids hadn't been in there that long but the little girl was that weak, and she had sandy blight in her eyes. The little boy was a bit older, and all he kept saying was, "Mummy, bubby cry all the time, bubby cry all the time." That was when I realised just how much my mum looked out for me. We took the kids all the way back to Perth, back to our house. It took ages of bathing before the little girl could open her eyes properly. Mum made them a really nice tea that night and put them to sleep in my room. Later on, when Mum went to check on them, they were fast asleep. The little girl still had a crust of bread in her hand from dinner and Mum went to take it out of her hand, but she just wouldn't let go. She was fast asleep, but she just wouldn't let go of that crust. Mum knew that the Department would be onto her, so the next day she got in touch with Sister Kate from Sister Kate's Home and when the kids were better they went out to Sister Kate's.

'Later on, when the girl was older, she came and stayed at our place for quite a while. I never mentioned that story about the crust to her till we met up years later when we were both older women, and it really upset her to think how she'd hung on to that crust.'

The incident never appeared in my grandmother's file. Not everything makes it into the records. Some incidents only remain in the minds of those who experienced or witnessed them. I believe that Sister Kate must have smoothed over any trouble in this instance. My grandmother became friends with Sister Kate, whose Home in Queens Park had been enthusiastically set up with Mr Neville's backing, for 'quarter-caste' children. As a child, my mother accompanied her mother on visits there.

'On Sundays we used to go to Sister Kate's Home. Our old woodman, Bert McNamara, used to take us out there in his truck. Mum used to give him petrol money and we'd stop on the way at Vic Park at this Greek fruit and veg shop. That's where she used to buy all the peanuts and mixed lollies, and the old Greek fella used to say, "You off to Sister Kate's lady?" and she'd say, "Yes, off to see the kids." Mum always used to take old newspapers with her. Dad would bring home from work what he could, and the store owners were always looking for it. Practically everything was wrapped in newspaper then, and this Greek shop owner used to say, "Well, do you want money for it or you want more fruit?" and Mum would always say, "Oh some more fruit, and some lollies as well." Then off we used to go to Sister Kate's. We'd get as far as Queens Park and you wouldn't see a soul. Then we'd come down Treasure Road and there'd be one kid, and as we rounded in towards the church they'd all come running out.'

My grandmother was regularly visiting Sister Kate's to keep an eye on the children of women she knew who were out working and unable to visit themselves. It was another institution of removal, and in recent years the abuse that children suffered in the 1950s and 1960s in this home has become well known. Whether such abuse occurred in Sister Kate's time, I do not know. Some people believe that these incidents started after Sister Kate died in 1946. In 1935 it seems that she was trusted by older women like my grandmother, for providing a better place for children than Moore River. If the women could have kept their children with them, or if my grandmother and other Aboriginal women could have fostered more children, such situations would not have been forced on Aboriginal mothers, and generations of children would not have had to pay so high a price.

When Moseley handed down his final report in January 1935, Neville was delighted. Moseley described how, in his view, 'half-castes' were 'the great problem confronting the community today.' And while finding biological absorption unpalatable and the removals of children unfortunate, Moseley actually recommended that the Department gain even greater control over an even larger number of Aboriginal people. In a letter to the Minister for Aboriginal Affairs, Mr Neville commented that, in regard to Moseley's Report, 'The views expressed by him as Royal Commissioner so nearly approach my own as generally tendered in evidence before him.'

Many charitable white groups that had earlier campaigned against the powers of the Aborigines Department also accepted the report with generally glowing responses. The Women's Service Guild wrote to the Department to 'express our appreciation of the action of the Government in appointing a Royal Commission on the Welfare of aborigines in Western Australia, and congratulate the Commissioner on a fine report submitted.' The Anti-Slavery and Aborigines Protection Society wrote to Neville stating their interest in 'the welfare of aborigines of Australia' and congratulating the government.

In September 1936, the amending legislative changes resulting from the Royal Commissioners' recommendations were placed before parliament. By April 1937 they had become law. Apart from minor articles in the press, the controversy that had been the 'half-caste problem' appears to have been solved for the wider public. It would be the Aboriginal community, already suffering greatly with massive unemployment, disastrous living conditions and racial segregation, that would have to deal with the consequences. The 1936 Native Administration Act was essentially the old 1905 Act in overdrive, with far greater powers for the Chief Protector, Mr Neville, who was subsequently promoted to the new role of Commissioner of Native Affairs.

The fact that the 1936 Native Administration Act allowed for any person of Aboriginal descent to be deemed a 'Native' under the Act would in reality make very little difference to most Aboriginal people. Under the 1905 Act, no matter how fair skinned, Aboriginal people were deemed to come under the Department's control merely by the act of association with other Aboriginal people. The government had always included provisions for being exempted from the Act, but these were conditional upon people divorcing themselves from their own people, their own immediate families and, in essence, their identity as Aboriginal. Many Aboriginal people applied for such exemptions, but they did so more to escape the provisions of the Act and the controls of the new Native Affairs Department than any desire to check their skins, or their families, at the door.

However, Section 8 of the 1936 Act would be particularly damaging.

> The Commissioner shall be the legal guardian of every native child notwithstanding that the child has a parent or other relative living, until such child attains the age of twenty-one years.

Essentially, this meant that every Aboriginal child, including my mother, could be removed by Mr Neville, without redress. Section 22 of the 1936 Act replaced Section 21 of the 1905 Act, the clause my grandfather had been threatened with by Mr Neville. It increased the penalty to a six-month prison term, for *suffering* 'any native to be upon any house, ship, camp, or other place in his occupation ... without the authority in writing of a protector or inspector.'

As the 1936 Act was being formulated, Mr Neville took the time in December to write to the Commissioner of Police yet again.

> I find that Mrs. J. Smith of 69 Glendower St., East Perth is still harbouring, boarding, or otherwise allowing half-castes to occupy her premises without the knowledge of this Department, or its approval. I shall be much obliged if these facts can be verified and Mrs Smith informed that any further breach of the Aborigines Act, in this connection, will be followed by prosecution without further notice.

Later, in January 1937, a note was made on my grandmother's file.

Mrs Smith called to see me today. She stated that the Police had been making enquiries regarding her and she wanted to know what was the matter. I told her and she admitted that William Noble and his wife (Dinah Sutton) had stayed with her and she stated that she had been visited by Carrie Layland, Elsie Gardiner, Sandy Harris and his wife, and Tommy Corbett. I told her that such visits must cease instantly otherwise the Department would take drastic action against her. She thanked me for the advice but gave me the impression that she was rather worried as to the action that she should take to keep these people away from her place. Eventually she said that she would tell them to keep away and if she had any trouble with them she would ring up the Highgate Hill Police. Finally, I told Mrs Smith that the Department did not propose to hesitate in action against her should she offend again and I gave her to understand that the future lay in her own hands.

My grandmother's strategy of playing for time was wearing thin. She had no intention of asking people to leave her house or return to the country, but she told the Department what she knew they wanted to hear. The police report that Mr Neville requested stated that,

It appears that half-caste women do visit Mrs Smith, of 69 Glendower Street, but whilst there they appear to conduct themselves well. The Police at this Station frequently pass the house in question. I have questioned them all in regard to the conduct of the place and they all state at no time have they seen or heard any unseemly conduct taking place there, nor has there been any complaint made at the Station re the conduct of the house or occupants. Should anything be brought under my notice, I will take suitable action to suppress same.

As the police seemed reluctant to act at Mr Neville's behest, he utilised his new powers to set up a Pass System for Aboriginal people entering the city as a means of controlling the community's movements. The Pass System came into effect from 1 July 1937 and applied to any Aboriginal person over the age of fourteen. Mr Neville dismissed his clerk's suggestion that the police handle the Pass System and insisted that all passes be issued only with his personal approval. These passes had gradations of access to the city which progressed from denial of access, to being allowed access only within daylight hours, and finally to unrestricted access, which meant that you had until 11.15 pm to get out of the Prohibited Area. The Department began with the issue of permits to domestic servants who worked within the boundaries of the area, inmates of the East Perth Girls Home and applicants who could prove they legitimately needed to pass through the city after hours.

Under the previous Prohibited Area system Aboriginal people were required to be out of the city by 6 pm if they were not in lawful employment. The police complained, however, that they had no way of telling whether people really were in employment or not. The new system solved this problem by requiring that to be anywhere within the Prohibited Area, night or day, you had to hold a pass approved by Mr Neville. The police simply had to ask to see your pass. No pass, you were out of the city. Even though police and Native Affairs inspectors were the only people entitled to check for passes, once knowledge of the system became common, any white person holding the merest sliver of authority could demand that Aboriginal people show their pass or leave. Some tram drivers, shopkeepers, and station masters took it upon themselves to demand to see passes. By 1939 the Pass System had been extended to include anyone camping in the entire metropolitan area, and police at Guildford and Fremantle were involved in a widening of the control of the community.

At this time Bella and Thomas Bropho were living in camps around the city, getting work wherever they could to support their family. Bella continued to work cleaning and scrubbing for white women around Swanbourne and Claremont where her family were camped. Thomas sold props all over the city, walking all day long calling out 'Props, props for sale', in working class areas, or if pounding the pavement of a more genteel clientele, 'Props, props, oh lady'. When Thomas paid visits to my grandmother's, he would have to sneak onto a train as he could not afford the fare.

Bella had to travel to the city to get rations when times were hard. She remembered the farce of having to apply for a pass to travel from the camps to the city. 'I used to have a little card to go from Perth Station to the Native Welfare. To get those passes you'd have to go to the Department and they'd

243

write it in a little book. You carried that little book in your bag all the time. A policeman could walk up to you and say, "Got your pass on you?" "Yeah I've got a pass here," and you'd pull it out and show it. "All right," he'd say, and tell you to be out of the town at a certain time.' The risks that Thomas Bropho and other Aboriginal witnesses had taken in giving evidence against the Department had been in vain.

In January 1938 an informant to the Department of Native Affairs met with Mr Neville at his head office in Murray Street. This person was not concerned with getting a pass to be in the city but had come to tell Mr Neville that my grandmother was caring for Ken and Alec Forrest without the Department's approval. My grandmother had cared for Ken and Alec since 1936 when their mother Kitty had asked Jessie to help while she worked as a cook in the Goldfields. Kitty had separated from her husband, Tom Forrest, and was supporting her boys as best she could. Most jobs didn't allow for children. In 1938 Alec Forrest set out to try and find work as a shearer in the Wheatbelt. Ken, who was younger, stayed with my grandparents and found a job in the city. But he was well under the age of twenty-one and, as such, was under the guardianship of Mr Neville, not my grandmother, or even his own mother. A note was made on the file.

> Highgate Hill Police visited Smith's house at 69 Glendower Street, and found that Ken Forrest and not Alex is staying there and is employed by the Pascomi Co. Perth. The C.N.A. instructed that Smith be prosecuted for breach of Section 22 of the Act.

The file does not record whether Edward was actually prosecuted. He may well have been fined. It was a rollercoaster ride of bluff, manoeuvre and counter call, but my grandmother continued to go about her life as she always had. What thwarted Neville was the reluctance of the local police to do anything about my grandmother's house. This was unusual. Police were the Native Affairs Department's front-line in dealing with the Aboriginal community. If my grandparents had not known the policeman on their beat well, a damaging report would have been forwarded and they would have been charged. But while my grandmother's own efforts, and her marriage to a white man, made her life exceptional for an Aboriginal woman in the Depression years, life for most Aboriginal families continued to be unremittingly harsh.

In August 1939 the same informant wrote again to Mr Neville. This poor Noongar woman's husband had left her and she couldn't get the maintenance that he owed her. She was down and tired and angry and spreading some of that anger around. 'The Police are hounding me, the West Perth coppers are bouncing me and bullying me every time they spot me.' She went on to name every Aboriginal woman living with a white man, and asked Mr Neville to deal with them as she'd been dealt with. She saved my grandparents for last.

> Jessie Smith has these women and a few more at her place drinking and carrying on with white men drinking up a treat ... Why are these whites allowed to cohabit with these half-castes and give them drink ... Nothing is said to these sinners ... So you know now what's going on at Jessie Smith's place.

Mr Neville moved into action again, and wrote to the Police Commissioner.

> I have heard that the home of Mrs Jessie Smith, 69 Glendower Street, Perth, is again becoming a place of resort for native persons ... I am told that drinking and taxi-riding are indulged in, and I have been particularly advised that two half-caste women ... and a white man ... are concerned. It is not desirable that drink should be available to natives, but Mrs. Smith is married to a white man who can obtain drink, and it may be available to half-caste women when they visit Mrs Smith; perhaps this rather than friendship is the attraction of Mrs Smith's house.

While Neville's investigation was under way, my grandmother was saying goodbye to one of her most valued friends. Anna Fielder passed away in 1938. Anna was only fifty-seven years old, and she and Jessie had known one another for more than seventeen years. Jessie attended the funeral at Karrakatta Cemetery, and a simple notice was placed in the *West Australian*. 'Dearly loved wife of Gerald Fielder, and loving mother of Jean, Keith and Hope, fond cousin of May and friend of Mrs Jessie Smith, North Perth.'

In late 1939 the Commissioner of Police responded to Mr Neville for the last time about his constant requests to hound the people visiting my grandmother's house.

> Relative to Mrs Jessie Smith of Glendower Street, Perth, it appears to me that as you have an Inspector attached to your Department, an inquiry of this nature could very well be undertaken by him.

Mr Neville, disappointed by the police response, asked the Deputy Commissioner of Native Affairs to 'Get Jessie Smith in and ask her straight out about the allegations,' adding, 'Previously she has assured me that nothing of the kind takes place there, but personally I am a bit doubtful.' The Deputy Commissioner made a note:

> Jessie Smith called and saw me yesterday afternoon. She denies emphatically that any misconduct was taking place at her home. She … expressed surprise that any complaints had been made to us.

I can just imagine my grandmother laughing as she told everyone that night how she had handled the Department.

My grandmother was not going to need her old tactics much longer. Neville was about to retire. As darker events were unfolding in Europe, the man who had personally and doggedly helped formulate and implement the most draconian legislation for Aboriginal people in Western Australia had finally run out of time.

Throughout 1939, Mr Neville attended various functions to mark his retirement. Blackfellas knew he was about to retire and were happy to see the back of him. But between work send-offs and the handover of the Department to his successor, Deputy Commissioner Francis 'Sonny' Bray, Mr Neville still managed to make a few plans for his own future that would continue to impact on the lives of Aboriginal people in Western Australia.

When Aunty Eileen Harwood smiles you can still see the Glamour Girl smile that she was famous for as a young woman. The smile that obviously beguiled Uncle George when he first came down to Perth from Broome all those years ago. It's the sort of 'pin-up beautiful' smile that would launch a campaign of some kind, that you might see on a billboard somewhere in the city. Aunty Eileen is white haired now, but her thick black eyebrows hint at the shock of curly black hair she was once so proud of. Even though she was taken away from Gidja country decades before, Aunty Eileen still speaks some language and has a Gidja way of speaking, modulating her sentences in a kind of singsong rhythm.

I've brought an image of Aunty Eileen with me that I want to ask her about. She hasn't seen this image in years, though she has a copy of it somewhere out the back in her boxes of belongings, and can remember the day it was taken in 1939. I copied this image from a book that was published in 1944. It was entitled *Australia's Coloured Minority* and was written by A.O. Neville. In those last months of his administration when he was busy creating pass systems and ordering prosecutions for cohabitation, Mr Neville was also collecting material for his book. It was to be his swan song, an immortalising of his views on the biological absorption of Aboriginal peoples into white Australia.

Aunty Eileen likes the image, but not the book that I retrieved it from. She had no idea that she was going to be used as Mr Neville's pin-up girl for biological assimilation. She was working in the city at the Avro Hospital when the directive came through. 'I got this letter telling me to come in and have my photo taken. I come into the studio and this man told me that it was for Mr Neville. I didn't think nothing of it till that book of his come out, years later, and there was my photo.' In the photograph she is seated in a studio. Her hair was fixed for the session, and she is smiling her best Glamour Girl smile.

Above the photo is one taken in the 1920s when she was a small child. Mr Neville, on his northern tour of inspection, was documenting suitable 'half-caste' children that he would remove to Moore River as soon as it was established. He spotted Aunty Eileen at Moola Bulla. He made her stand up against the feeding depot wall and asked her to smile, which she did, and took her photograph.

In his book, the caption to the Moola Bulla photo reads 'A Bush Waif', while the studio photograph of her in 1939 is captioned 'Half-Blood (First Cross), Identical with above child'.

These photographs, along with many others, appeared in the macabre centrefolds of Mr Neville's book. Every person in these images was a friend of my grandmother's. Each of these women, and some of the small boys mentioned, were part of the community of people that managed to survive the Neville years, only to be held up as positive examples of his theories of eugenics and the breeding out of colour.

They were the very same women who sat around my grandmother's table at mealtimes, who had driven Mr Neville in his continuous campaign against my grandparents. They were the women who met up with their boyfriends, family and children at my grandmother's house. They were women who, on their days off, would put in their money and shout my grandmother to a taxi ride into the hills.

In Neville's book the narrative of their lives was a simple one. Removed from their country, they were trained to become white, and they became white. His narrative, suggested by his series of 'before' and 'after' shots, falls insultingly short of appreciating the complexity of marda-mardas living as a community of extended Aboriginal families, bonded by complex systems of culture and respect for where we belong.

There is an image in Neville's book of Aunty Elsie Gardiner and Mary Cross. Mary was a good friend of my grandmother's. She was from Wyndham, near my grandmother's country, and had been brought down around the same time as Aunty Elsie, who was from Mount Gardiner Station. The studio images were taken at the same time as Aunty Eileen's. Mary and Elsie both sit looking straight into the camera with confidence. Above them is a photograph that Mr Neville had taken of two children, one of whom is Elsie at age five, before she was taken away from her family in the East Kimberley. Under the image of the children he has placed the caption 'As I Found Them'. Under the image of Elsie and Mary as grown women he has placed the caption 'First Cross Half-Blood Girls'.

Aunty Elsie Gardiner was everyone's favourite. She appears in all our family photographs, in early images of my grandmother with other domestic servants, in the Moore River Native Settlement, all over the state. Like my grandmother, she is described by women who knew her as having a way of attracting people, a woman that other women turned to in times of trouble. My mother loved Aunty Elsie, and she was known by almost everyone in the community. She was one of the first women to begin taking box brownie images of her friends and sharing around the photographs, and she left a valuable record of the women who were sent to work from one end of the state to the other.

The image that Mr Neville took of Elsie Gardiner and Mary Cross as children was taken on the same expedition in 1916 that he first noticed Aunty Eileen Harwood. Three years after returning to Perth, Mr Neville ordered a police report on the conditions of the children he had photographed in the north. The reports were duly sent. They noted the children's names, ages and the names of their parents. Unusual in the case of removals, Mr Williams, who was managing Mount Gardiner Station, told the police that he 'would take no part in the sending away of these two children.'

Constable John McLay was sent to remove the children, but informed Sergeant Crone of the Derby police that he also did not want any part in the removal, and Sergeant Crone agreed. Inspector Drewry of the Derby police subsequently wrote to Mr Neville informing him of their dissent.

> I desire to submit that this seizing and removing of these children is so obnoxious to the Police and I trust that some official of the Aborigines Dept. will be appointed to do it. I submit that behind the power of the Chief Protector to order such seizure lies the point 'for cause shown', yet, in these cases no cause has been shown; yet he can seize all aboriginal or half-caste children under sixteen years of age. No neglect has been shown by the mothers ... The Aboriginals Act does not demand that Police shall carry out duty such as the above, which I contend is not humane, the mother having cared for these children under circumstances where a white woman under similar circum-stances would have found an easy solution out of the difficulty. The children have the natural love for the mother.

This is another aspect of the complexity of our histories that the Mr Nevilles of the world like to gloss over when considering race issues. Aboriginal witnesses complained of the senselessness of Department policies at the 1934 Royal Commission. The Native Union spoke out against injustice in 1928. Here these police were refusing to accept blanket racist policies aimed at solving so-called 'Aboriginal problems'. Aboriginal communities and the problems they experienced were complex then, as they are now. Simplistic solutions based on ignorance and ingrained senses of superiority serve no one.

Mr Neville was incensed and wrote back to the Police Commissioner.

> If the duty of bringing in half-caste children is obnoxious to the Police, it is strange that this Department has not been previously advised of this, in view of the hundreds of cases that have had attention. I inspected these two youngsters when in Kimberley in

1916. I ask, therefore, that the removal be effected as early as possible. It is inadvisable that the Station should be advised beforehand of the date upon which the children are to be taken away, as this would undoubtedly lead to the mothers hiding the youngsters, and thereby causing the Police additional trouble.

In the 1934 Royal Commission, when critics claimed that hundreds of Aboriginal children had been taken away from their families, Mr Neville argued that it was perhaps only dozens of children. Yet his own records reveal that even by 1920, fourteen years earlier, he was aware that there had been hundreds.

There is a recent revision of Mr Neville's legacy by Western Australia's more conservative historical community, which has seen him as a 'man of his time', and Aboriginal criticisms of his regime of repression as 'naive and ill-informed'. I believe that these historians would do better to listen to the Aboriginal witnesses who knew this man, and the stories that they have passed on within our communities.

In December 1919, Aunty Elsie Gardiner was taken away from her mother. This is one story of the removal of women who featured in the centrefold of Mr Neville's book. There are others. Under an image of Lemmie Ah-kim as a child were the words, 'Half-Blood, Chinese-Aboriginal Girl'. Lemmie and her sisters Orange (Orrie), Winnie and Rosie were all taken away from their Chinese father in Wyndham after their mother died. He had cared for them on his own until the Department found out about them. Later, sitting in the adult Lemmie's flat, she told me that, though they never got to see him again, they had been informed of his death. He was a market gardener and a bird catcher on the outskirts of Wyndham. When he'd had enough, she was told he went and lay in a grave he'd dug himself and waited for death.

Under an image of Aunty Bessie Rutter, her daughter Hettie and her grandson Peter, are the words,

Three Generations. Reading from left to right, 1. Half-blood—Irish Australian Father: Full-Blood Mother, 2. Quadroon Daughter—Father Australian Born of Scottish parents, 3. Octaroon Grandson—Father Australian of Irish descent: Mother, No. 2.

Hettie and Auntie Bessie came to my grandmother's house. George was cared for by my grandmother while his mother worked at the Golden Eagle Tea Rooms.

There are many more women in Neville's book with equally insulting and disturbing labels under their pictures. They all have their stories of removal, of avoiding the Department and of having to deal with the obsessed actions of a detached, removed public servant.

Finally, in an image of three young girls taken in the studio is Aunty Eileen Shang. Aunty is barely old enough to be out at work. She is smiling into the camera without a clue as to how the photograph would be used. Below the image is the caption, 'Three Near-White Girls'. Mr Neville used these images as proof of his successes. He used them in a mounting narrative of racial management through biological absorption. It was the only story he knew.

In March 1940 Mr Neville was nearing the end of his reign. He was attending just one more retirement bash down at the East Perth Girls Home. It was hardly major news. The war was looming. Buried in the 'Woman's Realm' section of the *West Australian*, amongst the 'Social Notes' and items such as 'Easter Eggs', was an article entitled 'Native Girls—Mr Neville Farewelled'. A number of dignitaries had turned out for the affair. The Lieutenant-Governor Sir James Mitchell and Lady Mitchell were in attendance along with Minister Cloverley, Chief Secretary Mr Kitson, Sonny Bray, Mrs Campbell, Sister Wilkinson (who had replaced Mrs Campbell), and a number of other Perth luminaries. Speeches were made by Mr Cloverley and Mr Kitson praising Mr Neville's hard work in carrying out the unenviable task 'of a man trying to produce bricks without straw'.

There was no mention of any Aboriginal women present when the new matron, who had been a nurse at Moore River in the 1930s, stepped forward to outline the training aspect of the East Perth Girls Home. She presented Mr Neville with 'an album containing photos of some of the hundreds of girls who had passed through it.' Had he known he was going to receive this album, he might not have ordered the studio images of women for his forthcoming book.

When Mr Neville took the stand, he made his usual comments on the future of Aboriginal absorption into the community, adding that disaster would be the outcome if they were 'to let the native people of Australia go their own way.' Interestingly, Mr Neville told the gathering that his 'interest in the welfare of native girls could be traced to an encounter with two small half-caste children in the Kimberley.' One of these two children was Aunty Elsie Gardiner. He told his audience that, once brought to Perth, these girls had prospered; one was working for a well-known family and the other was married and in a home of her own. Expunged was the story of how he had pressed on with Aunty Elsie's removal despite clear reports from the police that she was being well cared for by her mother.

In lauding the work of the East Perth Girls Home he pointed out that there was a steady demand for domestic servants that the Department found 'impossible to fill', and that in his view, 'the girls had earned a fine reputation.'

Mr Neville had one final point to make about the virtue and success of his department and its policies. 'These girls,' he said, 'were more to be admired when the temptations that came their way, even near the East Perth Home, were taken into consideration.' I wonder if he had my grandmother's house in mind.

Aunty Eileen Shang had done her time in the East Perth Home and had no time for any party for Mr Neville. 'Well, Neville was a dictator. He dictated our lives, and white Australians couldn't see what he'd done. He was a powerful man. They didn't know, or they didn't want to know, what they did to us. They tried to kill the race out, but they couldn't.'

When the news spread that Mr Neville was really going, my grandmother and her friends decided to have their own party. In the back yard of Glendower Street they pulled out the chairs and set up the drinks. They invited a few blokes around and played music, and they danced to the news that they were finally rid of the man who had ruled over their lives for so long.

My grandmother's file that had grown so rapidly during the years of the Depression, well tended and fed by Mr Neville's surveillance of my family, now began to shrink and wither as succeeding administrators turned their attention to wider concerns.

The lights were about to go out across the city as blackout conditions were brought in during the war. Some of the men and women visiting Glendower Street pooled their money together to take my grandmother up into the hills for a last look at the lights before war descended. Henry Mippy was in the back of the taxi, which was crammed with all the people they could fit, as they headed up Greenmount Hill. Henry was staying at my grandmother's. His mother was Amy Mippy, one of the old girls my grandfather would seek out at White City for news of Jessie while she was in Moore River.

Years later when I caught up with Henry Mippy, he was an old man living in Wickham, just out of Roebourne. He told me the story of the night they took my grandmother up the hill. 'When we got up to Greenmount Hill you could see the lights of the city in the distance. We'd had a great ride out, having a ball in the back of the taxi, and Aunty was real happy. After we'd been up there a while, just looking at the city, the taxi driver says, "Okay to head back now, Missus?" But Aunty Jessie was loving it. She just said, "No, we go home when I'm ready."'

From their spot high on the hill they could see the ring of lights of Gloucester Park Trotting Track. Standing in the cool air, surrounded by the darkening sky, the lights of the city shone, floating in the distance. On a clear night it is a breathtaking vision. It must have seemed as if the whole world opened up and unfurled beneath my grandmother's slippers as the new decade was about to begin.

night lives

I'm waiting at the airport for Aunty Eileen Shang to arrive. Aunty always makes a big entrance. There doesn't always have to be an occasion, but in this case there is. Eileen Shang is returning to Perth for the first time in over forty years. She is coming back to set the story straight. During her self-imposed exile Aunty has gladly told anyone within earshot that Western Australia is the most racist state in all of Australia, and that wild horses wouldn't bring her back. The plane that is finally bringing her back is late, but what are a few hours when you've been away for forty years.

Aunty Eileen went back to the tiny town of Marble Bar soon after the Second World War. At that point she hadn't quite quit the state of Western Australia. Aunty Eileen had been taken from her mother by the Aborigines Department when she was still a baby. After years spent at the Moore River Native Settlement and even longer working for white people, she was fed up with the South and with the people who ran it. Aunty knew she was taking a chance, but she decided, in the post-war muddle, to risk the wrath of the Native Affairs Department and she fled the city. With her oldest boy Jimmy in tow she wanted to return to her country and her mother. But it was too late. Her removal from her country and her mother, and the damage that had resulted for her own mother in all the years between had made reconnection too difficult. She stayed in the North as long as she could, hoping that things would be resolved, but too much had changed. Reunions are seldom the wonderful and satisfying affairs that novelists and television producers like to portray. The homeland that once existed in the form of her family and her country was lost to her.

On returning to Perth in the early 1950s, Aunty Eileen was reminded of the other reasons that made her flee the city. At bus stops buses wouldn't stop for her. At shops shopkeepers wouldn't serve her. Aunty Eileen was tired of being trapped and marked in this backwater town. From being separated and sorted like cattle at the Moore River Native Settlement, to being beaten as a young teenager when sent out to work for white families, suffering police intimidation and the ever present eye of the Native Affairs Department, Aunty had seen and experienced it all. Aunty Eileen has a long memory of Western Australia. It is something she'd rather forget, but she refuses to let go, as if doing so would somehow signal some kind of defeat.

Eileen Shang fled the city for the last time in the 1950s and headed north to Darwin. In Darwin Aunty found refuge. Of course, there were still racial problems but, compared to Perth, she believed she'd found paradise. Aunty soon married and raised her large family. When Cyclone Tracy hit Darwin in 1974, Aunty was the last person out the window of her home, clutching her memories in an old biscuit tin. Memories, even those that you want to forget, are the first thing we reach for when the house comes down. Apart from the photographs of her good memories, of the children growing up, and of she and her husband's life together, the tin held the last remnants of her life in Perth. Images of close friends, images of my grandmother and of other old girls who had made life in Perth bearable. There were also the 'Dog Tags'. This was the 'identity card' that was forced on the Aboriginal community that Aunty wanted to show to her children. Here was her tangible proof of her experience of Perth and Western Australia, but as she crawled out of the window in the howling rain the tin of evidence was snatched from her hands by the wind.

Aunty has moved around a great deal since then, all over Australia in fact, but she never returned to Perth. After retiring she lived in reconstructed Darwin. She never did find the lost images. But you don't forget being taken from your family and treated as a less than second-class citizen. Memories resurface and smack you in the eye. Aunty Eileen was a Nor'wester and one of my grandmother's favourite claimed nieces. She is legendary in the stories that circulate about Aboriginal community life in Perth during the war years. Her house was a place of comings and goings of United States, British and Australian servicemen, of sly grog and illegal gambling. Her house was like my grandmother's house, as the two of them learned how to make up for life carefully under the watchful control of the Aborigines Department.

But it isn't wild horses that are dragging Aunty back to Western Australia, rather a request from me that she participate in a documentary film about Aboriginal experiences in Perth in the 1940s and 1950s. At first, Aunty wasn't too sure about it, but when I promised she would have the chance to tell things as she saw them, she was willing to give it a go. Mind you, it took me five years of asking and careful discussion to convince her, and in the end it was less my persuasion that swayed her, I believe, than her curiosity and her own desire to put this place to rest.

It turns out that it is not the plane that is late, but Aunty. Because she has to walk with a cane the airline have arranged to take her off the plane by wheelchair. When she finally rolls through the arrival gates, wheeled by a young male airport worker, the lines of disembarked passengers part like the Red Sea. Eileen Shang has landed. Waving good-naturedly to the people that skip out of the way of her wheelchair, talking loudly and floridly with the airport worker, who she has obviously managed to charm in the short time it has taken him to push her from the plane, Aunty is in her element. I can tell that she is nervous though. Her bravado is her way of clearing a space to give herself time to set the tone, sort out any opposition and position herself to deal with it head on. Some people get through life by saying as little as possible and blending into the background. Background is not a word that Aunty Eileen Shang recognises.

Covered in jewellery from head to toe, every finger of her hands covered with rings, Aunty is wearing a bright blue leather jumpsuit. She could outdo the arrival of Elvis. Aunty Eileen is well over seventy, but her long hair is plaited into a thick jet-black rope that cascades over her shoulder and rests in swirls on her lap. Aunty has always liked to dress up. When she was a young girl in Moore River she would wear berries tied like fake pearls around her neck. During the war years, when she was a young woman in Perth, Aunty dressed like there was no tomorrow. If the police were going to stop her in the street and make an exhibition of her then, she decided, she was going to be seen in style. Even in her wheelchair, on one of her regular trips to the casino with her old mates, it's make-up and jewels to the nines. Why should her arrival in Perth be any different? Aunty Eileen is not slipping back into Western Australia. Aunty is standing on Western Australia's doorstep, knocking loudly; ready to thump it good and bloody hard if it dares to complain.

After sorting out the luggage and fielding questions from onlookers wondering who this celebrity must be, we are out the doors and into my car. I want to get Aunty to the house of an old friend from Settlement days so she can rest. 'Rest?' Aunty Eileen says, 'What do I want to rest for, dear? Come on, you've got me here now, let's have a look at this place then.' It is late at night as we head for the city and Aunty is filling us in about the flight, about getting away from her flat, and anything else that comes to mind. But her eyes are watching, looking carefully at every building we pass as we head down the highway into the city. The city is completely transformed from the place that she remembered. We decide to do a lap.

Turning west we head along Newcastle Street. We pass Wellington Square where homeless Noongars still sleep; Northbridge, the remnants of what Aunty remembered as Northline, the area north of the railway tracks; past the faux-Tuscan city dwellings and the ghost tracks of the trams that used to run here, and arrive on top of the tunnel that now cuts its way east at the junction of Fitzgerald Street. Turning south down Fitzgerald Street we pass what was known by city blackfellas as Bungey Park, which has recently been transformed into a replica English park complete with a gazebo. Cutting through the new West End, cleaving through the new cool wealth and city apartments that are taking form all over the city, we arrive at the river.

We drive east along the Swan River, which smells of salt as the fresh waters merge with the saltwater tide. Turning north into Bennett Street takes us through the lower edges of town, past the fishing grounds and swamp that is Queens Gardens, over the hill of the old East Perth Cemetery and what were once traditional camping grounds, and down into the shining edifices of new East Perth. Winding our way through the freshly signposted streets, past the marina that was dug out of Claisebrook Creek, through the dwindling old black and white working-class industrial area that now houses apartments, we come to the junction of the railway that cuts the city in two, north–south. Aunty Eileen is not talking, just looking and nodding at all the changes, rubbing the rings on her hands that are tightly folded in her lap, and peering out at the lights that illuminate the shiny new city.

It is a large area that we have just travelled, easily five kilometres square. The streets have changed. Buildings have disappeared and been replaced by skyscrapers and shopping malls. Parks have been built over and tunnelled under. This square that we have just travelled represents the boundary of the Prohibited Area of Perth — officially, from 1927 to 1954, but unofficially for much longer than that. For Aunty Eileen the days of identity cards, dog tags and being stopped and moved on or threatened with arrest are still with her. That's why she is looking so closely, I suspect, to make sure that it really has gone.

Finally, we find ourselves at what is left of Bennett House in East Perth, where Aboriginal women were compelled by law to stay while in the city. Aunty Eileen had done time here in the 1930s. It is the place where she first met Jessie Argyle. Aunty Eileen is sitting in the car just looking at the building. It has been marked for demolition, a part of the old East Perth that has not been deemed worthy of preservation. We sit quietly for a long time with the motor running as we look at the Home. I ask Aunty if she wants to get out and have a look around, but she doesn't and motions with her hand for me not to turn off the engine.

She is looking at the building as if she can see all the women who ever passed through here, who have long since gone. She is looking at the building as if it is the embodiment of everything that she hates about Western Australia and all that it had done to her. I'm worried that I've done the wrong thing by bringing Aunty back here, but she is not. 'No dear, I had to come back. I'm gunna catch up with my mates and then I'll leave this dump as far behind me as possible.' As we pull away from the house, Aunty livens up. 'Hey, don't worry, Stephen. I've come back to have my say, and I'm going to bloody have my say. It's their shame job, not mine. Let them pull it down if they want. We know what we know and pulling it down won't wipe the slate clean. Come on, let's get some dinner ay?' The city passes by us, lit by pulsing blue pools of light, but the city of Aunty Eileen's and my grandmother's time can still be glimpsed in the alleyways, in the side roads and disused factories of a racially segregated Perth. You just have to know where to look.

East Perth, December 1943, Department of Native Affairs. The Native Affairs Department was active in East Perth on patrols with the Western Australian Police Department, and sometimes with the United States shore patrol. The Native Affairs Department was involved in the patrols because they were attempting to keep alcohol out of the Aboriginal community of Perth. The shore patrol just wanted to keep US servicemen out of trouble, and that meant keeping the local authorities happy. On this particular night in December 1943 the new Deputy Commissioner of Native Affairs, Mr McBeath, was pounding the pavement looking out for the supply of sly grog to blackfellas. Although it wasn't on the record, the mixing of African Americans and Aboriginal women was also on the list of boundaries to be enforced that night.

Bill Bodney, my grandmother's contemporary from the Swan Mission and well-respected Elder of the Noongar community, was making his way towards the Crystal Picture Theatre. He was most likely oblivious to the presence of the officers hiding in the shadows of the houses opposite, watching him as he made his way into the lobby. It was 8.30 pm and McBeath was half an hour into a two-hour stake-out of the picture theatre, on the lookout for clandestine meetings and unbecoming behaviour. The theatre was just outside the Prohibited Area, not more than five minutes walk from the East Perth Girls Home. It was an island of subdued light in the blacked-out suburb of East Perth.

Soon after Bill Bodney entered the theatre, three African American sailors rolled into the lobby and then came outside again. They waited for something or someone for half an hour or so before they called it quits and hopped on a trolleybus back to the city. Other Noongars attending the pictures that night or walking by, were duly noted and watched. In his report McBeath wrote, somewhat disappointedly, 'I am afraid we visited on an off night.'

An 'off night' meant they were unable to catch American servicemen meeting Aboriginal women in the park opposite. An 'off night' meant they weren't able to catch Jackie Layland or Wally Isaacs or any other young fellas selling grog on the sly to cashed-up Yanks looking for a card game and some girls to meet. Jackie Layland used to have a source who could get him whisky. He'd buy up as much as he could afford, gather together empties with good labels from hotels nearby in East Perth, and water down the liquor to sell to American sailors desperate for a drop after closing time.

The East Perth Girls Home was under particularly close watch. Women staying there were forced to return well before dark or face the wrath of the matron who oversaw them. Some women, like old Aunty Molly Ginger, told me they were afraid of the Yank sailors.

Aunty Molly was taken away from Myroodah Station and placed in the Moore River Settlement where she was named Molly Myroodah. After years of training Molly was sent south to the East Perth Girls Home for more training and a place to stay while she worked in the city. Sitting in her State Housing flat in Geraldton, Aunty Molly laughed as she thought back to how scared she had been of the Yanks. She believed the stories that she'd heard about sly grog laced with drugs, of knife fights, rapes and even murders. Just the sight of Yanks in the street would send Molly and some other Aboriginal women running back to the East Perth Home. The Americans might have been allies, but for many people in the relatively quiet backwater of Perth, they were seen as dangerous. The Department, it seems, was happy to reinforce these myths in the 'protection' of its female wards.

In the darkness of the blackout, East Perth was considered a sinister and dangerous part of town. The fact is, it was just poorer than the rest of the city. More trouble took place in Northline at the Roe Street brothels that stretched through to West Perth, but containment was considered to have solved potential problems in these areas. There were reports of prostitution involving Aboriginal women and white women in East Perth, along the Swan River and around the industrial parts of the Port of Fremantle, places out of sight and out of the way of the police. Aboriginal camps could be found on the outskirts of these poorer regions because Aboriginal families could only afford to live in these out-of-the-way areas. There was prostitution taking place, and the Americans were sometimes responsible for grog finding its way into the community. Yanks were also welcome at Aboriginal card games where they could splash around some money. To deny these facts would be naive, but to assume that every Aboriginal household, camp site, or dwelling was a site of 'immoral' activity is downright racist and reactionary.

Aboriginal East Perth was pinned down during the war years. Aboriginal families living in cheap rented accommodation or camping down at the 'Bull Paddock' were watched closely, as were relatives coming in from the country to stay. Each Aboriginal family member, every house and every camp was noted, tracked, regularly patrolled and occasionally raided. The Department, the police and the shore patrol didn't need grounds for a raid. A rumour of cohabitation or a suspicion of the supply of alcohol would be enough for them to come searching through a person's house. In later years they would send the bulldozers in to clear out the camps in East Perth as they sought to scatter the Aboriginal community out of the city and into the suburbs. But with the war on and resources stretched, the Native Affairs Department had to make do with whatever information it could gather as the means of controlling Aboriginal lives. Even so, after the retirement of Mr Neville in 1940, the amount of information gathered and retained thankfully diminished with each passing year.

The laws were as harsh as ever and the Department, when it decided to, could dramatically change a person's life forever, but the apparatus of control after Neville's leaving was less focused, though no less damaging. Removals were still common. Passes were still required to be in the city after dark. Permits were still required if you wanted to employ Aboriginal people. If men were caught with alcohol they received a stiff fine and six to fourteen days in the lock-up. If you were the sole breadwinner of your family it meant they went without while you worried about them from gaol. But with the focus of mainstream Western Australians shifting overseas to the war, small cracks opened up in the machinery of control of the Aboriginal community, and if you were a person like my grandmother who had spent your whole life seeking out the cracks as a means of evading authority, when the lights went down in the blackout, anything was possible.

There would be a knock at the door. It would be for Jessie. The publican of the Royal Standard Hotel had sent someone with a message. The Trump boys were at it again, and could my grandmother come down and sort them out. She occasionally headed down to the Royal Standard Hotel anyway, usually just before dark, about five o'clock. Edward would be home soon and then the boys in uniform would start floating in from the city.

Jessie would give my mother Betty instructions to watch the dinner, then she'd put on an old overcoat, slide her small dainty feet into her old slippers, and make her way down Glendower Street for the two blocks that it took to reach the Royal Standard Hotel. Jessie moved quickly for a woman of twenty-one stone. Her hands were small and dainty, but her arms were tight and firm inside the giant overcoats she wore. On the way out she would stop to collect the sturdy old cane pram that sat on the front verandah, tossing in a few blankets. She'd need them for cover on the way back. In another hour it would be dark, too dark for safety. She would have to sort the boys out quickly.

At the hotel the Trump boys would be ready to kill each other. They were known in the neighbourhood for their long-drawn-out, knock-down-drag-out fights that broke anything that came to hand. My grandmother had known them since they were small boys and had been sorting them out for their mother since they were unable to be pulled apart. She would leave the pram at the bar and motion to the barman to load it up—five fingers—five bottles. Without making any fuss she would announce herself to the boys. They would square off, circling, but she would make her way between them and grab their collars. They knew what was coming. They couldn't ignore my grandmother, especially when she kicked off her slippers. When Mum Smith took off her slippers it was known around the neighbourhood that there was no shifting her. It was as if cement had been poured between her and the earth. She'd take hold of whoever was fixing for a fight and hold them there in her iron grip and stay fast. If they didn't back down she'd literally knock their heads together. No one wanted their heads knocked together by Mum Smith. The Trump boys had had their share of it. When they were younger my grandmother would settle disputes by clearing a space in the vacant block next to Glendower Street, lay down the rules, provide the gloves, and let them at it. Whatever the problem, it usually resolved itself pretty quickly and enough steam would be let off that life could return to normal. That's how it was settled in Moore River between women or men. It worked there. It worked in the city.

While the fight was being broken up the barman would load up the pram with beer and put it on my grandmother's tally. Having sorted out the Trumps, my grandmother would cover the beer with the blankets she had brought and head back to Glendower Street as if she were walking the baby. Anyone who knew my grandmother knew that Mum Smith took in kids for women who couldn't care for them. Some kids stayed for years. Some kids were there until their mothers found good positions. It was not an unusual sight to see Mum Smith pushing a pram down the street around teatime. People who knew my grandmother well enough to be welcome at one of her all-night card games might guess what was in the pram and maybe decide to pay a visit later that night. Strangers who had no business in the neighbourhood, or people who didn't mix, would have no idea that she was running grog back to the house.

Edward would have returned home and would not be surprised to hear that his wife was breaking up a fight down the street. He would have already read the evening edition of the *Daily News* when it came off the press so would usually head into his room to listen to the radio until Jessie turned up, while Betty set the table. Twilight was time for the blackout. Even the tram lights were cut in wartime, but you could still hear them trundling towards you in the dark, and catch the odd spark trailing from the overhead wires as they made their way down Bulwer Street.

Turning into Hyde Park, the sounds of the street would fade to the sounds of geese, ducks, swans and frogs settling into the darkness under the canopy of Moreton Bay figs. The trees masked the darkening sky, blanketing Glendower Street in an early darkness that showed up the dull rectangles of curtained windows in the houses opposite and filtered the smells of grilled chops, fried rissoles and boiled cabbage bought with ration coupons. It would not be unusual to see human shapes emerge from the park just ahead of my grandmother, opposite her house. They could be police on the lookout for a blackfella just like her, slipping home with a pram full of grog. They could be blackout officers making their way through the park to check for blackout failures. Most likely, they would be Jessie's boys.

If she wasn't sure, all my grandmother had to do was whistle into the darkness of the park. If it was one of her boys he'd signal by whistling back, or making an owl call, or with one of the signals they learned in army training to look out for each other, easily adapted to looking out for the police or the military patrol. Bill Poland would be the most likely source of such a signal, and Jessie could be sure that he'd be at the gate well before her, keeping an eye out for her as she made her way down Glendower Street with her illicit load that could have seen her put away for two weeks in gaol.

Jessie Smith was as old as the century, forty-three years. By white standards she was middle-aged. By black standards she was an old girl. Black people died younger than whites—and still die younger. Making it to forty-three was no mean feat.

To be called 'Mum' Smith was to fulfil a role that cut across boundaries of family and into the wider circle of the Aboriginal community. My grandmother had been raised in the South-West community of Nor'wester and Sou'wester women who looked out for each other and each other's children and, when they had to, their men. It was a community that operated on a system of respect and shared responsibility. Being called

'Mum' was a sign of her place in her community, her role as keeper of family knowledge, carer of children, and someone to be relied upon when things went bad. And things were always going bad somewhere.

On any given night the lounge room of the Glendower Street house was covered with the bodies of sleeping Aboriginal servicemen.

The Poland brothers were Yamatji men from Shark Bay. They were regulars at my grandmother's house in the lead-up to the Papua New Guinea campaign against the Japanese. Bill Poland was the leader and elder of all the young men who stayed at the house. He kept an eye out for trouble and watched over everyone. He could hold his grog, get by with less than an hour's sleep, and was always ready with a joke or a comeback line. Bill had worked the lighters along Shark Bay when he was a boy. He knew hard work, he could sail, load and unload cargo, and had worked alongside my grandfather in 1925 when Edward had exiled himself to Hamelin Pool while my grandmother was imprisoned in Moore River. He was a skilled craftsman and his beautifully carved pearl shells were highly sought after in the community.

When war broke out, Aboriginal men like Bill saw their chance to serve and protect their own country while proving to the nation that they had earned their right to be treated without discrimination. What the uniform provided them in terms of conditional acceptance by white authorities was more than they had ever experienced before. In most places it opened up new avenues and a sense of equality that never existed before the war. But the uniform was not a guaranteed passport to acceptance, and for that reason and strong family ties, Aboriginal servicemen stuck together. Whites who accepted blackfellas as equals were accepted in return and these white men also found themselves accepted into the extended family of my grandmother's house.

I don't know how Bill first made his way to my grandmother's house but I imagine it was in much the same way that other younger men did. For some who were joining up from the country it was their first time in the city, and their mothers would tell them to look up Aunty Jessie Smith. Those who landed cold in town would hear through the black grapevine that there was always a bed and a feed waiting for them at Mum Smith's place.

There were three other Poland brothers from Shark Bay who joined up to fight along with Bill: Harold, George and Jack. Bill and his brother

Jack were known around town as the 'black detectives'. They were both good-looking men with an eye for good-looking women. They looked out for each other and when they were in trouble in the city, put their army training to good use with those secret signals and calls to warn of disgruntled husbands approaching bedroom windows or police on the lookout for black men in pubs and public houses. Sometimes they'd head into a pub with white mates prepared to stand up for them, but most times they looked out for themselves.

When the Second World War began, Aboriginal men were some of the first to join up, even though it was not exactly legal since they were not officially counted as 'Natural Born Australian Citizens'. Some of the white men who had been coming along to my grandmother's house in the 1930s also joined up and they formed easy and long-lasting friendships with many of the black servicemen down from Shark Bay, from Busselton or Kalgoorlie—from all parts of the state.

Jimmy McSkene was a white soldier who came to stay and became one of my grandmother's favourites. Jimmy had come along to the card games, stayed for the night, and it seems he never left. He had been a bagman in the Depression and first became known to my grandmother in the late 1930s when he came by asking if there was any work he could do for a feed. My grandmother gave him sandwiches and a bottle of tea because she couldn't stand to see a man go hungry, and told him to be on his way. But Jimmy wouldn't accept payment without work. He chopped the firewood and promised to be back the following week. He returned to chop more wood, again and again, until he was just one of the crew that made 69 Glendower Street their second home. Jimmy was living off and on at the Old Men's Home for most of this time, even though he was relatively young, something my grandmother seemed to see as a mark of his ingenuity. Like many men in his position, he probably went off to war to escape his dire situation, but like so many others, ended up in even worse circumstances. In Jimmy's case that meant years in Changi, the infamous Japanese prisoner-of-war camp.

Jimmy wrote to my grandmother from the front in New Guinea, and later from Changi. Jimmy was a machine-gunner in the reconnaissance unit of the Second Fourth ('2/4') machine-gunners, and he was somewhere in New Guinea when he wrote telling my grandmother that he had found himself a new girlfriend. Jimmy was described as a bit of a 'ladies' man'. He wasn't much to look at but he had a good sense of humour and a way of accepting absurdity that was disarming. But there was nothing disarming about his new girl. He carried her with him day and night, slept with her in his foxhole and owed her his life. She was cold as steel but he wouldn't be without her. He wrote telling Jessie that this new girl was 'the one' and that, 'when she kisses you goodnight, she kisses you goodnight forever.'

He addressed his letters to 'The Duchess of Glendower Street', and after a while everyone, including the postman, started calling Jessie 'The Duchess'. When he wrote from Changi though, he simply wrote to 'Mrs Jessie Smith', and was only able to say in the small space provided, 'Am doing fine.' Jimmy had a brother who joined up too, but no one knew where he was or whether he had survived the war. As far as family went, he only had my grandmother and grandfather.

Edward continued working at the *West* and enjoyed the comings and goings of the 'boys', children of the many women he had known through my grandmother from the 1920s. With Neville no longer hounding him with threats of prosecution, the mood in the house had shifted. He was not one for the cards or a friendly drink, but liked to catch up with people coming down from Shark Bay. As my grandmother had become 'Mum' Smith, Edward had likewise, in his mid fifties, become known as 'Pop' Smith and, to be honest, I'm not sure how he felt about that. When the cards started up, he seems to have been happy to leave the floor to his wife, and to busy himself with his radio, his books and a good night's sleep before his early start at the *West*.

Ironically, the images of our family's life became more joyous and free in wartime. There were gatherings for group shots in the back yard of Glendower Street, and larger numbers of people stood in Government Gardens for the requisite images of friends and loved ones. But for all the extra freedoms that emerged out of the miasma of war, small-minded petty racism was still prevalent.

Uniform or not, Aboriginal men could still find themselves thrown out of pubs for the crime of being black, or locked up for being within the Prohibited Area after dark. Aboriginal men and their white comrades in arms could likewise find themselves being asked to move on by police, or worse, locked up for what one white returned serviceman described as 'cohabitation', because of their interracial friendships. While cohabitation was supposed to imply a relationship of a sexual nature, it appears from the white male servicemen who were warned not to mix with fellow

Aboriginal servicemen, that it was generally used, in the wider public sense, to describe any kind of interracial mixing.

Aboriginal women could still be harassed for mixing with black servicemen or, as was going on at my grandmother's house, with white servicemen too. If Aboriginal women had an African American boyfriend on their arm as they walked through the city, they were certain to come under the scrutiny of the police, the Department, and sometimes the courts.

Young men came and went. The community became more mobile and while the older generation tried to survive at home, many of the younger generation went off into the world to fight for a land and a political system in which they weren't even entitled to vote.

After the Neville years the Aboriginal population of Western Australia, and particularly the South-West, emerged from the 1930s Depression in a terrible state. Having endured higher unemployment than whites in the south, they were denied the dole and other benefits that whites could fall back on in hard times. The majority of the population was destitute.

The farce of the 1934 Moseley Royal Commission into Native Affairs and the resulting 1936 Native Administration Act had made it nearly impossible in the late 1930s for Aboriginal people to obtain work due to the requirement that they be employed under strict permits which required employers to pay fees to employ them—an obvious disincentive. People in rural areas who could not find work would drift to the city where jobs could be found at the superphosphate works or in other light industry. The Department considered legislating to force people to remain in employment within their own areas, requiring that 'those who had taken up other occupations should be ordered to return.'

Some Aboriginal women were sent to National Service officers who would determine how best they could be engaged in the war effort at home. Generally this meant that they cooked, cleaned or laboured for some institution like a hospital or factory; certainly, there was no real shift in the type of employment offered to them. More work, there was, but it was generally more of the same as they had always done. Still, this increase in Aboriginal employment during the war meant that some people were able to obtain better employment and higher wages, even though the control of Aboriginal labour was still largely vested in the Native Affairs Department.

The war brought an end to the downward spiral that the Aboriginal community had been locked into during the Neville years. More money was beginning to float around the Aboriginal community and Mum

Smith was keen to see some of that pass over her card table. One old girl whose mother was a good friend of my grandmother's told me with more than a hint of wryness that, 'Jessie Smith was a ruthless old cardsharp who could smell money like a shark could smell blood.' She also laughed and told me how her mother had been lent more by my grandmother than she'd lost at the games and that it was understood that these loans were 'help-out money' that was never expected to be repaid.

The Glendower Street mob of the 1940s included the likes of the Mallard boys and, of course, the Poland Brothers, also the Mippys, Kellys, Ogilvies, Lockyers, Pooles and Prossers, and many other blackfellas from all over the state who had joined up. By and large it was the younger generation that joined up to fight. Older men like Bill Bodney and Thomas Bropho were too old to join up, although Tom Forrest, who had fought in the Light Brigade at Gallipoli, somehow managed to get in for the Second World War also, but this was rare.

The first Aboriginal person to join up was Cecil Fitzgerald on 10 October 1939, and by June 1940 more than seventy Aboriginal men had enlisted in the armed forces from all over the state. By the end of the war over four hundred Western Australian Aboriginal men had joined up to fight in joining thousands from all over the country.

The army became a black and white meeting point, and although no doubt there were tensions, black–white friendships, which never had the chance to develop before then, became possible through war. The Native Affairs Department and police were not sure how to deal with the new-found and enthusiastically exercised rights of Aboriginal soldiers. Legally there had been no change in rights; enlistment in the armed forces accorded no change in their status under the Native Administration Act. However, this did not stop them from exercising rights that they felt they had earned by enlisting. Previously segregated by law and culture, black and white serviceman could now unite against a common enemy—civilian authority. In the seemingly equal situation of the army, common ground could be found and differences overlooked. For Aboriginal men, and many white men in uniform, it seemed that a future of equality was possible. But in reality, what Aboriginal soldiers and white soldiers experienced was the common bond of mateship and loyalty in the face of adversity—it was not equality.

The police were in the tricky situation of wanting to prevent Aboriginal soldiers' access to alcohol, yet not wanting to arrest men who were enlisted to fight for their country. Soldiers able to get alcohol were supplying it to other Aboriginal people. It wasn't anything new but it was of great concern to the police and had always been one of the main reasons for Aboriginal incarceration in Western Australia. There were, of course, cases where Aboriginal soldiers were arrested, just like any other Aboriginal man caught drinking without an Exemption. Regardless, people still found ways around the police. In my grandmother's case, access to alcohol was well under control.

With the war in full swing and many Aboriginal men enlisted and away fighting, 69 Glendower Street had become a kind of centre of Aboriginal and non-Aboriginal interaction. Had Neville still been in power there would have been letters flying back and forth alleging prostitution, racketeering and immoral behaviour. There was no prostitution, but maybe a little racketeering in the form of sly grog and gambling. The behaviour wasn't 'immoral', it was simply the normal behaviour of a community of marda-mardas and whites who had been accepted into my grandmother's extended family getting on with their lives. And although the Neville years were behind them there were legacies of those times that never quite disappeared.

By 1943 my grandmother had buried some of her closest friends, attended the funerals of children she'd loved in Moore River and Swan Mission, and was rapidly becoming a prisoner of her own body.

This is not how she projected herself though. That wasn't her style. On the outside she was tough but fair, open but careful, and seemingly invincible. Her face was smooth, round and small above the mountain of her body. The problems that had begun in her left leg from a young age continued to dog her. In some photographs her bad leg has swelled to twice the size of her good leg. Her long curly brown hair was almost always swept back, neat but flowing over her shoulders, and when standing with my grandfather her shoulder cut in just under his arm so that when they held each other they seemed perfectly balanced despite his wiry body and her great large frame. They were made for each other.

Edward understood her completely. He understood that she could never be alone. She always had to have someone with her — a neighbour, a friend, friends, relatives. She understood that he needed his own space, a quiet place where he could read, listen to the radio, catch up on the latest electronics. He needed his own rhythms to be honoured, just as she needed hers. He never stayed up late for the card games. He never went to the pub. She was only to ever see him drunk once, and he wasn't even particularly fond of his yearly dose of Christmas sherry. Edward loved his wife and daughter. He would happily have shared the house with them alone, but he knew that Jessie needed people around her, so he was accommodating.

By this time Betty was already taller than my grandmother and almost as tall as my grandfather. They made a happy family in photographs, and Edward and Betty followed Jessie's directions to stand in front of her to protect her as much as she desired from the camera's gaze. Betty was growing up fast in more ways than my grandmother liked to admit. My grandmother protected my mother from the Department, from any interested young men and now from my mother's own growing sense of independence. Betty had developed film-star good looks. She looked a lot older than her fourteen years, and her years of growing up around extended family made her very confident in company. She had grown into the young woman that my grandmother had hoped she would be. She was well liked and happy. Even though the Department still ruled Aboriginal lives, Jessie knew that my mother's chances for a good life were far better than her own because of the start they'd given her and the extended family that my grandmother had gathered around her.

My mother had every chance and opportunity that my grandmother had not. Where my grandmother had little schooling, in 1943 my mother was attending the Perth Girls School in East Perth. Where my grandmother had her life tracked and controlled by the Department, with Neville gone my mother was relatively free of the eye of the authorities. Where my grandmother had once had to beg in writing for new clothing to be purchased on her behalf by the Department, my mother was well dressed, had a roof over her head, and wanted for nothing. Betty would never have to endure the privations her mother did, as long as breath filled my grandmother's lungs.

But there was a price that my mother paid for this security. My grandmother watched her like a hawk. My grandmother knew my mother's every move. She knew when she was due home and where she was at every moment that she wasn't under her watchful eye. At fourteen my mother had opportunities that my grandmother had never had, but she had become the sapling that strained towards the light beneath the branches of the taller tree that was Mum Smith.

As the war years raged and my grandmother grew in stature and strength, so too did the hold that she held over my mother. As 1943 slipped into 1944 my grandmother and mother posed for a photograph at Glendower Street. It was summer. The sunflowers that sprang wild from the seeds of the previous year's crop dwarf them as they stand side by side in the full light of a high sun. They look happy. My mother is a gawky beauty of a teenager. My grandmother is almost completely hidden by the huge leaves of the sunflowers, their clock-face flowers stretching up over her head. She always liked cover when a photo was being taken. But you can see the pride she feels towards her daughter, and the sense of protection in the large arm she has placed around my mother's waist. In the flat, hard light of the Western Australian sun and the black and white of the image, the difference in their colour is almost imperceptible. 'Coloured women' is how they referred to themselves and colour still mattered in their world of 1940s Perth.

As my grandmother worked to ensure that her daughter would not have to face the kind of racism and control that she had endured, it seemed my mother became a constant reminder of just how hard it had been for her. As Jessie kept an eye on my mother to ensure that she would not be removed to a Settlement, or sent out as a servant to white people, she was reminded of other children, children of women she knew and loved, that she had been unable to protect. And while she worked to create a sense of security and normality in the extended family of Glendower Street, it seems to me that my grandmother also came to resent the relative ease with which her daughter's life was unfolding.

However, my mother didn't see it as such an easy ride. Scrubbing the floors, preparing the meals, running home at lunchtime to do the shopping or helping my grandmother get a card game ready, Betty felt anything but free, but she knew better than to question her mother's judgement. They loved each other deeply, accompanied each other everywhere and knew each other intrinsically. But at the same time that Betty was growing into a young woman and beginning to experience her own youthful desire for freedom, Jessie's health was beginning to decline. The Glendower Street house was more popular than ever and her dependence on Betty grew.

Jessie's extended family of young Aboriginal men were regulars at Glendower Street when on leave, as were Nor'wester women needing a place to stay while passing through the city. Servicemen looking for an all-night game of cards made a beeline to the house.

In all this activity, Edward seems to have receded from the life of the house. He continued working at the *West*, brought home his pay packet like clockwork and operated in his own world within the world of their home. He hungrily gleaned any mention of London from newspapers and newsreels, and increasingly went to his room to tinker with his crystal radio set to catch the latest news — that is, the latest news after the censors had finished with it. When the war first broke out his mind must have been in another time and place that was tied to his personal experience of 1909, the last time he saw London.

In late 1941 a letter arrived from London from Bernie Bayly, the son of his old friend Jack Bayly, who had left England with him. The two families had kept in touch, although the Baylys were not regular visitors to Glendower Street. Bernard Bayly was in London having signed up. What managed to pass the censors' scissors was mostly bad news. Bernard had visited Iron Gates, the old house in Surrey. Sadly, he informed Edward, Uncle Alfred Graham had died several years previously. His aunt was alive and sent her best wishes, but she was frail. Bombs had fallen in the front and rear of Iron Gates and destroyed much of the neighbourhood. Edward's old school and the entire city was covered in darkness, and the staff and children of Emanuel had been evacuated to the countryside. The school had been hit by the bombing and there was a good chance it would suffer more in a London in which air raids were becoming a normal part of life. Working at the *West*, the news of bombings in England came through as daily reminders of the homeland he'd left behind.

Letters from Edward's family stopped soon after the war began and he had no news of his sisters' lives during the Blitz. But as the shape of the war shifted to the Pacific, and even closer to the northern ports that he'd worked on as a young man, he would have been becoming far more concerned about the tangible threat to the family he had devoted his life to — Jessie and Betty. Jessie and my mother had no idea what he was planning to do, but they'd learn soon enough.

In this uncertain but busy rhythm of the war years, the home opposite Hyde Park continued to witness many comings and goings. It remained an open house in many ways, although constrained by unspoken boundaries and the threads of unresolved family issues in the form of my grandmother's worsening health and her increased reliance on my mother.

In the evenings the family settled down to nights under the cover of the blackout. After listening to the radio (speeches by Pig-iron Bob were my grandmother's favourite, even though she never agreed with him, she loved the way he spoke), more people would arrive, the grey blanket would be brought out and thrown over the table and the cards would be warmed up for another round of poker. As the steel tops of the brown bottles of beer were snapped off, Edward would say goodnight to Betty before heading into his room for some late-night eavesdropping on the airwaves. As they each settled into their routines, 1944 was shaping up to be a year of great change.

It was well after teatime in the spring of 1944. My grandmother and my mother sat on the front porch shelling peas. At times like these, some people pace. Some people bite their nails. My grandmother shelled peas, and my mother knew not to ask too many questions. Edward had been gone all day and he was late home. He'd never been late home. Earlier that week he'd made up his mind. He was going to join up.

In a repeat of the First World War, I imagine that Edward had become swept along by a sense of duty, and perhaps even a little shame. As the war dragged on, younger men that he knew, young men his wife had cared for, who had stayed under their roof, had gone away to fight. Some returned wounded. Some were captured. Some were still fighting in New Guinea. Some were dead. Perhaps he stumbled upon his old prayer book with its special note to himself as a teenager. At the age of fifty-four, how many of his 'Clues to Success' did he still follow? Honesty, Industry, Temperance, Civility, Punctuality, Economy, Perseverance, Courtesy, Observance and Attentiveness? Even then, in the middle of the war, as he was about to wager his own chance of actually being accepted to fight, I think he still would have believed in these values. But even though the army was beginning to accept men from older age brackets, how was he to get around his whispering voice? Could he lie and say he had a cold? Could he convince them that he could be a signaller or something else that didn't require a loud voice? Perhaps he thought they were desperate enough to take him anyway, as gun fodder.

Later that night a US military Jeep pulled up abruptly outside 69 Glendower Street. It was filled with American servicemen. Propped up high in the back, drunk as a skunk and held up by the other men, was Edward Alfred Byron Smith. In full view of his wife and daughter, a staggering Edward made his way through the gate, up the steps and, without even glancing towards his family, saluted the Americans and stumbled into the house. The Americans were more than a little polite in what they knew was a difficult situation. They kept calling my grandmother 'Ma'am' as they respectfully related how they had come across the strange and downcast figure of my grandfather standing outside the recruitment office in Claremont.

Edward had signed the relevant papers and completed the required medical, but when all was done, his application was stamped REJECTED. He was to wear the badge of a rejected man yet again.

He was standing outside the recruitment station, about to make his way home, when the Americans turned up in their Jeep asking directions to an oval in Fremantle where they were expected for a cricket game, 'whatever that was.' Edward began telling them the way in his whispering voice, but they decided it would be easier to invite him to show them himself, with the promise of returning him to anywhere he wanted to go afterwards. He took them up on their offer of a ride. He also accepted their offer to play for their side in the cricket match, as well as their offer to knock back whisky after whisky as they waited their turn to bat. Before they brought him back to Glendower Street, Edward had taken up other offers of drinks, and provided the Americans with a guided tour of the city.

The Americans left him to his wife and daughter and screamed off down the road. I imagine Jessie knew that he wouldn't be accepted. I imagine she knew he had to do it, for pride or some such reason, so that he could at least say that he had tried, but I doubt that she was very happy about it. Although the Department was less personally involved in their lives then, my grandmother still took calculated risks in claiming for her home the kind of freedom that she wanted, and she knew well enough that it was not simply by her will alone that the authorities had begun to ease up on them. What my grandmother got away with in Glendower Street, North Perth, was immeasurably more than anyone could hope to have enjoyed who lived in East Perth. She knew of the raids on houses looking for grog, servicemen and gambling. She knew her home was protected in part by her careful management of the situation, keeping in good with neighbours, making sure not to be too obvious. But she also knew that the main reason she was able to get away with so much was the fact that she was married to a white man with a steady job who, when trouble came calling, always stood by his wife.

The day that Edward got drunk with his new-found American friends was the first and only time in his life that he let temperance slip from his motto. After this incident Edward settled back into his familiar life of family, work and the community of his home.

It was fortuitous that he didn't join up that summer. Jessie may have seemed invincible on those occasions when she broke up fights or sorted out other people's problems, but her health was seriously failing and now she was diagnosed with diabetes. Her illness made her listless and tired. She couldn't walk to the shops any more. Taxis had become her only form of transport. My mother was doing the housework before and after school, and doing the shopping at lunchtime. She would run from East Perth to North Perth to shop at the Brisbane Street shops, return home to help Jessie with any problems she was having with her leg or the diabetic ulcers that had begun to plague her, then run back to school. Betty was doing well in school and wanted to go right through to do her certificate, but someone had to help Jessie with the house and look after her. So my grandmother decided that my mother should leave school. My mother resented it terribly. She'd enjoyed school, was well liked by her friends, and thought there was more to the story of my grandmother's illness than met the eye.

Everybody knew that my grandmother couldn't stand being alone. At night the house was filled with friends and family but by day, unless there was someone down from the country, or a neighbour came by, Jessie was alone. Her illness became a kind of mixed blessing and an excuse that she used to control my mother and contain her growing desire for freedom. If my mother ever wanted to go out with a boy, my grandmother was suddenly ill. But if Eileen Shang, Eileen Gentle or Mary Forrest were keen on a card game, it was amazing how Jessie could spring to life. Just as the real illness of her leg, which still troubled her, was her passport back to the city in the 1920s to spend time with my grandfather, her diabetes became the weight that she strapped to my mother to ensure that she remained close to her in every way. My grandmother was genuinely very ill, but she was also a survivor.

Tensions grew within the household. One evening, after Betty had completed her chores and set the table for that night's collection of diners, my grandmother called out for her to come and fix something. Without thinking, my mother called out, 'In a minute.' As my mother entered the room my grandmother's fist came from nowhere, collected her jaw, lifted her body, and sent her flying across the newly polished dining room floor that she'd just finished that day. My mother never blamed my grandmother. She blamed the illness. She said it drove Jessie wild. It made her hit first and ask questions later. It was happening a lot around that time. It had happened before too, when my mother was eight. She'd played up and my grandmother went into a rage with an ironing cord. The doctor was called and couldn't believe the welts that had been laid across my mother's back. My grandmother's dainty hands at the end of those huge arms were deceptive. They could hurt, and they did. They lashed out in times of anger at the closest and dearest, my mother. The violence stopped for a time, but as the illness worsened, she began lashing out more often.

Dora Poole and Nellie Lyndon decided that my mother needed a holiday. She was fourteen years old, had just left school and was caring full time for her mother and for the people who passed through their home. Dora and Nellie were old Moore River women. They'd known my grandmother for decades and had stayed at Glendower Street off and on for years. They worked in Bridgetown for a white family who didn't mind if they brought a girl down from the city with them to stay for a few weeks. It was the first holiday my mother ever had. She loved Bridgetown. Nellie and Dora took her walking through the hills when they had time off, and at night they played cards and listened to the sounds of the bush. They took my mother across to the Old Rectory, where Jessie had worked for the Sherwoods as a girl not much older than Betty was then, and took her to meet other women who worked nearby and who had often visited when in Perth.

When Betty returned to Glendower Street my grandmother showered her with love and presents of dresses, and allowed her to go out with friends for a while. My mother made up her mind then, that she was going to have her own life separate from her mother. In 1940s Perth, the way most young women got away from their mothers was through marriage. It wasn't a plan, but she knew it was a chance which, if it ever came knocking, she would grasp with both hands.

card fever

As the war continued in the Pacific, the daily papers were filled with statistics of battle; numbers of lost submarines, of 'Japs', 'Huns' and 'Yanks' killed, sat alongside complaints about rationing, small-time criminal activity in the city, local car accidents, helpful hints on where to send Red Cross packages, or how to get letters through to loved ones imprisoned in Japan and Malaysia. Early in 1944 Sydney bookies were taking bets on the war ending in Europe by June. Much of the news was propaganda, some of it was accurate, and a lot of it was censored.

What had certainly become less prevalent however was the public's focus on the Aboriginal community. This is not to say there weren't continued racist attacks, insults or discriminatory policies that the Aboriginal community had to endure. The Native Affairs Department may have become less overtly controlling of my own family's life after Neville's exit, but families trapped at Moore River or on reserves would not have seen it this way. Also, the Department was planning a new push in its policy of assimilation, to catch up with the changes that the war had swept across the state. At Glendower Street, my grandmother and other women and men who called Jessie's place home were also focused on the war, on the men who had died in action and the ones who had been captured and imprisoned, as they waited for news of the ones they'd heard nothing of for months. The papers Edward brought home carried news of the distant war as a mixture of rumour, gossip and propaganda. There were other rumours too, closer to home, of new laws that were going to affect the lives of Aboriginal people throughout the state.

While the card games of the 1930s had been sedate affairs almost entirely patronised by Aboriginal women, the card games of the 1940s were generally for high stakes with bigger gamblers and they really got money moving. With the increase in money that was circulating in the community, along with the growth of the metropolitan Aboriginal population through people drifting into the city, the appearance of Aboriginal servicemen and the increase in sly grog, the card games began attracting people from different backgrounds.

Aunty Eileen Shang, who had been taken away from the Pilbara as a child and placed in Moore River, met my grandmother at the East Perth Girls Home. Jessie went to the Home because she would have heard that a new Nor'wester was in town; they became very close friends. Having suffered the worst of the Neville regime, Aunty Eileen gladly defied the Department that had controlled her life since she was a child.

It was through Aunty Eileen Shang that black American sailors began to come along to the card games and associate with the Aboriginal community. Most of them had come off the American submarines that operated from the Submarine Base at Fremantle. When they weren't on tour, they were off duty for some time, and a lot of Aboriginal women found themselves the focus of the black American sailors' affections. When I asked her if many Aboriginal people mixed with black Americans, Aunty Eileen Shang recalled, 'Oh, yes, yes, but we had to do it quietly, we weren't allowed to mix with the Negroes and I couldn't understand it because they were black and we were black. We couldn't understand why we couldn't associate with the whites, not that I liked white men, but we couldn't associate with them either, so I mean, we had to have someone.'

The black American sailors were welcomed at the card games. They had more money, they were charming, and they were black. Unlike some units of the American armed forces, these men were not part of a segregated unit and they often brought along their white shipmates, or sailors of other nationalities who were in port—Fremantle was also home to British and Dutch submarines.

At Glendower Street, and at other card houses in the metropolitan area, or at camps on the fringes of the city, whites and blacks found a space for coexistence, even if it was at times uneasy. At any one of the marathon card games at Jessie's you could find British servicemen, Dutch submariners, Aboriginal diggers and black US sailors sitting around the table. Like no other time before it, the war brought the world to Western Australia. Segregation was still the law, however the reality was that the Aboriginal community, usually isolated, now found itself exposed to other peoples, if not as equals, at least in a way that had certainly not occurred before the Second World War.

Still operating within the framework established by A.O. Neville, the Department was adamant about segregating Aboriginal women from black American servicemen. Indeed, the entire population of Perth was paranoid about black American servicemen interacting with whites, and the *Mirror*, the scandal sheet of the day, often ran stories about supposed liaisons between 'Negro' servicemen and white women. In a typical story, a white woman was charged with vagrancy for simply speaking with an African American man. The judge in the case was quite clear. 'The worst feature of this case is that people have seen you, a white woman, associating with a black soldier. If you are seen with a black man again you will go to prison.'

The *Sunday Times* reported the case of two white women who had simply talked with a black American sailor. Under the heading 'Women Talked to Negro', the story told of how the women were asked by police to give their names and when they refused to do so, were arrested. In court the women said they were members of the People's Security Party, and they were 'discussing politics with the Negro, an educated man.' Both women got off with a caution. There were also in the press many reported cases of abuse of Aboriginal women by black American servicemen. The *Daily News* ran a headline, 'Black Slave Traffic' and alleged that a white woman drove 'native women', young and old, around in her car, picked up 'Negro' sailors and took them to Point Walter 'to spend the night.' The Aboriginal women were reported as saying that the sailors gave them money, and also paid the woman in question. The woman was imprisoned for nine months for being in breach of the Native Administration Act.

However, not all contact was of the nature imagined by the Department, or as described in the cases mentioned above. Caught up in the segregatory laws of the Native Welfare Department, some Aboriginal women, like some white women, struck up relationships with African American sailors stationed in Perth. At card houses like my grandmother's, women could catch up with their boyfriends and there was also the chance for black American and Aboriginal servicemen to mix. Away from the card houses, Eileen Shang and other Aboriginal women would meet up with black American sailors in various pubs and wine saloons that would let them in. But to do this, the women still had to run the gauntlet of the Pass System.

Conditional citizenship was the new 'big idea' the Native Affairs Department had dreamed up to deal with the increased Aboriginal engagement with the wider community as a result of the war. The 'Dog Act', as it was known in the black community, came into being in 1944 as an amendment to the 1936 Native Administration Act, and was an attempt to allow greater rights of citizenship to certain Aboriginal people. These rights included the right to vote and to enter public places, exempting the holder from the provisions of the Native Administration Act. But these citizenship rights had to be applied for and, being conditional, could be removed at any time. The new rights operated alongside the Exemption Certificate, which was still in operation, as well as the Pass System that had operated in Perth from 1937. While Aboriginal people had become used to, if not resigned to, the discriminatory power of the police, some black American servicemen were indignant that their partners came under such laws of control and were outraged that they had to show their dog tags. Eileen Shang remembered this well. 'We used to go to a wine saloon, y'know, with our dog tags. We used to march in the wine saloon and show them and these Yanks used to say, "Hey baby, what's this for?" "Oh, shut up," we'd say, "this, you don't understand." "Oh, you can't have that," they'd say, and these Negroes tore a couple of the girl's things up. They got furious because they said it was wrong.'

George Harwood explained how he understood the attraction of black US servicemen for Aboriginal women, because on the arm of a sailor, they could get into places usually banned to Aboriginal people.

Of course, this did not always work. Eileen Shang remembered how she and another Aboriginal woman and their black American partners were stopped from going to the pictures. The ticket seller said, 'I'm sorry, but there's no room.' They were standing at the ticket booth with their money ready to pay. Two black men and two black women enjoying themselves out on the town. Their money was fine, their skin was the wrong colour. The other woman with Aunty Eileen had much darker coloured skin. Aunty Eileen's partner leaned forward and politely said to the ticket seller, 'I think you're making a mistake, lady.' This might be the way that they treat blackfellas in this town, but he wasn't going to be treated like dirt. 'All right, that's all right,' he said, and they left. 'I'll see the General,' was all he said. He didn't make it into the pictures that night, but the incident made it around the black grapevine the next day. I imagine that most of the population of Perth would have thought that it was quite right that he was refused, but while it didn't change anything for Aboriginal people having to endure such insults, it showed that standing up for yourself was possible.

African Americans didn't just bring money, good dance moves and sweet talking into the community. Their disbelief at the treatment of the Aboriginal people they were mixing with, and the stand they sometimes took, left a mark on the minds of those in the community who had long-term visions of equality. As Aunty Eileen Shang remembered, 'They just couldn't understand it, they really couldn't understand it, see, why we were treated like that, because they, American people too, they're fighters they're, they're very aggressive people. Aboriginal people are very humble people, they don't go to the extreme of doing what the American Negroes did, so that's the difference between them. This American Negro was telling me — all these other American Negroes too, they reckon — no, that's not the right way they were treating us. But of course we didn't know nothing, we just went along and did what they wanted us to, because we didn't know nothing.'

News of such acts of resistance circulated quickly around the Perth Aboriginal community, and there's no doubt that instances like these and others were closely observed by those seeking to test the boundaries.

Bill Bodney had been agitating against the control of the Aborigines Department and the Native Affairs Department since the 1920s and was still looking for ways to bring change for his people. Although of African descent, Bill married into Noongar society, worked all over the south mixing with Noongars, and was classed as Aboriginal under the 1905 Act. He was a well-respected member of the community with consider-able Noongar knowledge. Bill was known throughout the city for his distinctive presence as he made his way through the streets at his own slow pace with his Noongar walking cane. He wasn't a big one for gambling, but made it along to card houses to catch up on what was happening in the community and to share information about who was in prison, who was in need of a place to stay or who had been removed from their camp to the Moore River Settlement.

Efforts by the Native Affairs Department and the police did not stop at surveillance. Upon receipt of information that black American servicemen were meeting Aboriginal women on the creek in a reserve near the East Perth Gas Works, the police, in conjunction with the Native Affairs Department and the American shore patrol, increased their night inspections of East Perth. The Deputy Commissioner of Native Affairs once again left his desk to go out on patrol. They searched East Perth with torches: down to the Bull Paddock, along the Claisebrook, around the mouth of the river and along the empty streets of the industrial areas, peppered with poor housing. They had a map of the houses occupied by Noongars and having turned up nothing down by the creek, began searching house to house for alcohol and black Americans. In his report McBeath noted that they raided a Noongar house in which they thought they'd find American servicemen, but in the end had to report that 'the Patrol and inspection was without results and I suspect that the police informant also warned the Natives who in turn advised the servicemen to keep clear of the reserve.'

The *Mirror* tabloid was keeping its eye out for a good story. Interracial mixing, especially with black American sailors, was a seller. Even Aunty Eileen made it into the *Mirror*'s pages when she was arrested for cohabitation and brought before the court. In a farcical playing out of proceedings, she stunned the judge when being pushed to acknowledge her guilt for mixing with African Americans by responding with her own question. 'What's wrong with it?' she demanded. 'They're black and we're black so I don't see what all the fuss is about.'

Aunty Eileen Shang really could not understand what the problem was. 'It was dreadful, dear. They had so much control of us that, like I said, we didn't know nothing. We had no choice, we had to go along with the system. You had to be off the streets at six o'clock, otherwise we'd be arrested. Not the servicemen—we'd be arrested.' Eileen and other women didn't always go along with the system. 'It didn't matter how much the police used to threaten to put me in gaol, I used to put on a show because I had all the navy behind me, I didn't care, see. I always … I was always with servicemen, cause they [the police] used to say to you … "you have to be off the streets," and told the Negroes that too, and the Negroes told them to "get lost". We had nowhere to go and we were drinking and having a good time. I mean war was party time, I'm telling you, everybody did that, but we wasn't allowed to do it, see we wasn't allowed to do it because we were black.'

When six o'clock came, most people got off the streets. And it wasn't only from the Prohibited Area. It was an unwritten law that you had to be out of the way, pretty much anywhere in the metropolitan area, unless you were prepared to stand up to the police. This is when card houses would be filled. 'The card games weren't about the money really,' said Eileen Shang. 'They used to have all these complaints, but [the gambling] was never anywhere to make money, wasn't a profitable thing, it was only to pass the time away.'

There were a number of card houses around the city in East Perth and, once Aunty Eileen got her own place in Leighton, just near Fremantle, it was common to find a full house there too. My grandmother loved to go to Aunty Eileen's place when there wasn't a game on at Glendower Street. Like my grandmother's house though, Aunty Eileen's came in for surveillance and the occasional raid. You had to think quickly to avoid trouble. If the police came to Aunty Eileen's door she knew how to handle them. 'Well, there's nobody here,' she'd tell the police.

As she explained: 'All the sailors used to run down the beach — I lived right on the beach. Everything was all arranged, don't worry, we knew when the police were coming. We'd put it [the money] in the oven or put it in the copper, didn't matter where it was, they was always raiding us, but they could never catch us doing anything.'

The Americans also brought 'dice', as Aunty Eileen called it, or craps, which became popular. If the cards were a tense stand-off of skill and luck, dice was the release. Aunty Eileen remembered how gambling really took hold in the war years. 'We were always playing cards and playing dice too, we's always playing dice because the Yanks liked dice. Even Jessie, she'd say, "Roll 'em, roll 'em." We used to roll dice and play cards, roll dice and gamble, and then we'd all chip in for food and drinks and we'd have a party then. You know, just something to do because we couldn't go down the streets.'

The departmental file that had tracked my grandmother for most of her life ended on 4 December 1944 with a single word, 'FILE'. My grandmother's file was presumably sent from the Native Affairs Department to the archives, where rows upon rows of personal files that were kept on our community were simply left to gather dust. My family were of course oblivious to this fact and continued to live their lives by the reality of their experiences on a daily basis. The files had documented the overt control of the Department over my grandmother for more than half her life. Just because the file stopped tracking my grandmother it did not mean that she would no longer experience racism, or that my mother would be able to avoid it, or that Edward could be free of the fear of what could be done to his family by the Department.

Each Aboriginal person that came into my grandmother's house had a file. Each had their own story of being tracked and controlled. As their paths crossed my grandmother's, so too did she enter into the 'ACTIVE' files of others whose volumes had not been shelved. The all-pervasive nature of surveillance of the Aboriginal community in Western Australia meant that you were never really far from the Department's gaze. The reality of life in the Aboriginal community of 1944 meant that the Native Affairs Department were never far from someone's life, affecting all those who came into contact with them. For each file that was shelved, another was just as quickly created in its place.

My mother met Chuck Friese at a Red Cross dance. After she returned from Bridgetown she was able to gain small freedoms from my grandmother. One of these freedoms included attending Red Cross dances. My mother was a great dancer and took out jitterbug competitions with an older African American serviceman she'd met and come to know over a few weeks. It was while she was out there strutting her stuff for the little gold cup that Chuck must have noticed her. Chuck was a white boy from Texas. He was on a submarine patrolling the Pacific. He had Montgomery Clift good looks, and was hardly older than my mother. It was early 1945 when they entered into their whirlwind romance.

Chuck was all manners and handshakes when my mother brought him home to meet the family, and although it must have gone against everything that my grandmother had wanted for her daughter, she saw that he was a decent young man, and that he and my mother were determined. Edward came to like Chuck a lot. There was something innocent and sweet about the boy that caught people off guard. There is only one photo of Chuck. He's standing with Betty on his right arm and Jessie and Edward at his left at 69 Glendower Street. Chuck is dressed in his navy blues, and although he fills out the uniform well, he is a mere child of a man. My mother is wearing his giant black navy-issue winter coat. Chuck stands between my mother and my grandmother. He's the focus and the foil, the go-between that would act as a diffuser for the break for independence that my mother was wanting. He was perfect for it.

Chuck loved coming to Glendower Street when he was back from patrols. He loved the city of Perth. He loved the hills. He came from money, or at least enough to buy a decent spread, a good block of land in the hills, and that became his dream, and my mother's dream. Chuck talked about setting up a house in the hills when the war ended. He had it all worked out. They'd build themselves a place overlooking the city and have Jessie and Edward come to live with them. Maybe it was his sell to the family so that he could become a part of their family while he was away from his own. Maybe he was just a boy-man with big ideas, like Edward had been when he first arrived in 1909. Maybe the dream he created for his new girl and her 'mom and pop' was what he needed to believe to get through a patrol stalking Japanese ships and subs, screwed down tight in a tin can for days at a time. Whatever the real story might have been, everybody bought it. My mother wanted it badly. It sounded good to Jessie and Edward. The war was nearly over. It was all just around the corner.

Family life revolved around card games, visiting servicemen and friends from the country. Just as my mother had accompanied my grandmother everywhere as a child, now she accompanied her as her aid and companion. Aunty Eileen would ring up and say, 'Ay Jessie, get yourself down here. I got a real good game going.' My grandmother would try to convince 'Shangi' that she should bring them all around to Glendower Street where there was less chance of them being raided, but Aunty Eileen would have nothing of it. Shangi liked to come to Jessie's, but she liked her own place a lot better. There were usually more Americans for one thing, and that meant higher stakes. But it could also mean trouble.

There was a card game going down at Eileen Shang's place one weekend. My grandmother ordered the taxi, collected my mother and a couple of Betty's old school friends who were visiting, and headed through the city, down around the river, and south on Stirling Highway to Leighton. Soon after they arrived a fight broke out. One of the women at the table had been dating a black American sailor who she thought had left for sea not long before. In his absence, she'd found herself a British submariner to keep her company. They were all getting into a game when the American sailor turned up. His ship had returned to port with engine trouble and he'd been looking for his girlfriend. He'd heard on the grapevine that she was out and about with a British sailor and by the time he tracked her down to Aunty Eileen's place he had worked himself into a rage. The room went quiet.

My grandmother could see in the American's eyes that he was intent on seriously damaging this little British officer, who was seated at the table next to his girlfriend, unaware of what was about to happen. Only when the American lifted the Englishman from his chair and grabbed him by the collar did it finally dawn that the quietness in the room had something to do with him. My grandmother got up from the table and pushed herself between them, kicked off her slippers and faced the American. He took a knife from his pocket, flicked open the blade and said, 'Get outta my way Jessie. Don't stop me. I'm gonna kill him.' My grandmother stood her ground and told him plainly, 'Well, you can try if you want to but you'll have to cut through me first and there's a lot to cut through.'

The stand-off seemed to go on for ages, the American standing over my grandmother with his knife drawn, the other man not knowing what the hell it was all about. Then the American put the knife away, and slowly stepped back. My grandmother didn't move from her spot. 'What do you think you're doing,' she said to the American, 'fighting over a woman?' Sensing the heat had left the situation, Jessie turned on all the men at the table. 'You men, you fight each other at war and then you bring your battles here.' Swinging around to the British officer, Jessie let fly, 'And you, you've caused enough trouble here for one day. This wouldn't happen if you blokes stuck to your own. Get your things together—you're coming with me.'

Jessie made both men shake hands before corralling my mother, her friends and the British officer into a taxi and heading back across the river to Northline. In the taxi the officer couldn't thank my grandmother enough. He was still shaken when they got to Glendower Street where Edward took over minding him while my grandmother cooled down. It turned out the man was from Surrey, and he and Edward got on famously. He stayed that night and joined the circle of servicemen who called on the Duchess of Glendower Street when in port for a game of cards and some sly grog.

Family picnics to Naval Base were now occasional treats rather than the regular occurrence they'd been in the early years of the war. Rationing was taking hold, and there was the problem of my grandmother's health.

Saturdays became SP bookie days as Betty and Edward took turns at riding down to the betting shop to put bets on for my grandmother. Jessie was a student of the form guide, but also acted pretty much on intuition and the sound of a good name in choosing her horses. Edward kept an old Australian Army Divisional Race Meeting, Rodeo and Picnic flyer in his trunk. Circled are the horses that my grandmother felt were sure winners. For race one she liked 1. Suits-Me, 2. Dorrabelle and 3. Mona. For race four she liked 1. Stout Fella, 2. Rex and 3. Fox Trot. She bet on the rodeo, the boxing and even the foot races. Anything that a bookie would take a bet on, she'd lay her intuition against. Special trips like this required the aid of my grandmother's favourite taxi driver, Tom Robbie, who also didn't mind placing a few bets himself.

Uncle Gordon Dorey, who my grandmother had cared for as a small boy in Swan Mission, was also a regular at Glendower Street. He was unable to join up due to the limp that he carried from being kicked by a horse. He worked at Cardabia Station on the North-West Cape, and occasionally came down to the city. My mother loved Gordon. He was like Bill Poland, one of the older, quieter men who had an air of confidence about him that was comforting. However, she didn't like how he changed his shirts twice a day, which meant she had extra to wash and iron. On the station Uncle Gordon didn't care what he wore, but in the city he always wanted to look a million dollars. He was going out with Nellie Lyndon for a while, but for some reason it didn't last, and Gordon became one of the old bachelor cowboys of the community. He liked company, but wasn't a gambler. He had money and chipped in when he stayed, but he knew how hard it was to accumulate, and he wasn't going to part with it easily. He kept a jar by the bed for loose coppers.

There is a great photo of him with Aunty Eileen Shang and Uncle Sam Mitchell. The two old boys are flanking Eileen outside her place in Leighton. In the background is the grille of an old Chevy framed by mountains of forty-four gallon drums stored behind the white tin fence of a marshalling yard nearby. Aunty Eileen is dressed to the nines in a slinky black number with black ankle-strap shoes. Gordon's huge six-foot-six frame is leaning into Shangi on his good leg. They're casting long afternoon shadows behind them, gazing directly into the camera with a sense of confidence, as if staring into the light of a bright future. Things were tough, but the war was nearly over. The newspapers called it a 'War Against Tyranny', so shouldn't the end of the war mean the end of discrimination for Aboriginal people as well?

My grandmother's house was always a meeting place. I say my grandmother's house, because although it was Edward's house too, the house had come to be Jessie's refuge. As her health declined, her house became her means of connection with the rest of the community; her hospitality and her contribution. There were children staying to attend school or apprenticeships in town. Sometimes Eva and Norm Harris came down from the country for medical treatment or for Show Week. Like many of the people who came and stayed, Eva was an old friend of my grandmother's from the Mission and Settlement days. My mother became great friends with their daughter Myrtle and son Norm and his wife, Anne, and they have always remained great friends. This was the house's function for my grandmother — a place for community, for family, and to enjoy the small freedoms available away from the gaze of the public, the police and the Department. Jessie's house, and houses like it, played a crucial role in keeping communication and social gatherings alive. Blackfellas couldn't gather in public places, couldn't enter hotels, pubs or other meeting spaces, and the reserves were so closely watched that anyone deemed to be in town from the country without a good reason would find themselves shipped back by rail at the first chance. The card games and gatherings served the need for community, but they weren't enough in themselves to maintain it, or to effect any kind of direct change on the conditions that made the houses so important — the segregation imposed upon them.

Although the Communist Party and other left-wing organisations of the day held generally progressive views in terms of policies towards Aboriginal people, the reality was that some of these organisations were made up of people competing with Aboriginal people for work; the memberships were almost entirely white, and there appear to have been no Aboriginal people in positions of power.

In 1945 the war seemed to be coming to an end and the wider population was beginning to focus on the home world that soldiers were returning to. The Native Citizenship Act had been passed the year before to create a mechanism for Aboriginal citizenship in the emerging society that had been woken up by the war years. So much of the public's mind was concerned with events overseas, that the race debates of the 1930s had faded from the pages of the press.

Jimmy McSkene survived Changi. He returned to the only home that he knew, 69 Glendower Street. But Jimmy was never the same again. His health was wrecked, he suffered flashbacks and he couldn't sleep. At night my grandmother would wake to find him sitting at the end of her bed, just touching her foot. When she asked him what he was doing, he said that he was just making sure she was real. Jimmy would walk around and around Hyde Park all night. He'd circle the twin lakes aimlessly, then make his way to the back verandah of Glendower Street where my grandmother slept, before heading out again when he realised he'd woken her. Around and around the park again. Later, Jimmy lived behind Glendower Street in an old workers' cottage in Primrose Lane. He was a shadow of his former self, and a bit of an easy mark.

After all that time in Changi, Jimmy came out of the army a relatively rich man. He had put his next of kin as 'Aunty Betty Smith of Glendower Street North Perth' when he had joined up in 1940, even though my mother Betty was only ten at the time. Because there were no dependants, Jimmy's army pay for the years that he was imprisoned was put aside for him. When he was released he had a total of £984, a small fortune, as well as his pension. It didn't last long. Within six months he'd been duped out of his money by a woman with eyes only for his pension, so the story goes. Within a year Jimmy was in Ward Thirteen, Hollywood Hospital, the Repatriation Hospital for Returned Soldiers. He was suffering from anxiety, arthritis and both kinds of malaria. He was broke again and asked for his pension to be increased so that he could head north to warmer weather. He never made it. He ended up in the old men's home again, but this time it was for good.

A little item in the *Sunday Times* heralded the postwar return of public sentiment about Aboriginal people in the city. 'Natives Need Pass For City', the headline confidently announced, reminding white citizens of their civic duty to ensure Aborigines didn't enter the city without a damn good reason. Readers of the *Sunday Times* were reported as asking, 'Are natives permitted to enter the city?' Mr McBeath, the same man who'd been out on patrols of East Perth with the American shore patrol watching for Aborigines and African Americans mixing, was now in the top job of Commissioner of Native Affairs. He put their minds at ease. He informed them that Perth was indeed still a 'prohibited area for all natives except those lawfully employed here. Others must have a Dept. pass for the period they want to stay in Perth.' He further assured the wider public that any Aboriginal people down from the country without a legitimate reason were to be 'sent back to their areas' as soon as they were detected by police.

The lights of the city were coming on again, and the wider community of whites who inhabited the metropolis didn't like what they saw. The Americans went home, taking with them as war brides many of the white women they had struck up relationships with. This was not possible for Aboriginal women. While it was not easy for white war brides to go to the United States of America, for Aboriginal women it was impossible due to the US immigration authority's policy regarding 'coloured blood'. It would have been impossible anyway, as it was illegal for Aboriginal women to be removed from the state without the permission of the Commissioner of Native Affairs—and he had spent the war trying to keep Aboriginal women and American servicemen apart.

Many Aboriginal men gave their lives fighting for Australia against the Japanese. Of those who survived, some stayed in the army as long as they could. One old man I knew was part of the mop-up operations in Hiroshima. Some stayed in the army permanently, taking their chances there wouldn't be another war. Korea was just around the corner, but most were demobilised to the bright lights of Fremantle and Perth. They returned transformed in so many ways to a country that, as far as their rights were concerned, couldn't give a damn.

On their return the comradeship between black and white continued in some cases, but in the main the fight for rights was left to the Aboriginal ex-soldiers themselves, who very quickly learned that their new-found freedoms during the war were only temporary. Aboriginal people were looking for ways to move forward so as to retain the gains they had experienced, not as a side effect of a war taking the public focus off the community, but as basic given rights. Black servicemen learned that it was wise to keep hold of their uniforms if they wanted to be able to drink in pubs with their Aboriginal mates, or with the few white mates that would still associate with them. In the era of postwar reconstruction, whites again turned their focus to their own affairs, but there were some who would not forget what they had fought for, and the friendship they had experienced with their Aboriginal comrades. Back in civilian life, the Aboriginal ex-soldiers were just like any other Aborigines, and apart from the farcical Native Citizenship Rights that were the result of the 1944 Citizenship Act, little had changed in regard to the laws that held back the community.

Although the 1944 Citizenship Rights Act allowed for Aboriginal servicemen to be eligible to vote, H.D. Moseley, then Lieutenant Colonel in charge of the Security Service Intelligence Corps., Western Australia, decided that those who received citizenship under this Act, 'must be taught, much as a child is taught' about their responsibilities. Apparently, of the hundreds of Western Australian Aboriginal servicemen who fought, only two received their citizenship rights under this Act, and even they were subject to all the usual limiting provisions. One of these was Sam Isaacs, a regular at my grandmother's house. The Isaacs family was so large and well connected within south-west Aboriginal society that there was no way that he would have been able to meet the first prerequisite of keeping his rights, 'disassociating all tribal connections'.

Increased employment and economic improvements for the Aboriginal community during the war years gave way to jobs for white diggers. The benefits and opportunities available to white soldiers—pensions and access to war service loans—were not available to Aboriginal soldiers, and with the influx of immigrants from Europe, even the kinds of low-paid labouring jobs that Noongars could usually be guaranteed of getting were now subject to competition. However, through interest in left-wing political groups like the Communist Party and the Anti-Fascist League, Aboriginal people were gaining some access to a voice for their desire for change in their conditions and recognition of their human rights.

While segregation prevailed, the card houses remained the focus of the community, but after the promise of the war years, they were not enough. Apart from small gains, there was still no actual unified political movement within the Aboriginal community. They were still completely under the thumb of the police and the Department. Influenced by the changing political climate around them, and world events affecting the entire population, Aboriginal people were yet to see the changes they desired as their right.

Aunty Eileen Shang is leaving Perth for the last time. It's been a good trip, but a difficult one. She caught up with old friends around the city and paid her respects to some that hadn't survived. At my mother's house Aunty refused to believe that the older woman welcoming her at the door was little Betty. 'No way, you can't be little Betty,' she said. 'Must be wrong house ay,' and jokingly started heading for the car. It was a good visit. My sister took photos of the old girls laughing it up, but there was also a sense of great sadness at the loss of all those years between them that seemed to slip from them, and as they were catching up, the years were also slipping away.

At the war's end Aunty Eileen Shang received news that her partner, an African American serviceman, had died when his ship went down in the Pacific. Aunty Eileen stayed in Perth for a few years, then headed north to Marble Bar to find her mother before returning to Perth, and then leaving for good until I asked her to come back to set the record straight.

Like Aunty Eileen, my mother heard about her partner Chuck through a friend who had a boyfriend on the same ship. Betty was notified that the ship had gone down in one of the last naval battles of the Pacific. She was too young to be informed officially.

My mother also hasn't been back into the city in years, or to Hyde Park, but Aunty Eileen's visit has got her thinking about it. She hasn't laughed this hard in a long time.

Aunty Eileen Shang has had her say and given the place a once-over. The city has changed, but the spirit of the city — the sense of itself — exists as an accumulation of all its past histories, and for Aunty Eileen, its smell is as strong as the river on a hot summer's night. Heading through East Perth for the airport, it's as if Aunty Eileen could still sense that shift that was about to happen in the community in the postwar years when the lights went on and the Department swung back into gear.

border crossings

It was after sundown that they began their work. Amongst the thickets of paperbarks, river gums and balga grasstrees, pockets of light could be seen floating between camp sites. Family groups made their way through the bush by lantern or candlelight to gather at the houses of local leaders of Noongar communities to listen to the men from the city who had come to talk with them about citizenship rights. From Narrogin to Gnowangerup and all towns in between, Aboriginal reserves were off limits to anyone who didn't have a permit from the local protector or policeman, or the Commissioner of Native Affairs in Perth. Gathering together under the cover of darkness was a necessity. News of the growing struggle for Aboriginal rights was hard to come by in the southern reserves that served as dumping grounds for Aboriginal families in the postwar period. The only way to get the message through to those Noongars living on the reserves—the ones who were most affected by the Prohibited Area laws—was to actually go down south and risk being arrested for breaking these laws. News had spread of two men who had come to agitate for rights amongst Noongars in the south.

These men had come to speak about the Pilbara Aboriginal Pastoral Workers strike that was taking place in the North, and about new moves afoot within left-wing political organisations across the state to champion Aboriginal rights. Huddled in tin shacks on southern reserves, they spoke about a future of equality, of access to housing, of the right to free association and, of course, the right to vote. They came to speak and to listen, and to report back to the Native Welfare Committee, an amalgam of left-wing groups coming together under the banner of black–white equality, about the living and working conditions in the south. They came, they spoke, they listened, and they left people with a sense of hope when they moved on.

Thomas Bropho and Geoff Harcus made an unlikely pair. Thomas was still a good-looking man despite his years of rough living in camps on the outskirts of Perth. His well-darned coat, most likely one of my grandfather's that my grandmother had decided would look better on her brother's back, belied the poverty that he and his family endured. Tom had not joined up to fight in the Second World War, but stayed at home to join the growing voices of discontent about the treatment of his people. He had survived the 1934 Royal Commission at which he gave evidence against Neville, but his family was being closely watched. He was almost fifty and were it not for the energy that he garnered from the growing movement for social justice, he would probably have looked a lot older than he did. He was risking imprisonment by travelling south to reserves without permission, as well as further hardship for his wife, Bella, and his children back at the camps, but for him the struggle for real freedom was worth the risk.

Geoff Harcus was a skinny white boy who looked older than his early twenties. He had served in the army in Papua New Guinea, and on returning had decided that the racism against Aboriginal people he witnessed on the streets of Perth was not what he had gone to war for. He had gone to war to fight injustice. Geoff had enjoyed the company of Noongars from when he was a small boy growing up in the Perth suburb of Subiaco. His parents endured the wrath of neighbours for letting him play with Noongar boys from the neighbouring camps in the bush at Daglish. This background enabled Geoff to form friendships with Noongar servicemen in New Guinea when many of his white mates urged him not to. When the war ended Geoff, who was a signwriter by trade, had the job of writing the names of dead Australian soldiers on memorial crosses for war graves in New Guinea. Somehow he was left behind and ended up in a remote village with the indigenous people of the region for months. By the time he returned to Perth he had suffered severe malaria, and he was recovering from this when he and Tom began their trip south.

The start of their journey provided a poignant reminder of the importance of their trip. On trying to enter the train compartment in Perth they were told that Tom Bropho had to ride in the guard's van along with the freight. Geoff joined Tom in the guard's van, and so began his own journey into the reality of black life in the south of Western Australia. Geoff had booked accommodation in small hotels in the towns they were travelling to, only to find on arrival that while he was welcome, Thomas wasn't. News began to spread throughout the South of the strange young white boy travelling with the older black man as they began sleeping under railway bridges and on the outskirts of towns. Geoff became a pupil of how to avoid the authorities, stay low and keep out of trouble. Being white, at least he was able to be served in the shops, so they could eat.

Geoff and Thomas first met on the Esplanade in Perth, the site of open discussion and free speech in the city. Mostly left-wing groups used the grassed open area between the city and the river as their public meeting ground amid a sea of conservatism. Geoff was far from a left-wing advocate. He was a churchgoer and in many ways anti-communist, but he believed in a fair go and if there was anyone who didn't have a fair go in Western Australian society it was obvious to him that it was blackfellas. It was after listening to Thomas making a speech that Geoff introduced himself and their life-long friendship began. Thomas invited Geoff out to his camp at Guildford, but forgot to tell Bella that a white man might be visiting. When Geoff turned up one afternoon while Thomas was out selling washing-line props, Granny Bella thought he was from the Department and had come to steal the children. She chased him away with her broomstick. The misunderstanding was soon cleared up, and Geoff became a close friend of the family.

Thomas spoke at any public gathering that would have him, and in Perth in the late 1940s the only groups who showed any interest in Aboriginal issues were either white amelioration groups or left-wing political groups. Thomas spoke to both, but it was at public meetings that he came into his own.

A 1946 *Sunday Times* article with the headline 'Native Persecution is Denounced in Big Perth Protest', captured a sense of his skill as an orator, honed since his days at Swan Mission. The *Sunday Times* noted that the audience contained a 'large number of aborigines and half-castes who followed every word with the greatest attention.' When Thomas came forward to speak, the crowd erupted with a 'tremendous ovation'. Thomas didn't disappoint. He spoke of being a representative of his brothers, and their demand for 'at least similar privileges to the white man, and our freedom.' Thomas reminded the crowd that 'Not long ago the Aborigine fought for his country, fought and died side by side with your brave sons, gave up his boomerang and spear to use modern weapons for peace, justice and liberty.' The crowd roared. Geoff Harcus was sold.

Thomas introduced Geoff around the Aboriginal community and there was not a blackfella who didn't like him. They went to other meetings, and Thomas took Geoff to meet other people becoming active in the move for Aboriginal rights. He also took him to his sister Jessie Smith's place in North Perth, where Geoff lost a good amount of money and met even more Noongars. Geoff became a regular visitor to my grandmother's house, although he soon left the cards to the increasingly serious players that would gather around the table. What attracted him to Jessie's were the conversations that took place outside of the card games and the serious business of money changing hands. Geoff was pleased to find that many of the men he'd known in Papua New Guinea were staying with my grandmother—Henry Mippy, Sporty Jones, Wally Ogilvie, the Mallard boys and the Poland brothers. Geoff entered into our community and when the chance came to head south, he put his money where his mouth was.

Two weeks into their clandestine tour, Tom could see that Geoff was unwell, even though the younger man tried to hide the shakes that began to take over his whole body. Sleeping rough was something Thomas was used to, but it brought Geoff's malaria back with a vengeance. He almost died. It took him a month in hospital to recover from the episode, and the tour was curtailed.

It was August 1946 when he was discharged from hospital, only two months after having returned from New Guinea. In that short time he had become accepted into the black community and had visited Moore River Native Settlement on his own initiative, writing a critical report to the Native Affairs Department. When he recovered from his illness, he began circulating in the community again. The police were beginning to crack down harder on Aboriginal and white interactions and Geoff was arrested for cohabitation for speaking with a Noongar ex-serviceman, Sporty Jones, on a street corner in the city after the six o'clock curfew. It only served to harden his resolve to do something to change those kinds of racist laws. He learned that you had to keep a low profile if you wanted to avoid trouble, but he didn't believe in having to do so forever. He returned to places like my grandmother's house, and formed part of a new generation that was looking for real change.

The period of postwar euphoria was not to last. It would not be long before returned Aboriginal servicemen were to experience the same racism that had been so pervasive in their lives before they joined up. Even the wearing of the uniform began to lose its benefit as they found themselves once again banned from hotels and subject to the Prohibited Area legislation. The card houses were still a major haven of the community, but the momentum that had gathered during the war through involvement in political groups, interaction with black American servicemen and greater interaction with whites, had built up a hunger for greater freedoms.

Having sent their young men off to fight and having participated in manpowered work, the Aboriginal community had done its part for the war effort, but as usual there was no real benefit in return. Much of the press of the time was derogatory towards Aboriginal people, portraying the community as drunks and layabouts. Instances of minor offences in relation to the possession of alcohol made the news while, in general, the good work being done in the community by those seeking change was ignored. The *Worker's Star*, the newspaper of the Communist Party in Western Australia, was the only paper regularly reporting on developments in the north, on the Pilbara strike of Aboriginal stockmen and on the conditions the Aboriginal community endured. But this paper had only a small circulation. With the war over, the Communist Party and other left-wing groups were labelled as subversive, and were under constant attack by the authorities. For many Aboriginal people the marginalisation of the socialist movement was a good reason to avoid getting involved in their organisations. Aboriginal people were already subject to scrutiny and heavy-handed authority; throwing their lot in with these organisations would only risk bringing heavier penalties down on themselves.

There was an increasing desire within the Aboriginal community to control our own affairs. With the combination of newly honed indigenous voices, schooled in the political meetings of the left and the increasingly insulting segregatory attitude of the wider community, the climate was ripe for change. In a very short time allegiances would be formed that would bring about rapid changes for Aboriginal people. It would still take some years for the legislative changes needed to bring about legal, if not actual, equality, but the short term would see changes that would have immediate and lasting effects.

For some time after the war, life at 69 Glendower Street continued much as it did during the war. Large numbers of servicemen stayed, the police kept a watch on the illegal consumption of alcohol and the card games continued, though the Americans and their money had gone. Edward joined in the regular celebrations of returning friends and mourned the loss of those who didn't make it back, and continued to work at the *West Australian*. My mother recovered from the death of her fiancé and began working in a laundry in William Street, North Perth, for a friend of the family. She was able to fit her work around caring for my grandmother and the housework that was required in accommodating the large number of people passing through the house. Jessie, at the centre of her household, maintained her close watch on my mother, and began to gamble more heavily.

There were great shortages at war's end, but there was also a lot of army back pay circulating in a climate of abandon and release after the horrors and sacrifices. Card games continued as a social function of a community unable to meet in public, but some games, and these included the ones at my grandmother's house, began to attract a new level of interest, and that brought a new level of interest from the police. New gamblers were making their way to my grandmother's house. They weren't looking for community or a place to call home; they were in it for the money and my grandmother was happy to accommodate them. But in taking their money she was upping the stakes. Small games amongst the community were one thing, but if caught red-handed in high stakes gambling she'd be sent to gaol for sure.

Helena Clarke has been around long enough to know a good thing when she sees it, and to know when someone is trying to pull the wool over her eyes, or anybody else's. With regard to governments and their reactionary approaches to Aboriginal issues, she knows from solid experience when they're up to their tricks. Helena was an old woman when I finally tracked her down in Darwin in the 1990s, but she still retained the fire of the youthful Helena who had hitchhiked a series of trucks down to Perth from her home town of Port Hedland in 1942, in search of work and on the first leg of a planned trip around Australia. Never mind that she was supposed to get permission from the Native Affairs Department to go south of the 27th parallel. Helena wasn't one for following rules that she felt were wrongly applied to her people.

It was the same with the Native Title regime that was set up in 1993. Helena was invited to be a part of a claim that related to her own family's links to Thangoo Station in the Kimberley, but she decided not to get involved. 'If the rules are laid down for you by someone else, you're doomed,' she believes, and the pathetic state of negotiations that have resulted for Aboriginal claimants from this Native Title process have borne her out. For Helena, any process of negotiation has to be owned by the people who are going to be affected by it, or forget it. She doesn't need some court to decide whether or not she belongs to that country—she knows where she belongs. She doesn't need an anthropologist to decide whether she knows about 'spiritual cultural practices' as part of some proof of culture—just tell those anthropologists to check out the spirits and ghosts that are always following her around and bothering her. Maybe they could do her a favour, be useful, and get these spirits to go back to their country.

Speaking with Helena you know she's sharp, that she's paying close attention to every word you say, but you never quite know as she looks over your shoulder if she's glaring at some spirit to make it leave the room. When I first caught up with her in the 1990s, it was a welcome surprise to her. She isn't someone to dwell in the past, but surviving eighty years certainly gets you thinking about all those miles you've travelled, and all those people who were a part of your history. For Helena, some of them still come visiting, and as we sit to talk about her time in Perth, I get the distinct feeling that a few of them are sitting on the arms of her lounge chair as she quietly brushes the fabric as if to get them to sit somewhere else.

First impressions on meeting her in her Darwin flat are dominated by her wall-to-wall Elvis memorabilia. 'Don't you dare say a bad word about him,' she warned me as I slurped a cup of coffee and stared over her head at the life-size image on the wall. I assured her I had no beef with Elvis. I've known Helena for more then ten years now and the woman she presents to you when you first meet her is the woman she stays for the whole time you know her. She is well loved by her large and extended family, still travels from one side of Australia to the other with greater ease than some people her age walk down the street, and is still keenly interested in everything around her.

Stories about Helena and her role in political action in Perth have circulated in our community for decades, but no one had any idea what happened to her after she left Perth in the late 1940s. It was as if she rode into Perth on the sidestep of a truck, shook things up and then disappeared into the sunset, like Clint Eastwood, to sort out the next town. Since that time she has begun coming down to Perth regularly to visit her grand-daughters, who moved here for work and study, to catch up with old friends, and to see how the place has changed since she left in the late 1940s.

She's well into her eighties but she can remember the day she walked into my grandparents' house as if she'd just come from there an hour before. Helena was greeted at the door by my grandfather who whispered to her to come in. Thinking there must be a baby sleeping, she whispered back, only to be drawn soon after to the lively sounds of people gathering out the back. Helena had heard of my grandmother's house from other Nor'westers she'd made contact with in the city. My grandmother, and everyone else in the place, took to Helena instantly, and I can see why. She has an energy that is infectious.

Helena Clark arrived on my grandmother's doorstep in 1942. She wasn't a gambler, reckoning that she couldn't win a chook raffle if she was the only one in it, but came for the company, and to meet up with other Aboriginal people. Helen's brother-in-law had joined the air force and was away fighting, so Helena and her sister Sue were sharing a little workers' cottage in West Perth. Helena's walk into the city took her under the West Perth bridge, past the Roe Street brothels and into Northbridge. She walked all over the city, wearing a hole in her shoe that she patched with cardboard until she managed to get a job in the Florentine Café as a general hand. She picked up other cleaning jobs and soon became aware that Perth was a very segregated town.

Helena sensed that Noongars within the city lived under a pall of controlled manipulation that her own family in the north had fought to overcome. She was determined to do something about this. She started by responding to derogatory reports about Aboriginal people in the daily newspapers by writing letters to the editor. When she tried to join the air force she was rebuked and told that they did not accept Aboriginal women in the armed services. She experienced the same discrimination when she tried to join the land army. When she was finally manpowered to work at St Johns Hospital, Helena was indignant at having to comply with the order while, at the same time, she was being refused the basic rights of a citizen of the country.

Helena Clarke grew up in a political household. She was raised by her parents, Katherine and William Lawrence Clarke, to be both respectful of her elders and resentful of any impositions on her own and other Aboriginal people's freedoms. Her parents were very independent and brought their children up with the same attitude. Lawrence Clarke, known as Secretary Clarke, or Pop Clarke, in Port Hedland, was born on Thangoo Station in the Kimberley region in 1897. In 1934, Pop Clarke began the Euralian Club in Port Hedland, a club for Aboriginal people of European descent. Helena Clarke remembered that her father used to 'go around talking his head off about improving our lot, and he couldn't get much because there were so few elderly men, but as younger ones came he started the club, and the young ones were very keen because of the dancing, and this is what my dad did up in Port Hedland with his Euralian Club. No outside influence, no church creating—just us folks, the coloured people themselves.'

In Perth in the middle of the war years, Helena Clarke also began to seek change. 'I was always interested in politics—not that I ever wanted to be a politician, but there was all this problem with our people and I thought, if I go along I can find out how these people work. And at that time the only political party an Aboriginal person could join was the Communist Party.' Apart from attracting Aboriginal people from within the metropolitan area with its 'plank of complete economic and legal equality for aborigines,' the Communist Party was active in the Pilbara region as well. The Pilbara Aboriginal pastoral strike, which was conceived as early as the beginning of the war, was a crucial turning point in Aboriginal politics in Western Australia. While Helena Clarke was going along to meetings to hear what the various left-wing groups had to say about changing the conditions Aboriginal people lived under, her father's Euralian Club was becoming more politically active in the North. The police were keeping an eye on it too, complaining that Pop Clarke had the presumption to believe 'he is as good as any white man, and therefore he should enjoy all privileges and that there should be a common law for all.'

Agitation for the Pilbara strike started up in the early 1940s, and Don McLeod, a local white prospector who had agreed to assist the Aboriginal pastoral workers, approached Pop Clarke to get involved. Helena believed that her father, although supportive in principle, would not join because he was keen for Aboriginal control of Aboriginal matters. Perhaps if he had been approached by one of the Aboriginal organisers he might have joined up. Lawrence Clarke had no illusions about left-wing groups in Western Australia. He had been banned from holding a ticket to work on the wharves by the Australian Labor Party in their campaign for job preferences to go to white workers. The incident threatened the livelihood of his family and left him distrustful of the involvement of whites in Aboriginal politics. He was also well aware that Communist Party involvement in the stockmen's dispute would bring heightened attention from the authorities.

The Deputy Director of Security for Western Australia contacted the Commissioner of Native Affairs in the war years with a request that a register of Aboriginal agitators be kept, so that people like Helena Clarke and her father could be kept under observation. The interest of the authorities in watching the community so closely was due more to the growing involvement of Aboriginal people in political movements of the time. The Australian Aborigines League in the eastern states was critical of Western Australia's Native Affairs Department, and the government was keen to sideline any similar organised agitation developing in the west. In the early postwar years, Helena Clarke, Geoff Harcus, Bill Bodney and Thomas Bropho were well known within the Aboriginal community, and also by Native Affairs administration, for their activities.

Helena loved to go along to my grandmother's house for the companionship, to listen to music, share gossip and catch up with whoever had rolled into town and ended up at Mum Smith's. But she and the new generation of Aboriginal leaders also wanted political action — to change the laws and achieve the equality that their parents had never experienced — and they would use these occasions at Glendower Street to make plans, try out ideas and share information.

My grandmother had no objections to this, although having endured the Neville years, she operated with quite a different approach. Jessie had survived by trying to keep her head down and bluffing her way against authority. To many of her generation, the Department would always be there, somewhere, watching. Keep your head down, but do what you want, was her attitude, and if a gift horse came along, you didn't say no.

Helena Clarke believed that you got what was yours by fighting, and you made sure that everyone else did too. Whereas older women like my grandmother would take risks to steal kids from a place like Moore River, and hope that trouble didn't result, people like Helena wanted to get rid of the Settlements altogether. She believed that the only way they were going to do it was by getting the vote. There were some Elders who'd thought that same thing for some time and were keen to join this new wave that was forming in the years immediately after the war.

Older people such as Thomas Bropho, Bertha Isaacs and Bill Bodney rallied to Helena's desire for real change, and it was this combination of respected community Elders and youthful energy that was to ensure their success. But whereas older people like Bill, Tom and Bertha were keen to accept the support of any political group willing to come to their aid, the younger generation was more wary. For some of the older people, it was counted a success to have white support and a forum for their views. For younger people like Helena Clarke however, white leadership was cause for suspicion. She felt that participation in white groups left the community vulnerable to other political agendas. The Communist Party, for example, had an ideological structure for societal power that did not recognise Aboriginal eldership and control over Aboriginal issues. How then was it likely that through them Aboriginal people could solve their own problems?

George and Jack Poland were staying at my grandmother's house and attending the odd meeting down on the Esplanade. Their older brother, Bill, hadn't wasted any time getting back to Shark Bay when he returned from the war. In the absence of his older brother, Jack had reinvented himself from being one of the 'Black Detectives' to the singularly glamorous 'Black Prince'. He had grown sharper and harder since his war service. Gone was the knockabout character of his former self. In its place stood six feet of cool reserved intensity. Jack ditched his uniform sooner than anyone else. He was photographed in 1946 at Glendower Street with Edward, Jessie and Betty in two-tone, pinstriped, open-collar coolness. My grandmother stands hidden by my mother who is tucked under my grandfather's arm. Jessie is bigger than ever and happy to have one of her boys back from the war. Edward is posed so as to hide his scar from his welding accident in 1927, and my mother looks directly into the camera. The extended family of my grandmother's house was returning, but changed by their experience in war.

Jack and George Poland knew Geoff Harcus from the army, and they had kept in touch through my grandmother's house. Jack Poland worked with Helena Clarke's brother at Crescos, the superphosphate works in Bassendean where a lot of Noongars worked, and Helena and Jack had talked at gatherings at Glendower Street. Once Helena and Geoff Harcus met they hit it off right from the start.

Jack and George accepted an invitation to meet with a couple of white women in their flat in West Perth. I'm not sure how they came to meet the McIntyre sisters, but it was most likely at a meeting on the Esplanade. The McIntyre sisters were members of the Modern Women's Club, a progressive organisation that wanted to do something for Aboriginal people, and had the idea of organising a social function to be held at a hall in the centre of the city. This was intended to be the first in a series of functions aimed at providing a meeting space for Aboriginal people in the city.

Jack Poland decided that their new group would be called the Coolbaroo League, after the Yamatji word for magpie. Helena thought that Coolbaroo was symbolic of people like herself, people of mixed descent, and she agreed to join as long as no whites held positions of power. It had to be Aboriginal owned and run. Geoff Harcus thought that Coolbaroo stood for black and white people working together, but completely agreed that it should be Aboriginal run and owned. The Coolbaroo League was born.

By stipulating that the club have only Aboriginal people in positions of office, Helena was following the ideals of her father's organisation, the Euralian Club. As a policy, it made the club very different from the kind of white benevolent groups in operation at that time. Also, by setting the club up with Aboriginal leadership, they were echoing the work of the Native Union that had operated in Western Australia from 1928 to 1938. The circle had swung back to Aboriginal control of an Aboriginal organisation to respond to and meet the needs of the Aboriginal community. The tide of Aboriginal dissatisfaction and desire for political recognition had moved from small meetings in houses and camps into an organised body. It started as a dance and grew into a movement that would become a beacon for Aboriginal people all over the South-West. It achieved all this, even though the first dance was a flop. The dance failed because the hall was located within the Prohibited Area, at a hall organised by the Modern Women's Club, and no one was able to attend without having a pass to be in the city after six o'clock. Instead of folding however, they shifted the dances to a little hall in East Perth, just outside the Prohibited Area, and they were a huge success.

The Coolbaroo League dances first came under the notice of the police on a warm Saturday night in January 1947. Two constables stumbled on the community hall in East Perth at 8.30 pm, well after curfew, to find almost two hundred blackfellas having a great time. They'd followed some people they'd seen in the vicinity and couldn't believe their find. There were blackfellas on the door taking a silver coin entrance fee, Aboriginal musicians on stage and Aboriginal singers swinging their way through the latest American hits. Helena fronted up to the police, told them who she was and informed them that they weren't breaking any laws.

Mr McBeath, the Commissioner of Native Affairs who had pounded the same East Perth beat during the war years, initially took a stand against the dances, and would have shut them down if he could. But they were outside the Prohibited Area and he was hesitant to act.

For Helena Clarke the Coolbaroo League was exactly the organisation she had been wanting to create to fight for the changes that the community needed. Using the knowledge she had learned from her father's Euralian Club, and from her experience of various meetings in Perth, she was determined that this was going to be a non-political, non-sectarian Aboriginal organisation that would enable interaction with whites and basic freedoms for the people, all under Aboriginal control. Instead of seeking support from white amelioration groups, Aboriginal people now had their own organisation.

George Poland eventually moved back home to Shark Bay, and even though Jack was still around town he did not stay involved with the League. Geoff Harcus remained. In fact, he felt that this was exactly what he had been looking for since his return from the war—to be able to mix with Noongars and do something to dismantle segregation. And he liked it that Aboriginal people ran the show.

The dances attracted people from all over Perth, from the 'town blacks' in East Perth to the 'campies' at Bassendean or Lockridge, and even as far out as nearby country towns like Northam. Regardless of divisions within the community, whether you were a 'campie' or a 'townie', a Noongar or a Nor'wester, poor or well off, old or young, the Coolbaroo League dances united the small and dispersed group that made up the urban Aboriginal population of the time. Naturally, too, most of the people attending the League dances were related in some way or another, and a sense of ownership quickly developed in the community.

The Department continued to try to shut them down. As the lights went up at the Coolbaroo League dances, the police settled in nearby, almost out of sight, to watch for any sign of sly grog changing hands. But Helena and others worked hard to ensure that the police and the Department couldn't touch them. Despite the efforts of the Department the League continued to grow, members raised their own money, organised their own meetings, and began to send deputations to the Minister over issues of deaths in custody and the right to vote, and called for an end to the Prohibited Area.

Initially my grandmother would head along to the dances on a Saturday night and gave a hand with the food. My mother went along to help her, and was roped in to giving lessons for dances she'd learned at Red Cross dances with African American servicemen. But after a while Jessie went less often. The cards took hold again and Saturday nights were good game nights.

At 69 Glendower Street the grey blanket went up in the window signalling to those who were in the know that a card game was on. Another grey blanket would be spread over the table, food prepared by my mother would be placed out for the punters, beer put on ice in the trough, and slowly but surely, the table would fill with eager players. While the police were keeping an eye on the League, Glendower Street was relatively untroubled. Other card houses were being raided in the city, but Mum Smith's games seemed untouchable.

There was a knock at the door of 69 Glendower Street. My mother and grandmother opened the door to a fresh-faced young man who, from the way he was dressed, didn't come from their neighbourhood. The young man was from the Electoral Office and he had a problem. He was responsible for ensuring that the spouses of husbands listed on the electoral role were assured of their responsibility to vote, but he had no listing for Mrs Edward Smith, although he was aware that Mr Smith was married. 'Yee-ai-sss,' my grandmother said.

The young man with the clipboard explained he was there to ensure that she, Mrs Smith, was aware of her responsibility to vote in any state and federal elections and that she should register immediately. He was very adamant that she must comply. The way my mother tells it, my grandmother thought there must be a mistake. She stepped forward onto the verandah and reminded him that she was Aboriginal and therefore wasn't allowed to vote. He stopped, checked his paperwork, looked a bit perplexed and stood his ground. 'No, Mrs Smith, you've *got* to vote.' I wonder what was running through my grandmother's mind as she weighed up how to handle this one. Was she amazed at the absurdity of the situation? Was she worried that perhaps she'd missed something, that after all these years of being under Native Affairs, of being tracked and controlled and managed by them, that she had got it wrong? Then again she may have simply thought, 'Why not.' She didn't have to sign up for an Exemption. She didn't have to apply to a magistrate. This young boy was going to 'give' her the vote.

The paperwork was filled out there and then. My grandmother asked him where she was supposed to carry out this responsibility. He explained that she would have to go down to where the local polling booths would be located. She explained that she couldn't get around like she used to. That was no problem for the young man. He would arrange a car. And so it was that at election time, my grandmother had a car come and collect her, take her to the polling station and bring her home afterwards. My grandmother believed that life was a gamble and you took what you could while the going was good.

After finding Jimmy McSkene's old house in Primrose Lane behind Glendower Street, my mother's spirits have lifted. 'Poor old Jimmy,' she says, 'he ended up marrying again but he was never the same again. I heard years later that he was living in an old men's hospital when he died in the sixties.' Walking down Primrose Lane brings me, my mother and my sister Beverley to 250 Lake Street. In the late 1940s the house at 69 Glendower Street was sold. My grandparents moved just around the corner, less than fifty feet away, and rented this place in Lake Street. It is part of a block of four two-storey terrace houses at the very top of Lake Street as it enters Glendower Street. From the upstairs verandah you can still see Hyde Park in the distance. The house where my mother spent her early twenties is for sale. It is the last place in the city that they, as a family, would really call their own. My mother is looking at the large photographs on the 'For Sale' sign as if they're written in another language. The interior has been transformed into new-millennium inner-city cool.

I don't tell her that they want almost half a million dollars for this place. When the family rented it in the 1950s it was definitely on the slide. The original red brickwork, which has been smoothed over with coloured rendering, was visibly cracked and worn when they lived here. There wasn't much to it but it became their new family home and people making their way up Lake Street to Mum Smith's had a little less distance to travel.

As the children my grandmother looked after grew up and went out to work, or headed back to the country after finishing their apprenticeships, other people came to take their place. Una Ashwin, out from Sister Kate's, came to stay while she worked at the Boot Factory in Lake Street, now an exclusive gated series of inner city apartments. Rachel Bowers, the young girl taken from my grandmother and placed in the Salvation Army Girls Home with her brothers by the Department, came and stayed while she completed her nursing certificate. She was like a sister to my mother, and my grandmother loved having Rachel around. Johnny Winder, one of the boys from Shark Bay, was staying while he completed his apprenticeship in the city.

The family photographs shift from the back yard of Glendower Street to the front of 250 Lake Street, although there are occasional gatherings in the back yard. I've brought images with me to line up the past with the contemporary edifice of their old lives. Here is Aunty Mary Mallis, my mother's best friend in school and one of my grandmother's favourites, dressed as if she's ready to dance the tango. Here is Nellie Lyndon and Dorothy Ring, arms folded and eyes half closed, looking lazily into the camera as if they're guarding the portals to a card game inside. All the younger ones are lined up with Jack Poland in the back yard: Myrtle and Norm Harris, Tommy Watson, Shirley Minson, and several others from my mother's generation. Sadly, too many of them are gone today.

But the photographs don't catch everything that's going on inside and surrounding the house. They don't catch the card games that spill from one day into the next. They don't catch the bottles piling up on the back porch. They don't show that Edward has receded further from the action, spending more and more time reading in his room or listening to the radio, tuning into life on the airwaves while his wife's card games attract higher stakes gamblers. They don't show that my grandmother was beginning to drink a little too heavily, or that the diabetes which caused her to put on even more weight is hampering her ability to care for herself, and that she is relying a little too much on my mother for help. They do not show my grandmother's desperate manipulation of my mother's emotions, pretending to be sick so that my mother won't go out to a dance and leave her alone. And when my mother does go out, and comes home early wracked with guilt, she finds my grandmother up and lively, half stung and enjoying a game of cards with a bunch of old girls who've dropped in.

When the family lived here my mother was working at the drycleaner's on William Street, not more than two hundred metres down the road. This suited my grandmother well. Although she was then a grown woman, my mother tells me that my grandmother still had a great hold over her. I find this difficult to imagine. When I was growing up my mother was no

312

shrinking violet. When I say this to her, she just looks at me and points across the road. 'See that corner shop over there?' My sister Bev and I look at it. 'If I went out to a dance I'd have to be home by a certain time. I used to catch the 22 tram back from the city and, I tell you, if I missed that tram I was running all the way behind it. I used to be that bloody scared to be late that I'd run the whole way and if I was a minute late your grandmother would be sitting on the steps of that shop with a wooden stick in her hand.' My sister and I know this story well. 'She never used it, but I tell you what, she would have.'

When people hear this story they often can't understand why my mother still loved my grandmother so fiercely, but she did, and still does. My mother never blamed my grandmother when this happened. She never blamed anyone. She just accepted it as part of what happens when your mother grows up in a mission, where she suffered the same kind of treatment. She also decided that she would never lay a hand on her own kids, and she didn't, not once. My mother loved my grandmother enough to be there for Jessie as her health began to deteriorate. She loved Jessie enough to hide things that she knew would hurt her.

There is a series of images of Betty with cars or, I should say, Betty with a ute, because they're all images of my mother driving the same vehicle, a ute that belonged to a local neighbourhood boy named Bill. 'Boy' seems the wrong tag to attach to Bill. He looks much older than my mother. He was a thickset 1950s-looking white man fond of wide-brimmed hats, fond of his ute, and fond of Betty Smith from Lake Street. My grandmother knew Bill well. He sometimes came to the house. She seems to have liked the idea of Bill and Betty. Maybe she liked the sound of their names together. Most likely he was just a decent guy when he visited. Also there was the added bonus that he lived nearby with his mother. I believe he was a butcher, or at least he looks like a 1950s butcher, as if he would look comfortable wrapped up in a striped apron with a sharp knife in one hand and a sharpening steel in the other. 'Bill the Butcher'. Maybe it was the thought of free beef and a solid income for her daughter. Whatever it was, my grandmother was nice to the guy and encouraged the union.

Bill and my mother went out for a long time in the early 1950s, long enough to take all those photos of Betty at the wheel, Betty standing by the open door, Betty leaning on the front grille, Bill standing, one leg crooked onto the bumper bar, framing the chrome work that was polished

313

to perfection. They went out long enough that he asked Betty to marry him. My mother was excited. Young women then seemed to say yes to the wrong men too easily, and became married before they had a chance to get out in the world. She was going to say yes. Then Bill placed a little condition on the marriage proposal; Betty was never to see her mother again. It must have come like a clap of thunder out of the blue. Bill got on well with both Jessie and Edward. He had even come along on some of the family picnics. It must have been a shock that the man my mother thought she loved could say something like this. Betty said no. She chose her mother. In choosing her mother she was also choosing self-respect.

I don't know how my mother managed to keep it from my grandmother, especially when quite a few of the older women knew about it. Aunty Eileen Harwood never forgave Bill and neither did any of the other old girls. In rejecting my grandmother they felt he was also rejecting them. Aunty Eileen said it was 'a mean thing they done to us, to Aunty … he dumped Betty cause she wouldn't stop seeing us, and her mum.' The old girls knew about it, but Betty didn't want Jessie to know. She made out as if they just didn't get on any more and broke it off.

Although Helena Clarke saw a divide between the political meetings and the social dances, with hindsight it must be said that the most simple and yet politically successful achievement of the Coolbaroo League was the creation of an overtly Aboriginal space in a white city. But, if the question of such a space was not on Helena's mind, it was certainly being considered by the police and Native Affairs.

From the time the police became aware of the Coolbaroo League the dances were under constant surveillance. Not content with watching the club for any misbehaviour or, more commonly, for catching Aboriginal people in possession of alcohol, the Commissioner of Police wrote to the Native Affairs Department stating that 'The question of being in a Prohibited Area should also receive consideration.'

Thankfully, the police were unable to act. The problem for the police was that, regardless of the powers they were able to exercise over the Aboriginal community, and even with the abuses that took place in the name of the law, the Coolbaroo League dances were outside the Prohibited Area. Attendance did not contravene any law. The Pensioners Hall in East Perth was located just across the railway line which formed the dividing line between where you could set foot and where you could not. Regardless of this, the patrols became more frequent and in the first six months of the League dances one hundred and thirty-one Aboriginal people were charged at the Perth Police Court for minor offences. By comparison, only thirty-two people were similarly charged in the same court for the six months prior to the dances starting up.

There is no doubt that there was occasional trouble at the Coolbaroo dances and in most cases it was due to alcohol. The dances themselves were supposed to be 'dry', and in the main most people supported or at least went along with this, but there were always young fellas who would try it on and for these young fellas there were plenty of police around to pick them up. Helena Clarke had in fact tried to organise an open police presence from the outset, to keep the peace and keep out undesirable whites. The League were well aware there would be people turning up with alcohol and they did not want this to jeopardise a community dance. So, in a move to assure the authorities there would be no trouble, Helena approached the Police Commissioner and requested a couple of officers on the door. It was agreed that this would happen and the League was to pay one pound per officer per night. But although they paid for them to come, Helena recalled hardly ever spotting them during the course of a night. 'We had them there for a couple of nights, or they showed up, put it that way. Apart from walking around and checking on them, I couldn't say whether they were there or not.'

Although they had been invited, even paid to attend, they instead chose to keep the dances under strict surveillance from a distance. Helena, who was too busy inside the hall, wasn't aware of what was going on outside where there were between five and six police on any night, some even hiding up trees to clandestinely spy on the dances.

If they weren't up trees, then they would be hiding in bushes, or in the shadows of the Post Office. Sometimes, they would be spying from the front room of a disgruntled white home owner near the hall. The dances attracted Noongars from all over, and they also attracted a lot of complaints to the police from local residents and local businesses about the increased presence of Aboriginal people in East Perth.

Within six months the dances were a regular beat on the police's Saturday night patrol.

Patrolled the city and outskirts, visited Blue Room, Coolbaroo Club, East Perth, City Ball Room, Anzac House and Y.A.L. dance rooms.

Plenty of signs of liquor on natives around Coolbaroo Club, but they were all orderly.

The police were arresting any Aboriginal person they believed had consumed alcohol and very occasionally young men were arrested for disturbing the peace. In the main the police were concerned with the more organised grog drops. These were highly sophisticated affairs with a system of 'nit keepers' (lookouts) keeping an eye out for any sign of the police. In one instance the police followed a white man suspected of supplying alcohol all the way to Guildford train station, but they lost him when he jumped the train and made off through Guildford Park.

After a while, small fights began breaking out at the dances, usually over petty things, but sometimes an eruption was related to a serious family feud. There'd be a bust-up and the police would be nearby to bear witness. Coupled with complaints by neighbours, these incidents did not help the situation. A further blow to the survival of these early dances came when Helena left the city to return to Port Hedland in 1949. Her mother was unwell and the strain of getting the dances and political meetings together each week was showing. Unfortunately, just at that time a combination of police surveillance, community infighting and grog was about to explode. My mother and grandmother were there the night it happened, and Geoff Harcus got caught up in the fracas.

Geoff remembered the night. 'It was a family feud, and really went mad, they went flying everywhere, chairs flying across the room and swearing, windows broken and smashed, and the old pianist kept playing. She was an old, dear old pensioner, she was playing in the corner, playing the piano and somebody threw off a shoe, hit someone in the middle of the hall, the person in the hall ducked and the pianist got it in the back of the head and went donk, on the piano. So, anyway it ended up there was fighting outside.'

As the fighters moved outside, other young men leapt into the fray to stick up for their mates. They were ripping pickets off nearby fences and clubbing each other with them. When the fight spilled out onto the railway line the police were there in a flash. As the police were heading in to break it up, my grandmother bundled my mother and a few others into a taxi and they were off, back to Lake Street.

After the big fight the dances were closed down. The League couldn't get a hall anywhere and the police, who still held incredible control over the lives of Aboriginal people, now had their excuse. They weren't going to give the League an inch. It had been a good fight, a real spectacle, but the short-lived excitement of a few people fighting gave way to the long-term loss of something that had benefited everybody. The dances would remain dormant until the early 1950s, when Bill Bodney, Geoff Harcus, Ronnie Kickett and a new generation of Noongars would get them up and running again.

When the Coolbaroo League dances recommenced my grandmother was no longer able to go along at all. She was far too unwell. My mother attended with the younger people from the house, with Aunty Eileen Harwood and sometimes the Kinnane brothers. Steve and Kevin were two Irishmen from East Perth. Before long my mother was dating Steve Kinnane. He had been recently discharged from the navy and he liked a good party. Betty was enamoured with his enthusiasm for a good time, and the fact that he did not reject her mother. My grandmother, however, had her reservations. Steve Kinnane was eleven years older than Betty and he had already been divorced. What really sealed his fate though, was that he liked showing off on the mouth organ, and he had once beaten her at cards. Not a smart move if he was trying to impress a potential mother-in-law. Jessie made it clear to my mother that she wasn't happy about her dating Steve, but for the first time in her young life, my mother stuck to her guns.

With the Coolbaroo dances up and running again Bill Bodney would pop into Lake Street to visit Jessie. Aunty Bertha Isaacs, another integral member of the League, came by to check on my grandmother, but being busy with the League, she didn't see her as often as she used to. Some nights they'd visit before a dance night and my grandmother would help bake food for the supper, but as she became weaker, these preparations took place at other houses.

While Betty was off out with her new boyfriend, my grandmother, on nights when she was in good form, would be running a card game, sometimes for high stakes, and sometimes just for enjoyment like the games of the 1930s that were 'old girls' affairs. Once my mother came home to find her and some of the other old girls trying a new cold remedy, getting drunk and eating chilli sandwiches, their feet in a tub of hot water trying to sweat the cold out. They were playing the gramophone, singing country and western songs, a bunch of old crows out of tune.

By 1954 my grandmother's leg had become a serious problem and regular bathing in the salty warm waters of the traditional Noongar hot spring at Nedlands helped to ease the pain. Her taxi driver, Tom Robbie, and his wife Rita would pick her up from Lake Street and head around the river at dusk for a dip, before it became too dark and others made their way down to the pool. The 'hot pool' was, apparently, as much a favoured rendezvous for illicit lovers as a restorative spring.

Tom Robbie probably saw more of my grandmother than most other people. He and Rita also took her to the races at Belmont on a Saturday. They would park the car in the car park, where she'd sit listening to the radio while they laid bets for her. My mother had often been the runner on these trips when she was younger. The gatekeepers knew Betty well enough never to charge her as she ran in and out placing bets for her mother with the bookies. In later years Tom and Rita would be in on the bet and keen to put Jessie Smith's horse sense into action. This love of the horses is something that skipped my mother and landed on my brother, the thrill of riding a horse home on a bet.

Edward was nearing his sixty-third birthday in 1954. He had become a second-storey dweller in his house, the ground floor belonging to his wife, to visitors and to those who were staying awhile. He was working his way quietly to his retirement and had begun a regular correspondence with his remaining sister, Lily, in England. His younger sister Blanche had passed away years before. He was never to return to his own homeland. He had that fact in common with Jessie who, I imagine, he was becoming increasingly alarmed about as the condition of her leg worsened.

Edward and Jessie. Cully and Miff. Whispering Smith and the Duchess of Glendower Street. Mr and Mrs Smith. They were getting old. Their daughter was a young woman. The world was changing rapidly around them.

Aunty Janie Winder arrived from Carnarvon with her son Ken at around nine o'clock at night. They'd just caught the plane down so that Ken could stay with Mum Smith while he settled into college. His brother John, and other boys from Carnarvon, used Lake Street as their stop in the city. There was a card game in progress. Mum Smith was dealing the cards, Betty was making food for the gamblers, who included Aunty Eileen Harwood, George Harwood, Mary Cross and two other cooks from the Avro Hospital, Millie and Kitty, Betty's boyfriend, Steve, and some of the neighbours. It was the cooks' night off at the Avro Hospital and they had a good kitty going.

George and Eileen called it quits, said their goodbyes and headed home. Aunty Eileen loved an all-night game, but she had work the next morning. Aunty Janie was sitting in the lounge room watching the game in progress, when she heard some noises from the back yard. 'We could hear this rumbling outside.' It was only a few minutes after Eileen and George had gone so they thought nothing of it. Then, in a flash, Steve got up from the table and opened the back door. As the police rushed in, he rushed out past them, somehow managing not to get caught as he leapt over the back fence, into the laneway, and was gone. Everyone grabbed their money and threw it on the floor, anywhere but on the table. Aunty Janie got the shock of her life as the money went everywhere, police filled the room and they were ordered to stay where they were. 'Mrs Smith sat there, she never had no money because she put the money under her bosom you see, and of course she was a big woman, Mrs Smith. He asked for the money, he said, "You're gambling." She said, "No we are not gambling, there's no money, we've got no money."'

The police scooped up the money from the floor, and made everyone empty their bags. Mary Cross only had one black sixpence in her bag, and she told them they could have it; to her surprise they took it. They took everything. Aunty Janie was taking her boy upstairs when the police ordered her back. As she stopped she saw Edward Smith coming down the stairs in his pyjamas. He'd been sleeping. When he realised what was going on he stepped quietly back up the stairs. The police let Aunty Janie off because they knew her husband in Carnarvon, and they knew that she'd only just arrived, because they'd been watching the house for some time. The noise that everyone had heard was the sound of the police in the dark knocking their heads against a bucket hanging up in the back yard.

They called in the paddy wagon and took everyone except Mrs Winder and Edward down to the station and booked them. They even took my mother. When my grandmother and mother were in the lockup my grandmother pulled out the cash from under her bosom and laughed, but the raid had taken it out of her. Edward came down and paid the ten pounds bail each, a tidy sum, to get them out. Everyone who'd left the table that evening was suspected of informing, especially Betty's boyfriend. Although my grandmother made light of it at the time, she was no doubt shaken. In all the years she'd been gambling, her card games had never been raided. It seemed like the old Duchess was losing her touch. It was the beginning of the end of Mum Smith's card house.

Hyde Park, North Perth. The leaves of the trees fill with the story of my family's years living so near to the earthy park in the centre of the city. Now they were leaving the area. My mother grew up here. My grandparents grew old here. It was where they stopped to face the Department. It was where my grandmother was given the vote by a smooth-faced white boy, even if she was not supposed to. It was where Jimmy McSkene had circled the park in search of his sanity. It was where they farewelled young boys who didn't make it back from the war. They loved this park and wouldn't have left it if they didn't have to. It was the backdrop to their lives and the witness to their stories. It was a refuge in a city of prohibition and starkly drawn boundaries designed to separate black from white.

The Smiths were to move away from the city that had been the heartbeat of their lives. With rental shortages of the postwar period they were forced out over the river to the suburb of Victoria Park.

amputation

My grandmother knew my mother would be coming to the hospital. She waited for her daughter each afternoon. I'm sure Jessie would visualise Betty finishing work for the day, tidying up at the Grand Pictures Milk Bar, walking down the plush carpeted steps into Murray Street, and turning east towards the hospital. Jessie could well imagine the sound of her daughter's heels on the city pavement, each step along the footpath, over Pier Street, past the old Aborigines Department and beneath the giant Moreton Bay figs that straddled the entire street. My grandmother had all the time in the world to imagine my mother's movements as she lay in her hospital bed day after day. Just as she had monitored my mother's movements in Lake Street, waiting for her on the corner at the number 22 tram stop, now she waited for Betty to arrive at the hospital. It was as if Jessie had turned those afternoon visits, the ones that took place in the later part of her time in Royal Perth, into a kind of test of my mother's love for her.

That is how my mother remembered those visits. My mother would climb the stairs to my grandmother's hospital ward, walk determinedly towards the ward and then stop. She would wait just beyond the door to her mother's ward, out of sight in case she could be seen, but knowing full well that Jessie knew she was there. Betty felt she had to be there, she was waiting for her mother's forgiveness. Betty was pinned. It was exactly where Jessie wanted her. As my grandmother lay in her bed staring at the door, it seemed she could sense the outline of her daughter, pacing, sitting, waiting, and she was just going to let her stay there. My mother wanted to go into the ward, but would never dare to, not even an inch, without a word or a gesture, or a message that this is what Jessie wanted. Betty could see glimpses of Jessie as the ward door opened and closed, but that is as far as she could even think of looking. My mother knew that my grandmother was angry with her and that the best thing she could do was stay out of her way. Betty was twenty-five years old but still very much held by her mother's will.

I believe my grandmother wanted my mother to come in, but I can imagine her thinking that not enough time had passed yet, deciding to let my mother wait.

My mother was engaged to marry Steve Redmond Kinnane, and he, Edward and Betty were living in the East Victoria Park house. She was a working woman in that winter of 1955 when she made her regular trips to the hospital to receive the cold shoulder from her mother. As much as she knew that the brush-off would pass and that Jessie would calm down and learn to cope with the result of Betty and Edward's decision, she also knew that this would only happen in her mother's own good time. Jessie allowed Edward in to visit, and he pleaded with her to see their daughter, but she wouldn't budge. I can imagine my grandmother looking at the place where her leg had once been, and the anger would just well up inside her.

The episodes had started in East Victoria Park. They had not been living in the new place long when my mother began to notice that my grandmother was acting strangely. At first she imagined that Jessie was reacting to the stressful changes they had all experienced in such a short space of time. They were thankful to have a house at all. It was difficult for anyone to find houses in the city then, which is why they had to move so far out, to 948 Albany Highway, East Victoria Park. In reality it was not that far from town. It was a short ride into the city on the East Vic Park tram, the same tramline Edward had been welding when he had his accident. But for my grandmother, it was another world. North Perth had become her centre. The neighbourhood was a part of her self that she had not wanted to give up.

When the house in Lake Street was sold in 1954, Jessie, Edward and Betty were taken in by Mary Mallis' family who lived at the bottom of Lake Street, right in the centre of Northbridge. It was a welcomed kindness, but for my grandmother, who had become so used to her own house, it was a great loss. The family were not living in bad conditions and they were grateful for the shelter. There were plenty of blackfellas who were much worse off, but for my grandmother the lack of independence in living under somebody else's roof was too much. She seemed to age quickly, and the poor health and pain that she had tried to keep from my grandfather and mother became too difficult to hide. Although they soon found the house in East Vic Park, for my grandmother it was never to be the same.

East Vic Park was too far out of the city for people to visit her easily, it was too far from the action. Her leg was very bad now and she found she was unable to care for herself while Betty was at work. My mother had started work at the Grand Theatre as an usherette and wound up working behind the counter of the Milk Bar. It was good work and the owner was thoughtful. On days when she had to return home early to tend to Jessie, her boss understood and never docked her pay.

Edward paid an old friend to come and cook for my grandmother and stay with her, without telling Jessie the nature of the arrangement. My grandmother hated to be alone with no one to talk to. All her life she had tried to be independent, had called the shots and looked out for others. Now she had become someone who needed serious health care to get through her day. My grandmother started to crave water. She could not get enough of it. She would sit with jugs of water within easy reach, constantly refilling her glass. Her diabetes was a serious problem but she refused to see a doctor.

Betty was at home the day it happened. My grandmother began talking and simply couldn't stop. Betty realised that something was seriously wrong. Jessie's eyes were unblinking. Her talking gave way to twitching. The twitching gave way to biting the side of her mouth and she began to fit violently. The doctor was called immediately. An ambulance was called and took my grandmother to Royal Perth Hospital. She was to spend the next eighteen months of her life there. Ironically, she was back in the centre of the city again, but not in circumstances that she would have chosen. My grandmother hated the hospital. She had always avoided doctors, fixing any illness with one of her sure-fire cures, like drinking beetroot juice for anaemia. Those early years of coming to Perth for the treatment of her leg had built up a resistance to hospitals. Her world was slipping rapidly from her grasp. She was stuck in the one place that she would rather not be.

The old wards of the hospital now house the administrative blocks under the canopy of the giant Moreton Bay figs that straddle Murray Street heading east. They are directly opposite the old Native Affairs office that was once the Aborigines Department office. My grandmother regularly lined up outside these offices for passes to travel by rail to and from the city when her leg first began to cause her pain in 1920. From the windows of the wards and rooms that she occupied for those eighteen months she had plenty of time to look over her life, and the very building that had held the Department that had watched her all those years. She was in a good position to be watching the watchers.

The eloquence of these older buildings has been replaced by 1960s biscuit brick modernity. But even though the Aborigines Department is long gone, blackfellas can be found moving steadily along Murray Street to the Royal Perth foyer. It is one of the city's most accessible and well-used hospitals. It is almost as popular an Aboriginal meeting place as the 'Big House' — the Casino — on a Friday or Saturday night, as people from all over the state come here for treatment, finding their way here from the outlying areas of the city.

In my grandmother's day they *had* to come down to this part of town to see Mr Neville, but if they had had their choice they'd make their way anywhere else but here. Following the arcades that run north–south like escape tunnels through the city, spilling out into the main streets of Hay and Murray, they could wind their way to the railway station and meet up with any blackfellas that were passing through the city, especially at the White Seats opposite the railway station. Even into the 1940s, before the serious onset of her illness, my grandmother would gather herself into her big overcoat, take my mother and meet up with her old mate Mary Forrest, a self-proclaimed 'city blackfella' who knew every turn, back alley and side lane there was as she made her way through the city with her own daughter Thomasisha, from one card game to another.

Mary Forrest had known my grandmother since the 1920s when they were domestic servants together staying in and around the city. In the 1940s Mary Forrest's place in East Perth was another card house where people could meet up. In the 1950s Mary camped on the river at Maylands for eighteen months until State Housing came up with a house in Bentley Park. It was miles from the city — out beyond East Victoria Park — but it was a house. And when Jessie Smith moved out that way in 1954, Mary made sure to drop in for a quick game of cards. But it was never the same. It was never the same as cutting across the city to Jessie's to sit at her giant oval table with a good number of players and a decent kitty. Mary's husband would arrive home to find his wife gone and know that she'd be at my grandmother's. If Mary won they had fish and chips and violet crumbles. If she lost, she kept the fact to herself.

Sitting in her hospital bed my grandmother had plenty of time to think over the shifts in her life. Women friends came to visit when they could, but the relaunched Coolbaroo League was going from strength to strength and the women found their time taken up with meetings, putting together newspapers, organising deputations. The stakes were higher than the older generation had envisaged, and younger more politically minded people were negotiating directly with the white power structure. With this new approach came a style that did not fit easily with the old timers.

They'd come in visiting hours and take her bets for the week's races, spend time, maybe even have the odd game just for the fun of it, but then they would leave and she was trapped there. Gradually, as the first months in the hospital stretched into twelve and beyond, it must have seemed as if she would never leave. Before long, Mary came to say that she was heading north with her family. As time passed and people got on with their lives, my grandmother became Aunty Jessie in the hospital, rather than Mum Smith.

A nurse gave my grandmother an overdose of insulin by mistake and laughed as she fitted. My mother rebuked the nurse, who laughed and replied, 'She's only a native.' My mother demanded the nurse be shifted, and she was, to another ward. In creating a life around her own house, my grandmother had been able to avoid these sorts of incidents.

Away from her own created place and community of protection, of people who came to see her, valued her, and respected her, she was isolated.

A doctor asked my grandmother if he could photograph her feet. It was an odd request but she let him photograph them. My grandmother had never heard of such a thing, photographing a woman's feet, but she conceded. Oddly, they seem to be the only parts of herself that she didn't mind being photographed. She had seen the bones of her feet once. At Alex Kelly's shoe store you could slip your feet under an X-ray machine for nothing and look at your skeleton for as long as you liked. But she never did see the picture of her feet that the doctor had taken.

It must be out there somewhere now, probably in some box tucked away, or filed within some old medical records or lecture papers—the image of her feet. Mr Neville would have known just the right title for it: 'Exhibit JA 325/55—Photograph—Feet of half-caste native female from the northern portions of the Kimberley region of Western Australia.'

The infection in my grandmother's leg could not be treated and the doctors decided that it would have to be amputated. My grandmother refused. She became worse. My mother pleaded with her to let them operate, but she wouldn't budge. 'When I go,' she said, 'I go in one piece, and that's that.' The decision was taken from her. When my grandmother went into a diabetic coma, Edward and Betty signed the release papers allowing them to remove her leg, against her wishes. Her leg was severed just below the knee. My grandmother blamed my mother for the decision and this is why she refused to see her.

The operation had not removed all the infection and my grandmother's illness became worse. The doctors were planning to remove the rest of her leg, several inches above the knee. Visiting my grandmother the night before the operation, my mother was surprised. My grandmother wanted to see her. They talked for a long time about what would happen when it was all over. Corrie, one of the Sherwood children, had kept in touch and through her husband had arranged a special wheelchair for my grandmother. The operation, everyone believed, would see an end to the infection and the problems she had endured. My mother was trained to give my grandmother her insulin injections. Jessie's life was being planned around wheelchairs, injections, carers and special beds. The people who loved her just wanted her alive.

That night my grandmother asked my mother to take her wedding ring. She removed it from her finger and slipped it into my mother's hand. My mother assumed this was in preparation for the operation. My grandmother said nothing about the operation. Later, my mother believed that my grandmother knew it wasn't going to take place. My grandmother was wearing that cheeky smile of hers. It was how she looked when she knew she had a winning hand. It was the last image that my mother saw as she left the ward. It was the last night of winter.

On the first day of spring 1955, aged fifty-four, my grandmother went into a coma. Betty and Edward were having dinner at a friend's house near the city, planning to head straight over to the hospital to be with Jessie after the operation. The hospital knew where they would be all that day, in case of an emergency. The doctors worked on my grandmother, but she could not be revived. Infection swarmed through her body, her organs began to shut down. Edward and Betty were telephoned. On the way to the hospital, the speeding car was flagged by police. When the police understood it was a race to the hospital, Betty and Edward were given a police escort, but they still became jammed in afternoon traffic. While they were stuck on the Horseshoe Bridge, my grandmother's heart stopped beating.

At the hospital, my mother could see my grandmother's still body on the hospital bed. My mother was numb. She couldn't move. Edward made Betty touch her mother's body to make real what she couldn't believe. My mother kissed my grandmother goodbye. Jessie was still warm. As she left the room in shock, Edward knelt over his wife's body and cried. When they cleaned out my grandmother's bedside cabinet, they found the antibiotic pills that she was supposed to have taken. Jessie had been pretending to take them, slipping them under her tongue and then hiding them in the cabinet when no one was looking. It appears that she made her own decision in the end. She had taken back control of what was left of her life, freed herself from her body, and gone.

When the sun set on the first day of spring, a full moon was rising over the hills that surrounded the city to the east. As Jessie's body was carried away by the undertakers, the news of her death was spreading across the city, from one neighbourhood to another, along the railway lines and out to the camps. For the next five days Edward and Betty prepared Jessie's funeral. On the fifth day of spring, as the moon was beginning to wane, my grandmother was interred at Karrakatta cemetery.

It was a huge funeral. All the old girls were there, all the women like herself who had been taken away from their families.

My mother was numb with grief. The day swept past her in a blur. Because Edward worked at the *West*, a reporter friend attended. On seeing the hundreds of people following the car from the gates of the cemetery to the plot, he could not believe the diversity of the people attending. There were people of all nationalities, and their families, Noongars, Nor'westers, Greeks, Italians, Jews, Chinese.

My mother looked up as my grandmother's coffin was lowered into the earth. She looked beyond the grave and, in the distance, beneath a box tree, his head bowed, she saw my grandmother's brother, Thomas Bropho. He stood alone, away from the crowd. When my mother looked for him later, he was gone. Thomas and Jessie had watched out for each other since they were taken away as children, from the ranges of Miriwoong country, across the ocean and south to the city.

IV

SHADOW LINES

cheeky spirits

Edward would return from working at the *West* to find the house in Victoria Park completely empty. They would never settle in this house. It was a house associated with death, it was in the wrong part of the city. I imagine Hyde Park drawing Edward back across the river each day.

His work enabled him to return to the city without giving away his true reasons. Edward had decided that he would be the strong one. His silence had nothing to do with his broken voice. His routine of working and moving forward, one step after the other, was both his salvation and his cover.

He probably would have given anything to have been able to ride his bike up William Street, enter the house in Glendower Street, or even Lake Street for that matter, and find Jessie at the table and something so simple and comforting as a meal in the oven. It's strange how it's the small routine comforts that we miss the most. Moments of simplicity that are private and yet intensely personal. He would see the other women sitting around the table and the pile of money in the pot. He would sense the intense concentrated delight of gamblers at work as the cards were leaved through just one more time before the final call. I imagine these were his simple desires, to feel that his life had returned to some sense of normality, with his wife's strength of presence.

But instead of heading north, each day after work he would head south. Instead of passing the neighbours, riding along streets that he had known for decades he would head south, over the Causeway and the river, to the house on Albany Highway. Jessie had only lived here a short time. There was no real sense of her there for him. The special bed, the wheelchair, the syringe containers and other medical paraphernalia that were brought in preparation for Jessie's homecoming were left untouched, soon to be returned to the hospital. I imagine that while he worked, while he concentrated on the electrics of the printing press and counted each minute until he would have to leave what seemed normal, for what was completely abnormal, his mind was able to put Jessie's death aside.

I imagine that he could feel his wife's imprint as she called to him from across the city. He was keeping his pain to himself, but he was cut adrift as much as my mother. When death came visiting, the rhythm of the city slowed, shifted and then sped up again in an unrecognisable beat that he could never get used to. The silence that comes with death is eventually lifted by the world that continues around us, but that part of our lives that has been left behind tugs at us, leaving us with a constant sense that there is something that we have forgotten, until it reminds us, and the world slows again where we exist. At first it would have seemed a transitory phase, a part of his grieving. But it did not leave him. Perhaps he was close enough to the city for it to bring him reminders of his life with his wife and partner. My mother was also trying to be strong for her father, but was failing badly.

The first time that he came home to find the house empty it must have seemed confusing for him. Steve was not expected home from work until later. Their house had never been empty. Even as a child, Edward had slept in dormitories that were never empty, where privacy was a treasured moment's peace. When he married Jessie and they began their own family, it had so quickly become her extended family's home too. There was always someone with Jessie, a neighbour, a friend, a gambler or three at the table, or Betty. 'Betty was not in the house.' I imagine it registering as simple as that once he realised what was wrong. Betty was not in the house. Betty was not just down the shops. Betty was nowhere to be found in the city. Betty, he soon learned, was also being called by the loss of her mother. At twenty-six years of age and pregnant with her first child, Betty would find herself drawn back to her mother's grave.

Have you ever lost someone so close that part of you died with them? It is a strange and vulnerable realisation when it strikes. When they have gone you realise that there was a part of you that you never knew existed outside yourself. It was such a natural part of yourself that you weren't even aware that it existed. And when you reach for it, it's not there

It is a dangerous time when you lose someone that you loved dearly. You can find yourself wishing to be with them. You can find yourself calling their spirit back against your own better judgement. In calling them, you call their cheeky spirit back across the waters, like the women of my grandmother's country called the children who were taken away, back across the Indian Ocean.

They're tricky things, those cheeky spirits. Their dreams can become your own. They will invade your sleep, and you'll feel their restlessness. You can try to beat them by staying awake, by defying sleep. But you have to give in sooner or later, and there they are again, taking hold of you with that part of yourself that you can't let go of. In your sleep you will have their scattered dreams of fragility, pain and loss. You'll find yourself flying over the land as if driven by a storm, up, over, around, into the ground, through walls, roof spaces, hallways. They go everywhere those cheeky spirits. Grief makes us follow them, but we shouldn't.

They're tricky all right those cheeky spirits. I met an old man in Warman once who could remember before he was born. He spoke five languages, this old man who's left us again, but only had English to share it with me. There is a language that Miriwoong and Gidja can use to describe this state. It's a high language, like a special lingo to describe the experience of death. He could remember flying low though the landscape, over the country, into one form after another. He could see his country from above, through ravines and dry lake beds, from the inside of ant beds and the tips of boab trees. And then one day, he saw his mother's face and he was human again.

He was a wonderful old man. His sister had raised him in the Bungle Bungles, south of my grandmother's country, but close. When I came looking for family, he thought that my grandmother was his sister's daughter who had been taken away, but she was later, after my grandmother. It's such a common story all over this state, and all over this country, the stealing of Aboriginal children. There are just too many who were taken away. Maybe they'll make it back through spirit. Maybe they'll dwell where they were taken away to for a while. Maybe they'll be drawn back by relatives calling their cheeky spirits back, against their better judgement.

It was Mrs Gorringe, their new next-door neighbour who gave Betty's secret away. She told Edward all about it. When he came home from work to the empty house, his neighbour told him about his daughter's daily ritual. Each day my mother would be drawn from the house. She would take a rose from Mrs Gorringe's garden and catch a bus into the city. She was being called, but it was not the city or the houses of Glendower and Lake Street that called her. She did not head to Hyde Park as I have done when needing some place to right myself. My mother was being called by her mother, back to Karrakatta.

From the city, Betty would catch the train to Karrakatta. From the train stop my mother would walk through the main gates to the cemetery. She would pass the well-tended and watered lawns where the better-off families of the colony were buried. Unknowingly, she passed close by Mr Neville's grave, where he lay buried within the leafier sections. Eventually, she would make her way to where my grandmother lay, sit quietly beside her, and simply speak with her. She would talk with her as the sun screamed over the horizon, slipping behind the tall pines and peppermint trees. She would clean away any leaves and just sit quiet and still in that hidden part of the cemetery, and feel comforted by the closeness of her mother. It was her way of righting her world.

My mother was ordered by her doctor not to visit the grave as he felt it was distressing her. Her baby's time drew near. The family decided not to think of the past. They focused on the imminent birth of Jessie and Edward's first grandchild. Aunty Bertha Isaacs, Aunty Elsie Gardiner, Aunty Eileen Harwood, Annie Sewell and Kitty Wilson came out by taxi for a visit when they could.

It had been a year since my grandmother's death. My mother woke to find my grandmother standing at the foot of her bed, her arms outstretched. She said nothing. My mother sat bolt upright with her eyes wide open, tears streaming down her face. Jessie held out her hands. My mother held out her arms and called her mother's name, and then Jessie was gone. It was the last time my mother would see her mother.

When the baby was born, she was a breech birth, just like my mother had been for Jessie. The baby was born at St Ives Hospital, a small private hospital just around the corner in Victoria Park. My sister was named Jessica, after our grandmother.

the whisperer

Edward would rise early on pension day. From his sleep-out he could hear the sounds of the magpies that sang from a lone giant tuart tree in the back yard. The louvred windows opened out onto the breaking light and the cool salty breeze. Some nights, when the density of the air was just right, he could lie silently on his bed and hear the ocean in the distance. This was not a faint distant sound like the sound you hear when you place a shell against your ear. Some trick of the night amplified the sound of the waves crashing on the beach. From the sleep-out at the back of 29 Bower Street, Scarborough, three kilometres from the ocean, Edward could close his eyes and hear the sea swirling around him. On some nights the sound of the sea was so overpowering he could have sworn it was advancing up the hill to the small State Housing home they had moved to from East Victoria Park five years previously in 1957.

I wonder if it invaded his dreams like it invaded mine when it was my turn to inhabit the room that had once been his. I wonder if it carried the memory of the day he arrived in Fremantle on the *Orontes* ocean liner, a boy-man of the Empire, his head swimming with plans and visions of his bright future. I wonder if, on some nights, it smelled like the lonely outpost of the pump house in Derby where he found himself counting out the few possessions he carried with him in his trunk, as the tide ebbed and flowed and the heat turned his blood sticky and sweet as it pumped a little slower and more rhythmically through his arteries.

I like to think that he dreamed of the days that they all drove to Naval Base in the war years. I like to think that his mind played over the images he had captured with his camera of Jessie, Betty, Sarah Lowe, Maggie Little, Sporty Jones, Ken Forrest and the rest of their large family floating, smiling into the camera in the briny Indian Ocean. I wonder, and like to imagine too, that he could have dreamed of easier days, like the day when he decided to show off a little at Trigg Beach on the Olympic rings.

They had travelled out during the war years for a day at the sea. It was practically undeveloped then. Hidden within the dunes was a small park that contained some new play equipment and exercise rings. He approached them like a professional, lifted himself from the earth and turned himself into the shadow of the gymnast he'd once been as a young boy in Emanuel School. He surprised everyone that day, and delighted the onlookers who oohhed and ahhhed at the sight of the old man, in shorts too big for his skinny legs, twirling like an acrobat. Jessie had watched, half smiling, half turning her eyes to the sky at the spectacle, but my mother could see she was secretly proud of him. Maybe that is what he dreamed of on the days when he would rise early and prepare himself for a trip to the city when pension day came around. Well, I like to think so.

Edward would take hours to prepare himself. He removed his implements of grooming from the trunk that had accompanied him for more than fifty years. He applied his theatrical make-up so as to hide his scar, but with less layering than he had once done as the scar had begun to fade with age. In the mirror he meticulously shaved himself to old Englishman perfection. He put on his best suit, combed the remaining hairs over his bald dome, and I could just see him, at the close of this long and detailed ritual of cleaning and preening, striking that same crooked pose — arms crossed, thumbs in lapels, head cocked just so to the left, hat tipped forward over his scarred face. Click. Ready for the city.

He would leave early to begin his journey back to the city. He loved the Scarborough house they had moved into. It was small, but the raised verandah looked over the wide blue horizon of the Indian Ocean in the distance. He could sit there most days, after busying himself with something to help Betty out, and just let his mind wander. He could follow the curve of the ocean as it raced east towards Africa and imagine his now distant and never-to-be-returned-to homeland of England, somewhere out there in all that blue water.

He loved to do the shopping for Betty. He loved to stroll down the small street, descending into the valley of tuart trees that had recently been a series of dunes before the postwar reconstruction had begun, to pick up the day's parcels. He was a well-worn seventy-one years then. The accidents that he had attracted to him like a magnet had taken their toll on his body. He looked much older than he was, and in 1962 was a man of another era. He was the sort of man that was easily noticed in a working-class street of a small outlying suburb, dressed in his suit, walking very smartly towards the shops. He would be gone for hours. When my mother became worried, she would look out for him down the street and, more often than not, see him walking back up the hill with one of the young shopkeepers, arm in arm, talking. They loved him down there. He hadn't lost his charm.

Being so far from the city, it was harder for the women to visit, but they still came when they could to see how Betty and Edward were doing, and to see young Jessica. Eva and Norm Harris moved down from the country and lived with their daughter Myrtle in a house two blocks away. Eva used to visit with Myrtle, who would have been driving her all over the coast for the day. For Jessica, the arrival of the aunties meant fuss and presents. Aunty Bertha Isaacs was Aunty 'Birthday' to my sister Jessica because she always brought something for Jessie's grand-daughter, just a little gift. For my grandfather it was a chance to hear what was happening around town, where he looked forward to returning every fortnight.

Having prepared himself, my grandfather would make his way to the nearest bus stop to begin his day's journeying back into the city. As he travelled closer to the city he could smell the diesel trains that fed its centre. As each kilometre of suburb gave way to older, larger streetscapes, he began to recognise the places that were part of the city of his little Wandsworth-by-the-sea. Passing the end of Scarborough Beach Road, the bus turned south into Fitzgerald Street, sweeping past the remains of the Rosemount Picture Theatre where he had once taken Jessie. Moving down Fitzgerald Street, the bus passed the end of Glendower Street, the centre of all of their lives and, I would wager, being the man that he was, he wouldn't get off just yet. He would let that one wait while he let the bus carry his rickety self down past the scrap metal works on the corner of Fitzgerald and Roe streets that always smelled of acrid rust from the nearby factories, over the railway lines that have always dissected the city and into the Central City Bus Station.

The city had been completely transformed. Perth had begun to shape-shift. His little Wandsworth-by-the-sea was fast disappearing. From the bus terminal he would make his way into the city along William Street and down to the *West Australian*. At the corner of Murray and William he would be reminded of the crowds and hear the cheers for Montgomery as he was paraded through the streets at the close of the war. He had stood at this corner and snapped a blurred moving image of his favourite Brit of the time. Hands reached out in front of him as he slipped the box brownie above the crowd. Standing on the corner in 1962, the events of postwar Perth are a lifetime away. Walking on further, he would make his way to the Terrace to Newspaper House and descend into the bowels of the printing rooms.

He was always warmly welcomed back. They all knew him at the *West* and would take time out to chat with him in the loading bay. He had become one of the city's occasional identities. While they knew him there as Whispering Smith, and would take time out for the old gentleman who seemed never to be able to leave, in the wider city, which was still just a big country town, he must have seemed an oddity. But in this sense, he was not alone. The city was filled with identities who have always formed an important part of its fabric. They inhabit the city within rules of their own making, and lift its sense of place simply through having existed within it.

There was 'The General', who marched the city and the entire length of sprawling Perth, stopping regularly to salute the west. There was 'Hats', the hat lady, who liked to wear different hats for each day as she walked the city taking seats in cafes and restaurants—a skipper's hat one day, a bonnet the next, a yellow rain hood in the middle of summer. There was 'The Duke', in my mother's memory, who liked to inhabit the older Art Deco picture theatres of his time. He would always take the front seat, and when they played 'God Save the Queen', he would rise, face the audience, and bow to receive their good wishes. There was 'Percy Buttons' who the *Mirror* once dressed up and photographed in formal evening wear and asked its readers if they knew who he was, before the page was turned revealing it was old Percy, ex-Vaudeville performer, town street identity, arrested regularly for collecting street alms, born the same year as Edward, in 1891, in the same city, London.

Edward would wander the streets of the city, dressed neat as a pin, taking time out to sit in Forrest Place, or at the remnants of the White Seats by the railway station, and just watch. I wonder, when he stopped at Baird's tobacconist to buy some refills for his pipe, or when he stopped at Boans Department Store for a rejuvenating cuppa, if, on hearing him speak, they also came up with a name for him, something simple like 'The Whisperer' perhaps, or maybe even something with a little more spin, like 'Rowdy Jim', or 'Chatterbox'. 'Here he comes again, The Whisperer, every fortnight like clockwork, stocking up on his tobacco. Where does he live? Where does he come from? How did he lose his voice? What's his story?'

Dressed in his neat suit, 'The Whisperer' walked the streets of the city that had eventually captured him in 1909. Like the images of London at the turn of the century that he seemed to inhabit at the edge of every frame, The Whisperer continued to be the eternal observer, the silent whispering man who had watched the city for more than half a century from the edges of its boundaries. His voice had marked him. His manner was unusual for the rougher Western Australian lifestyle that he so loved and was attracted to.

Walking up Murray Street, Edward would have passed the remains of the Aborigines Department. He had come here with Jessie to plead their case for the nine years that they circled each other trying to be together before, miraculously, they had been deemed a suitable experiment by the Chief Protector and allowed to marry. The city still contained its boundaries. He would not be arrested for talking with any blackfellas that he might have come across at the White Seats in 1962, but he would certainly have been frowned upon, seen as an even more obvious oddity for having anything to do with blackfellas in the street.

Walking further along Murray Street, he would pass the old section of Royal Perth Hospital where Jessie had decided it was time to put an end to the restrictions that overcame her own short life. It was only seven years since Jessie had passed away on the first day of spring 1955. Standing under the shade of the giant Moreton Bay fig, whose roots have torn through the pavement and tarmac in defiance of the lines and boundaries that the city has placed over it, he would have looked up to the old part of the hospital where she had died and where he had stood by her bed as his daughter cried for her mother. I imagine he could easily remember the still warm body of his wife covered by a sheet, and the depression of white cotton in the place where her leg should have been. The smell of the hospital, mingled with the earthy smell of the Moreton Bay fig, would have brought it all back for him, brought it back to the surface again, as he moved on, back into the city.

From the railway line the curve of the Horseshoe Bridge has become obscured. Walking past what were once avenues of taxicab drivers whose names he had always known, the deep din of the city must have been a comforting sound. It was in his blood. It surrounded him at birth; the resonant sound of all those lives existing, surrounding, colliding with his own in the distant city of London. Walking through the city, he passed the remains of the old arcades that had so delighted him on his first sighting in 1909 when he had finally stopped roaming the Wheatbelt. Passing the site of the old White City, where he and Jessie had danced around the police, the Aborigines Department and each other, he would find nothing but ruins.

Returning to the Terrace, and back towards the centre of the city, he would pass the scaffolding surrounding the wide and gaping holes of his town, as skyscrapers began to dominate the skyline. There was no room for history in the city of his final years. The mineral boom and the promise of untapped riches in the North, in my grandmother's country and in the countries of all those people who had been taken away, was fuelling the city's new wealth. As new images were being made of the glass, concrete and steel towers, in the crowds of eager onlookers, somewhere just out of the frame, is The Whisperer, Edward Smith.

They are always with us, the people of other eras that exist alongside our own, quietly watching the new psyche of the city take form as the world that they inhabited is redrawn, torn down, reclaimed and redeveloped. Their presence is fainter, less vociferous than it was when the city was theirs, but they still shadow it, and feed into it.

There are lives and spirits and maps and boundaries that they follow which newcomers cannot see. Edward would follow these trails of the making of his life in this place so far from where he began, quietly walking the streets, watching the changes, noting the rhythm, but never able to completely yield to it. The new rhythm was someone else's. He was following a different call, leading him north again, across the railway line, along Lake Street, out and over the ridge of the edge of what was once a freshwater swamp, to what remained of Hyde Park.

The house at Lake Street was still there as he made his way to the cool shade of the park, finally resting on one of its benches, taking time to catch his breath, filling his lungs with that fertile air that swirled around the twin lakes.

When my grandmother appeared to my mother, she had marked a turning point in their lives. For each of them, her apparition was a sign that it was time for them to allow her to become an accepted part of their past. Edward had been the strongest advocate of accepting this shift. To relieve my mother's grief, he urged her to let go, to accept the coming birth of Jessica as a new beginning, and to put the pain of the recent past behind them and 'to remember only the good times.' But Jessie had not disappeared completely, for either of them. They did not visit the grave because they believed that she was always near, although they did not say that to each other. They avoided her presence because of its continuing resonance for both of them. They carried the sense of Jessie, each in their own way, still connecting her to them, and to that part of themselves that she had taken with her. In this way, they did not lose that part of themselves. It simply became a more subtle part of their lives, like the grief that they both pretended to move beyond, but in reality, carried with them. They carried it because it reminded them of the way back to that part of themselves that Jessie carried within her cheeky spirit. They carried it forward until it became something to be cherished as a part of her living as much as a part of her death.

Hyde Park shadowed Edward as he rested beneath its branches. It continued to record his story in its fibre as he walked around the lakes one last time before making his way to the bus stop and heading west towards the sea. The diffused light through the trees cast shadow lines of story across his path as he walked beneath and through it, and linked his story to all the others that had been carried within its living memory.

The hard, inflexible boundaries that are laid down by narrow definitions of race, nationalism and religion are shadowed by the boundaries that we create as we try to make sense of the world. The stories that we create in our lives are not neatly divided and separated by these demarcations. The shadow lines of story that we create as we go about our daily lives connect us in ways that we can't even fathom, until they are made clear to us through the inability of the rigid boundaries that circumscribe us, to contain, describe and give sense to our lives. Within the piercing light of Western Australia, such lines were ruled north–south, dividing my grandmother's country into Federated Western Australia and the Northern Territory. Within the sheer, sharp light of this land, such lines were ruled around us to describe our race, around settlements to contain us, around prohibited areas to segregate us, and through our families to engineer us.

If power is the ability of others to make you inhabit their story of you, this power can only be contained by the rigidity of ignorance and the inability to question and to learn. Shadow lines are wide lines of negotiation that we all use to make sense of our differences and our inter-connections. They shift and change, break and re-form, swell and divide into spaces and patterns within the honesty of those of us who, like Jessie and Edward, choose to ignore the straight, hard lines and choose to step into a place where our stories have room to move, to dance and exist. These lines of story shadow all of us. They are not always eloquent, or enlightening. Some are rough and difficult to reconcile.

While the shadows of accumulated stories were playing over Edward's life, his own story was beginning to slip away as he returned to his home that he loved by the sea. His grand-daughter, my sister Jessica, screamed in fright when she found him slumped on the floor of the sleep-out that filled with the sounds of the ocean. His story faded as he was rushed to hospital by ambulance, all the way back to the city. His arteries collapsed. His heart finally gave way. He died on the operating table at Royal Perth Hospital. My grandfather's story, like my grandmother's story, became a shadow line to my own.

On cool summer evenings, Karrakatta is a haven and an oasis within the heart of a city that has stretched and grown. The wind rises off the river to the south, moving the tall date palms and straight pines side by side as the crows and magpies keep watch over the dead. Almost all of the stories of the people who inhabited my grandparent's story have also ended here. Boundaries have been drawn again, based on religion, on class, on how much you can afford to bury a loved one. Turning east at the main entrance I'm passing them all as I walk towards the back of the cemetery on All Saints Day. A half moon is rising in the east, peeking over the ridges that ringed the city that captured them both. It's a mischievous thing to do, to come here on a day when the spirits are supposed to be so close to our world. They are both here together, Edward, the boy-man from London escaping his birth city of familial death, and Jessie, the child who was taken away from her mother, her people and her country. They were not supposed to be together. The hard lines and boundaries that set so much of their lives in train did not prevent them from coming together. Laws of race and segregation that existed in their lives did not stop them from staying together.

Some Noongars believe that the spirits of the dead pass into the moodjar tree before being released. Many of us Nor'westers believe that when a person passes away their spirit dwells nearby in the earth, travelling through the land for a time, until it is released and returns to its proper country. Some people do not speak the name of the dead for fear of bringing on the cheeky spirits.

I like to believe that Jessie and Edward's spirits returned to their countries. For Edward, he would have found a city transformed by war; laid out much as he remembered it but also changed beyond recognition. For my grandmother, returning to her lands in Miriwoong country, she would find the landscape of her childhood, of red earth and wild rivers, about to become submerged beneath the waters of Lake Argyle. My grandmother's skin was concealed when she was a small child, but we have retrieved it, reconnected with it, and with the story of her removal which was meant to be wiped clean.

Sometimes when I walk around Hyde Park of an evening, I like to think that Jessie and Edward are somehow still around us all. I break with my Nor'wester traditions here, I like to call their names.

Epilogue

I'm heading north again. I pass Hyde Park heading out of the city, heading out of the Swan Valley. I pass Moore River heading into sky country. The earth begins to change from white sand to brown clay and finally, blood-red earth. The sky opens up as I pass fields of ant beds that stand solid in the spinifex landscape, like giant women sitting in the waving spinifex outcrops, watching me pass. I pass the groves of upside down boab trees as I turn east from Derby. I pass through plain country, over giant rivers, until I am finally following the Ord Valley, heading towards Lake Argyle.

I am returning to a place where our skin means more than just colour. I am from this place. I am tracking all of my histories through this country, and the way is opening up, like the lines of story that crossed this land, that remain hidden within flooded valleys and transformed landscapes—unless we are willing to read them. Miriwoong women sang songs to try and spirit the children back to their country. The women's voices carried their despair, flowing through the valley and out to sea. Some were able to come back, many haven't. Some created new lives for themselves against the lines of stories that were written for them, and they linked these stories back with the ones that were denied them. I am wondering if, in spirit form, my grandmother found her way back here after all.

Notes on Sources

Chapter One: *skin*

The historical narrative of this chapter is drawn from research of primary Police, Aborigines Department, and manuscript notes based in the Western Australian State Records Office (SRO) and the J.S. Battye Library of Western Australian History (Battye Library). These primary sources form the basis of much of the history within this book, and have been used with due care for individual family members mentioned within them.

Research for this chapter was completed at the Battye Library of Western Australian History, the State Records Office of Western Australia, the Australian Archives, Perth and Darwin, and the Mitchell Library, Sydney.

Throughout the book I use Noongar to name the peoples of the south-west of Western Australia. Alternative spellings include Nyungar, Nyoongar, Noongah, and Nyungah, to name a few.

The narrative of my grandmother's removal is taken from the journal of Constable Hill 'Whilst on Escort Duty to Wyndham,' 30/06/06–23/07/06, Police File (4729/1906). Other key primary sources include the *Royal Commission on the Condition of the Natives,* Report (1904) by W.E. Roth, and the resultant legislation, *Act No. 14 of 1905,* referred to as the *Aborigines Act* (1905). Newspaper reports in the *West Australian* for 1905 and 1906 document parliamentary debates regarding the 1905 *Aborigines Act.* My grandmother's removal from Argyle is also referred to in the Aborigines Department file, *Swan Mission as an Industrial and Reformative School* (231/1906). This file refers to an older Aborigines Department file, 46/1906, that has been destroyed, but Colonial Secretary's Office (CSO) letters inwards and outwards registers confirm correspondence regarding the removal between the Department, Wild Dog Police and the Inspector of Police for the Kimberley.

Guddia, more recently spelled *kartiya,* is a Kimberley Aboriginal term for non-Indigenous peoples. I use *guddia* as I consider it closer to the pronunciation of older generation East Kimberley relatives who are mentioned in this story.

Many people have written of the East Kimberley frontier in what is known collectively across the Kimberley by Aboriginal peoples as the 'Killing Times', and these secondary sources also provided invaluable insights. Andrew Gill's paper, 'Aborigines, Settlers and Police in the Kimberleys, 1887–1905' (1977), was particularly relevant to understanding Police mechanisms of control and in particular, the, 'economy of the cow.' Tim Rowes' paper, 'Were You Ever Savages? Aboriginal Insiders and Pastoral Patronage,' (1983) was relevant in its exploration of 'inside' and 'outside' power relations that were set up in the East Kimberley with the coming of the guddia. Mary Durack's two books, *Kings in Grass Castles* (1967) and *Sons in the Saddle* (1983), provided a valuable non-Indigenous perspective through documentation detailing Durack family holdings and history within the East Kimberley region. Gordon Broughton's, *Turn Again Home* (1965) also provided useful information on the region. Jack Sullivan's collaboration with Bruce Shaw, *Banggaiyerri: The Story of Jack Sullivan as told to Bruce Shaw* (1983), provided an invaluable Aboriginal community history and Aboriginal perspectives about the place, people and time of my grandmother's life at Argyle Station. Another invaluable source in understanding Aboriginal relations in Western Australia was Anna Haebich's fantastic and formative work, *For Their Own Good: Aborigines and Government in the Southwest of Western Australia, 1900–1940* (1988).

The contemporary narrative is based on returns to my grandmother's country in 1988 and 1989. Within this period, many of the elders mentioned were still alive and their memories, guidance, shared stories and experiences form the basis of the contemporary narratives within this chapter. All of the community members mentioned have since passed away and I use their skin names, Nangala, Namidge, Nangari, Nannagoo and Nambijin as a mark of respect. I make mention of Banggaiyerri in particular, as he recorded his story in print, and I also acknowledge Three Day Joe for his reminiscences.

Other contemporary descriptions of the East Kimberley are based on subsequent returns to Miriwoong country over the years. My grandmother's removal from Wyndham to Perth was registered in the State Shipping Records Passenger Lists under the name, Gipsy, WA Inwards Shipping Registers: Cons 457 Vol 11.

Information about the *Bullarra* was gained through archival images, as well as a description of the ship in J. Thomson's *Nor'West of West* (1908), and via a description of voyages by Abbot Torres in 1905 in, R. Pratt and J. Millington, *The Torres Diaries, 1900–1914* (1987).

Chapter Two: *life lines*

The historical narrative documenting Edward Smith's last days in London in 1909 is based on personal primary records, particularly his *Ruby Pocket Diary* of 1909, as well as secondary documents. Personal documents such as notes, receipts, wills, memoriam cards, letters and tickets were used to flesh out this period. Birth, death and marriage certificates for the Smith and Graham families aided in tracking his history, while searches of the censuses helped track their lives within the city.

Research for this chapter was completed at the Westminster Archives, Westminster Abbey Archives, Westminster Library Records Office, London Metropolitan Archives, Brompton Cemetery Records Office, the Public Records Office Chancery Lane and the Emanuel School Library. Interesting notes were also obtained on London burial practices and patterns from the London Museum.

The contemporary narrative informing this chapter is based on three trips to my grandfather's country and London in spring 1996, autumn 1998, and the summer of 2002. These were invaluable in understanding both his past and my connection to this city.

Searches of *The Times* of January and February 1909 informed the descriptions of London, including the particularly cold winter from which Edward escaped.

These were also useful in illuminating the diversity of experiences on offer within the city and the various escape routes via sea travel.

Descriptions of photographs were made from personal family photographs of that period, as well as images from published sources. To this end I relied on two books from the *Archive Photographs Series*, on Wandsworth and on Battersea and Clapham, both compiled by Patrick Loobey (1994). Equally useful regarding London transport and infrastructure was Brian Girling's *Westminster Villages* (1996).

Descriptions of life at Emanuel School were informed by a visit in 1996, and research of the *Emanuel School Magazine* for 1901–1906, kindly aided by Marian Bradnock, the School Librarian, as well as Edward's personal photographs and some archival photographs from the Emanuel School Archive. Roger Marjoribanks' history, *The Noble Aim: Emanuel School 1594–1994,* Wilfred Giles and Bernard Slater's *Emanuel School, the history of 1594–1964* (1964), and Henry Maskell's *Recollections of Emanuel School* (1904) also provided information.

Ordinance Survey Maps of Wandsworth (1894), Wandsworth Common (1893), and Chelsea (1894) also provided a means of retrieving Edward's London from the maze of contemporary London. In Edinburgh I stumbled upon a seat commemorating the life and work of Gertie Gitana, and further information regarding her career was obtained from Edinburgh Library Archives—under 'Memories' in the *Evening News*, 29 September 1967.

Information regarding the Chelsea Women's Hospital was drawn from archives of the Greater London Records Office, *Records Transferred by the Medical Records Officer,* Acc 2653, and Annual Reports of the Chelsea Women's Hospital for 1892, 1897 and 1901.

Information regarding older photographic techniques and aiding the deciphering of remaining chemicals in Edward's trunk was found in Elizabeth Martin's *Collecting and Preserving Old Photographs* (1988).

Chapter Three: *captive souls*

Much of this chapter is based on archival research of the Swan Mission from its inception in 1889 to its closure in 1921. The old Swan Mission School buildings and grounds still exist within the precinct of Swanleigh School. Swanleigh records of the site were described as being destroyed in a flood some years ago. Aborigines Department records from 1898 to 1921 consequently formed the basis of primary research into this history. This included a search of all inmate register files, baptism records and annual reports. My grandmother's baptism is recorded in Swan Parish Baptism Records for 1906, Battye Library 2467A/249.

Other references for life at Swan Mission included A Peterkin's *The Noisy Mansions* (1986), John Harris' *One Blood: 200 Years of Aboriginal Encounter with Christianity: A Story of Hope* (1990), Bronwen Watkins' thesis 'History of Swanleigh Anglican Hostel' (1966), Peter Biskups', *Not Slaves Not Citizens: The Aboriginal Problem in Western Australia 1898–1954* (1973) and of course, Anna Haebich's *For Their Own Good: Aborigines and Government in the Southwest of Western Australia, 1900–1940* (1988). Comparisons of Mission subsidies were discussed in detail by Haebich (1988) and were the subject of the 1904 Roth

Royal Commission in which Swan Mission's more generous subsidies were discussed.

Sally Morgan's *My Place* (1987) contains a story by inmate Albert Corunna about the brutal treatment he received in Swan Mission and his escape from there as a child. This incident was followed up and referenced to a newspaper report in the *Sunday Times*, 'Swan Native Mission ... Management by Muscle,' 21 May 1911. Information regarding 'The Storm' that struck the Mission in 1915 came from stories handed down by my grandmother to my mother, as well as newspaper reports including 'The Storm' in the *West Australian*, 7 March 1915, 'The Greatest Storm in the History of Perth,' and 'A Tragedy at Swan Native Mission,' in the *Daily News*, 26 February 1915,' 'Perth Visited By a Great Storm,' in the *Sunday Times*, 28 February 1915, and 'Sensational Storm—A Young Girl Killed,' in the *West Australian*, 27 February 1915.

The names, periods of employment and styles of staff administration at the Mission is taken from Swan Mission Annual Reports, Aborigines Department files and correspondence, as well as some of the secondary sources related previously.

Descriptions of my grandmother's time at Swan Mission were greatly informed by interviews with uncle Bob Dorey (Carnarvon 1988), an inmate of the Mission; Baby Jones (Perth 1996), daughter of Mr and Mrs Jones, missionaries during some of my grandmother's time at the Mission; and Grannie Bella (Isobel) Bropho (Perth 1988–91), Thomas Bropho's wife, who shared her husband's stories of life at Swan.

This chapter was also influenced by stories told to me by my mother, Betty Kinnane, remembering stories told to her by my grandmother of her experiences at Swan Mission.

Information on the Dorey Brothers' removal was provided by the interview with Bob Dorey, and also by the Aborigines Department file of their removal.

The image of Thomas Bropho and Mary described in this chapter was found in the Sydney Mitchell Library General Photograph Collection; it had been deposited by Reverend Price. The history of Mr and Mrs Jones is directly informed by the interview conducted with their daughter, 'Baby' Jones (Perth 1996) and through memories of them passed on to my mother by my grandmother.

The saying, 'God made the white man, God made the black man, and the Devil made the half-caste,' was in common usage to describe Aboriginal people of mixed descent and was discussed in an interview with Helena Murphy (Darwin 1992). Numbers of deaths of children at the Mission were obtained from Anglican Church records listing the names, dates of death, and ages of children buried in the St Mary's graveyard at Swanleigh.

Chapter Four: *reinvention*

Records of Edward's work in theatres around Perth were taken from his personal diaries, lists of payment and hours worked, and descriptions of timings of various stage actions. A search of the *West Australian* for the dates mentioned in 1909 confirmed the plays and performances discussed in his diaries.

Edward's brush with diphtheria and subsequent loss of voice are based on letters between himself and his family in England and my mother's reminiscence of Edward's descriptions of falling ill. Treatments for diphtheria in Australia at the time of Edward's illness were gleaned from Jennifer Hagger's *Australian Colonial Medicine* (1979), in which it is related that no antitoxin for diphtheria was developed until 1917.

Haebich (1988) cites the droughts of 1911 and 1914 as impacting upon the abrupt downturn of agricultural production in Western Australia at that time Jacobs' *Mister Neville* (1990) describes the economic downturn as being particularly related to the drought of 1912, as outlined in *The Selector's Guide* (1912). According to *The Macquarie Encyclopaedia of Australian Events* (1997), the boom that followed Federation was curtailed by environmental forces in the form of droughts, as well as political forces in the form of the oncoming World War.

Edward was recorded as being found to be medically unfit in his *Application to Enlist in the Australian Imperial Force*, for his 'Defective Voice,' at Perth on 7 September 1916 (Register No. 141.3.16). Edward's *Medical Certificate of Unfitness* listed him as being likewise 'rejected on grounds of physical unfitness,' ref. (W 66 333). For the description of Mr Campbell's military background I have drawn on Haebich's (1988) extensive research into the personnel of the settlement at this period.

The trunk described in this chapter still exists and continues to carry the remnants of my grandfather's past.

Chapter Five: *in service*

A.O. Neville's appointment as Chief Protector of Aborigines in 1915 is well documented by Haebich (1988) and Jacobs (1990). My own take on Neville's performance as an administrator is based on viewing many primary records in which his overtly controlling style is evident and from interviews with several Aboriginal women under his charge including Alice Nannup (Geraldton 1988–92), Isobel Bropho (Perth 1988–91), Jean Hill (Geraldton 1988–90), Liza Isaacs (Perth 1989), and Clara Jackamarra (Mogumber, 1995). Many other community members who had dealings with Neville found him to be a highly problematic character. Jacobs' (1990) biography of Neville provided information about the machinations of the Aborigines Department, and Neville's belief in his 'duty' to the Aboriginal peoples of Western Australia. This duty was certainly noticed by me in many files, including my own grandmother's personal file, where his methods of 'protecting' Aboriginal peoples through control and management were powerful in their ignorance.

Haebich (1988) outlines Neville's disdain for Missions and relates the closure of Swan Mission and other similar church-run institutions as part of Neville's plan to take over management through the government settlements at Carrolup and Moore River.

Much of this chapter, and the subsequent tracking of my grandmother's life under the various departments created to manage and control the Aboriginal peoples of Western Australia, is based on the more than three hundred pages of my grandmother's personal file, 'Jessie Smith and Family. Personal File,'

(312/1926, 346/1931). We received this file from the then Department of Community Services in 1989.

Norm Harris, a former Native Affairs employee, described the incineration of files that took place within recent memory in an article in the *West Australian* on 8 April 2000.

For further information regarding the creation, destruction and management of Aborigines Department files created to monitor and control Indigenous peoples of Western Australia see Lauren Marsh and Steve Kinnane's 'Ghost Files: The Missing Files of the Department of Indigenous Affairs Archives' (2003).

Information regarding Noongar response to non-Indigenous encroachment upon their lands and territories came from Len Collard's MA Thesis, 'An Analysis of Nyungar Influences in South West Western Australia' (1996). Noongar country boundaries were derived from Len Collard's *Interpretive Maps of Nyungar Country* (1998).

Background to the life and people of Bridgetown was aided by a search of the *Blackwood Times* for 1918–1921, as well as Bridgetown Historical Committee Records, Bridgetown Roads Board records, the dairies of John Allnutt, William Walter's scrapbook of family photographs and newspaper cuttings (1887–1903), Donald Breen's *The Wheatley Family of Bridgetown* (1958), and Colin Gaines' *Bridgetown: One Hundred Years of History* (1970), which was particularly useful in providing a time-line of the encroachment of non-Indigenous peoples into Noongar territories.

The quote by Mr Roberts on Empire Day regarding the symbolism of the flag was from the *Blackwood Times*, 31 May 1918. Advertisements calling for previously rejected men to enlist were from the *Blackwood Times*, 14 June 1918.

Details of the Sherwood family history are based on an interview with Betty Davies (1988), follow up telephone conversations and a subsequent meeting with Betty Davies and Corrie Forbes (1998). The drowning of young Enid was described by Mrs Davies, and also described in the article 'Drowning Fatality' in the *Blackwood Times*, 10 September 1920, and the results of the inquest published in the *Blackwood Times*, 17 September 1920.

Chapter Six: *isolation*

The phrase 'out of sight and out of mind' came into common usage when describing Moore River as a segregationist detention camp on the outskirts of mainstream society, through the work of Bill Bunbury in his 'Hindsight' interviews for Radio National.

Details of Edward's employment in the settlement are based on remnants of diaries, letters from family, the letter of offer from Mr Campbell to Edward, and the subsequent letter of reference supplied by Mr Campbell, 26 September 1922. The photographs described in this chapter were taken by Edward in 1922 and the glass plate negatives form part of his collection.

Much of this chapter is informed by interviews with Grannie Bella (Isobel) Bropho (Perth 1988–91), Ralph and Lizzie Dalgety (Geraldton 1995), Clara Jackamarra (Mogumber 1995), Jean Hill (Geraldton 1988–90), Alice Nannup

(Geraldton 1988–91), and discussions with Mr Peter Toms, an inmate during Edward's time at the settlement. Grannie Bella's story is also recorded in 'The Stockrider's Daughter,' in Jan Carter's *Nothing to Spare* (1981). For an intimate description of life on the inside in Moore River, also see Alice Nannup, Lauren Marsh and Stephen Kinnane's *When the Pelican Laughed* (1992).

The influenza epidemic that gripped Moore River during my grandmother's time there was described by Haebich (1988), and further evidenced by an increase in deaths that impacted upon the Settlement population, as discovered through a search of Aborigines Department records for 1917–1940, and from Moora Courthouse records of death.

Information regarding staff difficulties, the reading of letters and inmate petitions, came from Aborigines Department files such as *Nurse V. Ryan Personal File*, 1003/1923, *Farm Assistant*, 1746/1923, *Matron Brodie: Personal File*, 461/1924, and *Superintendent Brodie: Personal File*, 387/1924. The episode of the fire sticks around Elbow was recorded in Edward's diary of that period on 24 March 1922.

Chapter Seven: *prohibited areas*

Much of the tracking of my grandmother's life during the period covered by this chapter is based on the official correspondence and documents within her Aborigines Department Personal File.

Descriptions of East Perth as a place of escape outside the prohibited area in the 1940s and 1950s were provided in interviews with Frank Bropho and Gladys Bropho (Perth 1995). Descriptions of old Noongar East Perth were provided in an interview with Thomasisha Passmore (Perth 1992–95), who was raised in East Perth and spent much of her life there, and from my mother's reminiscences of East Perth from her many visits with my mother.

The reference to the walls having eyes is taken from *When the Pelican Laughed* (1992).

Information regarding the clearing out of Aboriginal tenements from East Perth in the 1960s came from the Native Welfare file, *East Perth Native Matters* (1312/1943).

Anna Fielder's history and descriptions of Anna are based on my mother's memories as well as searches of Swan Mission Aborigines Department files. Anna was an 'old girl' to my grandmother while she was at Swan Mission, going out to service while my grandmother was still a child. Anna was known to my father's family who also lived in East Perth in the 1920s. Anna wore horseshoes inside her long coat when betting on the races, one on each side of the shoulder as good luck shoulder pads, and was also superstitious and would never place a bet if her path 'crossed a cross-eyed' person.

Information about Aboriginal women working in domestic service came from came from interviews with many people who worked as 'domestics', and their children, including Betty Kinnane (Perth 1988–92), Alice Nannup (Geraldton 1988–92), Jean Hill (Geraldton 1988–90), Liza Isaacs (Perth 1989), Lemmie AhKim (Perth 1990), Isobel Bropho (Perth 1988–91), Thomasisha Passmore (Perth 1992–95), Clara Jackamarra (Mogumber 1995), and discussions with many older women who were sent out as domestic servants, including Ethel Clinch, Alice Stack, Minnie van Leeuwen, and Marie Harris.

The photographic images described in this chapter that were taken by Aboriginal women of that time form the bulk of our family photographic collection. Basil Gardiner's mother, Elsie Gardiner, was particularly active in documenting other Aboriginal women working as domestic servants.

The description of Con's café as one of the many meeting places used by Aboriginal domestic servants was described by Alice Nannup in interview (Geraldton 1988–92), and information about other meeting places within the city, and the way in which Aboriginal women used various strategies to foil the Department, were described in interviews with Alice Nannup (Geraldton 1988–92) Jean Hill (Geraldton 1988–90), Liza Isaacs (Perth 1989), and Isobel Bropho (Perth 1988–91).

Edward's visits to White City are noted in his diaries. White City is the particular focus of A.O. Neville's efforts to have Aboriginal people banned from the city for visiting this amusement park in 1927. Information relating to this action, including Police correspondence and descriptions from patrols came from the Aborigines Department file, *City of Perth Prohibited Area* (38/1927). References to 'Cooee City' were also found in the article, 'Coo-ee City first tie in WA the Chair-o-plane,' *Mirror*, 6 November 1926. Descriptions of White City are also based on archival images within the State Archives and the Western Australian Newspaper publication, *Stage Screen and Stars* (1992), which described White City as, 'two acres of fairground which provided a popular night out in the Roaring Twenties.'

The story of the smuggled letters between Jessie and Edward was told to my mother by my grandmother. The frequency of letters between Jessie and Edward over this period is based on Edward's personal diaries.

Descriptions of Isobel Bropho's time at Dulhi-Gunyah were based on interviews with her (Perth 1988–91). This period of Isobel Bropho's life is also mentioned in Jan Carter's *Nothing to Spare* (1981), and in an interview with Ronda Jamieson (1989) deposited with the Battye Library, ref. (H2086). The removal of Isobel Bropho and her siblings to Dulhi-Gunyah is documented in the Aborigines Department file, *A. R. Pries, Busselton: re railway pass for Clara Leyland and 6 children* (1027/1906).

The story of the night of Mr Campbell's death and the events surrounding it came from interviews with Isobel Bropho (Perth 1988–91) and Clara Jackamarra (Mogumber 1995). The story of Thomas Bropho and Jessie Argyle singing in the church is also based on these interviews, and both of these stories are mentioned in Clara Jackamarra and S.M. Kelly's *A Proud Heritage* (1980).

Wadjella is a Noongar term used to describe non-Indigenous peoples. It is often spelled different ways including *wetjella, watjella* and *wedjella*.

Information regarding the old and new Moore River Cemetery sites was obtained primarily from the Aborigines Department file, *Mogumber Cemetery* 1916–1964 (149/1948). Information regarding previous locations of pre-contact burial sites was provided by Mrs Clara Jackamarra (Mogumber 1995). Information regarding the numbers of people buried, dates of deaths, frequency of deaths and causes of death came from Moora Courthouse records of deaths, as well as *Cemetery 1916–1964* (149/1948). Information describing burials and beatings of Aboriginal women by Superintendent Brodie came from interviews with Isobel Bropho (Perth 1988–91), Alice Nannup (Geraldton 1988–92), and Jean Hill (Geraldton 1988–90). Information regarding Aboriginal women seeking to avoid being sent to the settlement to give birth came from the file *King Edward Memorial Hospital and Government Hospital—Admission of Native Women* (271/1943).

Chapter Eight: *dangerous love*

The incident of Jessie and Edward's letters being passed on to the Aborigines Department was recorded in my grandmother's personal file. Information regarding Edward's rejection by Mr Sherwood came from an interview with Betty Davies (Perth 1988), and my own mother's recollections of that story as told to her by my grandmother. Descriptions of their meetings and rendezvous are based on Edward's diaries.

Information about Mrs Mulvale's Boarding house for Aboriginal women came from my grandmother's personal file and interviews with Alice Nannup (Geraldton 1988–92), as described in *When the Pelican Laughed* (1992).

Cohabitation Cards described in this chapter were created by the Aborigines Department under A.O. Neville and are stored within the State Records Office, ref. (Acc 5404/ vol 1784/ 1–7, 1926–1959). For further information see 'Ghost Files' (2002).

Details of the internal machinations of the Aborigines Department regarding control of departmental files and budgets were found in Haebich (1988) and Jacobs (1990).

I have also viewed hundreds of departmental administrative files and discussed the administration with many of those who came under the Department, including some who have since received their personal files, which all reveal a similar pattern of pedantic control and surveillance.

Information regarding Edward's employment and movements of this time is taken from his personal papers including notes, receipts, and union contribution cards. The story of Jessie and Edward meeting regularly in the city is evidenced in his notes and was related by my mother, as told to her by my grandmother. Alice Nannup also described Edward and Jessie meeting in the city in *When the Pelican Laughed* (1992). Descriptions of Edward's routine of applying theatre make-up to hide his scar are from my mother's recollections.

Further information relating to the Prohibited Area, including police correspondence, descriptions from police patrols and Neville's complaints regarding women staying out late was came from the Aborigines Department File, *City of Perth Prohibited Area* (38/1927).

Information regarding the Native Union was found in Haebich (1988), as well as evidence provided in the *Royal Commission into the Treatment of Aborigines, 1934* (333/1933). The photographic image of the Native Union men appears in *Truth*, 11 June 1927.

Chapter Nine: *glendower street*

Information regarding letters from A.O. Neville, police reports and Edward and Jessie's responses to the Department is found in my grandmother's personal file.

Boodjamooling is the Noongar term for what is known currently on mainstream maps of the city as Hyde Park, and is prominently displayed on signage interpreted by the North Perth Park Historical Society.

Haebich (1988) cites over six hundred letters and articles dealing with Aboriginal issues in the press between 1930 and 1934, leading up to the 1934 Royal Commission. Information regarding Neville's letter-writing campaign under A. O. N. comes from Jacobs (1990). Information regarding Neville's approaches to biological absorption is based on numerous references within administrative files, but in particular to his own book, *Australia's Coloured Minority: Its Place in The Community* (1948). Descriptions of Neville's card system are based on research of the remaining cards stored within the State Records Office, ref: (Acc 5404/ vol 1784/ 1–7, 1926–1959). Jacobs (1990) and Haebich (1988) also provided useful information regarding the internal management of the cards and files.

Information regarding Thomas Bropho's life and political action from the 1930s to the 1950s was obtained from interviews with Isobel Bropho (Perth 1988–91), and Geoff Harcus (Northam 1992–93), as well as transcripts of Thomas Bropho's evidence to the 1934 Royal Commission. Grannie Bella's Personal Card, obtained in 1989, revealed information regarding the departmental tracking of Thomas and his family. Each of these people remarked on Thomas' oratory, as have many others, including Clara Jackamarra and S.M. Kelly in *A Proud Heritage* (1980), in which Clara Jackamarra also discusses how Thomas Bropho removed a whip from a tracker and hid a rifle so as to prevent bloodshed in Moore River.

The removal of Aboriginal people to Northam in which Section 12s—which ordered the removal of Aboriginal peoples from the Northam Camp to Moore River—were supplied for every individual, was recorded in the file *MRNS Admission of Northam Natives* (21/1933). This incident, along with the figures for one hundred and fifty-four Aboriginal people in the Metropolitan area in the 1930s, is related in Haebich (1988).

Interviews with Eileen Harwood and George Harwood (Canberra 1990, 1992) inform much of this chapter. Eileen Harwood's removal is based on these interviews and on the file *Removal of Half-Caste General File* (16/20), in which Neville's views regarding the desirability of removing women from their countrymen are found. Eileen Harwood's removal is also mentioned by Neville in *Australia's Coloured Minority: Its Place in the Community* (1948), in which she is pictured in the 'before' and 'after' shots discussed. Information regarding the East Perth Girls Home came from Haebich (1988).

A.O. Neville's use of personal files in attacks against witnesses to the 1934 Royal Commission is discussed by Haebich (1988) and Jacobs (1990), and is evident in the transcripts of evidence in which he routinely hands in personal files for consideration of the Commissioner as a means of discrediting witnesses in *Royal Commission into the Treatment of Aborigines, 1934* (333/1933). The evidence in support of the findings of the 1934 Royal Commission came from the file *Royal Commission into the Treatment of Aborigines 1934, Findings* (131/1935).

Death figures for Moore River are based on research of deaths of inmates from the Moora Courthouse records. Conditions of Moore River in the 1930s are detailed by Haebich (1988) and were also recorded in primary departmental files. Death rates for the settlement are based on research of the Moora Courthouse Records. The effects of the resultant *Native Administration Act 1936* on the Aboriginal community of Western Australia are well documented by Haebich (1988).

The story of my grandmother heading to Moore River to retrieve children from the dormitory was told to me by my mother.

Information regarding my grandmother's visits to Sister Kate's home was based upon my mother's recollections. Information regarding the setting up of the home is well documented by Haebich (1988).

The Pass System and its introduction are recorded in the file *Establishment of a Pass System in Metropolitan Area* (162/1938). Descriptions of suffering under this system in which many white people arbitrarily felt it within their power to check people's passes are based on interviews with Isobel Bropho (Perth 1988–91) and Eileen Clarke (nee Shang) (Adelaide 1992; Perth 1995), as were descriptions of life in the city during the Depression under the Aborigines Department. Elsie Gardiner's removal is documented in an earlier removal file *Particulars of H. C. Children on Nor' West Stations Who Require to be Removed* (973/1916). Lemmie AhKim told the story of her father's death to me in 1992. Lemmie is listed as being taken away and placed in Moore River in 1925 in the file *Removal of Half-Caste General File* (16/20). Lemmie's father is listed in Wise's Postal Directories of Wyndham as a bird-catcher and Market Gardener.

Information on Neville's retirement bash came from 'Native Girls, Mr A. O. Neville Farewelled,' *West Australian* 16 March 1940. Descriptions of Jessie's trip to Greenmount Hill came from an interview with Henry Mippy (Wickham 1988).

Chapter Ten: *night lives*

Much of this chapter of life in Perth and at Glendower Street in the War years is based on my mother's stories and on interviews with Isobel Bropho (Perth 1988–91), Eileen Clarke (nee Shang) (Adelaide 1992; Perth 1995), Henry Mippy (Wickham 1988), Eileen Harwood (nee Gentle) and George Harwood (Canberra 1990, 1992), Liza Isaacs (Perth 1989), Geoff Harcus (Northam 1992), Helena Murphy (Darwin 1992; Perth 1995), and Bill Poland (Carnarvon 1988). Bill Poland also remembered Edward from his time working with him in Shark Bay when Bill was a young lad.

The description of the surveillance of the Crystal Picture Theatre in East Perth, including details of police raids in East Perth and joint patrols between the Department of Native Affairs, the Police and the Shore Patrol, and the focus on the prohibition of alcohol, arrest rates, and raids on Aboriginal houses in East Perth, were drawn from the file *East Perth Native Matters* (1312/1943). Biskup (1973) was helpful for statistics relating to servicemen who joined up to fight, as was R. Hall's *The Black Diggers* (1989). Information regarding Manpowering policies toward Aboriginal people came from Helena Murphy (Darwin 1992) and CSO file (3312/1911).

The state of destitution experienced by the Aboriginal population of Western Australia in the Depression has been well documented by Haebich (1988).

Information regarding the restrictions of returning war brides was provided by Annette Potts and Lucinda Strauss in *For the Love of a Soldier* (1987).

Stories of Jimmy McSkene are based on my mother's reminiscence, on Jimmy's Military Service file held in the Australian Archives, Perth, and personal papers.

Thomas Forrest's war record was recorded in his Aborigines Department personal file and information regarding his earlier war service was related in interview with Thomasisha Passmore (Perth 1992, 1995). Information regarding Cecil Fitzgerald being the first Aboriginal man to enlist in the Second World War, as well information regarding enlistment numbers and increased Aboriginal employment opportunities that occurred with the outbreak of war was from Biskup (1973).

The letter from Bernard Bayly informing Edward of the effects of the war on London, including the evacuation of Emanuel School, was sent on 12 January 1941.

Chapter Eleven: *card fever*

Much of this chapter is informed by interviews with Eileen Clarke (nee Shang) (Adelaide 1992; Perth 1995), Helena Murphy (Darwin 1992; Perth 1995), Geoff Harcus (Northam 1992), and my mother's recollections.

Incidents of segregation of African American servicemen and white women in *The Mirror* are well documented by Davidson (1994). Specific incidents referred to in relation to white women being charged for mixing with African American servicemen and alleged prostitution are from 'Woman Talked to Negro,' *Sunday Times* 18 February 1945, and 'Black Slave Traffic,' *Daily News*, 26 August 1944.

The information regarding the imposition of the pass system and the introduction of the conditional 1944 Citizenship legislation came from the files *Legislation Citizenship* (463/1944) and *Establishment of Pass System in Metropolitan Area* (162/1938). Bill Bodney's political agitation is documented in Haebich (1988), and was mentioned in interviews with Geoff Harcus (Northam 1992), George and Eileen Harwood (Canberra 1990, 1992), Corrie Bodney (Perth 1995), and Eileen Clarke (nee Shang) (Adelaide 1992; Perth 1995), and is documented in the file *Coolbaroo Club* (146/1947) as well as in the volumes of the *Westralian Aborigine* newspaper published by the Coolbaroo League, between 1952 and 1957.

Other stories relating to the life of the house at Glendower Street, including the story of Chuck Friese, were based on my mother's recollections.

Language in newspapers of the war period describing 'Huns' and 'Japs' and so on was revealed in a search of the *West Australian* for 1944 which also included references to the 'War Against tyranny.' Biskup (1973) documents the increased surveillance of Aboriginal people across the state that occurred with the onset of the Second World War. Specific reference to the only two Aboriginal returned servicemen who received Citizenship Rights, one of whom was Wally Isaacs, is in Biskup (1977).

Departmental policy of keeping people out of the metropolitan area and returning any that were in unlawful employment was recorded in *Establishment of Pass System in Metropolitan Area* (162/1938), and in 'Natives Need Pass for City,' in the *Sunday Times* (11 February 1945). Information regarding the involvement of the Communist Party in Indigenous issues is documented in Biskup (1973) and was also came from searches of the *Workers Star* and interviews with Helena Murphy (Darwin 1992; Perth 1995) and Geoff Harcus (Northam 1992).

Chapter Twelve: *border crossings*

The stories of Geoff Harcus and Thomas Bropho's journey into the south-west to speak on citizenship rights, Geoff's relationship with the Bropho family, and his association with the Coolbaroo League, are based on an interview with Geoff Harcus (Northam 1992).

The surveillance of the Bropho family was evidenced in their Personal Cards citing their location, living conditions and so on. Thomas Bropho's speeches in Perth and Fremantle were reported in the articles, 'Native Persecution is Denounced in Big Perth Protest,' *Workers Star*, 31 May 1946, and 'Fremantle Backing for Native Rights Struggle,' in the *Workers Star* 30 June 1946. Geoff Harcus' illness was also documented in his Military Service Record.

Helena Murphy's story of her involvement in the Coolbaroo league, Perth Politics, the Pilbara Pastoral Workers Strike, the Euralian Association and her father's political agitation during this period come from interviews in 1992. Information regarding Pop Clarke's statements regarding equality comes from his personal file, provided to me by Helena Murphy, and from the document *Port Hedland Euralian Association—Request by Deputy Director of Security for Information Regarding members, and Activities of* (796/1943) regarding the Euralian Club and economic and legal equality. The request of the Deputy Director of Security to the Native Affairs Department to provide a list of Aboriginal people for observation was found in Biskup (1977). The story of my grandmother receiving the vote, by accident, was based on my mother's recollections.

The story of the Coolbaroo league is based on the file *Coolbaroo Club* (146/1947), which included much of the correspondence between the Police and the Native Affairs Department, as well as in the volumes of the *Westralian Aborigine* Newspaper published by the Coolbaroo League, 1952–57, *East Perth Native Matters* (1312/1943), numerous newspaper reports in the press, and interviews with Helena Murphy (nee Clarke) (Darwin 1992; Perth 1995), Geoff Harcus (Northam 1992) and many others. References to 'town blacks' or 'townies' and 'camp blacks' or 'campies' are based on interviews with Gladys Bropho and Frank Bropho (1995). The story of the card raid was based on my mother and father's recollections and on interviews with George and Eileen Harwood (Canberra 1990, 1992), and Janie Winder (Carnarvon 1988).

Chapter Thirteen: *amputation*

Once again, this chapter is based on my mother's memories of this period of her life, including the stories of Alex Kelly's shoe store and the X-ray box.

Information regarding Mary Forrest came from interviews with Mary's daughter, Thomasisha Passmore (1992, 1995). Grannie Isobel Bropho (1988–91) recalled that Edward paid her sister to care for my grandmother part time, unknown to my grandmother, or my mother, at the time.

The White Seats are legendary and mentioned by many as a meeting place throughout this period. Even when the seats were eventually removed from this corner of the city it continued to be known as Noongar Corner and was a popular rendezvous point, as described in interview by Gladys Bropho (1995), Frank Bropho (1995), Geoff Harcus (1993), and Thomasisha Passmore (1992).

Chapter Fourteen: *cheeky spirits*

This chapter is primarily based upon my mother's recollections of the time soon after my grandmother's death. The story of the power and movement of cheeky spirits was told to me by a Kija elder who has since passed away, Paddy Williams (Warman 1992).

Mr Neville passed away in 1954 and his grave is, ironically, not that far from my grandmother's.

Chapter Fifteen: *the whisperer*

This chapter is primarily based on reminiscences of my mother and my sister Jessica of my grandfather's last years when the family moved to the house at 29 Bower Street, Scarborough.

Information about particular identities within the city is based on family stories and my own observations. Information about Percy Buttons is based on Ron Davidson's *High Jinks at the Hot Pool* (1994). Percy Button's age and birth date were taken from information accompanying a mug shot of one of his arrests in the Police Gazette.

The reference to the idea of power being the ability of others to make you inhabit their version of your story was inspired by Phillip Gourevitch's book, *We wish to inform you that tomorrow we will be killed with our families* (1998).

Select Bibliography

PUBLISHED SOURCES

Berndt, R.M. and Berndt, C.H. (eds), *Aborigines of the West: Their Past and Their Present*, University of Western Australia Press, Nedlands, 1979.

Biskup, P., *Not Slaves Not Citizens: The Aboriginal Problem in Western Australia 1898–1954*, University of Queensland Press, St Lucia, 1973.

Breen, D., 'The Wheatley Family of Bridgetown,' Thesis, Graylands Teachers College, 1958.

Bridge, P.J. (ed), *Aboriginal Perth Bibbulmun and Legends*, Daisy Bates, Hesperian Press, Perth, 1992.

Broughton, G., *Turn Again Home*, Jacaranda Press, Sydney, 1965.

Byrne, G., 'Other Overlanders: Kilfoyles in Grass Castles,' in *Australian Frontiers*, University of Queensland Press Journal of Australian Studies, No 49, 1996.

Carter, J., *Nothing to Spare*, Penguin Books, Ringwood, 1981.

Collard, L., 'An Analysis of Nyungar Influences in the South West Western Australia,' Murdoch University MA Thesis, 1996.

Davidson, R., *High Jinks at the Hot Pool*, Fremantle Arts Centre Press, Fremantle, 1994.

Durack, M., *Kings in Grass Castles*, Corgi, London, 1983.

—— *Sons in the Saddle*, Constable, London, 1959.

Emanuel School Magazines, 1901–1907.

Fraser, B. (ed), *The Macquarie Encyclopedia of Australian Events* (rev ed), Macquarie University, NSW, 1997.

Gaines, C., *Bridgetown: One Hundred Years of History*, Graylands Teachers College, Perth, 1970.

Giles, W.S., and Slater, B.V., *Emanuel School, the history of 1594–1964*, The Old Emanuel Association, London, 1964.

Gill, A., 'Aborigines, Settlers and Police in the Kimberleys, 1887–1905,' in *Studies in Western Australian History*, Vol 1, June 1977.

Girling, B., *Westminster Villages*, Chalford Publishing, St Mary's Mill, UK, 1996.

Gourevitch, P., *We wish to inform you that tomorrow we will be killed with our families*, Picador, London, 1998.

Hall, R., *The Black Diggers*, Allen & Unwin, Sydney, 1989.

Haebich, A., *For Their Own Good: Aborigines and Government in the Southwest of Western Australia, 1900–1940*, University of Western Australia Press, Nedlands, 1988.

Haebich, A., Gammage, B, & Markus A (eds), 'On the Inside: Moore River Native Settlement in the 1930s,' in *All That Dirt. Aborigines 1938*. Canberra: History Project, 1982.

Hagger, J., *Australian Colonial Medicine*, Rigby, Port Melbourne, 1979.

Harris, J., *One Blood: 200 Years of Aboriginal Encounter With Christianity: A Story of Hope*, Albatross Books, Sutherland, NSW, 1990.

Jacobs, P., *Mister Neville*, Fremantle Arts Centre Press, Fremantle, 1990.

Kelly, S.M. and Jackamarra, C., *Proud Heritage*, Artlook Books, Perth, 1980.

Kaberry, Phyllis, 'Trade routes Map, Kimberley Region, 1936,' AIATSIS Unpublished Manuscripts, Canberra, Australia, 1936.

Loobey, P., *Battersea and Clapham, The Archive Photographs Series*, The Chalford Press, Bath, 1994.

——*Wandsworth, The Archive Photographs Series*, The Chalford Press, Bath, 1994.

Marjoribanks, R., *The Noble Aim: Emanuel School 1594–1994*, The Ludo Press, London, 1994.

Marsh, L., and Kinnane, S., 'Ghost Files: The Missing Files of the Department of Indigenous Affairs,' in, C. Choo and S. Holbatch (eds), *History and Native Title, Studies in Western Australian History*, Vol 23, 2003.

Martin, E., *Collecting and Preserving Old Photographs*, Collins, Melbourne, 1988.

Maskell, H.P., *Recollections of Emanuel School*, Endowed Schools Office, London, 1904.

Morgan, S., *My Place*, Fremantle Arts Centre Press, Fremantle, 1987.

Nannup, A., Marsh, L., and Kinnane, S., *When the Pelican Laughed*, Fremantle Arts Centre Press, Fremantle, 1992.

Neville, A.O., *Australia's Coloured Minority: Its Place in the Community*, Currawong Publishing, Sydney, 1948.

Old Ordinance Survey Maps, London Sheet 87, Chelsea, 1894, The Godfrey Edition, Godfrey Maps, London, 1984.

Old Ordinance Survey Maps, London Sheet 124, Wandsworth Common, 1893, The Godfrey Edition, Godfrey Maps, London, 1992.

Old Ordinance Survey Maps, London Sheet 114, Wandsworth, 1894, The Godfrey Edition, Godfrey Maps, London, 1989.

Pratt, R., and Millington, J., *The Torres Diaries 1900–1914*, Artlook Books, Perth, 1987.

Potts, A., and Strauss, L., *For the Love of a Soldier*, ABC Books, Sydney, 1987.

Reynolds, H., *With the White People*, Penguin Books, Sydney, 1990.

Rowse, T., '"Were you ever savages?" Aboriginal Insiders and Pastoral Patronage,' *Oceania*, Vol 158, No 1, December 1987.

Roth, W.E., *Royal Commission on the Conditions of the Natives, Report*, Western Australian Government Printers, 1905.

Stage, Screen and Stars, West Australian Newspapers Ltd, Perth, 1992.

The Stolen Generation Enquiry: Human Rights and Equal Opportunity Commission, 1996/1997.

Sullivan, J., and Shaw, B., *Banggaiyerri: the story of Jack Sullivan as told to Bruce Shaw*, AIAS Press, Canberra, 1983.

Tdoobalin, Ruby, *Ruby's Story, Kimberley Land Council News*, Vol 2. 1988.

Thomson, J., *Norwest of West*, Gordon & Gotch, Perth Western Australia, 1908.

Walter, W., 'Scrapbook of family photographs and newspaper cuttings (1887–1903)'. Battye Library, PR 2202.

Watkins, B., *History of Swanleigh Anglican Hostel*, Thesis, Graylands Teachers College, 1966.

ORAL HISTORY INTERVIEWS
(Conducted by Lauren Marsh and Steve Kinnane. Deposited with the AIATSIS).

Corrie Bodney, Perth 1995.
Isobel Bropho, Perth 1988–1991.
Frank and Gladys Bropho, Perth 1995.
Mr Jimmy Clarke, Helena Murphy (nee Clarke), Frankie Alberts, Darwin 1992.
Mrs Eileen Clarke (nee Shang), Adelaide 1993.
Mrs Betty Davies (nee Sherwood), Perth 1989.
Ralph and Lizzie Dalgety (nee Rae), Geraldton 1995.
Robert Dorey, Carnarvon 1988.
Mr Geoff Harcus, Northam 1991, 1992.
Mrs Eileen Harwood (nee Gentle), Canberra 1990.
Mr George Harwood, Canberra 1990.
Mrs Jean Hill (nee Walker), Geraldton 1989–91.
Mrs Liza Isaacs (nee Barron) Perth 1989.
Mrs Clara Jackamarra (nee Roe), Mogumber 1995.
'Baby' Jones, Perth 1996.
Mrs Betty Kinnane (nee Smith), Perth 1988.
Mrs Helena Murphy (nee Clarke), Darwin 1992.
Mrs Thomasisha Passmore (nee Forrest) Perth 1990, 1992, 1995.
Mrs Janie Winder, Carnarvon 1988.

NEWSPAPER SOURCES
(Chronological)

West Australian, 5 October 1905, H. Prinsep's Report.
West Australian, 20 December 1905, letter to the editor Re 1905 Act.
West Australian, 9 July 1906, letter to editor, J. Corbett complains of the Connor Doherty and Durack monopoly.
Sunday Times, 21 May 1911, 'Swan Native Mission ... Management by Muscle.'
Daily News, 26 February 1915, 'The Greatest Storm in the History of Perth' and 'A Tragedy at Swan Native Mission.'
West Australian, 27 February 1915, 'Sensational Storm—A Young Girl Killed.'
Sunday Times, 28 February 1915, 'Perth Visited By a Great Storm.'
West Australian, 7 March 1915, 'The Storm'.
Mirror, 6 November 1926, 'Coo-ee City first tie in WA the Chair-o-plane.'
West Australian, 3 August 1935, M.P. Durack, letter to the editor.
Blackwood Times, 1918–1921.
Blackwood Times, 31 May 1918, re: the flag.
Blackwood Times, 14 June 1918, re: enlistment calls.
Blackwood Times, 10 September 1920, 'Drowning Fatality.'
Blackwood Times, 17 September 1920, re: the Inquest.
West Australian, 16 March 1940, 'Native Girls, Mr A. O. Neville Farewelled.'
Daily News, 14 August 1944, 'Mistresses Convicted', re: Black American Servicemen.

Daily News, 23 August 1944, 'Black Slave Traffic.'
Sunday Times, 11 February 1945, 'Natives Need Pass for City.'
Sunday Times, 18 February 1945, 'Woman Talked to Negro.'
Workers Star, 31 May 1946, 'Native Persecution is Denounced in Big Perth
    Protest.'
Workers Star, 30 June 1946, 'Fremantle Backing for Native Rights Struggle.'
Daily News, 18 March 1947, 'Aborigines, Half-Castes Have Weekly Dance,
    Social.'
West Australian, 24 May 1947, 'An Evening at a Native Social.'
Daily News, 20 December 1947, 'Planning Their Own Utopia.'
Sunday Times, 18 January 1948, 'Big Brawl in East Perth.'
West Australian, 8 April 2000, re: destruction of files.

FILES AND PRIMARY RECORDS
(Chronological)

(Aborigines. Refers to Aborigines Department Files. Police. Refers to Police
Department Files. Native Affairs refers to Native Affairs Department Files. All
housed within the State Records Office, Western Australia).

Police. 1315/04. Northam Letter to *Sunday Times*—PC Hill (517) suspected of
    writing.
Police. Kimberley Occurrence Books, 1903.
Aborigines. 53/05. R.M. Wyndham: re Relief Issued at Argyle Police Station.
US and Naval Astronomical Records, 1906.
WA Inwards Shipping Registers: Cons 457 Vol 11.
Police Annual Report, Commissioner of Police, 1905.
Police Annual Report, Commissioner of Police, 1906.
Police. Hall's Creek Report Books and Journals.
Journal Const Richardson: 12 March 1905 – 1 April 1905.
Aborigines. 52A/05. R.M. Wyndham, Native Affairs, 1905.
Police. 4051/06. Kimberley District Annual Report, Acting Sub Inspector
    McCarthy to 30/06/06.
Aborigines. 47/00. James Sharpe, Complaining of Sentence Inflicted on Boy.
Police. 1906, Sub Inspectors Annual Report East Kimberley.
Act No 14, 1905, proclaimed in Western Australia on 23 December 1905
    (Commonly referred to as the 1905 Aborigines Act).
Police. 458/06. Inspector Troy's Report on Roth evidence, 1906.
Police. 4035/06. Journal PC Hill on Prisoner Escort to Wyndham.
Aborigines. Protest Over White Men Marrying Aboriginal Women. 827/06
Aborigines. 231/06 AAD, Swan Mission and 46/06 Colonial Secretary
    Office—Removal.
Aborigines. 1004/06. 'Half-Caste Girls Annie and Topsie from Wyndham.'
Durack, M.P., Diary. 4587A/21. Battye Archives.
Aborigines. 06/05. Ill treatment of Natives.
Aborigines. Olivey, Travelling Inspector's Report, 1903.
Aborigines. 105/06. Resident Magistrate Wyndham.
Swan Parish Baptism Records: 2467A/249.

Swan Parish Baptism Records 2467A/122–359.

Aborigines. Swan Mission Quarterly Summary: 955/99.

Aborigines. Removal of Half-Castes General: 16/20.

Aborigines. Swan Mission: 444/08.

Colonial Secretary's Office, Swan Mission Exemption Half-Caste Women: 810/06.

Aborigines. Swan Mission Quarterly Summary: 995/10.

Aborigines. Swan Native and Half-Caste Mission: 178/02.

Aborigines. Swan Mission Annual Reports: 178/02, 31/09, 915/10, 1496/11, 1354/13.

Aborigines. Rail Pass for Half-Caste Richard Dorey and Three Children: 811/11.

Aborigines. Swan Annual Report: 1354/13.

Swan Parish Burial Records: 2467A/124. There is also a Plaque in St Mary's Cemetery, Middle Swan.

Aborigines. Jessie Argyle Personal File: 312/26.

Aborigines. Particulars of H. C. Children on Nor' West Stations Who Require to be Removed (973/1916).

Aborigines. Swan Mission Old Girls re: Oversight Of: 597/18.

Edward Smith Application to Enlist in the Australian Imperial Force at Perth on the 7 September 1916 (Register No. 141.3.16).

Edward Smith Medical Certificate of Unfitness ref. (W 66 333).

Aborigines. Salvation Army Girls Home, Kalgoorlie: 118/27.

Letter from DCP to St Brodie, MRNS, April 1924. J. Argyle Personal File: 312/26.

Aborigines. Superintendent Brodie Personal file: 387/24.

Aborigines. Matron Brodie Personal file: 461/24.

Aborigines. Farm Assist MRNS: 1746/21.

Aborigines. Children's Art MRNS: 1003/23, 2619/23, 1365/23.

Aborigines. MRNS Admission of Northam Natives, 21/1933.

Aborigines. Nurse V. Ryan Personal file: 1003/23. Petition from inmates protesting to replacement of Nurse Stewart with V. Ryan.

Smith Family: private archives.

Smith Family: archival photographs.

Aborigines. Mogumber Cemetery 1916–1964: 149/48.

Letter by E. Copping, Secretary Aborigines Depart. Jessie Argyle Personal file: 312/26.

Handwritten letter by Jessie Argyle. Jessie Argyle Personal file: 312/26.

Letter from Ernest Copping dated September 1924. Smith Family private archives.

Aborigines. City of Perth Prohibited Area: 38/27.

Handwritten letter by Jessie Argyle, January 1929. Jessie Argyle Personal file: 312/26.

Jessie Smith and Family Personal file: 346/31.

Handwritten letter by Edward Smith to CPA Aborigines Department, March 1930. Jessie Smith and Family Personal file: 346/31.

Anonymous handwritten letter of complaint to Department. Jessie Smith and Family Personal file: 346/31.

Aborigines. Royal Commission into the Treatment of Aborigines, 1934, 333/1933.

Aborigines. Royal Commission into the Treatment of Aborigines 1934, Findings 131/1935.

Native Affairs. Establishment of Pass System in Metropolitan Area: 162/38.

Native Affairs. East Perth Native Matters: 1312/43.

Native Affairs. Port Hedland Euralian Association—Request by Deputy Director of Security for Information Regarding members, and Activities of 796/1943.

Native Affairs. Legislation Citizenship: 463/44.

Native Affairs. The Coolbaroo Club: 146/47.

Native Affairs. Lawrence Clarke: 1366/17. Port Hedland Police.

Australian Security Service: A 367/1–C79568, Canberra.

War Record Geoff Harcus: WX41275.

DIA Card System. Acc 5404/ vol 1784/ 1–7, 1926–1959.

Photographs

Photographs are from the collection of Stephen Kinnane unless otherwise indicated.

Acknowledgements

Shadow Lines would not have been possible without the work, support and advice of many people to whom I owe a great deal. Shadow Lines began in 1988 as a collaboration between my partner Lauren Marsh and myself. Originally planned as an anthology of Aboriginal women's stories, this work grew into the recording of dozens of community stories, volumes of research, and hours of time spent with wonderful people willing to share their lives and stories with us. The book When the Pelican Laughed and the film The Coolbaroo Club, both of which Lauren and I co-wrote, were part of this journey. Much of the research used in writing Shadow Lines is based on the collaborative work that Lauren and I completed together and this work has greatly influenced this book. Whether sifting through mountains of archival records, tracking people across the state, lurching across swollen rivers in an old Valiant, or being there for our friends and relatives at the end, Lauren has completed the journey of this book and my life with me, for which I am forever grateful. I am also deeply indebted to Lauren for her insightful editorial advice. I would also like to thank my mother, Betty Kinnane, for sharing her history and my grandparents' history with me from when I was a child, instilling in me a great respect for our pasts and the power of our individual and community stories. I would also like to thank my family for their support.

The research and writing of Shadow Lines has been assisted by the Commonwealth Government through the Australia Council, its arts funding and advisory body, through the support of the Aboriginal and Torres Strait Islander Arts Board and the state of Western Australia has made an investment in this project through ArtsWA via the assistance and support of the Aboriginal Arts Panel. Research towards this book was completed under related research projects supported by the Australian Institute of Aboriginal and Torres Strait Islander Studies (AIATSIS) in Canberra, and permission to use material from the AIATSIS research project, 'Card Fever', was kindly granted. I would also like to thank the Western Australian History Foundation for support of a related research project dealing with the history of the Swan Native and Half-caste Mission.

Many individuals within these organisations have aided this work over the years and I would like to thank arts agency workers Carol Innes, Yvette Alger, James Wells, Barbara Pilot and Lesley Fogarty for their advice and support. I would particularly like to thank Penny Taylor (formerly History Officer of AIATSIS) for her support of research towards this book, and for her commitment to cross-cultural histories. I would also like to thank Dr Kingsley Palmer, Dr Stephen Wild, Dr Mary Edmunds, and Jackie Lambert of AIATSIS for their support of the project.

Whilst based on archival research, the genesis of *Shadow Lines*, and much of the information that it is informed by, lies in the sharing of story, by word of mouth, from witness to listener. I am deeply thankful to all those who have shared their stories with me, stories that have directly informed this book. In no specific order, I would like to thank and acknowledge my mother, Betty Kinnane, as well as Alice Nannup, Jean Hill, Isobel Bropho, Eileen Harwood, George Harwood, Eileen Clarke, Helena Clarke, Geoff Harcus, Janie Winder, Bob Dorey, 'Baby' Jones, Bill Poland, Henry Mippy, Jack Sullivan (Banggaiyerri), Mary (Nangari), Luddie (Nangari), Gypsy (Namidge), Ruby (Nangala), Katherine (Yerribee) Barney, Daisy, Three Day Joe, Thomasisha Passmore, Betty Davies and Corrie Forbes. I would also like to thank and acknowledge Gladys Bropho, Frankie Bropho, Corrie Bodney, Frankie Alberts, Jimmy Clarke, John Winder, Alice Stack, Ron Farmer, Mary Tickle, Shirley Lathbury, Frank Lathbury, Kevin Kinnane, Ethel Clinch, Una Ashwyn, George Augustine, Clara Jackamarra, Mary Mindamurra, Hazel Nellie, Lemmie AhKim, Myrtle Mulally, Billy and Molly, Liza Isaacs, Bess Jones, Steve Redmond Kinnane, Jessie Cross, Tommy Watson, Basil Gardiner, Molly Ginger, Minnie van Leeuwen, and Marie Harris whose reminiscences of my grandparents and their time have indirectly aided the telling of this story.

Many friends have helped *Shadow Lines* along through discussion, advice and all- important moral support. I would particularly like to thank Mark Turton for his support and friendship to Lauren and I over the years. I would also like to thank Anna Haebich, Anne Bellman, Sarah Irwin, Jenny Mogridge and Marion Benjamin, and my Murdoch colleagues Denise Groves, Len Collard and Kathy Trees.

Staff at the State Records Office, the Battye Library of Western Australian History, the Australian Institute of Aboriginal and Torres Strait Islander Studies Library, the Indigenous Affairs Department Library (Western Australia), Swanleigh Library, the Australian Archives (Northern

Territory, Canberra, and Western Australia), the Mitchell Library (Sydney), the Moora Courthouse, the Mogumber Heritage Photographic Collection, the Westminster Archives (London) and the Emanuel School Library (London) for their assistance with accessing their collections. I would particularly like to thank Sue Beverly, Penny Tinsley, Harry Taylor, Tom Reynolds, Gerard Foley, Jenny Mogridge, Jenny Carter and Marion Bradnock for their support of research towards this book.

Many people helped with support and advice with research, places to stay while following the story, and help with getting around. For this support I would like to thank Penny Taylor, my family, John and Katiya Wilson, David Newry, Frances Kofod, Ian Kirkby, Bob Hannan, Una Augustine, the Pilbara Land Council, the Pilbara Language Centre, the Mogumber Heritage Committee, Jenny Mogridge, William Worrell, Ray Minniecon, Wol Saunders, Ruth Park, Len Collard, Sandra Harwood, Nick Thieberger, Maryanne Jebb, Anna Haebich, Fiona Skyring, Cathie Clement, June Thomlinson, Sally Morgan, Jack McPhee, Angela Bignell, Mark Lester, Zita Murphy, Thomasisha Passmore, Joanie and Phillip Bradshaw, Fred Murphy, Helena Murphy, Waringarri and the Mirama Dawang Woorlab-gerring Language and Culture Centre.

Finally, I would like to thank the Fremantle Arts Centre Press who agreed to publish *Shadow Lines* some years ago. I would like to thank them for their patience, as well as their support of cross-cultural and Aboriginal history and stories. I would like to thank all the staff of the Fremantle Arts Centre Press involved in the publication of *Shadow Lines*, including Helen Kirkbride, Clive Newman, Marion Duke, Vanessa Bradley, Leone Dyer and Stephanie Green. I would particularly like to thank my editors Ray Coffey and Janet Blagg for their thoughtful and detailed edit of the many and various stages of the manuscript.

Index

More classics of Indigenous literature

Oceanic in its rhythms and understanding, brilliant in its use of language and image, moving in its largeness of spirit, compelling in its narrative scope and style, *Benang* is a novel of celebration and lament, of beginning and return, of obliteration and recovery, of silencing and of powerful utterance. Both tentative and daring, it speaks to the present and a possible future through stories, dreams, rhythms, songs, images and documents mobilised from the incompletely acknowledged and still dynamic past.

'*Benang* is brilliant. It is a mature, complex, sweeping historical novel which will remind people of Rushdie, Carey and Grenville at their best. This is an absolute page turner and in the end we are left with a sense of joy and gratitude that such stories are still possible—that the silence has been broken.' *Sydney Morning Herald*

fremantlepress.com.au and all good bookstores

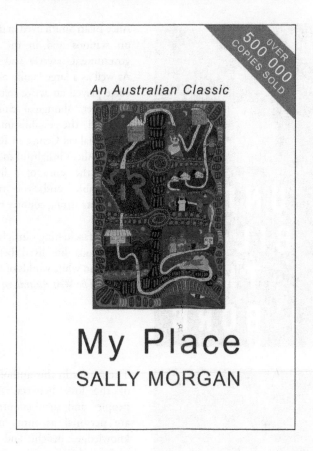

More Indigenous stories from Fremantle Press

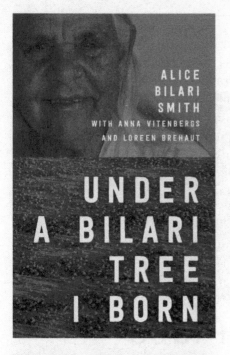

Alice Bilari Smith lived in the Pilbara, on stations and in the bush, on government reserves and in towns. As well as a large family of her own, Alice played an active role in caring for other Aboriginal children and initiated the establishment of a Homemakers Centre in Roebourne. This is Alice's insightful and inspiring story—the story of a life that is remarkable and yet typical of Australia's strong country women.

'... a fascinating insight on an Indigenous life lived between the black and white worlds of the North-West.' *The West Australian*

The stories in this anthology speak of the love between Aboriginal peoples and their countries. They are personal accounts that share knowledge, insight and emotion, each speaking of a deep connection to country and of feeling heartsick because of the harm that is being inflicted on country even today, through the logging of old growth forests, converting millions of acres of land to salt fields, destruction of ancient rock art and significant Aboriginal sacred sites, and a record of species extinction that is the worst in the world.

fremantlepress.com.au and all good bookstores